The
PORTABLE
MBA
in
PROJECT
MANAGEMENT

The Portable MBA Series

The

PORTABLE

MBA

in

PROJECT

MANAGEMENT

EDITED BY

ERIC VERZUH

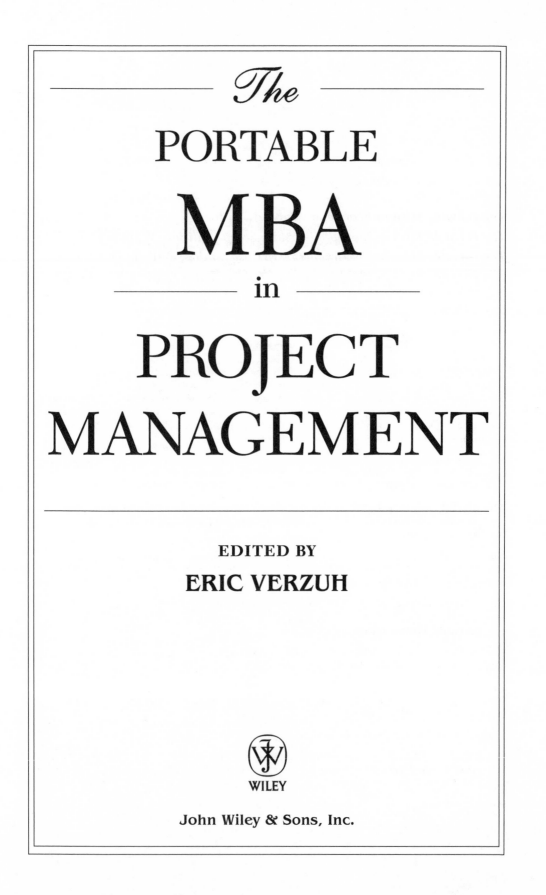

WILEY

John Wiley & Sons, Inc.

To my parents, Jim Verzuh and Julie Welle Verzuh, and to my parents-in-law, Larry and Fran Kissler, whose lives and accomplishments continue to be an inspiration.

Preface

In the 1990s, project management moved from a little-used industrial engineering discipline to the engine of managing America's work. Prior to 1990, project management techniques were unknown to most corporate managers who considered projects to be the realm of engineers or the IS department. In universities, with few exceptions, the only place to learn project management was the industrial and management engineering program—not even "real engineering." Fast forward to 2003 and project management has leapt to center stage. Corporations are using the "project management office" to implement consistent project management practices across the enterprise and manage mission-critical strategic initiatives. From the CEO's office down to the frontlines, business and government organizations have "projectized" their work and are looking to the classic discipline of project management to give them greater productivity and faster response to changing market conditions. This shift has not gone unnoticed on campus where business schools now offer masters programs in project management and many graduate and undergraduate curriculums include at least one course on project management. What prompted this revolution? The American economy is increasingly characterized by change and change means projects; project management is the tool set of the twenty-first century.

The growing use of project management mirrors the growing number of projects we find in our workplace. In every industry and profession, organizations find a greater proportion of their time and resources are committed to projects, giving rise to *the project-based organization*. In the past, many firms considered themselves project based. Consulting firms, construction-related businesses, aerospace companies, and agencies such as the U.S. Army Corps of Engineers can find that 80 percent to 100 percent of their revenue/budget is attributable to projects. However, a firm need not be completely devoted to projects to face the challenges of managing multiple projects or to gain the benefits of applying the project management discipline. If even 20 percent of your organization's budget or revenue is represented by projects, consider yourself a project-based organization. That isn't suggesting you try to jam the operations of your entire department or company into the project mold—it is suggesting that if one-fifth of your budget/revenue is project-based, significantly improving the performance of your projects will have an impact on your overall bottom line.

This book is intended for the leaders of this emerging entity known as the project-based organization. CIOs, department managers, program managers, and senior project managers being challenged to implement project management—to formalize the processes of managing projects—will find strategies and standards for leveraging the proven discipline of project management.

For our purposes, the project-based organization can be a department, division, or entire company. Government agencies and nonprofits should consider themselves candidates as well as for-profit businesses. The traditional project-based firms often focused on a few very large projects or programs. The new breed of multiproject enterprise is often comprised of many smaller, independent projects. Optimizing performance on one project is already difficult. Optimizing performance across many concurrent projects requires a conscious method of management. As we optimize the project portion of the business, we cannot afford to ignore the nonproject side. The goal of this book is to provide the methods and framework necessary to run an organization that must successfully deliver many independent projects.

The discipline of project management is well developed. There exist, literally, hundreds of books intended to help us better manage a project. The body of knowledge for managing a multiproject organization is far less developed. This book, intended as a resource for leaders of the project-based organization, must address both topics. It is impossible for a CIO, engineering director, vice-president of new product development, or owner of a construction or consulting firm to optimize their organization's project performance if she or he cannot speak the language of project management. At the same time, the discipline of project management is insufficient for managing the entire firm. Therefore, the strategy of this book is to provide a condensed view of the traditional project management topics and to assemble the guidelines for managing the organization.

Part One introduces the dual tiers of project focus and enterprise focus. It provides an introduction to the project management discipline and also exposes the opportunities available to firms who choose to focus on project management as a strategic advantage. You'll be able to assess the strategic benefits of project management to your organization and have a vision for the components of a successful project-based organization.

Part Two contains the proven discipline of project management including project selection, detailed planning, project control, quality management, and risk management techniques. These chapters are designed to present enough detail for executives to understand the techniques their own project managers should be using. In these chapters, the focus is on the methods for managing a single project, but the role of the executive is always stressed. With this level of understanding, leaders of the project-based organization will understand what processes and activities should be taking place on projects as well as their own critical contribution to project success. Experienced project managers should be able to use these chapters as a condensed resource outlining the *must have* project management activities. Be aware, however, that if you are seeking detailed tips and how-to advice for managing projects, that is better found in my previous book, *The Fast Forward MBA in Project Management*, also published by John Wiley & Sons.

Part Three addresses the human dimension of project success. No experienced project leader or manager can deny the importance of a unified team and a positive atmosphere. Nor can we ever discount the value of a driven, can-do team attitude. To some, achieving these environmental team factors far outweighs the importance of critical path analysis or risk planning. Rather than argue over their relative importance, this book presents both the *science* of project management (Part Two) and the *art* of team leadership (Part Three) as essential to a successful project. As with Part Two, Part Three presents well-established principles, but it differs in one important respect: The books on building successful teams outnumber even those on project management. Topics in this section were specifically chosen because they serve the project environment—temporary teams, often composed of people who work in different organizations (sometimes different companies) and who may even be geographically dispersed. Because of their unique perspective, these three chapters address the heart of building a successful project team.

Good project management is essential for project success, but it is not enough for the project-based organization. Part Four presents the macro view of the project-based organization: the processes and systems required to oversee multiple projects, the leadership challenge involved in formalizing project management practices, and the other capabilities—beyond project management—required for a successful project-based organization.

One-third of the content of this book has been previously published, reflecting the fact that project management is a mature discipline. Rather than rewrite what has been previously well done, we have compiled it. Other sections are necessarily new: They either present classic techniques with a new perspective (Chapters 4, 5, 6, and 7 condense large topics to provide a detailed overview) or they represent some of the newest thinking on the topic of managing the project-based organization.

If you read only one book about project management, you cannot hope to understand all there is to know about the topic. As with any good project, this book has a specific purpose that has limited its scope. Because the book attempts to cover a broad scope, it is prevented from covering all its topics in great depth. The target reader—experienced project managers, project office personnel, and leaders of multiproject organizations—do not want all the details of how to manage a project. Likewise, certain valuable project-related topics such as procurement and estimating were ultimately determined to be too specialized.

Devotees of the Project Management Institute's *A Guide to the Project Management Body of Knowledge* (PMBoK) will notice that all of the content of this book is in alignment with the PMBoK. The terminology used in this book does not conflict with PMBoK definitions. However, the scope of this book is different than that very thorough glossary, so not every topic found in either book can be referenced to the other.

Ultimately, the content of this book rests on my observations about the challenges of managing a project-based organization. For over a decade, my firm has been delivering the time-tested principles of project management to firms across the economic spectrum. We have seen huge changes in the enthusiasm for project management and the organizational assets committed to formalizing its practice. Firms that were initially hesitant to purchase a few days of training later have staffed a project management office with full-time, experienced project leaders and invested in enterprise project management software.

For those of us who work in this field and see the potential for project-based organizations, the momentum is both gratifying and cause for alarm. Our satisfaction is easy to understand. Our alarm stems from the dangers associated with management fads. Nearly everyone with more than 10 years of work experience has seen at least one fad wash over his or her organization—complete with training, slogans, and accompanying software—only to have the new ideas and better ways disappear as everyone "got back to work." That can happen with project management, too.

Leading the charge to building a better project-based organization makes sense for many organizations, but that doesn't make it easy. This book is intended to make that journey a little bit straighter, a little less painful, and, ultimately, to improve the quality of work life of every person who is working in the project environment.

Eric Verzuh

Acknowledgments

On every project, one of my greatest pleasures is recognizing the people whose individual contributions lead to the ultimate success of the team. Particularly in this case, I am privileged to have my name on the cover of a book that is the product of many, many hands. To all those who have given me their time and trust, I offer my thanks and these acknowledgments:

Larry Alexander and Karen Hansen of John Wiley & Sons, Inc. conceived this project.

Paula Sinnott of John Wiley & Sons, Inc. assisted me with editorial duties and handled the administration necessary to secure permissions for portions of this book that were previously printed. Her commitment to quality ensured we kept our standards high.

Denis Couture, Robert Cooper, and Ned Hamson contributed hard-won expertise in the form of their individual chapters. Their content is golden.

Previously printed works appear in this book courtesy of their publishers. I thank the authors: Elaine Biech, Jack Meredith, Samuel Mantel, Neal Whitten, Randall Englund, Robert Graham, Deborah Duarte, and Nancy Tennant Snyder. I read many books in my search to build the best content for this book and your writings were selected for their enduring value and accessible style.

Michelle Actis and Greg Smiley are members of the Versatile team who made it possible for me to build a book and hold down a job. Michelle developed many of the diagrams and Greg assisted in writing Chapter 5.

I am fortunate to have many colleagues who have provided insights, encouragement, and, importantly, criticism. Tammy Bare, Fred Black, Patrick Bryan, Denis Cioffi, Mandy Dietz, Kristian Erickson, Jeff Lynch, Donna McEwen, Jean Miller, Clive Schuelein, Larry Spallanzani, Pen Stout, and Kim Ring all offered their time and shaped some aspect of this book.

Sam Huffman, Cynthia Actis, Dave Bush, and Thomas "TJ" Filley are colleagues at Versatile. They have contributed to this work through their ideas, criticism, and day-to-day examples of commitment to excellence.

Barbara Lowenstein and Norman Kurz are my agents. They have been invaluable in making this project possible.

Marlene Kissler, my wife, has once again proved herself a partner for all occasions. On this project, she acted as critic, editor, and coach. Together, Marlene and I manage a portfolio of projects that include a business and a family. I could ask for no stronger, more reliable, more joyful partner in any endeavor.

E. V.

About the Editor

Eric Verzuh is president of The Versatile Company, a project management training and consulting firm based in Seattle, Washington. His company trains thousands of professionals every year in the proven principles of project management including how to get the most out of Microsoft Project®. Versatile's consulting practice focuses on helping firms establish consistent, practical methods for managing their projects. The company's client list includes large corporations such as Adobe Systems, General Electric, and Lockheed Martin, as well as government agencies and small businesses. Verzuh is a frequent keynote speaker at conferences on project management.

Verzuh is the author of *The Fast Forward MBA in Project Management*, also published by John Wiley & Sons. He has been certified as a project management professional (PMP) by the Project Management Institute. He can be reached via his company's Web site at www.versatilecompany.com.

About the Contributors

Elaine Biech is president and managing principal of Ebb Associates, an organizational development firm that helps organizations work through large-scale change. She has been in the training and consulting fields for 22 years working with for-profit and nonprofit organizations such as McDonald's, Land's End, the U.S. Navy, and the IRS. Author and editor of two-dozen books, and recipient of the 1992 National American Society for Training and Development (ASTD) Torch Award, Elaine Beich has presented at numerous national and international conferences.

Robert G. Cooper, PhD, is a world expert in the field of new product management. He has been called "the quintessential scholar" in the field of new products in the *Journal of Product Innovation Management* and is a Crawford Fellow of the Product Development & Management Association. Mr. Cooper is the father and developer of the Stage-Gate™ process, now widely used by leading firms around the world to drive new products to market. He is also the developer of the NewProd™ system for screening and diagnosing new product projects, also used by a number of companies.

Cooper has written six books on new product management, including *Winning at New Products: Accelerating the Process from Idea to Launch,* which has sold over 100,000 copies. He is president and cofounder of The Product Development Institute, Professor of Marketing at the School of Business, McMaster University in Hamilton, Ontario, Canada, and also ISBM Distinguished Research Fellow at Penn State University's Smeal College of Business Administration.

Denis Couture, PMP, is president and cofounder of the pci group, a consulting firm based in Troy, Michigan, that specializes in project and portfolio management, business consulting and training. His company trains hundreds of individuals each year at such corporations as General Motors, Daimler-Chrysler, and ADP in the application of project management best practices, including the steps required for increasing project management maturity. The pci group's consulting practice focuses on helping firms build an effective project management environment, based on the three cornerstones of success: process, organization, and information technology. Couture can be reached via his company's site, www.pcigroup1.com.

Deborah L. Duarte, PhD, is an expert in the areas of leadership development, knowledge management, virtual project team leadership, performance management, and organizational culture change. She consults in these areas with a number of private and public organizations, including the National Aeronautics and Space Administration (NASA), the Federal Aviation Administration (FAA), the United Nations, Whirlpool Corporation, NORTEL Networks, Johnson & Johnson, and Gap, Inc. Duarte is a faculty member at George Washington University and teaches courses in leadership, organizational learning, and research methods. She also teaches at the Singapore Institute of Management and at the International Space University in France. She holds a doctorate in Human Resource Development from George Washington University, and is a frequent presenter at conferences and workshops, and has published extensively in the areas of global and virtual teaming leadership, project management, and knowledge management.

Randall L. Englund, MBA, NPDP, CBM, is an author, speaker, trainer, and consultant. He is a partner in a new advanced project management training venture called Madeline Learning and an associate to the Human Systems Knowledge Network and the Strategic Management Group. He was a project manager for Hewlett-Packard Company (HP) in Palo Alto, California, for 22 years. As a workshop facilitator and consultant, he draws on his experience releasing high-technology products, developing a system product life cycle, resolving computer system architectural issues, researching effective practices for project success, and designing management processes, courses and Web shops. Englund is a member of PMI and a former board member for the Product Development and Management Association (PDMA), and is a certified New Product Development Professional (NPDP). With Robert J. Graham, he co-authored the book *Creating an Environment for Successful Projects: The Quest to Manage Project Management.* Their next book is *Creating the Project Office: A Manager's Guide to Leading Organizational Change.* Graham and Englund also present executive briefings for Stanford University, Project-World, Strategic Management Group (SMG), and PMI.

Robert J. Graham is an independent project management consultant and senior associate with the Strategic Management Group. Graham was a senior staff member at the Management and Behavioral Sciences Center at the Wharton School, University of Pennsylvania. He taught in the MBA and PhD programs and the Wharton Effective Executive program. With Randall L. Englund he co-authored the book *Creating an Environment for Successful Projects: The Quest to Manage Project Management* and *Creating the Project*

Office: A Manager's Guide to Leading Organizational Change. Graham and Englund also present executive briefings for Stanford University, Project-World, Strategic Management Group (SMG), and PMI.

Ned Hamson is currently a strategic innovation consultant. He served as editor of the *Journal for Quality and Participation* from 1985 to 2002, and has co-authored three books: *Managing Quality* (Wiley, 2002); *Global Innovation* (Wiley, 2002); and *After Atlantis: Working, Managing and Leading in Turbulent Times* (Butterworth-Heinemann, 1997).

Samuel J. Mantel Jr. is the Joseph S. Stern Professor Emeritus at the College of Business Administration at the University of Cincinnati, where he taught courses in Operations Management and Project Management. He holds A.B., M.P.A., and Ph.D. degrees from Harvard University.

Prior to his 20 years of service on the faculty of the University of Cincinnati, he also served on the faculties of the Georgia Institute of Technology and Case Western Reserve University. At CWRU he was Director of the Economics-in-Action program. He also founded and directed the University of Cincinnati's Graduate Center for the Management of Advanced Technology and Innovation.

Mantel has published over seventy papers on the application of economics and quantitative methods to the management of projects, research and development, technological change, and the operation of service agencies. He has published in such journals as *Project Management Journal, IEEE Transactions on Engineering Management, Technology Management,* and *Operations Research.* He currently serves on the Editorial Board of the international journal *Technovation.*

He has conducted more than three hundred seminars at universities across the United States and consulted in the areas of operations management and project management to more than 200 for-profit and not-for-profit organizations. He co-wrote the article on Project Management for the *International Encyclopedia of Business and Management* (2001), published by Thomson Learning, London, and he has co-authored several books, including two popular college textbooks—*Project Management in Practice,* and *Project Management: A Managerial Approach* (2003), now in its fifth edition—both from Wiley.

Jack R. Meredith is Professor of Management and Broyhill Distinguished Scholar and Chair in Operations at the Babcock Graduate School of Management at Wake Forest University. He received his Ph.D. and MBA degrees from the University of California, Berkeley. He has worked as an astrodynamicist for Douglas Aircraft Company and TRW Systems Group on the Viking, Apollo, and other space programs. His current research interests are in the areas of research methodology and the strategic planning, justification, and implementation of advanced manufacturing technologies. His recent articles have been published in *Management Science, Operations Research, Journal of Operations Management, Sloan Management Review, Strategic Management Journal, Decision Sciences,* and others. He has co-authored five popular college textbooks: *Operations Management for MBAs* (Wiley), *Quantitative Business Modeling* (South-Western), *Project Management: A Managerial Approach* (Wiley), *Operations Management: A Process Approach with Spreadsheets* (Wiley), and *Project Management in Practice* (Wiley). He was the founding editor of *Operations Management Review,* and is currently the Editor-in-Chief of the *Journal of Operations Management,* and a member of the editorial advisory board for *Production and Operations Management.*

Nancy Tennant Snyder is vice president for leadership and strategic competency creation at the Whirlpool Corporation, based in Benton Harbor, Michigan.

Neal Whitten, PMP, is a speaker, trainer, consultant, mentor, and author in the areas of both project management and employee development. He has over 30 years of front-line experience in project management, software engineering, and human resource management. In his 23 years at IBM, Whitten held both project leader and management positions. He managed the development of numerous software products, including operating systems, business and telecommunications applications, and special-purpose programs and tools. For three years, he also managed and was responsible for providing independent assessments on dozens of software projects for an Assurance group. He is president of The Neal Whitten Group, created shortly after leaving IBM in 1993. He is also a contributing editor for the Project Management Institute's *PM Network* magazine.

Contents

PART ONE

THE CASE FOR PROJECT MANAGEMENT

Modern project management has been in use since the early 1950s, yet it experienced explosive growth during the 1990s. Firms in every sector of the economy, including nonprofit and government agencies, discovered this proven discipline as though for the first time. The shift toward project management reflects many other shifts in the workplace: global competition, the increased use of temporary labor at all levels of the organization, and the rapid pace of technological advancement.

To a certain degree, the project management discipline is stable and ready for service. The fundamentals of managing a successful project have not changed much over the past 25 years. Project leaders can look to existing tools and texts to understand how to set up and manage a project. But many firms have already reached the limits of the discipline: The principles of managing a single project are insufficient for managing a collection of independent projects. The nature of projects—each is unique in its duration, budget, product, personnel requirements, and risks—is magnified as the number of projects grows. As departments and entire firms spend a greater proportion of their time, budget, and personnel on projects, they need to master the principles of managing a project and a project-based organization.

To fully understand the problem, we need to understand how we arrived here. Management theory was born and raised in the twentieth century. Frederick Taylor, Peter Drucker, Alfred Sloan, W. Edwards Deming, and many others developed and practiced theories of managing organizations that became the foundation of the world's leading businesses.

Along the way, project management techniques were developed, the first in the mid-1950s.

For the most part, project management was ignored by schools teaching management and by professional managers because most people weren't working on projects. That began to change by the mid-1980s. Economic and technology factors combined to increase the number of projects in many firms. Initially, the problems of projects were considered the domain of engineers, programmers, and others who actually worked on project teams. The answers were found in the existing project management discipline. Today, however, executives are taking an active interest in projects and project management.

What has changed is not only that more people are working on projects, but also that the proportion of budget and/or revenue attributable to projects has jumped significantly. When projects represented less than ten percent of our activities, they could be treated as anomalies. The fact that they are difficult to estimate and demand cross-functional staffing is challenging, but the project management tool set addresses these problems. When projects become 30, 50, or 70 percent of a department's activities, they demand a different kind of attention.

Executives trained in the theories of twentieth-century management recognized a gap—theories of economies of scale and process improvement were focused on getting better at doing the same thing. But projects are always doing something new. The disciplines we use to make the trains run on time are not necessarily the ones that will help us build a new railroad.

Here's another way to view the problem: When our work is primarily repeatable activities (manufacturing is a classic example), the old metaphor for an organization as a machine where the structure and processes are cogs and gears serves a purpose. Fine tuning the machine means analyzing and improving specific processes or authority structures. But imagine that the cogs and gears are constantly changing size and speed, and they come and go on a seemingly random basis. How do we manage that kind of machine?

Part One of this book helps us understand the problems of the project-based organization, the answers provided within the project management discipline, and the new directions that firms have chosen to capitalize on the opportunities created by projects.

Chapter 1 provides an overview of project management. It begins by explaining why managing a project is different from managing an ongoing operation and why a separate management discipline has evolved to address these differences. We see, at a high level, how a project is selected; how the project manager establishes a clear direction for the effort, including detailed action and risk management plans; and how these upfront activities become the basis for successfully managing and delivering the product.

The shift to project-based work has brought opportunities as well as challenges. Chapter 1 also poses the question of whether a firm's ability to manage projects is merely a tactical competency or actually forms a strategic competitive advantage. If it is a strategic capability, that means understanding project management is important to executives and that the firm is justified in adapting its structure and processes to further improve project performance.

Chapter 2 provides a vision for an environment conducive to successful projects. Authors Graham and Englund identify the organization structure and processes necessary to foster project success. They also emphasize the critical role that upper management plays in a project-based organization: Consistent project performance relies on honest, consistent management support.

The transformation to a project-friendly organization has dangers. Chapter 2 also describes the risks associated with large-scale organizational change and provides insights into the change process and the attributes of the successful change agent.

By the end of Part One, you will understand the case for project management—the relative importance of projects to your firm and what constitutes a successful project-based organization.

PROJECT MANAGEMENT IS A STRATEGIC STRENGTH

1

Eric Verzuh

The dawn of the twenty-first century is characterized by pervasive change throughout the global economy. The ability to rapidly adapt to change and, more importantly, *drive* that change, has become a survival factor for firms across the economic spectrum.

This chapter describes how the project management discipline has evolved to be a strategic capability in firms of every size as we all adapt to the increasing pace of change. The content of this chapter is broken into two parts: The first part provides a general overview of the discipline of project management; the second part demonstrates why project management is a strategic capability and what firms are doing to leverage project management techniques.

THE PROJECT MANAGEMENT DISCIPLINE

The basis of understanding project management is the understanding of *project*. A project is defined as "work that is temporary and produces a unique product or service." Temporary work has a beginning and an end. When the work is finished, the team disbands or moves on to new projects. Producing unique products or services is why projects are often referred to as *one-time shots*.

It is often easiest to understand what projects are by also stating what they are not. If projects are temporary and unique, ongoing operations are neither; for example:

- Developing a more accurate weather forecasting software model is a project; using the model to forecast the weather week after week is an operation.
- Implementing a software package to process loan applications at a credit union is a project; processing the loan applications becomes an ongoing operation.
- Installing robots to paint automobile bodies at an assembly plant is a project; painting cars is an operation.
- Writing a professional development class on risk management is a project; presenting the class repeatedly to many customers is an ongoing operation.

THE NEED FOR A DIFFERENT DISCIPLINE

The definition of a project gives us clues as to why projects can be so troublesome—if we get only one chance to do it right, how can we ever hope to succeed? Refer to Exhibit 1.1 and consider the challenges inherent in managing one-time shots:

- *Staffing.* As the project has a start and a finish, so does the project team. The more unique the project is to your firm, the greater the difficulty in assembling a team with the appropriate skill mix. Compound that problem by trying to run many projects simultaneously, all with different durations and different team size requirements. You may have the need for 500 people to work on projects this quarter but need only half that many next quarter. Where do the people come from? Where do they go? Balancing the projects undertaken against the staff and resources available is a critical organizational capability.
- *Budgeting.* Most budget cycles are set to reflect accounting cycles dictated by the Internal Revenue Service and other government agencies. However, projects are driven by other factors and often cannot wait for the next budgeting cycle. If you are beginning your fiscal year and find

EXHIBIT 1.1 Projects versus operations

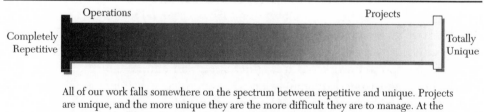

All of our work falls somewhere on the spectrum between repetitive and unique. Projects are unique, and the more unique they are the more difficult they are to manage. At the extreme end of the scale, research projects attempt to manage discovery. At the other extreme, work that is almost completely repetitive has been automated and is performed by computers or robots.

out your nearest competitor is gearing up to release an improved product, you don't want to wait until next year's budgeting process to find money to launch your own product development effort.

- *Authority.* When "politics" gets in the way of project progress, we usually mean that the authority structures set up to manage the ongoing operation aren't serving the project. That's not surprising, given that projects often require cooperation and participation across the normal functional boundaries within the firm. The unique nature of projects means that a single vertical line of authority is more the exception than the norm on projects.

- *Estimating.* As new projects are considered, deadlines and budgets are estimated to set financial goals such as return on investment. However, given that estimating requires forecasting the future, these cost and schedule goals are often built more on assumptions than facts. The project team is being asked to create something unique; that means it will solve new problems and encounter unexpected obstacles. Even projects that are similar to previous efforts can be difficult to forecast because most projects contain so many variables.

- *Communication.* If people are the engine of accomplishing work, communication is the heart of true productivity. It is easy to understand why "constant effective communication among everyone involved in the project" is considered a project success factor.[1] Projects that require cooperative, concerted effort from temporary, cross-functional project teams must re-create basic communication channels on every project.

As challenging as it can be to manage a project, the problem is magnified when a firm or department has tens or even hundreds of projects. Each project has its own risks, stakeholders, communication channels, and resource requirements. The project management discipline has evolved to address the challenges of individual projects and continues to evolve to address the problems faced by project-based organizations.

A BRIEF HISTORY OF PROJECT MANAGEMENT

Although human history is marked by projects—from the Roman aqueducts to the American transcontinental railroad—project management was not developed as a separate discipline until the mid-twentieth century. Beginning with the nuclear weapons programs after World War II, specific techniques emerged for planning and managing their enormous budgets and workforce. The most well-known, PERT (Program Evaluation and Review Technique) and CPM (Critical Path Method), have become synonymous for project scheduling techniques. (Both PERT and CPM were much more than scheduling techniques, but the scheduling graphics they produced, called *PERT charts* and *Critical Path charts,* were so distinctive that many people have mistakenly equated project management with PERT and Critical Path charts.)

PERT and CPM evolved through the 1950s and 1960s to become commonplace on major space and defense programs, but they saw limited use beyond those industries. From the mid-1960s through the mid-1980s, project management methods grew and matured but still found a relatively limited audience. Even at universities, project management was usually taught on a limited basis in some engineering schools. However, in the 1990s, interest in project management soared because of a convergence of several factors. Computer technology was making a huge difference in the way we worked. More powerful computers and software also made it easier to use the classic project management techniques. Project management methods today are not that much changed from a generation ago, but they have become commonly accepted in every industry.

FUNCTIONS OF PROJECT MANAGEMENT

The project management discipline covers a broad spectrum of concepts, tools, and techniques designed to enable the best possible project selection and execution. Exhibit 1.2 breaks down the discipline of project management into the major functions an organization must perform to take a project from concept to delivery.

EXHIBIT 1.2 Project management functions

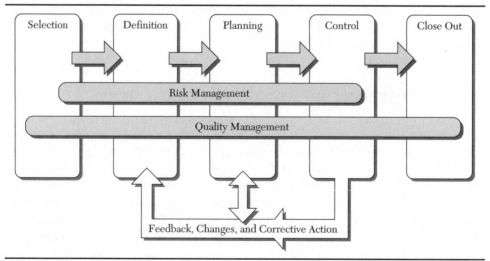

Selection

Pursuing the correct projects is easily as important as the effectiveness with which the project is carried out. Project selection contains the following activities:

- *Create a business case for the project.* The business case describes the project's purpose and benefits in relation to the goals of the firm; identifies financial targets for the project such as return on investment, internal rate of return, and payback period; and estimates resources in cost and personnel. It serves as a basis for documenting commitment to the project.
- *Align the project's goals in the organization.* Aligning the project tests project goals against strategic goals for the firm and other involved stakeholders. For instance, if multiple departments must cooperate to accomplish a project, understand how the project will help the departments meet their goals.
- *Prioritize the project relative to other projects and ongoing operations.* Every firm has limited time, people, and money to spend on projects. Therefore, each new project must be weighed against existing commitments and available resources.

It is important to recognize that the project manager responsible for delivering the project is rarely involved in any of the selection activities. Operational or product managers typically develop the business case and test the project for goal alignment. Executives prioritize the project. That is a risk for the project, the project manager, and the organization, which is why the risk management function overlaps project selection.

Definition

After a project is selected, a project manager is assigned and goes to work building the foundation for the project's success. Project definition activities include the following:

- *Identify all stakeholders on the project and document their goals and involvement.* Stakeholders include customers, vendors, core team members, and supporting management in the firm.
- *Develop a relationship with the project sponsor.* A sponsor is an executive in the organization who is responsible for the success of the project. While the project manager performs the day-to-day oversight of the project, the sponsor provides the executive authority necessary to overcome organizational obstacles.
- *Record the goals and constraints of the project using a statement of work or similar document.* Goals and constraints can include the scope, budget,

key schedule milestones, authority structure for the project, measures of success, communication standards, and other facts or assumptions that will affect the project. This document is then signed by the project stakeholders, establishing a baseline agreement.

Project definition is the foundation for success because it establishes a common understanding of the goals and constraints of the project. Without it, the project team is shooting at a moving target.

Planning

With a clear goal in place, documented by the statement of work and business case, the project manager builds the action plan that describes the who, what, when, where, and how of accomplishing the project. Planning typically includes the following activities:

- *Develop a detailed description of the work on the project using a work breakdown structure (WBS).* The WBS breaks the overall work of the project into small, individual tasks, much the same way an organization chart for a company breaks down authority.
- *Analyze the sequence of the tasks.* For all the tasks on the WBS, understand which tasks have to be performed before others. The classic diagram for this analysis is called a *network diagram.* (Both PERT and Critical Path charts are forms of network diagrams.)
- *Estimate the tasks to determine the required skills, effort, equipment, and materials.* Even though the business case provides a high-level cost estimate, it is necessary to have detailed estimates to assign resources to accomplish tasks.
- *Use the detailed information derived from the work breakdown structure, network diagram, and task estimating to create "bottom-up" estimates for the project.* In other words, add up the cost, and schedule estimates of the individual tasks to determine the cost and duration of the entire project.
- *Establish detailed project schedules documenting specific start and finish dates, responsibilities, and completion criteria for each task.*
- *Determine the number of people on the team and what skills are necessary.* For part-time team members, identify the dates their skills and effort are required. Staffing the project team often requires negotiating with other project managers or functional managers.
- *Prepare contracts for vendors who are participating in the project.*

Control

The control function can be likened to driving a car: The driver monitors the vehicle and the environment, intentionally steers toward the destination, and takes corrective action as obstacles or unexpected events arise. For project managers, driving the project includes:

- *Monitor the progress of the project against the plan.* Projects are typically too large for subjective assessments of progress to be valuable. Instead, we need specific measurements, such as the percent of the budget consumed to date. The detailed nature of the project plan allows for detailed measurements of cost and schedule progress. We can see which tasks are late, which are early, and which are consuming more or less effort than was estimated.

- *Communicate with the project team and stakeholders.* Because life and projects rarely go as planned, continuous, purposeful communication is necessary to keep all project participants informed and working together in harmony. Stakeholder communication includes formal reporting to customers and management.

- *Form the project team and attend to its health.* Forming the team means assembling a disparate group of people into a team with a shared goal. Consciously build and maintain trusting relationships within the team. Monitor the quality of team decision making to ensure appropriate participation and productivity.

- *Maintain the cost-schedule-quality equilibrium.* During project selection and definition, the stakeholders agreed on what to create, how much to spend, and when it had to be delivered. The greatest threat to that balance comes from adding scope (additional work) during the project. Any changes to the project that affect the cost, schedule, or product must be approved by the project manager, customer, and other affected stakeholders.

- *Take corrective action to keep the project on track.*

Risk Management

Because every project is unique, every project includes a high degree of uncertainty. Risk management is the systematic practice of identifying and reducing the threats that exist in the project and the project's environment. Planning for risk begins during the development of the business case and continues through definition and planning as each successive function provides a more detailed view of the project. During the control function, risk management activities mirror the other control activities as we monitor and communicate each risk and, if necessary, take action to respond to the risk.

Quality Management

Delivering the correct product or service, which performs as the customer expects, is no accident. Practices developed and established within the quality discipline (as defined by Deming, Crosby, et al.) can be applied to the project management discipline. This integration begins as the project is conceived and carries forward until the outcome of the project is created and is accepted by the customer. These practices focus on clearly understanding what the customer wants and consciously planning to deliver it, including methods for ensuring the product will be correctly built.

Close Out

Project completion goes beyond delivery of the product. In addition to ensuring customer acceptance, the project manager will disband the project team and dismantle the project infrastructure. A significant goal of project close out is capturing the lessons of the project so that they can be passed on to the organization.

As demonstrated in Exhibit 1.2, the functions of definition, planning, and control are ongoing throughout the project. It is important to recognize that no matter how well a project is defined or planned, during the course of the project, changes can occur that require the scope, cost, schedule, or some other constraint to be modified. When that happens, the project manager will revisit the activities included in project definition and planning.

PROJECT SUCCESS: THE TRIPLE CONSTRAINT

The functions of project management provide for gaining agreement on what should be built, the cost or price of the product, and when it must be delivered. In project management jargon, we term this the cost-schedule-quality equilibrium or *triple constraint*. These three variables define the overall goals of a project; therefore, any project that is "on time, on budget, high quality" is declared a success. The difficulty, however, exists in their relationship to one another. The term *equilibrium* sums up the challenge: The quality of the product we create depends on the time and money we are willing to spend. After a balance between these variables is struck, a change to one will affect the other two.

Achieving the proper balance of cost, schedule, and quality is beyond the control of the project manager alone. All stakeholders, particularly those involved in project selection, influence the choices and trade-offs that make up the triple constraint.

PROJECT MANAGERS MUST BE LEADERS

The discipline of project management can lead us astray. With all its structured methods and specialized reports, it can create the illusion that if a person learns the discipline, he or she will surely lead successful projects. Projects are much too messy to be ruled merely by organized documentation. The methods and mechanics of project management are essential, but they are not sufficient.

Forming a team to build something from nothing requires a range of leadership skills and characteristics. Effective project managers are able to:

- *Communicate a vision.* Projects start with problems and finish with products. They begin with fuzzy ideas and result in tangible services. To lead all the stakeholders on this journey requires the ability to communicate the destination and the path to achieve it.

- *Motivate and inspire the team.* Every project—from the daunting to the mundane—benefits from a motivated team.

- *Build trust within the team.* A fundamental component of a high-performance team is the trust that enables team members to rely on one another both for support and appropriate criticism. Project managers set the tone that fosters open communication and honesty, which fosters trust and strong relationships.

- *Influence stakeholders beyond the project team.* Customers, vendors, other projects, and senior management all contribute to the project but do not report directly to the project manager. Gaining cooperation outside official authority is essential for project managers.

- *Make abstract things concrete.* Transforming a concept to reality requires the ability to sift through assumptions and generalities to take meaningful results-oriented action.

- *Demonstrate persistence and determination.* Not every project is tough, but few are easy. Projects are full of unexpected problems, which require a leader who will not give up easily.

- *Manage and resolve conflict.* Conflict is a natural part of change. As people struggle to invent new products and processes, the project team must not run from conflict; rather it must work through it to reach the best decisions while respecting and maintaining team relationships.

- *Know when to make a decision.* Balance the need for more information, more participation, and the urgency of the situation.

- *Maintain the big picture perspective while organizing details.* Project managers are responsible for achieving the overall goals by directing the details.

This list could go on. The nature of projects makes them unruly and prone to chaos. It takes a firm, disciplined hand at the wheel to keep the project and all the stakeholders moving in a purposeful, concerted direction toward success.

The discipline or "science" of project management makes up an essential tool set. The "art" of leadership lifts the human component of the project to its potential. Neither the art nor the science is sufficient on its own. Together, they form a powerful force that overcomes great adversity and enables us to accomplish any goal.

PROJECT MANAGEMENT IS A GROWTH INDUSTRY

Projects are temporary and produce unique products. Both of these character-istics make managing projects not just difficult, but different from managing ongoing operations. The project management discipline contains methods, tools, and concepts that were specifically developed to ensure that each project meets cost, schedule, and quality goals.

The use of project management methods has grown tremendously over the past decade, and all indications are that the trend will continue. Computer-based project management tools continue to add powerful features that make it more practical to apply the classic techniques. Growing demand for project managers has led to explosive growth in the number of universities offering de-grees or certification in project management. However, these factors are merely proof that this discipline is becoming a necessary skill in most organizations. The root cause of the growing use of project management is the increasing rate of change in our economy and our places of work.

PROJECT MANAGEMENT AS A STRATEGIC STRENGTH

What is the single largest factor driving the increased use of project manage-ment methods? The ever-present, ever-increasing pace of change present in our world today. Whether you work in health care, banking, professional ser-vices, manufacturing, aerospace, computer hardware and software, telecom-munications, or entertainment, you feel the changes all around you. You can be employed by a government agency, nonprofit firm, small business, or Fortune 500 corporation, and you will experience the constant change that comes from rapidly growing computing power and global competition. The number and va-riety of changes surrounding us have many sources, and each change spawns others, creating an ever-growing web of change.

This climate of ever-faster change has created new challenges and new opportunities. All firms are challenged to keep up with the pace or risk being left behind. The opportunities for the quick and agile are exemplified by tech-nology companies that started from scratch and made their founders billion-aires within a decade or less. However, the opportunities are not limited to wireless telecommunications, computer networking, or software businesses. Starbucks, the Seattle-based coffee retailer, has grown from a few friendly shops in Seattle to a worldwide chain in less than ten years.

Business gurus and corporate chieftains noticed this shift in the late twentieth century:

- Tom Peters characterized the challenge in the title of his 1987 book, *Thriving on Chaos.*
- Andy Grove, CEO of Intel, titled his 1996 book, *Only the Paranoid Survive.*

- Peter Senge described the "learning organization" as the new paradigm for corporate survival in his landmark book *The Fifth Discipline*, published in 1990. He quotes an executive as saying, "The ability to learn faster than your competitors may be the only sustainable competitive advantage."[2]
- Jack Welch, of GE, perhaps the most respected CEO of the 1990s, observed in 1994, "I'm in my 14th year of running a global company, and I've been wrong about a lot of things in those 14 years; but one prediction I've made at least 14 times that has always come true is that things are going to get tougher; the shakeouts more brutal and the pace of change more rapid."[3]

As change becomes a constant, the project management discipline moves to the forefront of organizational capability *because change is accomplished through projects.* The ability to properly select and effectively execute projects is as integrally tied to the success of a firm as its choice of products and markets.

A NEW STRATEGIC STRENGTH

Effective execution of projects has always been important. It has never been acceptable to be over budget, behind schedule, or delivering the wrong product. In the past, however, project management has been seen as a *tactical* strength. In the words of Steve Weidner, president of Program Navigators, executives' attitudes toward project management was "I hire people, who hire people, who hire people to manage projects." Because projects were carried out far from the strategic planning sessions in the executive offices, senior management could ignore the details and discipline of project management.

Has anything really changed? Are CIOs and CFOs paying attention to project schedules? Can the ability to manage projects actually become a competitive advantage?

Before we assess whether project management is a strategic strength for your firm, we must first define the term itself. *Strategic strength* refers to a competitive edge that influences the strategy of the firm. At best, it is such a dominant strength that it keeps competitors from entering the marketplace, shaking their heads, and exclaiming "I can't compete with that!"

Consider some strategic strengths of the past:

- Economies of scale allowed manufacturers to produce more products at a cheaper rate. Henry Ford pioneered this idea, and it was refined throughout the twentieth century. By 2000, this strength was cited by banks and entertainment companies, such as Bank of America and Disney, as they rapidly acquired or merged with their competitors.
- Large, established distribution networks provide channels for delivering products to the customer. U.S. automakers have a much larger share of rural U.S. markets because their dealer network is stronger than that of

foreign competitors. Coca-Cola and McDonalds also enjoy worldwide distribution networks.

- Specialized skills and processes enable a firm to produce better products less expensively. Sony has proven repeatedly that it is the master of consumer technology. Sony's products often work better and are more user-friendly even though they are cost competitive.

Can project management capability be as important to an organization as these strategic strengths have been in the past? The determining factor is how dependent the firm is on successful projects.

TACTICAL OR STRATEGIC?

Project management is not a strategic strength for every firm, because not every firm is project-based. For example, it would be difficult to make a case for most retail stores to focus on project management as a strategic competency. The following factors help you assess the relative importance of projects to your firm and your career. The more that these factors are true for an organization, the more project management will be a strategic competency. Realize that these factors may be assessed for the entire enterprise or for a specific division or department. The statements are organized so that the first five assess the importance of projects to your career and the last six apply to your firm.

Respond to the following statements as to strategic importance of project management skills to your career:

- *Project management is an important tactical skill for me.* If you manage projects, project management is an important tactical skill because it helps you perform your current job better. The more projects you manage and the larger the projects are, the more important this skill becomes.

- *My organization has a high proportion of budget or revenue attributed to projects.* If your firm derives a significant portion of revenue from project-based work, your ability to manage projects well is a direct reflection of your value to your firm. This is also true if your firm has a high proportion of its budget allocated to projects because you will be instrumental in creating the most value for the money spent. If you work for a consulting firm or general contractor whose primary source of revenue is delivering project-based services, this factor applies to you. However, you could also agree highly with this statement if you work in a project-based support group in a nonproject-based company. For instance, most information technology (IT) departments have a high proportion of their budgets devoted to projects, even though the company as a whole might be a manufacturer or a retail chain.

- *My profession is driven by projects.* This factor applies to you if most people in your profession or with your skill set work a large proportion of their time on projects. For instance, engineers tend to spend much of their time on projects, so any engineer will find his or her career opportunities expand as he or she masters project management skills. Because fewer professionals are spending their entire careers with a single employer, this factor has an even greater impact on your career.

- *I have many projects under my span of control.* Ironically, strong agreement with this statement has often been associated with people who don't understand project management principles. They prefer "to leave the details to the people managing the projects." However, if you have many projects that you are responsible for, your ability to monitor and mentor multiple project managers will improve if you use project management techniques.

- *I have career goals to significantly increase my responsibilities.* Whether you work in a project-based organization or not, your ability to manage a new initiative, pioneer a new product, or solve a unique problem will make you stand out among your peers. The career ladders are packed with people who are competent at the normal requirements of your firm; you will distinguish yourself because you can handle what isn't normal.

As these factors are considered, it may be useful to distinguish between the overall purpose of a company or agency and the purpose of a department. As noted in the previous questions, a support department can be very project-driven while the business as a whole is not. It is useful to respond to these statements from both perspectives.

Respond to these statements about project management as a strategic competency for your firm:

- *Project management is an important tactical skill for my firm.* If there are projects in the firm, it is at least a tactical skill because it is always important to execute tasks efficiently.

- *My firm has a high proportion of budget/revenue attributed to projects.* The connection here is obvious. If the business derives a large proportion of revenue from project-related work, project management capability will make the firm more competitive; it will be able to provide lower cost, higher quality products to customers. Similarly, when a significant amount of the budget is spent on projects, strong project management gives a firm more value for the money spent.

- *My industry is driven by projects.* When your industry is driven by projects, your competitors are also engaged in managing projects. Who will be faster to market? Who will have the better product or the more competitive cost? A number of factors cause an industry to be driven by projects:
  —If your firm and your competitors deliver project-based services, your industry is driven by projects. A wide variety of service businesses, from construction to accounting to information technology, falls into this category.

—Shelf life and complexity of your products drive projects. In the software product industry (e.g., Microsoft, Novell, Adobe, Oracle), the products are complex and difficult to create (though simple to manufacture), and they have a relatively short shelf life with significant new releases coming out every 18 to 30 months. Therefore, these firms are constantly engaged in product-development projects.

—The complexity and uniqueness of your products drive projects. Aerospace and pharmaceutical companies have these factors in common. Military aircraft and cancer-fighting drugs are tremendously expensive and take years to develop. In these industries, shaving 10 percent off a budget can generate millions of dollars in savings.

—If you are in a growth industry, it is driven by projects, because at the least you are rapidly adding capacity. However, growth industries are typically characterized by innovation as well—meaning you will need to change rapidly to stay in the game.

—Industries associated with technology are forced to change rapidly and constantly as they either produce new technology or use it to leverage other competitive strengths.

- *My firm has many independent projects.* Independent projects—where the products or customers are unrelated—magnify the challenges of managing projects. Compare managing a wide variety of unrelated projects to juggling a basketball, an apple, a golf shoe, and a flaming torch. Juggling is difficult enough, but the difference in weight, size, and shape of all these items compounds the difficulty. So, too, with a variety of projects, all of which ultimately share the same set of corporate or department resources.

- *My firm has significant growth goals.* Growth comes through change, and change is accomplished by projects. Too often, a company with a hot product is choked by its inability to grow its infrastructure to support the demand. When that happens, the revenues grow but the costs grow faster, cutting the profits and squeezing cash flow.

- *My firm has important projects whose failure will cripple the firm.* If you have strategic projects, the ability to carry them out is a strategic strength.

Many of these factors probably apply to you. For firms with many of these factors, project management is more than a tactical strength—it is a capability that can fundamentally change the organization's ability to compete.

THE STRATEGIC ADVANTAGE

The factors outlined previously show that projects play a large role in an organization. However, just because a firm has many projects, and many important projects, how does that make project management a strategic strength? There are two fundamental answers to that question: outperforming your competition and reducing risk.

In athletic competition, a coach often emphasizes the fundamentals of the game during all practices because of the obvious reality that no game plan can succeed without mastery of the fundamentals. Projects in every endeavor share this emphasis on fundamentals. No matter how good our strategy, poor execution causes us to fail, which is a tactical issue. It becomes a strategic strength when the consistency and speed of our execution enables us to change our strategy. The following examples demonstrate how project management— once considered mere "blocking and tackling"—can change the game plan:

- Through the use of good project management and process improvement methods, a financial services firm was able to slash its product development cycle from 14 months to 8 months. Now this firm can deliver a new product in about 60 percent of the time it takes a competitor. That provides a cost advantage (therefore, a profit advantage), but the strategic advantage is the ability to always be first to market when new opportunities appear.

- There is perhaps no better example of the strategic importance of speed than in computer hardware and software development companies. *Moore's Law* has postulated that computing power doubles every 18 months. So far, it is holding true. The implication for firms that develop hardware is that they need to constantly be designing and developing new products, often with two or more generations of products in development at the same time. Software development companies are in the same situation. They are constantly working on the next release of their product to take advantage of new processing power and memory capabilities, as well as re-sponding to shifts in the marketplace. In this never-ending product development race, the firm that can consistently deliver the best product to the market window has the advantage. When firms fail to maintain this pace, they not only fall behind, they are out of the race. Project management is one of the fundamental abilities that enable a firm to consistently deliver a better product faster and at less cost.

- One of the factors fueling the economic expansion of the 1990s was im-proved productivity. New technology enabled firms to accomplish more with fewer people. The firms who have mastered project management quickly take advantage of new cost-saving ideas without throwing their op-erations into an uproar. On the other hand, firms that struggle with every new project often spend far more implementing the new idea than they will ever realize from the cost savings. For instance, companies that have installed so-called enterprise resource planning systems (ERP systems such as PeopleSoft, Baan, SAP, and many others) reduce information sys-tem costs and, importantly, gain greater understanding of their operations through more integrated information management. ERP systems enable these firms to fine-tune operations and produce significant cost savings.

Implementing these productivity tools and processes is often complex; therefore, good project management is essential. Too many firms have spent millions of dollars on the software and services required to implement these ERP systems yet have nothing to show for it. They are mired in the complexity of adjusting their way of doing business and matching it to the new computer system. It is a complete lose-lose situation, wasting money and failing to gain the competitive advantages that an ERP system can provide.

- Hospitals and health-care networks also face the need to morph rapidly for survival. They are refining and updating internal business practices to rein in costs and improve service. Organizations that have been successful with these reengineering initiatives have become the new leaders—while those that fail have had to merge with or be taken over by competitors.

These examples demonstrate how effective project execution allows a firm to adopt more aggressive growth goals. When every project costs less and is consistently performed faster, we can take on more new initiatives—whether they are for efficiency, customer satisfaction, or new products and markets.

Outperforming the competition is one reason project management is a strategic competency. Risk management is the other reason.

Every new endeavor—from ERP system implementation to new product development—is filled with uncertainty, both good (opportunities) and bad (risks). Often, the greater the opportunity is, the greater the risk. The uncertainty is why we tend to get nervous while working on projects. Then add to the problem that most projects are initiated based on more assumptions than facts, and the project-based organization begins to look like a high-stakes gamble. However, avoiding all projects to reduce risks also means avoiding all opportunities. The answer is being able to engage in projects and to better manage the associated uncertainty—to play the game but improve our odds of winning.

The gambling analogy is apt. Casinos with blackjack tables know the odds are in favor of the house. But those gamblers who have learned to "count cards"—by some method, remember the cards that have already been dealt—tip the odds in their favor. They don't win every hand, but they win more than they lose—enough so that when a card counter is recognized, the casino may not allow him or her to play.

Project management techniques are methods for reducing uncertainty and, therefore, improving our odds of success. Whether you manage a cost center or a profit center, every time you take on a project, you take on a risk. The more projects you have, the more the risk can be magnified or reduced, depending on your ability to plan and manage projects. Project management techniques reduce risk in three fundamental ways:

1. *Forecasting the future:* When you can see the future, you improve your odds dramatically. That's why good sailors watch the weather reports so carefully. Project management techniques do not provide a clear picture

of the future. Rather, they are like weather forecasting techniques; they leverage past experience to understand the present and provide a range of probable outcomes for the future.

2. *Early problem recognition:* Simply put, small problems are easier to solve than big ones. The structured tools of project management enable early problem recognition and resolution. That includes canceling or dramatically redirecting projects that have gone off track or no longer make sense. The difference is that these problem projects are found earlier, after spending less corporate resources, therefore reducing the loss.

3. *Improved communication:* There is no more common cause of project failure than communication breakdowns. Whether the misunderstanding is over what, why, or how to build the product, communication failures lead to wasted effort, time, and money. Every facet of project management improves communication, from techniques to gain early stakeholder cooperation, to scope management and cost control methods. The discipline provides a structured, systematic way to know and agree on every what, why, when, how, where, and who.

Reduced risk makes project management a strategic competency because it alters the opportunity-versus-risk equation. It changes the long-standing financial rule that high returns require high risk. Because of that, it allows firms to play in high-stakes games and win more consistently.

In summary, project management can be a strategic strength because it makes firms stronger competitors. It produces consistently better project performance, more accurate cost and schedule forecasts, and early problem recognition. That, in turn, improves the ability to manage the project portfolio—to select the projects with the greatest return and cancel those that are not living up to expectations. A strategic strength is an ability that provides a competitive advantage. In this world of rapid change, it is increasingly difficult to sustain operational advantages, making it all the more important to master the discipline of change.

STRATEGIC COMPETENCIES

Firms that have recognized project management as a strategic competency are responding by adding three primary components: project portfolio management, consistency in project management tools and techniques, and a project management office.

Project portfolio management refers to the methods used to select and oversee projects. The term *portfolio management* conjures up the appropriate analogy to managing an investment portfolio because each project is an investment of the firm's limited resources. The project portfolio management capability typically has four components:

1. *Project selection criteria:* Consistent criteria are used to accept projects and to set performance measurements. The first sign the selection criteria are working is that some proposed projects are rejected.
2. *Goal alignment:* The people charged with project portfolio oversight clearly understand the overall goals of the firm and ensure that all projects support these goals.
3. *Resource planning:* Projects are prioritized and chosen with the knowledge that the firm has limited people and budgets available. Most firms that lack this component find they are working on far more projects than they can accomplish—therefore, they get only partial completion on all but a few projects.
4. *Ongoing oversight:* Given that projects are unique, changes in budgets, schedules, and priority are to be expected. Regularly scheduled progress reports allow the portfolio management team to spot run-away projects early, cancel projects that no longer meet selection criteria, or divert additional resources to projects that increase in priority.

Consistent project management tools and techniques are the basis for improving overall project performance. Early in the chapter, we established that many of the challenges of managing projects arise from the fact that projects are, to some degree, unique. Exhibit 1.3 illustrates the goal of using consistent project management practices on all projects in a firm—that consistent project management practices leverage what is similar about projects, thereby making them less unique. This, in turn, should reduce some of the challenges inherent in managing unique work. Exhibit 1.4 lists potential project management tools that could be standardized in an organization. Firms seek several benefits from these consistent tools and methods:

- A common vocabulary exists across all projects. Mistakes caused by miscommunication are reduced as all project participants use common terms to discuss project issues.
- The ability to exchange project data, particularly to combine data from multiple subprojects to gain an overall "super project" view.

EXHIBIT 1.3 Project management maturity

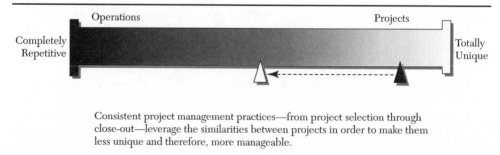

Consistent project management practices—from project selection through close-out—leverage the similarities between projects in order to make them less unique and therefore, more manageable.

EXHIBIT 1.4   Potential standard deliverables by project phase

Define

- Charter
- Statement of work
- Responsibility matrix
- Communication plan
- Order-of-magnitude estimating guidelines

Plan

- Risk profiles
- Risk log
- Risk management plan
- Work breakdown structure
- Guidelines for task size
- Network diagram (PERT)
- Gantt chart
- Cost-estimating worksheet

Execute

- Status reports for different audiences
- Cost and schedule tracking charts
- Meeting agendas, including open task reports
- Cost-tracking guidelines
- Issues log
- Change request form
- Change log

Close Out

- Postproject review agenda and guidelines
- Postproject review report
- Client satisfaction assessment
- Project history file guidelines
- Project summary report

- Consistent format improves communication with management and customers.
- The common methods and decision points form the firm's project management process. After a baseline process is established, it becomes possible to improve the common process based on the successes and failures encountered on individual projects.
- Common practices form the basis for building project management skills.

A project management office (PMO) is some organizational unit that is responsible for the project management capabilities of the firm. In practice, this office has been called a variety of names and has a range of responsibilities, which are described in Exhibit 1.5. Whatever the overall responsibilities of the PMO, the fundamental reason a PMO must exist is that it gives some person or

EXHIBIT 1.5   Project office forms and responsibilities

Responsibility	Center of Excellence	Project Support Office	Project Management Office	Program Management Office	Accountable Project Office
Maintain standards	●	●	●	●	●
Organize training	○	○	○	○	○
Mentoring and consulting support	○	●	●	●	●
Schedule and budget analysis		●	●	●	●
Enterprise project information		●	●	●	●
Make project management decisions				●	●
Supervise project managers			○		●
Meeting project objectives			○	○	●
Career growth for project managers	○	○	●	○	●
Supply project managers to the organization			○		●
Participate in project portfolio management	○	○	○	●	●

Legend: ● = Full responsibility
   ○ = Partial responsibility
   Blank = No responsibility

group ownership of the project management process. Without a PMO, any efforts to create consistent project management practices will be viewed as optional and will soon become out of date. It is almost impossible to think of a firm having a portfolio management capability in place without some form of PMO to create and enforce the necessary project initiation and reporting standards.

How does a department or entire firm implement these capabilities? That is the subject of this entire book. The chapters that follow detail both the discipline of project management and the path to project management maturity.

SUMMARY OF PROJECT MANAGEMENT AS A STRATEGIC STRENGTH

The opening of the twenty-first century is characterized by an increasing pace of change, and change is accomplished through projects. Whether you work in government, nonprofit, or large or small business, your firm must adapt; it must either drive change or, at a minimum, keep up with your peers.

The increasing pace of change causes greater uncertainty for all organizations. The discipline of project management can reduce the risks of uncertainty. This discipline uses proven techniques to select, plan, and execute projects to reduce the cost and schedule required and to improve the quality of the result.

As firms are increasingly driven by projects, the ability to manage projects consistently and competently is changing from a tactical competency to a strategic competency. Firms that recognize project management as a strategic capability—an ability that gives them a competitive advantage—are viewing project management as a process that can be defined and consistently improved. These firms are focusing on three components:

1. A rigorous portfolio management process to correctly choose which projects to invest in and to oversee existing projects.
2. Consistent project management methods so that each project is using reliable techniques for planning and managing.
3. A project management office responsible for maintaining and improving the portfolio management process and project management methods.

This book describes the proven discipline of project management and how project-based organizations can use that discipline to thrive.

NOTES

1. Eric Verzuh, *The Fast Forward MBA in Project Management* (New York: Wiley, 1999), p. 8.

2. Peter Senge, *The Fifth Discipline: The Art and Practice of the Learning Organization* (New York: Doubleday, 1990), p. 4.

3. Janet Lowe, *Jack Welch Speaks: Wisdom from the World's Greatest Business Leader* (New York: Wiley, 1998), p. 98.

LEADING THE CHANGE TO A PROJECT-BASED ORGANIZATION

2

Robert J. Graham and Randall L. Englund

Most future growth in organizations will result from successful development projects that generate new products, services, or procedures. Such projects are also a principal way of creating organizational change; implementing change and growth strategies is usually entrusted to project managers. However, project success is often as much a result of the organizational environment as of the skills of the project manager. As the size and importance of projects increase, the project manager becomes the head of a complex development operation with an organizational dimension that can make important contributions to project success or failure. That this organizational dimension may help explain project performance has been strangely neglected in the literature, a problem addressed here by examining the role of upper management in creating an environment that promotes project success.

All too commonly, people become project managers by accident. One way to become a project manager is to ask a question at a meeting and then be told, "That's a good question. Why don't you take on the project of dealing with that problem?" Or somebody comes up with an idea and is tapped to make it happen, or the generator of the idea looks around for the first person in sight to whom it can be assigned for implementation. Experience indicates that in the process of developing projects, upper managers often appoint inexperienced or accidental project managers (APMs), given them a project to manage—and then systematically undermine their ability to achieve success. Upper managers do not usually undermine APMs on purpose, but too often they apply assumptions and

26

methods to project management that are more appropriate to regular departmental management. Projects are in many ways a totally different beast. Everyday management generally is a matter of repeating various standard processes, but projects create something new.

In addition, upper managers are often unaware how their behavior influences project success or failure. Because previous examinations of project success focus almost exclusively on the functions of the project manager, there is an understandable lack of awareness of the importance of the project environment and the behavior of middle and higher managers in organizations—those managers of project managers that we refer to as *upper managers.* It is important to understand the impact of their behavior on the future survival of organizations. Roles and responsibilities are changing as organizations become organic and project-based—that is, driven by internal markets and team accountability for specific results. Any lapses by upper managers in the authenticity and integrity of their dealings with project managers and with managers in other departments are likely to have a severe impact on the achievement of project goals.

A SCENARIO

Many upper managers voice increasing frustration with the results of projects undertaken in their areas of responsibility. They lament that despite sending people out for training and buying project management software, projects seem to take too long, cost too much, and produce less than the desired results. Why is that? To help understand the problem, consider the following scenario.

An upper manager gets an idea, perhaps from reading a book or attending a conference, and has a vision of a product or service that the organization can offer. This vision may differ from what the company normally provides, so creating the product becomes a special project. Talking it over with associates, the manager is delighted when one of the best engineers becomes interested. To get the concept rolling, the manager asks this engineer to manage the project. They both figure the project can be done quickly because the engineer has achieved good results on past work. The new project manager talks to a few friends, and soon a team of engineers begins working on the design. After a while, the team comes back to the upper manager with good news and bad news. The good news is that one needed technology is available inside the organization; it was developed in another division, however, so the team needs to borrow a few people from there to get it. The bad news is that another needed technology is not available in the organization, so new people will have to be hired. The upper manager arranges to borrow people from the other division and authorizes the new outside hires.

Delay begins about here. The new hires must be approved by the executive committee and then must have job descriptions defined and developed by the personnel department. As these new people know the latest technology, they are expensive; even so, once on board it takes them longer than expected to become productive because they are not used to the ways of their new employer. Eventually, however, the whole group gets working—until a manager from the other division, for which this special project is not a priority, takes back the borrowed engineers. Work slows again as the upper manager tries to negotiate their return. Some engineers are finally freed for the project, but not the same ones as before, so there are more delays until they are brought up to speed.

When work finally resumes, questions arise about marketing the new product and about using patented technology to create it. The upper manager must therefore add people from the marketing and legal departments to the project. Sure enough, the lawyers ascertain that the new hires inadvertently used a technology patented by another company; the upper manager must decide if it is cheaper to pay for its use or develop an alternative technology. The new project team members from marketing are difficult to communicate with because marketing uses a different e-mail system than that of engineering and legal. Decision making is further delayed as upper managers argue over a number of manufacturing issues that had come up on previous projects but were never resolved.

The team grows disgruntled as it becomes clear that the great engineer is not skilled in planning and conflict management; the situation is not improved when the engineer disappears for several weeks to fix problems that have arisen from a previous project. Elsewhere in the organization, people begin to grumble that the project is costing lots and accomplishing little. The upper manager spends time justifying the project to other department managers but cannot avoid finally being called before the executive committee to explain why it is taking so long and costing so much.

If this scenario seems at all far-fetched, consider this letter received by one of the authors:

> I work in a planning and distribution organization. My duties include leading efforts that are called projects and generally I'm fixing a problem with a process or system. Rarely do I get due dates or objectives . . . and when I press my sponsor[s] on this point they tell me essentially that they just want it done. Coupled with this the department has difficulty achieving the full intent of the objectives, and we are pretty unproductive (we don't get many projects completed in a year). We are putting together a proposal including development of dedicated project managers in the organization whose entire job is to lead the projects of the organization (as opposed to the current method of choosing people whose work is closely aligned to the project).
>
> Unfortunately, some managers feel strongly that they do not want their resources utilized by the project managers (and subject to the project manager's discretion). Plus they want to have access to their people to pursue their own objectives (this includes assigning one of their people as project lead[er] regardless of skill). At this point we need help in convincing these managers to support the process of project management. . . .

You can almost hear the voice trailing off in a sigh of frustration.

Another problem is the assumption that project work should take about as long as traditional work. This sets expectations that can never be met, so projects always seem slower and more costly than other activities. Actually, they should take longer; project work represents something new and different, so the inevitable unknowns, such as those in the scenario, should be factored into the expected length. It is also a false assumption that project work can be handled in the same way and using the same organization and the same people as other work. In reality, because project work is different it requires a project-based organization. The project in the scenario failed because upper management had not created an environment for project success.

CREATING AN ENVIRONMENT FOR SUCCESSFUL PROJECTS

What environmental components foster successful projects? Many misconceptions develop into folklore over time, such as the Humpty Dumpty nursery rhyme (see Box 2.1). The king's men may not have been able to put Humpty's pieces together, but the key pieces needed to create a picture of a supportive project environment (see Exhibit 2.1) can be readily assembled.

A word of caution: the pieces we are assembling will not stay together without glue, and the glue has two vital ingredients: *authenticity* and *integrity*. Authenticity means that upper managers really mean what they say. Integrity

---

Box 2.1

A Challenge

Humpty Dumpty sat on a wall
Humpty Dumpty had a great fall
All the King's Horses
and all the King's Men
couldn't put Humpty together again.

The character in this nursery rhyme is usually represented as an egg that falls and breaks. In reality, a humpty dumpty was a type of military cannon. During a battle it was put up on a wall. When the cannon was fired, the recoil sent it off the wall to the ground, where it came apart. The king's horses were the cavalry, and the king's men were the army. They were there to win the battle, but they couldn't put Humpty the cannon together again: they were not able to put together all the pieces required for success.

EXHIBIT 2.1   The components of an environment for sucessful projects

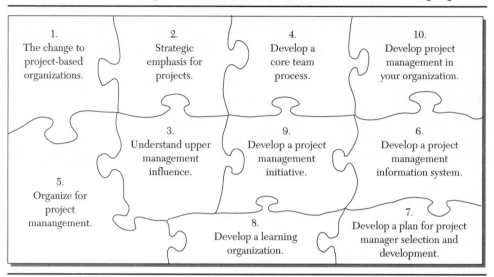

means that they really do what they say they will do, and for the reasons they stated to begin with. It is a recurring theme in our experience and our writing that authenticity and integrity link the head and the heart, the words and the action; they separate belief from disbelief, and often make the difference between success and failure.

1. *Change to project-based organizations.* The balance of this chapter examines a process for changing organizations and discusses the requirements of change agents. Changing to a project-based organization requires changes in the behavior of upper managers and project managers. For example, a project-based organization must also be team-based; to create such an organization, upper managers and project managers must themselves work as a team.

2. *Emphasize the link between strategy and projects.* It is important to link projects to strategy. Upper managers must work together to develop a strategic emphasis for projects. One factor in motivating project team members is to show them that the project they are working on has been selected as a result of a strategic plan. If they instead feel that the project was selected on a whim, that nobody wants it or supports it, and that it will most likely be canceled, they will probably (and understandably) not do their best work. Upper managers can help avoid this problem by linking the project to the strategic plan and developing a portfolio of projects that implements the plan. Many organizations use upper-management teams to manage the project portfolio; this approach would certainly have reduced the problems and delays depicted in the previous scenario.

Chevron, for example, developed the Chevron Project Development and Execution Process (CPDEP), which provides a formalized discipline for managing projects.[1] A key element of CPDEP is the involvement of all stakeholders at the appropriate time. In the initial process phase to identify and assess opportunities, a multifunctional team of upper managers meets to test the opportunity for strategic fit and to develop a preliminary overall plan. The project does not proceed from this phase unless there is a good fit with the overall strategy.

3. *Understand top management influence.* Many of the best practices of project management often fail to get upper-management support. Many upper managers are unaware of how their behavior influences project success. To help ensure success, they are advised to develop a project support system that incorporates such practices as negotiating the project deadline, supporting the creative process, allowing time for and supporting the concept of project planning, choosing not to interfere in project execution, demanding no useless scope changes, and changing the reward system to motivate project work.

4. *Develop a core team system.* A core team consists of people who represent the various departments necessary to complete a project. This team should be developed at the beginning of the project, and its members should stay with the project from beginning to end. Developing a core team system and making it work are essential to minimizing project cycle time and avoiding unnecessary delays. Important as they are, however, core teams are rarely implemented well without the implicit and explicit support of upper management. Firms that have used core teams, however, often report dramatic results; Cadillac, for example, found that core teams can accomplish styling changes that previously took 175 weeks in 90 to 150 weeks.[2]

5. *Organize for project management.* In the scenario earlier in this chapter, much of the delay can be attributed to the lack of an organizational design that supports project management. In contrast, the decentralized corporate culture of Hewlett-Packard (HP), for one, gives business managers a great deal of freedom in tackling new challenges. Upper managers have a responsibility to set up organizational structures that support successful projects.

6. *Develop a project management information system.* In the past, organizational policies, procedures, and authority relationships held things together. The project-based organization lacks much of that structural framework; instead, the project organization is kept intact by an information system. For example, HP executive vice president Rick Belluzzo envisions a "people-centric information environment that provides access to information any time, anywhere . . . and that spurs the development of a wide range of specialized devices and services that people can use to enrich their personal and professional lives."[3] Upper managers need to work in concert to develop an information system that supports successful projects and provides information across the organization. In this regard, online technological capabilities are increasingly attractive and important but do not replace the need for upper management to determine what information is necessary and develop a system to provide it.

7. *Develop a plan for project manager selection and development.* Future organizations will see the end of the accidental project manager. Project management must be seen as a viable position, not just a temporary annoyance, and

project management skill must become a core organizational competence. This requires a conscious, planned program for project manager selection and training. HP, Computer Science Corporation (CSC), Keane, and 3M are among the companies that have spent large amounts on project manager training and development. The development emphasis of these organizations seems justified because the project managers of today will become the leaders of the project-based organization of tomorrow. This is such an important topic that Bowen, Clark, Halloway, and Wheelwright have advised organizations to "make projects the school for leaders."[4]

8. *Develop a learning organization.* One key to organizational learning is the postproject review, which helps project participants and the rest of the organization learn from project experiences. Although its value may be priceless and its cost nil, this learning process takes place only if upper managers set up a formal program and require the reviews. When they do, many tools for project improvement can be developed that can help eliminate frustrating delays. For example, British Petroleum (BP) has operated a postproject appraisal unit since 1977, and BP managers attribute dramatic results to it; by learning from past projects, they say that they are much more accurate in developing new project proposals, have a much better idea of how long projects take, and thus experience less frustration at perceived project delays.[5] Learning from project experience becomes a major emphasis in project-based organizations and can be seen as a competitive advantage.

9. *Develop a project management initiative.* HP has an ongoing initiative to continually improve its project management practices. Dubbed the Project Management Initiative, it is part of senior management's breakthrough objective to get the right products to market quickly and effectively. The initiative group works with upper managers and project managers to increase project management knowledge and practice throughout the organization. Project management has become very important to HP's success because more than half of customer orders now come from products it introduced within the previous two years. Shorter product life cycles mean more new projects are needed to maintain growth. Marvin Patterson, a former director of corporate engineering at HP, says, "Due to my experience since I left HP, I would say that HP probably has the best project managers in the world, or at least in this hemisphere. The Project Management Initiative made a huge contribution to this success."

10. *Apply project management concepts to any organization that needs them.* For example, Honeywell developed a global information technology project management initiative, based on its chief information officer's desire to have modern project management disciplines throughout Honeywell Information Systems be "the way of doing business" and a "core competency." To accomplish this, the initiative group developed a project management focus group of fifteen people from different departments to discuss the basis of good project management. With input from this group, the initiative team developed a project management model, a project management process, and a

supporting training and education curriculum; it also promotes a professional project manager certification process. The team's vision is for Honeywell Information Systems to be recognized "as a world-class leader in modern Information Technology Project Management principles, processes, and practices."[6]

3M has developed a Project Management Professional Development Center, which consists of people and services from three information technology organizations. The center offers consulting help for project teams, research on the latest best practices and help in applying them, and a project management competency model supported by a project leader curriculum. It also sponsors a project leader forum, where project leaders can meet in person to share stories and problems. An "electronic post office," a communications network linking all project managers enhances communication.[7]

All of these examples represent significant efforts on the part of major corporations to meet the challenge of developing project management expertise. Such major effort is needed because the change to project management means changing some ingrained habits of organizational behavior. Many cherished and highly rewarded practices must be replaced by new practices, and this often requires major upheaval.

Major upheaval requires authenticity and integrity on the part of upper managers. Most change efforts do not fail from lack of concepts or from lack of a description of how to do it right. Most change programs fail when upper managers are hoisted on their own petard of inauthenticity and lack of integrity. This failure happens because people involved in the situations where managers violate authenticity and integrity sense the lack of resolve, feel the lack of leadership, and despair of the situation. When upper managers speak without authenticity, they stand like the naked emperor: they think they are clothed, but everyone else sees the truth. When upper managers lack integrity they do not "walk the walk," they only "talk the talk," and people sense the disconnection and become cynical. Management cannot ask others to change without first changing themselves. Implementing the concepts in this chapter depends on upper management's resolve to approach the needed changes with authenticity and integrity.

THE NEED FOR PROJECT MANAGEMENT

Forces outside the organization are pushing the need for project management. An important shift in the marketplace is that customers who were formerly content with products now demand total solutions to problems. In the past, customers bought an array of products to solve their problems; the functional or bureaucratic organization provided standard products, each of which was a partial solution to problems. Thus, bureaucratic organizations put out products and the consumers moved across organizations to put together solutions to their problems.

But to provide today's customers with total solutions, project-based rather than product-based organizations are best. The new organization uses multidisciplinary project teams that move across the organization on the customer's behalf to provide a total solution. This continuing trend means that project management is the future of organizational management.

The project management concept is based on cross-functional teams that are assembled to achieve a specific purpose, usually in a specific time and within a limited budget. These teams are temporary; once they achieve their objective, they are disbanded and the team members assume traditional work or are assigned to yet another project. Because project teams cut across traditional functional lines, they are best suited to provide total customer solutions. Typically, one person is in charge of the team: the project manager or project leader.

Project management is fairly new in organizations. In the past, the staff of the functional organization developed new products. But with increasing pressure to get products to market, special project teams were formed; they also proved useful in developing systems solutions for customers. People in organizations suddenly found themselves working on many special projects.

There seems to be general agreement that project management is a trend that will continue to accelerate in the twenty-first century. During workshops and consulting engagements with numerous participants, the authors find that more and more people, from administrative assistants up to CEOs, are doing project-based work.

The role of upper management is of paramount importance in developing a project-based organization. Such development involves a lot more than moving lines and boxes on an organization chart, sending a few managers out to training, and telling them to "do project management." The process of developing a project-based organization mirrors the desired new organization because the process is itself a project. It requires a vision of how the organization will function and what it will achieve. It requires that upper managers act as a team among themselves and with project managers to change the organization. It requires a change in behavior, as an organization is not a chart but rather the sum total of the behavior of the people who work in it. It also requires a plan and the participation of important stakeholders, such as customers.

A shift to projects cannot be accomplished simply by adding projects to department work because there are substantial differences between department and project work. For one, departments do not foster change; the hallmark of a good department is repeat processes or products, and good department management involves setting procedures that allow the repeat work to be done as efficiently as possible. This is not conducive to doing something new, because departments support the status quo—in fact, they are the status quo. Projects, however, foster change and thus disturb the status quo.

Furthermore, departments normally are not cross-functional, whereas projects require a cross-functional view of the entire organization because the target of projects is often a system (i.e., payroll, customer profiles, customer interface, or a set of products) that is itself part of a larger system, or at least connected to some other system. For a project to be successful, its effects on all other systems must be considered. People skills in departments are more often focused on production rather than on developing processes to achieve unique new results. Tales of failures caused by unexpected consequences are legend in any new operation. It takes a total view of the organization to ensure successful projects, and this requires a cross-functional team. This wide view is normally not found in departments.

Also, departments are assumed to last forever, whereas projects have a limited life. Because projects are temporary, they are not seen as the departments "real work" and so are given low priority and not assigned the best people. This is a recipe for project failure.

Departments are also level-conscious. Much of the power and leadership in departments depends on the level in the hierarchy. Projects require multilevel participation. The power should flow to the person who can get the job done, and this may often require that people work for someone below their level. This could be difficult to achieve in departments.

Organizations have found cross-functional project teams to be very effective for project work. For example, when Chrysler went to a platform team for its cab-forward design, it cut the new model development time from three and a half or four years down to only two years. In addition, the number of people necessary went from 1,500 to 700. When PECO Energy attempted to refuel nuclear reactors using a departmental approach, it took 120 days. With a cross-functional team approach, PECO set a company, U.S., and world record for refueling time of just under 23 days in February 1995.[8] Refining the team approach, they set another world record in October 1996, completing the refueling in 19 days and 10 hours. PECO officials attribute this achievement to two years of planning, superb coordination, and great teamwork. Examples like this are commonplace when organizations begin to take the project management approach seriously. Clearly the payoff is well worth the effort.

TOWARD THE PROJECT-BASED ORGANIZATION

In initial attempts to respond to the need for project management, many organizations attempted to integrate projects into a functional organization by using the matrix approach, in which functional managers (designated as FMs in Exhibit 2.2) control departments such as engineering and marketing while project managers (PMs) coordinate the work across functions.

But in general, the matrix organization tended to cause more problems than it solved. The major fault was that it was a marginal change—a mere modification to the old hierarchical organization. This meant that many of upper management's assumptions were based on the functional organization or mechanistic model. As a result, many of the behaviors that were rewarded by upper management were actually counterproductive to successful projects. Project team members felt that organizational rewards favored departmental work and that

EXHIBIT 2.2 Matrix organization

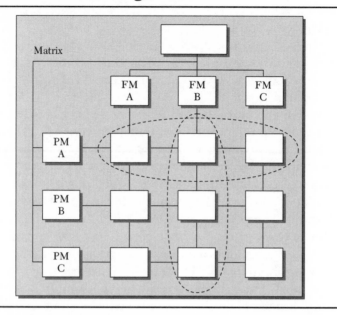

working on projects was actually bad for their careers. Many people working in a matrix complained of being "caught in a web" of conflicting orders, conflicting priorities, and reward systems that did not match the stated organizational goals (see Exhibit 2.3). Effective behavioral change requires a change in the reward system, and this did not occur in many matrix organizations.

The use of a matrix for project management is a classic case of rewarding one behavior while hoping for another; that is, rewarding departmental work

EXHIBIT 2.3 Caught in a web

while hoping for project work. Although people were told that working for two bosses would be beneficial to their careers, experience proved to them that doing project work decreased their chances for promotion. Because people did not see project work as compatible with their personal interests, the project work suffered. The rewarded behaviors were those the organization wanted to discourage, and the desired behaviors were those that went unrewarded. Such organizational perversity is an example of the type described in Kerr's classic article "On the Folly of Rewarding A While Hoping for B"[9] (see Box 2.2).

Because the matrix approach represented only a marginal change, the typical problems of bureaucracy often appeared. In many cases, the money continued to reside in the departments, with projects having limited budgets. Project members were treated as second-class citizens. In addition, individual positions and promotions continued to reside in the departments, making those groups much more important for long-term career success. Even if projects were given budget authority, conflicts over priorities continued to arise. Rules were then needed to resolve conflicts, and these rules tended to accumulate. Whenever a mistake was made or a conflict noticed, a rule was made to prevent its recurrence. As a result, operational responsibility tended to drift upward and conflict resolution required top management involvement. Finally, the rules began to guide behavior and became a concern in themselves. People

---

Box 2.2

Organizational Perversity

Steven Kerr realized that individuals seek to know what activities will be rewarded by the organization and then carry them out "often to the virtual exclusion of activities not rewarded." However, he found numerous organizations where the types of behavior rewarded are those that the rewarder is actually trying to discourage, even as the desired behavior is not being rewarded at all.

Kerr cites examples such as universities, where "society hopes that professors will not neglect their teaching responsibilities, but rewards them almost entirely for research and publications," as well as "sports teams [that] hope for teamwork but usually reward based on individual performance" and "business organizations [that] hope for performance but reward attendance." We, the authors, have experienced organizations that say they want upper managers to oversee and mentor projects but reward them based on the number of people in their department. They are, in other words, organizationally perverse: their organization members say they want one behavior but reward activity that will ensure that it cannot be accomplished.

acted with concern for the rules, not with concern for the success of the whole. This is classic bureaucracy in action.

The weakness of bureaucracy brings the tenets of the organic organization into focus. The organic organization is one in which everyone takes responsibility for the success of the whole. When this happens, the basic notion of regulating relations among people by separating them into specific predefined functions is abandoned. The challenge is to create a system where people enter into relations that are determined by problems rather than by structure (see Exhibit 2.4). In essence, people market their services to those projects inside the organization that need them and are capable of paying for those services.

The tenets of such an organization are described in *The Post-Bureaucratic Organization,* in which the basic building block is considered to be the team.[10] Consensus on action is reached not by positional power but by influence—the ability to persuade rather than to command. The ability to persuade is based on knowledge of the issues, commitment to shared goals, and proven past effectiveness. Each person in the group understands how his or her performance affects the overall strategy.

Ability to influence is based on trust, and trust is based on interdependence—an understanding that the fortunes of the whole depend on the performance of all participants. The empowered manager assesses the level of trust and agreement that exists with another person and plans an approach to that person that leverages the strengths of that relationship.[11]

EXHIBIT 2.4   Organic organization: A market-based approach to projects

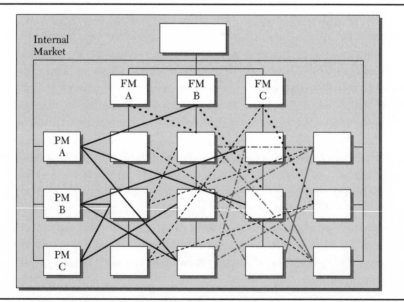

Highly effective people in this organization can influence without authority by using reciprocity as the basis for influence. People need to learn to exchange "currencies" based on respective needs, leading to win-win situations.[12] Communications need to be explicit and out in the open.

A strong emphasis on interdependence and strategy leads to a strong emphasis on organizational mission. In order to link individual contributions to the mission, there is increased emphasis on information about the organizational strategy and an attempt to clarify the relationship between individual jobs and the mission. This calls for a new type of information system where information linking individuals to the strategic plan is readily available.

Guidelines for action take the form of principles rather than rules. Principles are based on the reasons why certain behaviors contribute to the accomplishment of strategy. One important principle is a relatively open system of peer evaluation, so that people get a relatively detailed view of each other's strengths and weaknesses. This calls for a change in the evaluations and reward system. In addition, the organization of the future has no boundaries. There is far more tolerance for outsiders coming in and insiders going out. The boundary between the organization and its customers blurs and the boundaries between levels and departments within the organization disappear. In addition, the postbureaucratic organization eliminates the idea of permanence, where decisions are final. The emphasis is now on decision processes.

Because this type of structure is currently embodied in project teams, the organization of the future will be project-based. Customers want to buy solutions, not standard products, and the organizational unit that can respond to this market is the customer-oriented project team. The team works to understand the customer's problems and what the team should achieve. With this understanding, the team can develop new solutions, perhaps ones that the customer had not imagined. This requires a new relationship between the company and the customer: the customer becomes a vital part of the team.

Customer-driven teams abandon the level-consciousness prevalent in many functional organizations. Project leaders are appointed because of their expertise in running projects, not because they have attained a particular level in the organization. Because the ability to influence is not based on position, level-consciousness decreases. In addition, as there are fewer levels, position becomes less important. A team member may be one or two levels above the project manager on the organization chart but still report to the project manager for that project (as in Exhibit 2.4). Team members no longer think of themselves as members of a particular function but as members of a team that is doing something for the good of the entire organization. Several customers may become members of the team, as was the case on the Boeing 777 airliner project.[13] Many team members may be from outside the organization, doing work on contract for that particular project. The project manager thus assembles the project team based on what is best for the project, not on what people the organization can spare.

Becton-Dickinson, an organization that embodies this trend, provides innovative technology and advanced solutions in flow cytometry systems.[14] In designing an organization to be more responsive to the needs of development programs, this company found that embedded functional management was delaying the cycle time. To help reduce cycle time, it eliminated functional managers and their departments. The important tasks of functional managers were put into focused groups, and a project management office was established to develop direction for project management in the new organization.

In the future, most organizations will consist of a smaller group of full-time employees and a large contractual fringe of individual contractors or strategic alliances that provide goods or services for given projects. In other words, the customer-based team properly comprises a small core of employees plus relationships with outside experts who work contractually for all or part of a project.

The new internal market organizations are based on areas of expertise and have profit and loss responsibility. Each area provides services to other areas in exchange for a fee. Rather than having their performance measured by how well they stick to a budget, these areas are measured according to how well they complete an internal project that helps the rest of the organization achieve its mission. In this way, everyone knows how their actions affect both profitability and the attainment of a mission that is stated in a strategic plan.

Moving to a project-based organization presents unique challenges to upper managers, as outlined by Wilson and others:[15]

- *The leader has little or no "position power."* The position power inherent in functional organizations has to change as the project-based organization is introduced. The team leader has little direct control over the career path of team members. Instead, team members require an independent career path over which they themselves have control and to which the project work can contribute. Developing such a scheme is similar to the development of individual retirement accounts where the individual has control of the fund and the employer merely makes contributions. This type of scheme has been used in universities for years; it allows professors to move easily from place to place, taking their retirement account with them. Now organizations need to make it easy for team members to move from project to project, taking their career path progress with them.

  Asked by a gathering of project managers whether the project management skill set was transferable to other functions in HP, CEO Lew Platt (1994) replied: "I think if you learn the skills of project management that you can manage a project in manufacturing, or a project in IT, or a project in marketing just as easily as you can manage a project in development. The issues are different, but I think the basic skills are pretty much the same. . . . In these times, it is quite important that you actually do think about moving around from one function to another as a way of getting a fresh set of experiences, re-igniting your interest in the job. . . . It's a tremendous growth experience."

Upper managers need to develop project managers and project management so that the project managers can lead based on influence rather than positional authority.

- *Conflicts over team member time and resource requirements.* Thus, upper managers must have a good plan and work out priorities. Alternatively, internal market pricing may be used to allocate scarce resources—individuals or organizations pay with internal charge accounts, sometimes called location code dollars, for services they find valuable. Value-based pricing mechanisms are a feature of internal market-based organizations.

- *Organizational boundaries are unclear.* Project management often requires quantum leaps in the level of cooperation among organizational units. If people see evidence that cooperation is not valued, then achieving cooperation is almost impossible. The alternatives to cooperation are turf wars and as-needed appeals to higher authorities, neither of which is beneficial in the long run. Upper management needs to create a structure where cooperation is rewarded.

- *Time and organizational pressures abound.* Upper management must be ready to support the best practices that allow reduction in cycle time. This includes developing a core team system, developing project goal statements, allowing time for project planning, not interfering with project operations, facilitating communication with customers, and supplying necessary resources. In addition, an adequate project time frame must be negotiated so that the team has a chance for a win.

- *Team members do not know one another.* Effective project teams require unprecedented levels of trust and openness. The climate of trust and openness starts at the top. If upper managers are not trustworthy, truthful, and open with each other, there is little chance that project team members will be so with one another. Trust and openness are the antithesis of most bureaucratic organizations. Upper managers coming from a less trusting organization may have difficulty developing high levels of trust.

- *Team members are independent and self-motivated.* Because team members may not even work for the organization, project managers need to develop influence skills, and upper management must support that process.

All these challenges require that upper managers work together to develop a process aimed at encouraging new types of behavior. Members of the organization look to the upper managers for guidance in both strategy and behavior, and if there is a lack of integrity between what is said and what is done, skepticism rises and morale falls. How can upper managers expect good teamwork when they are fighting among themselves? Organizational change requires not just a concept of a new organization but the resolve to create it. If upper managers expect team members to change their behavior, they should be ready to change their own behavior as well. Sending people to project manager training is not enough; the shift to a project-based organization requires a concerted effort from all upper managers.

A MODEL OF ORGANIZATIONAL CHANGE

The revitalization process model described by Wallace considers the time and processes necessary to change behavior.[16] He uses this model to describe a society moving through a series of temporally overlapping but functionally distinct phases of change. Any group of people may be said to have a culture—a set of beliefs, values, norms, and practices that help the group solve its problems. Business organizations are groups of people and thus have a culture; because this is so, the revitalization model can be used to describe the phases of change in organizational cultures. For changes in organizational culture to occur, behavioral changes in the people that make up the culture must be brought about.

However, the steps to achieve actual change in behavior are difficult indeed. Few believe in the benefits of change until they actually experience them. Change agents often feel like the person described by Plato (see Box 2.3), particularly when their visions of the future only provoke ridicule. When new ideas provoke ridicule in an organization, it usually means that the people

---

Box 2.3
Response to Change Agents

[According to Plato's *Republic*] human beings are like prisoners chained to the wall of a dark subterranean cave, where they can never turn around to see the light of a fire that is higher up and at a distance behind them. When objects outside the cave pass in front of the light, the prisoners mistake as real what are really shadows created on the wall. Only one who is freed from his chains and leaves the cave to enter the real world beyond can glimpse true reality. . . . Once he habituates himself to the light and comes to recognize the true cause of things, he would hold precious the clarity of this new understanding. . . . Were he required to return to the cave and contend with the others in their usual activity of "understanding" the shadows, he would likely only provoke their ridicule and be unable to persuade them that what they were perceiving was only a dim reflection of reality.

Source: Tarnus, R., *The Passion of the Western Mind* (New York: Ballantine, 1991, p. 42).

in it are not ready for change because they do not yet see the need. If upper managers start a change process before they really believe change is necessary, others will sense this lack of authenticity and the process will fail. A change process is effective when the change leaders believe it is necessary and show the way to others. The revitalization process acknowledges this fact and describes the stages an organization goes through until the majority of its members are ready for change.

The stages of the revitalization process are shown in Exhibit 2.5. The basically successful organizations develop procedures that allow them to achieve a steady state such that the organizational system handles any problems that arise. But as the environment changes, continued use of the old procedures causes people to enter a period of individual stress. If this is allowed to continue, the organization falls into a period of cultural distortion, where the procedures cause many problems. However, enlightened upper managers can bypass that state and go directly to a period of revitalization, in which new procedures are adopted to match the problems in the new environment.

The Steady State

Every organization begins with a set of problems that need to be solved in order to carry on its business. (The case of early AT&T is a good example; see Box 2.4.) Successful organizations develop a culture—a set of beliefs, values, norms, and practices—that help the members of the organization solve these problems. This

EXHIBIT 2.5   Stages of the revitalization model

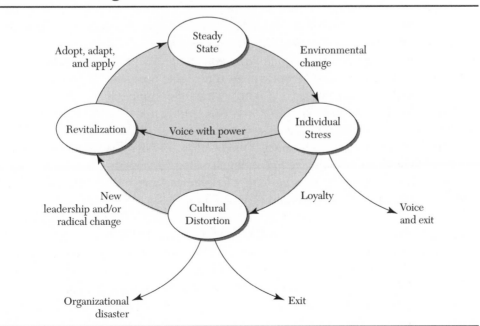

Box 2.4

Procedures at AT&T

Functional organizations were a necessary step in the evolution of organization design. For example, consider the American Telephone and Telegraph Company, a forerunner of today's AT&T, which was established on February 28, 1885. It was formed to operate long-distance telephone lines to interconnect local exchange areas of the Bell companies. Although it must have seemed incomprehensible in 1885, the plan was to extend those lines to connect "each and every city, town and place in the State of New York with one or more points in each and every other city, town or place in said state, and each and every other of the United States, and in Canada and Mexico . . . and by cable and other appropriate means with the rest of the known world."[*]

Such a lofty goal required massive generation of and attention to standard procedures. Without each and every city, town, and place following the same procedures, there is no way the AT&T network could have been completed. The procedures helped to solve problems. After all, there was no way to call to discuss and fix connection problems until the phone was actually connected. So bureaucracy was created by necessity, allowing the next generation of organizations to emerge from it.

[*] Shooshan, H. M. III, *Disconnecting Bell: The Impact of the AT&T Divestiture* (New York: Pergamon, 1984).

---

culture is embodied in a set of organizational rules that are passed on from one generation of workers to the next. Application of these rules keeps the organization in a state of equilibrium. Each year looks much like the last, as the organization produces similar products through repeatable processes. The members of the organization become more and more efficient at applying the rules, and the organization thrives. This is the steady state, which we could equate to the mechanistic or functional model of organizations.

To keep an organization in the steady state, a control system must be developed. Whenever outside disturbances threaten the equilibrium of the organization, the control system is capable of detecting and interpreting them and setting in motion practices that counteract them.

Control systems are both internal and external. The external control system attempts to regulate the environment in a way favorable to the organization, such as by gaining patents, monopolies, or other favorable government rulings. The internal control system regulates members' behavior and works to eliminate any threat to the smooth functioning of the organization. Organizations in the steady state are characterized by large and onerous control systems that, as we shall see, become their undoing.

During the steady state the organization is usually successful and often able to affect its environment more than the environment is able to affect it. This is often due to some patent, monopoly, or new process the organization has developed that is not yet general knowledge. When this is so, there is little time pressure on projects; the control system acts to fend off the need for change. As a result, project management is not really necessary. Projects wend their way through the bureaucracy in due course.

For example, AT&T reached its steady state in the period 1934–1960.[17] By 1934, the Bell system had operating companies in most major American cities and AT&T could proceed to tie them together and provide the dream of universal service. To provide this service, AT&T was given a telephone monopoly in the United States. Given the lack of competition, AT&T developed a steady, stable, predictable, and military-like culture that allowed the efficient realization of the goal. The antitrust cases brought against AT&T during this period were defeated.

The Period of Increased Individual Stress

Over time, the environment of an organization changes such that the existing culture is no longer appropriate to the problems it faces. When, for example, customers begin to demand new and different products and solutions, the assumptions on which the organizational culture was built become increasingly invalid. Following old procedures at such times begins to cause problems rather than solve them. Some individuals in the organization begin to realize that major changes are necessary, but they often go unheeded as others continue to find success using the old ways. During this phase the organization continues to be successful—it may even experience its most successful period—so it is not surprising that many members of the firm do not see the need for change.

The problems are exacerbated because those who see the need for change and sound the alarm are often forced out of the organization (as Dagwood learns in Exhibit 2.6). In the process of exit, voice, or loyalty described by Hirschman, people who see the need for change often leave the firm (exit) and join other organizations where the change has already been made or is being implemented—firms that are already in their period of revitalization.[18]

An alternative to exiting is to voice strong opinions about the needed changes. This is often followed by exiting; as other members of the firm do not see the need for change, the advocate of it is likely to be accused of not being a team player. If the individual still does not want to exit, the final alternative is loyalty—succumbing to pressure and going along with the others. No change takes place; the fate of potential change agents during the period of increased individual stress is that they leave the organization or join the majority.

During this period, individual managers may see the need to improve project management in order to cut cycle time. The usual response is to send some engineers to training so they can learn the latest best practices. But when

EXHIBIT 2.6   Exits

Blondie

© 1994 King Features Syndicate. Reprinted with special permission of King Features syndicate.

they return, they find they cannot practice the new ideas because others in the organization still see no need for it. They know that best practices require cooperation from all parts of the organization, and because they cannot practice what they know is best, they leave the organization (exit) or decide to ignore the practices (loyalty).

For example, in 1961 AT&T set up a school to teach customized sales. However, managers who finished the course returned to find that noncustomized, mass sales were still what really counted in the organization. The frustration level was such that 85 percent of the graduates quit, and AT&T disbanded the school.[19] As a result, the best practices were never implemented. This is why sending individuals out for training but not supporting the new practices they bring back is so notoriously ineffective.

During the time of increased individual stress, the organization continues to decline as its practices become increasingly outmoded. If the leaders realize the need for change at this point and are ready to make them, they can skip directly to the period of revitalization and direct the change process themselves. This path is shown as "voice with power" in Exhibit 2.5. It is possible even for individuals to invoke the voice-with-power path if they are willing, have skill as change agents, learn how to communicate with upper management, and are able to "speak truth to power."[20] However, the leaders should realize that organizational forces are working against them, which is why organizations often fall into the next phase, cultural distortion, before meaningful changes occur.

AT&T experienced its period of increased individual stress from 1960 to 1974. By 1960 the goal of universal service had been reached, so the AT&T monopoly was no longer necessary; many competitors wanted to enter the telephone business but AT&T fought them off in the courts. Between 1960 and 1970, however, it lost a number of legal battles, culminating in the "Above 890" decision that opened the way for microwave communication and competition in long-distance service. During this period, several attempts were made to make

AT&T a marketing organization, but as all the company's marketing organizations were structured in typical AT&T mode, they were never elevated above the operations department and thus were never effective. The process of using old structures for new applications is typical of the period of increased individual stress and typically ineffective.

The Period of Cultural Distortion

In this period, old practices begin to cause more problems than they solve. The number of organizational inconsistencies becomes so great that people begin to suffer marked decreases in productivity. The organization may begin to lose money for the first time in its history.

During this phase there may be a concerted and systematic effort to teach and implement best practices for project management. However, it is usually done only at the lower levels of the organization; upper managers do not change their behavior, or do so only ever so slightly. In addition, typically no change in the reward system is made to support the new practices—indeed, the system usually continues to reward and support the old practices, and the people in the organization experience the perversity of Kerr's folly.[21] In effect, upper managers are systematically undermining the efforts of project managers. The project managers quickly discover that their efforts are not rewarded, so they leave and things get worse.

The period of cultural distortion is usually accompanied by the failure of one or two large and highly visible projects. The response is often to find and fire one person, usually the project manager, who is thought to be obviously responsible for the failure. As indicated by Cohen and Gooch (see Box 2.5), however, this usually merely demonstrates a lack of understanding of the real causes of misfortune.[22] In complex situations, such as large projects with many players, many conflicting stakeholders, and many different departments involved, failure is rarely due to one person's poor judgment. Firing a scapegoat may make upper managers feel good, but because it reflects no understanding of the true causes of failure, it certainly will be woefully inadequate in preventing future failure. So as heads roll, morale sinks and problems continue to get worse.

At this point the members of the organization face a crisis. Things are so bad that they now realize radical changes must be made. Perhaps this phase is necessary to increase the upper managers' level of authenticity, for now when they say change is needed they really mean it. Sometimes the needed changes are so radical that upper managers are unable to make them and the organization dies, or the organization installs new leadership. New leadership, if needed, will be most effective if brought in from outside the organization.

AT&T experienced its period of cultural distortion from 1974 to 1983. In 1974, the U.S. Justice Department filed suit, seeking to break the company up. The AT&T response was to fight it in the courts, a tried and true method.

Box 2.5

Causes of Misfortune

Cohen and Gooch studied military misfortunes in an attempt to avoid them in the future. Much of the interest in similar studies of project management comes after a disaster on one or more projects. Part of the solution to a disastrous project is understanding what caused the disaster so it can be avoided in the future.

When military disaster happens, how can it be understood and explained? The "man on the dock" approach is common, which is the notion that disaster occurs because one person, typically the commander, commits unpardonable errors of judgment. But this assumes that the person in charge has control over all pertinent variables, which is not usually true. The modern commander is much more akin to the managing director of a large conglomerate; he is the head of a complex military operation, and as its size has increased, the business of war has developed an organizational dimension that can make mighty contributions to triumph or tragedy. In project management, not all failure can be laid at the project manager's feet. Often an organizational component is also important.

The "man on the couch" view says that failure is due to some collective way of thinking that blinds people to the correct actions. Cohen and Gooch argue, however, that if this were true, disaster would be much more common than it is, and the problem would be to explain the reasons for success. Because this is not the case, any collective way of thinking of military leaders is of limited use in explaining misfortune.

The "collective incompetence and the military mind" explanation says that simply living in and serving a hierarchical institution such as an army encourages and intensifies potentially disastrous habits of mind. However, analysis indicates that supposed collective incompetence is more a result of the reward system than of supposed deficiencies of the military mind. Cohen and Gooch recommend looking instead to the organizational systems within which such minds have to operate.

"Institutional failure" is another possible explanation. When the blame cannot be put on one person, it is often given to an entire institution, such as the U.S. Navy. However, knowing what the Navy is does not explain how it works, and explaining failures requires knowing how it works. Thus, Cohen and Gooch say we must think of the armed forces not as institutions but as organizations.

They point to the interaction of people, systems, and organizations to explain failure. People cannot be put aside in explaining failure, but they respond to the organization and the characteristics of it that determine how tasks are approached, that shape decisions, and that affect the management of disaster. In addition, organizations have systems that sometimes go awry when failure in two or more components interact in unexpected ways. When this happens people lose control of the system, and their response is often dictated by the organizational procedures. Examining this interaction of people, organizations, and systems is most fruitful in explaining misfortune.

However, some people saw the futility of fighting and began to establish some new patterns aimed at developing a competitive organization. To accomplish this, the marketing department was expanded and many people were brought in from other organizations. By design, these people had different assumptions, values, and practices that often clashed with those of traditional Bell system managers. As the process continued, it became increasingly clear that the culture was internally distorted and the elements not harmoniously related. The group that wanted the monopoly maintained could not continue to exist alongside the group that wanted competition. Something had to give.

The Period of Revitalization

During this period, leaders are able to eliminate old practices and behaviors. When the organization gets to this point, things are so bad that its members usually bring in a new leader to make changes. The new leader installs a new behavioral code to bring company practices in line with today's problems. There are two phases to this period; the first involves establishing a new code for behavior and the second involves adopting the code as the new organizational norm.

The first phase begins with a new leader, often from outside the organization, who paints a picture of the new process that the organization must adopt in order to survive. This new code normally includes an increased emphasis on projects and satisfaction of customer expectations. The new code for behavior must then be communicated to all members of the organization. This communication is typically accompanied by a change in the organization's structure to help accomplish the objectives of the new code.

The second phase is directing the process of adapting the new code. People need to learn to discard old behavior patterns and adopt new ones. This phase involves training people in the new behavior and then directing the process of cultural transformation so that the new code becomes natural and routine.

The period of revitalization is often traumatic to members of the organization. If the process has followed its normal course through the period of cultural distortion, the organization is near collapse. Typically, the new leader brings in new upper managers who trumpet a behavior code that is so radical that 30 to 50 percent of the organization members leave, in one way or another.

AT&T entered its period of revitalization in 1983 with the consent decree that separated the competitive aspects of the business from the remaining aspects of the Bell system. As of January 1, 1984, those who wanted free market competition could go with AT&T, and those who wanted monopoly could remain with the local Bell operating companies. This change was traumatic for those who went with AT&T, for it required implementation of entirely new ways of looking at the business. During the next ten years, AT&T laid off many employees and hired many new people who had never been exposed to the old Bell ways. The transformation continues to this day.

Part of the reason for the turmoil at AT&T was that its managers did not make the necessary changes back in 1970, during the period of individual stress. If they had, members of the organization could have spent time getting ready for the change rather than fighting it. When upper managers see the need for change during the period of individual stress, it can be accomplished more rationally and with much less upheaval. The authors feel that for most organizations, the time for the change to project-based organizations is now.

The New Steady State

Here, the organization is again in harmony with its environment. This stage continues until new changes in the environment force the revitalization process to begin again.

THE SUCCESSFUL CHANGE AGENT

Any successful change requires a successful change agent. History is replete with agents of change who were killed by the very individuals they were trying to help. As shown in the last section, part of a change agent's success is timing. People who offer advice during the period of individual stress are often unheeded, but those who offer the same advice during the period of revitalization are seen as heroes. This occurs because during the period of cultural distortion, more people begin to vividly see the need for change and to seek the very advice they previously shunned. To skip the period of cultural distortion, upper managers must act together as change agents and direct the change before distortion begins. According to Rogers, successful change agents fill seven critical roles:[23]

1. *They develop the need for change.* Change agents show others what the problems are and convince them that they can and must grapple with these problems in order to improve. The successful change agent leads the organization around the period of cultural distortion. After one or two

project failures the change agent must argue that this is not just an aberration or the fault of a single project manager. Change agents take the lesson of Cohen and Gooch that failure is not usually caused by just one person but is the result of a combination of problems. Repeated failure is a systematic problem, one that needs to be tackled by the entire organization.

2. *They make others accept them as trustworthy and competent.* People must accept the messenger before they will accept the message. Upper managers must act with integrity and authenticity, or they will be seen as incompetent; if they "talk the talk" but do not "walk the walk," they will not be seen as trustworthy and their attempts to bring about change will most likely fail. This has been the fate of many a change process.

3. *They diagnose problems from the perspective of their audience.* Successful change agents must see problems from the project manager's point of view. If they regard the project manager as the culprit, the upper manager will never see the project manager's point of view. This indicates that the best project managers in the organization should be involved in the change process.

4. *They create the intent to change through motivation.* Lasting change cannot be dictated from a position of power; it comes from motivating people to solve their problems. Change that is seen as helping to solve the project manager's problems while contributing to the organization's welfare will be enthusiastically applied because the participants are motivated. Change that is seen as benefiting only upper management, however, will be resisted. The change agent motivates the entire community by showing that the change benefits everyone. People readily adopt practices that are in their best interest.

5. *They work through others in translating intent into action.* A team of project managers who can translate the intent of the change into action is necessary.

6. *They stabilize the adoption of innovation.* All too often, change leaves with the change agent. Upper managers may put in a set of procedures to help make project management more effective, but then their attention gets directed to other matters. When this happens, the changes often fade. An initiative team can outlast the change initiators and help stabilize the adoption of the innovation throughout the organization.

7. *They go out of business as change agents.* If all the previous steps have been successful, the need for the initial change agents vanishes. So should they.

The successful complete upper manager understands the influences that shape organizations, embraces the changes that are required for continued vitality, takes on the role and responsibilities of change agent, and works to develop the postbureaucratic organization through the project management function. If done right, the project management function of today will become the postbureaucratic organization of tomorrow.

THE COMPLETE UPPER MANAGER

The successful complete upper manager:

- Understands the need for better project management in organizations of the future.
- Understands that the role of upper management is critical in developing successful project management practices throughout the organization.
- Understands that past organizational forms, such as the functional or matrix organization, may be detrimental to developing good project practices.
- Embraces the tenets of the postbureaucratic organization that emphasize teams, consensus action, empowerment, trust, and open communication.
- Believes in and behaves with integrity and authenticity as a requirement for leading others.
- Leads an organization through the revitalization process.
- Acts with other upper managers as a team of change agents to develop an environment that supports project management.

NOTES

1. D. Cohen and J. Kuehn, "Navigating between a Rock and a Hard Place: Reconciling the Initiating and Planning Phases to Promote Project Success." Paper presented at the Project Management Institute 27th annual seminar/symposium (Boston, 1996).

2. Cadillac Motor Company, *Information Book* (Detroit, MI: Cadillac Motor Company, 1991).

3. R. Belluzzo, Presentation at the IDC European IT Forum (Paris: September 1996).

4. K. H. Bowen, K. Clark, C. Halloway, and S. Wheelwright, "Make Projects the School for Leaders," *Harvard Business Review* (September/October 1994): 131–140.

5. F. R. Gulliver, "Post Project Appraisals Pay," *Harvard Business Review* (March/April 1987).

6. J. W. Koroknay, "Global Information Technology Project Management Initiative." Paper presented at the Hewlett-Packard Project Management Conference 1996 (San Diego, CA: April 1996).

7. R. Storeygard, "Growing Professional Project Leaders," *Proceedings of the Project Management Institute 26th Annual Seminar/Symposium* (Upper Darby, PA: Project Management Institute, 1995).

8. "Company Sets Industry Standard with Limerick Refueling Outage," *Perspectives: PECO Energy Company Newsletter* (February 1996).

9. S. Kerr, "On the Folly of Rewarding *A* While Hoping for *B*," *Academy of Management Executive* (February 1995). (Original work published 1975 in *Academy of Management Journal.*)

10. C. Keckscher and A. Donnellon, *"The Post-Bureaucratic Organization: New Perspectives on Organizational Change* (Thousand Oaks, CA: Sage, 1994).

11. P. Block, *The Empowered Manager: Positive Political Skills at Work* (San Francisco: Jossey-Bass, 1987).

12. A. R. Cohen and D. L. Bradford, *Influence without Authority* (New York: Wiley, 1989).

13. C. G. King, "Multi-Discipline Teams: A Fundamental Element in the Program Management Process," *PM Network,* vol. 6 (1992): 12–22.

14. R. Stoy, "Experiment with Reducing Cycle Time," *Proceedings of the Project World Conference,* Session C-11 (Washington, DC: August 9, 1996).

15. Jeanne M. Wilson, Jill George, Richard S. Wellins, and William C. Byham, *Leadership Trapeze: Strategies for Leadership in Team-Based Organizations* (San Francisco: Jossey-Bass, 1994), pp. 253–255.

16. A. Wallace, *Culture and Personality,* 2nd ed. (New York: Random House, 1970).

17. R. J. Graham, "Organizational Culture Change and Revitalization at AT&T." Unpublished master's thesis (Philadelphia: University of Pennsylvania, Anthropology Department, 1985).

18. A. Hirschman, *Exit, Voice, and Loyalty: Responses to Decline in Firms, Organizations and States* (Cambridge, MA: Harvard University Press, 1970).

19. "Corporate Culture," *BusinessWeek* (October 27, 1980): 148, 154.

20. R. J. Graham and R. Englund, "Communicating with Upper Management: The Problems with Speaking Truth to Power," *Proceedings of the Project Management Institute 26th Annual Seminar/Symposium* (Upper Darby, PA: Project Management Institute, 1995), pp. 462–468.

21. See note 9.

22. E. Cohen and J. Gooch, *Military Misfortunes: The Anatomy of Failure in War* (New York: Free Press, 1994).

23. E. Rogers, *Diffusion of Innovations,* 3rd ed. (New York: Free Press, 1983).

PART TWO

THE PROJECT MANAGEMENT DISCIPLINE

To many people, project management equates to the scheduling graphics they see in popular project management software. Gantt charts and critical path analysis are certainly well-known techniques developed specifically for managing projects, but the discipline of project management extends far beyond these scheduling methods.

Project management is a discipline. It contains well-developed, repeatedly proven principles, methods, and techniques. These concepts are well documented in textbooks, consistently presented at colleges and universities, and automated in software programs. There is debate over which topics are within the discipline and which are related. For example, effective project teams need sound decision-making processes but that is true of any work group. The chapters in Part Two represent the accepted core of the discipline, the techniques that have been developed specifically to handle the unique challenges of managing projects.

The structured, sometimes mathematical, nature of many of these processes causes some to distinguish them from the soft or more human factors in managing projects. This duality is important to recognize because both the structured methods and the human factors are important in project success. But it is equally important to recognize that both the soft and hard side of project management is mutually dependent. Successful projects need clear communication and commonly understood goals and detailed plans. They also need teamwork, mutual trust, and accountability from all sides. Methods that facilitate specific, detailed agreements and rational decisions go a long way toward establishing all these success factors. The principles and techniques described in Part Two form a foundation that is complementary to the human and teaming factors described in Part Three.

The mechanics of project management have another benefit. Because of their structured nature, they can be learned by individual project managers, standardized within the organization, and clearly visible to other stakeholders. In other words, these methods can become a known, repeatable process for managing projects. If your firm is attempting to standardize project management, it will be able to add an element from every chapter in Part Two.

Each chapter in this section presents a set of mature processes and techniques that address some challenge of the project environment. Let's look at how they all fit together in a systematic process that takes a project from concept through delivery.

Pursuing the correct project is easily as important as the effectiveness with which the project is carried out. Chapter 3 presents several methods for assessing ideas before they become projects.

The detailed action plan, replete with work breakdown structure, Gantt chart, and critical path is almost a cliché for project managers. These are the methods we use to break down the big picture into specific, manageable actions. Chapter 4 presents the step-by-step model for analyzing the project and building the action plan—the foundation for every successful project. These are the tools that enable rational, fact-based decisions about achieving the optimal cost-schedule-quality equilibrium.

Every project manager who swears by the necessity of a detailed plan will also, in his or her next breath, caution that plans never match reality. Chapter 5 shows us how to use the plan—despite its limitations—to steer the project to completion and success. Since success is in the eye of the project stakeholders, the chapter begins with identifying and understanding who our stakeholders are, in order to design our control systems to measure what is important to the customer.

The calculations used in project selection and project planning have one weakness: They assume an ability to accurately forecast the future. Since this ability is rare, the savvy project manager will continuously seek out the hidden dangers and unexpected problems that derail our careful plans. Chapter 6 presents a process known as *project risk management,* which is used to systematically identify and manage the uncertainty inherent in our projects.

The trilogy of project success has long been *on time, on budget, high quality.* On time and on budget are easily measured with a calendar and a checkbook. The quality of our deliverables, however, is too frequently debatable. If your team has ever struggled with the challenge of "how good is good enough" or had your budget and schedule blown away by rework, you'll find the quality management framework in

Chapter 7 invaluable. This chapter translates the discipline of quality management—which is often associated with mass production—into its application in the project environment.

Projects are managed by project managers, and that's who will primarily apply the techniques in these chapters. But every project needs management support. These chapters are designed to give the manager overseeing multiple projects a thorough overview of the techniques he or she should use to communicate with the project manager and project team.

Given the long history of project management (well, relatively long—since the mid-twentieth century) it might seem that these methods are actually at risk of becoming out of date. Yet nothing could be further from the truth. Active application by professionals in every field continues to prove the value of the fundamental principles of project management.

3 PROJECT SELECTION*

Jack R. Meredith and Samuel J. Mantel Jr.

Project selection is the process of evaluating individual projects or groups of projects, and then choosing to implement some set of them so that the objectives of the parent organization will be achieved. This same systematic process can be applied to any area of the organization's business in which choices must be made between competing alternatives. For example, a manufacturing firm can use evaluation/selection techniques to choose which machine to adopt in a part-fabrication process; a television station can select which of several syndicated comedy shows to rerun in its 7:30 P.M. weekday time-slot; a construction firm can select the best subset of a large group of potential projects on which to bid; or a hospital can find the best mix of psychiatric, orthopedic, obstetric, and other beds for a new wing. Each project will have different costs, benefits, and risks. Rarely are these known with certainty. In the face of such differences, the selection of one project out of a set is a difficult task. Choosing a number of different projects, a *portfolio,* is even more complex.

In the following sections, we discuss several techniques that can be used to help senior managers select projects. Project selection is only one of many decisions associated with project management. To deal with all of these problems, we use *decision-aiding models.* We need such models because they abstract the relevant issues about a problem from the plethora of detail in which the problem is embedded. Realists cannot solve problems, only idealists can do

---

* This chapter has been abridged. It can be found in its entirety in Meredith, Jack R. & Samuel J. Mantel Jr., *Project Management: A Managerial Approach,* Chapter 2. Hoboken, NJ: John Wiley & Sons, Inc., 2002.

that. Reality is far too complex to deal with in its entirety. An "idealist" is needed to strip away almost all the reality from a problem, leaving only the aspects of the "real" situation with which he or she wishes to deal. This process of carving away the unwanted reality from the bones of a problem is called *modeling the problem.* The idealized version of the problem that results is called a *model.*

We live in the midst of what has been called the "knowledge explosion." We frequently hear comments such as "90 percent of all we know about physics has been discovered since Albert Einstein published his original work on special relativity"; and "80 percent of what we know about the human body has been discovered in the past 50 years." In addition, evidence is cited to show that knowledge is growing exponentially. Such statements emphasize the importance of the *management of change.* To survive, firms must develop strategies for assessing and reassessing the use of their resources. Every allocation of resources is an investment in the future. Because of the complex nature of most strategies, many of these investments are in projects.

To cite one of many possible examples, special visual effects accomplished through computer animation are common in the movies and television shows we watch daily. A few years ago they were unknown. When the capability was in its idea stage, computer companies as well as the firms producing movies and TV shows faced the decision whether or not to invest in the development of these techniques. Obviously valuable as the idea seems today, the choice was not quite so clear a decade ago when an entertainment company compared investment in computer animation to alternative investments in a new star, a new rock group, or a new theme park.

The proper choice of investment projects is crucial to the long-run survival of every firm. Daily we witness the results of both good and bad investment choices. In our daily newspapers we read of Cisco System's decision to purchase firms that have developed valuable communication network software rather than to develop its own software. We read of Procter and Gamble's decision to invest heavily in marketing its products on the Internet; British Airways' decision to purchase passenger planes from Airbus instead of from its traditional supplier, Boeing; or problems faced by school systems when they update student computer labs—should they invest in Windows®-based systems or stick with their traditional choice, Apple®. But can such important choices be made rationally? Once made, do they ever change, and if so, how? These questions reflect the need for effective selection models.

Within the limits of their capabilities, such models can be used to increase profits, select investments for limited capital resources, or improve the competitive position of the organization. They can be used for ongoing evaluation as well as initial selection, and thus are a key to the allocation and reallocation of the organization's scarce resources.

When a firm chooses a project selection model, the following criteria, based on Souder,[1] are most important:

1. *Realism:* The model should reflect the reality of the manager's decision situation, including the multiple objectives of both the firm and its managers. Without a common measurement system, direct comparison of different projects is impossible. For example, Project A may strengthen a firm's market share by extending its facilities, and Project B might improve its competitive position by strengthening its technical staff. Other things being equal, which is better? The model should take into account the realities of the firm's limitations on facilities, capital, personnel, and so forth. The model should also include factors that reflect project risks, including the technical risks of performance, cost, and time as well as the market risks of customer rejection and other implementation risks.

2. *Capability:* The model should be sophisticated enough to deal with multiple time periods, simulate various situations both internal and external to the project (e.g., strikes, interest rate changes), and optimize the decision. An optimizing model will make the comparisons that management deems important, consider major risks and constraints on the projects, and then select the best overall project or set of projects.

3. *Flexibility:* The model should give valid results within the range of conditions that the firm might experience. It should have the ability to be easily modified, or to be self-adjusting in response to changes in the firm's environment; for example, tax laws change, new technological advancements alter risk levels, and, above all, the organization's goals change.

4. *Ease of use:* The model should be reasonably convenient, not take a long time to execute, and be easy to use and understand. It should not require special interpretation, data that are difficult to acquire, excessive personnel, or unavailable equipment. The model's variables should also relate one-to-one with those real-world parameters the managers believe significant to the project. Finally, it should be easy to simulate the expected outcomes associated with investments in different project portfolios.

5. *Cost:* Data-gathering and modeling costs should be low relative to the cost of the project and must surely be less than the potential benefits of the project. All costs should be considered, including the costs of data management and of running the model.

We would add a sixth criterion:

6. *Easy computerization:* It must be easy and convenient to gather and store the information in a computer database, and to manipulate data in the model through use of a widely available, standard computer package such as Excel®, Lotus 1-2-3®, Quattro Pro®, and like programs. The same ease and convenience should apply to transferring the information to any standard decision support system.

In what follows, we first examine fundamental types of project selection models and the characteristics that make any model more or less acceptable.

Next we consider the limitations, strengths, and weaknesses of project selection models, including some suggestions of factors to consider when making a decision about which, if any, of the project selection models to use. Finally, we comment on some special aspects of the information base required for project selection. Then we turn our attention to the selection of a set of projects to help the organization achieve its goals and illustrate this with a technique called the *Project Portfolio Process*.

THE NATURE OF PROJECT SELECTION MODELS

There are two basic types of project selection models, *numeric* and *nonnumeric*. Both are widely used. Many organizations use both at the same time, or they use models that are combinations of the two. Nonnumeric models, as the name implies, do not use numbers as inputs. Numeric models do, but the criteria being measured may be either objective or subjective. It is important to remember that the *qualities* of a project may be represented by numbers, and that *subjective* measures are not necessarily less useful or reliable than so-called *objective* measures.

Before examining specific kinds of models within the two basic types, let us consider just what we wish the model to do for us, never forgetting two critically important, but often overlooked, facts.

1. Models do not make decisions—people do. The manager, not the model, bears responsibility for the decision. The manager may "delegate" the task of making the decision to a model, but the responsibility cannot be abdicated.
2. All models, however sophisticated, are only partial representations of the reality they are meant to reflect. Reality is far too complex for us to capture more than a small fraction of it in any model. Therefore, no model can yield an optimal decision except within its own, possibly inadequate, framework.

We seek a model to assist us in making project selection decisions. This model should possess the characteristics discussed previously and, above all, it must evaluate potential projects by the degree to which they will meet the firm's objectives. To construct a selection/evaluation model, therefore, it is necessary to develop a list of the firm's objectives.

A list of objectives should be generated by the organization's top management. It is a direct expression of organizational philosophy and policy. The list should go beyond the typical clichés about "survival" and "maximizing profits," which are certainly real goals but are just as certainly not the only goals of the firm. Other objectives might include maintenance of share of specific markets, development of an improved image with specific clients or competitors, expansion into a new line of business, decrease in sensitivity to business cycles, maintenance of employment for specific categories of workers, and maintenance of system loading at or above some percent of capacity, just to mention a few.

When the list of objectives has been developed, an additional refinement is recommended. The elements in the list should be *weighted*. Each item is added to the list because it represents a contribution to the success of the organization, but each item does not make an equal contribution. The weights reflect different degrees of contribution each element makes in accomplishing a set of goals.

Once the list of goals has been developed, one more task remains. The probable contribution of each project to each of the goals must be estimated. A project is selected or rejected because it is predicted to have certain outcomes if implemented. These outcomes are expected to contribute to goal achievement. If the estimated level of goal achievement is sufficiently large, the project is selected. If not, it is rejected. The relationship between the project's expected results and the organization's goals must be understood. In general, the kinds of information required to evaluate a project can be listed under production, marketing, financial, personnel, administrative, and other such categories.

Exhibit 3.1 is a list of factors that contribute, positively or negatively, to these categories. In order to give focus to this list, we assume that the projects in question involve the possible substitution of a new production process for an existing one. The list is meant to be illustrative. It certainly is not exhaustive.

Some factors in this list have a one-time impact and some recur. Some are difficult to estimate and may be subject to considerable error. For these, it is helpful to identify a *range of uncertainty*. In addition, the factors may occur at different times. And some factors may have *thresholds*, critical values above or below which we might wish to reject the project. We will deal in more detail with these issues later in this chapter.

Clearly, no single project decision need include all these factors. Moreover, not only is the list incomplete, also it contains redundant items. Perhaps more important, the factors are not at the same level of generality: *profitability* and *impact on organizational image* both affect the overall organization, but *impact on working conditions* is more oriented to the production system. Nor are all elements of equal importance. *Change in production cost* is usually considered more important than *impact on current suppliers*. Shortly, we will consider the problem of generating an acceptable list of factors and measuring their relative importance. At that time we will discuss the creation of a Decision Support System (DSS) for project evaluation and selection.

Although the process of evaluating a potential project is time-consuming and difficult, its importance cannot be overstated. A major consulting firm has argued[2] that the primary cause for the failure of R&D projects is insufficient

EXHIBIT 3.1 Project evaluation factors

Production Factors

1. Time until ready to install
2. Length of disruption during installation
3. Learning curve—time until operating as desired
4. Effects on waste and rejects
5. Energy requirements
6. Facility and other equipment requirements
7. Safety of process
8. Other applications of technology
9. Change in cost to produce a unit output
10. Change in raw material usage
11. Availability of raw materials
12. Required development time and cost
13. Impact on current suppliers
14. Change in quality of output

Marketing Factors

1. Size of potential market for output
2. Probable market share of output
3. Time until market share is acquired
4. Impact on current product line
5. Consumer acceptance
6. Impact on consumer safety
7. Estimated life of output
8. Spin-off project possibilities

Financial Factors

1. Profitability, net present value of the investment
2. Impact on cash flows
3. Payout period
4. Cash requirements
5. Time until break-even
6. Size of investment required
7. Impact on seasonal and cyclical fluctuations

Personnel Factors

1. Training requirements
2. Labor skill requirements
3. Availability of required labor skills
4. Level of resistance from current workforce
5. Change in size of laborforce
6. Inter- and intragroup communication requirements
7. Impact on working conditions

Administrative and Miscellaneous Factors

1. Meet government safety standards
2. Meet government environmental standards
3. Impact on information system
4. Reaction of stockholders and securities markets
5. Patent and trade secret protection
6. Impact on image with customers, suppliers, and competitors.
7. Degree to which we understand new technology
8. Managerial capacity to direct and control new process

care in evaluating the proposal before the expenditure of funds. What is true for R&D projects also appears to be true for other kinds of projects, and it is clear that product development projects are more successful if they incorporate user needs and satisfaction in the design process.[3] Careful analysis of a potential project is a *sine qua non* for profitability in the construction business. There are many horror stories[4] about firms that undertook projects for the installation of a computer information system without sufficient analysis of the time, cost, and disruption involved.

Later in this chapter we will consider the problem of conducting an evaluation under conditions of uncertainty about the outcomes associated with a project. Before dealing with this problem, however, it helps to examine several different evaluation/selection models and consider their strengths and weaknesses. Recall that the problem of choosing the project selection model itself will also be discussed later.

TYPES OF PROJECT SELECTION MODELS

Of the two basic types of selection models (numeric and nonnumeric), nonnumeric models are older and simpler and have only a few subtypes to consider. We examine them first.

Nonnumeric Models

The Sacred Cow

In this case the project is suggested by a senior and powerful official in the organization. Often the project is initiated with a simple comment such as, "If you have a chance, why don't you look into . . . ," and there follows an undeveloped idea for a new product, for the development of a new market, for the design and adoption of a global data base and information system, or for some other project requiring an investment of the firm's resources. The immediate result of this bland statement is the creation of a "project" to investigate whatever the boss has suggested. The project is "sacred" in the sense that it will be maintained until successfully concluded, or until the boss, personally, recognizes the idea as a failure and terminates it.

The Operating Necessity

If a flood is threatening the plant, a project to build a protective dike does not require much formal evaluation, is an example of this scenario. XYZ Steel Corporation has used this criterion (and the following criterion also) in evaluating potential projects. If the project is required in order to keep the system operating, the primary question becomes: Is the system worth saving at the estimated cost of the project? If the answer is yes, project costs will be examined to make sure they are kept as low as is consistent with project success, but the project will be funded.

The Competitive Necessity

Using this criterion, XYZ Steel undertook a major plant rebuilding project in the late 1960s in its steel-bar-manufacturing facilities near Chicago. It had become apparent to XYZ's management that the company's bar mill needed modernization if the firm was to maintain its competitive position in the Chicago market area. Although the planning process for the project was quite sophisticated, the decision to undertake the project was based on a desire to maintain the company's competitive position in that market.

In a similar manner, many business schools are restructuring their undergraduate and MBA programs to stay competitive with the more forward-looking schools. In large part, this action is driven by declining numbers of tuition-paying students and the stronger competition to attract them.

Investment in an *operating necessity* project takes precedence over a *competitive necessity* project, but both types of projects may bypass the more careful numeric analysis used for projects deemed to be less urgent or less important to the survival of the firm.

The Product Line Extension

In this case, a project to develop and distribute new products would be judged on the degree to which it fits the firm's existing product line, fills a gap, strengthens a weak link, or extends the line in a new, desirable direction. Sometimes careful calculations of profitability are not required. Decision makers can act on their beliefs about what will be the likely impact on the total system performance if the new product is added to the line.

Comparative Benefit Model

For this situation, assume that an organization has many projects to consider, perhaps several dozen. Senior management would like to select a subset of the projects that would most benefit the firm, but the projects do not seem to be easily comparable. For example, some projects concern potential new products, some concern changes in production methods, others concern computerization of certain records, and still others cover a variety of subjects not easily categorized (e.g., a proposal to create a daycare center for employees with small children). The organization has no formal method of selecting projects, but members of the Selection Committee think that some projects will benefit the firm more than others, even if they have no precise way to define or measure "benefit."

The concept of comparative benefits, if not a formal model, is widely adopted for selection decisions on all sorts of projects. Most United Way organizations use the concept to make decisions about which of several social programs to fund. Senior management of the funding organization then examines all projects with positive recommendations and attempts to construct a portfolio that best fits the organization's aims and its budget.

Of the several techniques for ordering projects, the Q-Sort[5] is one of the most straightforward. First, the projects are divided into three groups—*good, fair,* and *poor*—according to their relative merits. If any group has more than eight members, it is subdivided into two categories, such as *fair-plus* and *fair-minus.* When all categories have eight or fewer members, the projects within each category are ordered from best to worst. Again, the order is determined on the basis of relative merit. The rater may use specific criteria to rank each project, or may simply use general overall judgment.

The process described may be carried out by one person who is responsible for evaluation and selection, or it may be performed by a committee charged with the responsibility. If a committee handles the task, the individual rankings can be developed anonymously, and the set of anonymous rankings can be examined by the committee itself for consensus. It is common for such rankings to differ somewhat from rater to rater, but they do not often vary strikingly because the individuals chosen for such committees rarely differ widely on what they feel to be appropriate for the parent organization. Projects can then be selected in the order of preference, though they are usually evaluated financially before final selection.

There are other, similar nonnumeric models for accepting or rejecting projects. Although it is easy to dismiss such models as unscientific, they should not be discounted casually. These models are clearly goal-oriented and directly reflect the primary concerns of the organization. The sacred cow model, in particular, has an added feature; sacred cow projects are visibly supported by "the powers that be." Full support by top management is certainly an important contributor to project success.[6] Without such support, the probability of project success is sharply lowered.

Numeric Models: Profit/Profitability

As noted earlier, a large majority of all firms using project evaluation and selection models use profitability as the sole measure of acceptability. We will consider these models first, and then discuss models that surpass the profit test for acceptance.

Payback Period

The payback period for a project is the initial fixed investment in the project divided by the estimated annual net cash inflows from the project. The ratio of these quantities is the number of years required for the project to repay its initial fixed investment. For example, assume a project costs $100,000 to implement and has annual net cash inflows of $25,000. Then

$$\text{Payback period} = \frac{\$100,000}{\$25,000} = 4 \text{ years}$$

This method assumes that the cash inflows will persist at least long enough to pay back the investment, and it ignores any cash inflows beyond the payback period. The method also serves as an (inadequate) proxy for risk. The faster the investment is recovered, the less the risk to which the firm is exposed.

Average Rate of Return

Often mistaken as the reciprocal of the payback period, the average rate of return is the ratio of the average annual profit (either before or after taxes) to the initial or average investment in the project. Because average annual profits are usually not equivalent to net cash inflows, the average rate of return does not usually equal the reciprocal of the payback period. Assume, in the example just given, that the average annual profits are $15,000:

$$\text{Average rate of return} = \frac{\$15,000}{\$100,000} = 0.15$$

Neither of these evaluation methods is recommended for project selection, though payback period is widely used and does have a legitimate value for cash budgeting decisions. The major advantage of these models is their simplicity, but neither takes into account the time-value of money. Unless interest rates are extremely low and the rate of inflation is nil, the failure to reduce future cash flows or profits to their present value will result in serious evaluation errors.

Discounted Cash Flow

Also referred to as the net present value method, the discounted cash flow method determines the net present value of all cash flows by discounting them by the required rate of return (also known as the *hurdle rate, cutoff rate,* and similar terms) as follows:

$$\text{NPV (project)} = A_0 + \sum_{t=1}^{n} \frac{F_t}{(1+k)^t}$$

where
  F_t = the net cash flow in period t,
  k = the required rate of return, and
  A_0 = initial cash investment (because this is an outflow, it will be negative).

To include the impact of inflation (or deflation) where p_t is the predicted rate of inflation during period t, we have

$$\text{NPV (project)} = A_0 + \sum_{t=1}^{n} \frac{F_t}{\left(1 + k + p_t\right)^t}$$

Early in the life of a project, net cash flow is likely to be negative, the major outflow being the initial investment in the project, A_0. If the project is successful, however, cash flows will become positive. The project is *acceptable* if the sum of the net present values of all estimated cash flows over the life of the project is positive. A simple example will suffice. Using our $100,000 investment with a net cash inflow of $25,000 per year for a period of eight years, a required rate of return of 15 percent, and an inflation rate of 3 percent per year, we have

$$\text{NPV (project)} = -\$100,000 + \sum_{t=1}^{8} \frac{\$25,000}{\left(1 + 0.15 + 0.03\right)^t}$$

$$= \$1,939$$

Because the present value of the inflows is greater than the present value of the outflow—that is, the net present value is positive—the project is deemed acceptable.

Internal Rate of Return

If we have a set of expected cash inflows and cash out-flows, the internal rate of return is the discount rate that equates the present values of the two sets of flows. If A_t is an expected cash outflow in the period t and R_t is the expected inflow for the period t, the internal rate of return is the value of k that satisfies the following equation (note that the A_0 will be positive in this formulation of the problem):

$$\frac{A_0 + A_1}{\left(1 + k\right)} + \frac{A_2}{\left(1 + k\right)^2} + \cdots + \frac{A_n}{\left(1 + k\right)^n} = \frac{R_1}{\left(1 + k\right)^2} + \frac{R_2}{\left(1 + k\right)^2} + \cdots + \frac{R_n}{\left(1 + k\right)^n}$$

The value of k is found by trial and error.

Profitability Index

Also known as the benefit–cost ratio, the profitability index is the net present value of all future expected cash flows divided by the initial cash investment. (Some firms do not discount the cash flows in making this calculation.) If this ratio is greater than 1.0, the project may be accepted.

Box 3.1

PsychoCeramic Sciences, Inc.

PsychoCeramic Sciences, Inc. (PSI), a large producer of cracked pots and other cracked items, is considering the installation of a new marketing software package that will, it is hoped, allow more accurate sales information concerning the inventory, sales, and deliveries of its pots as well as its vases designed to hold artificial flowers.

The information systems (IS) department has submitted a project proposal that estimates the investment requirements as follows: an initial investment of $125,000 to be paid up-front to the Pottery Software Corporation; an additional investment of $100,000 to modify and install the software; and another $90,000 to integrate the new software into the overall information system. Delivery and installation is estimated to take one year; integrating the entire system should require an additional year. Thereafter, the IS department predicts that scheduled software updates will require further expenditures of about $15,000 every second year, beginning in the fourth year. They will not, however, update the software in the last year of its expected useful life.

The project schedule calls for benefits to begin in the third year, and to be up-to-speed by the end of that year. Projected additional profits resulting from better and more timely sales information are estimated to be $50,000 in the first year of operation and are expected to peak at $120,000 in the second year of operation, and then to follow the gradually declining pattern shown in the table at the end of this box.

Project life is expected to be 10 years from project inception, at which time the proposed system will be obsolete for this division and will have to be replaced. It is estimated, however, that the software can be sold to a smaller division of PSI and will thus have a salvage value of $35,000.

PSI has a 12 percent hurdle rate for capital investments and expects the rate of inflation to be about 3 percent over the life of the project. Assuming that the initial expenditure occurs at the beginning of the year and that all other receipts and expenditures occur as lump sums at the end of the year, we can prepare the Net Present Value analysis for the project as shown in the table below.

The Net Present Value of the project is positive and, thus, the project can be accepted. (The project would have been rejected if the hurdle rate were 14 percent.)

Just for the intellectual exercise, note that the total inflow for the project is $759,000, or $75,900 per year on average for the 10 year project.

The required investment is $315,000 (ignoring the biennial overhaul charges). Assuming 10 year, straight line depreciation or $31,500 per year, the payback period would be:

$$PB = \frac{\$135,000}{\$75,900 + 31,500} = 2.9 \text{ years}$$

A project with this payback period would probably be considered quite desirable.

Year A	Inflow B	Outflow C	Net Flow $D = (B - C)$	Discount Factor $1/(1 + k + p)^t$	Net Present Value D (Disc. Fact.)
1996°	$0	$125,000	$−125,000	1.0000	$−125,000
1996	0	100,000	−100,000	0.8696	−86,960
1997	0	90,000	−90,000	0.7561	−68,049
1998	50,000	0	50,000	0.6575	32,875
1999	120,000	15,000	105,000	0.5718	60,039
2000	115,000	0	115,000	0.4972	57,178
2001	105,000	15,000	90,000	0.4323	38,907
2002	97,000	0	97,000	0.3759	36,462
2003	90,000	15,000	75,000	0.3269	24,518
2004	82,000	0	82,000	0.2843	23,313
2005	65,000	0	65,000	0.2472	16,068
2005	35,000		35,000	0.2472	8,652
Total	$759,000	$360,000	$399,000		$18,003

° $t = 0$ at the beginning of 1996

Evaluating Profitability Models

There are a great many variations of the models just described. These variations fall into three general categories: (1) those that subdivide net cash flow into the elements that comprise the net flow; (2) those that include specific terms to introduce risk (or uncertainty, which is treated as risk) into the evaluation; and (3) those that extend the analysis to consider effects that the project might have on other projects or activities in the organization.

Several comments are in order about all the profit-profitability numeric models. First, let us consider their advantages:

1. The undiscounted models are simple to use and understand.
2. All use readily available accounting data to determine the cash flows.
3. Model output is in terms familiar to business decision makers.

4. With a few exceptions, model output is on an "absolute" profit/profitability scale and allows "absolute" go/no-go decisions.

5. Some profit models account for project risk.

The disadvantages of these models are the following:

1. These models ignore all nonmonetary factors except risk.

2. Models that do not include discounting ignore the timing of the cash flows and the time–value of money.

3. Models that reduce cash flows to their present value are strongly biased toward the short run.

4. Payback-type models ignore cash flows beyond the payback period.

5. The internal rate of return model can result in multiple solutions.

6. All are sensitive to errors in the input data for the early years of the project.

7. All discounting models are nonlinear, and the effects of changes (or errors) in the variables or parameters are generally not obvious to most decision makers.

8. All these models depend for input on a determination of cash flows, but it is not clear exactly how the concept of cash flow is properly defined for the purpose of evaluating projects.

A complete discussion of profit/profitability models can be found in any standard work on financial management—see Moyer[7] or Ross, Westerfield, and Jordan,[8] for example. In general, the net present value models are preferred to the internal rate of return models. Despite wide use, financial models rarely include nonfinancial outcomes in their benefits and costs. In a discussion of the financial value of adopting project management (that is, selecting as a project the use of project management) in a firm, Githens[9] notes that traditional financial models "simply cannot capture the complexity and value-added of today's process-oriented firm."

In our experience, the payback period model, occasionally using discounted cash flows, is one of the most commonly used models for evaluating projects and other investment opportunities. Managers generally feel that insistence on short payout periods tends to minimize the risks associated with the passage of time. While this is certainly logical, we prefer evaluation methods that discount cash flows and deal with uncertainty more directly by considering specific risks. Using the payout period as a cash-budgeting tool aside, *its only virtue is simplicity*, a dubious virtue at best.

Numeric Models: Scoring

In an attempt to overcome some of the disadvantages of profitability models, particularly their focus on a single decision criterion, a number of evaluation/

selection models that use multiple criteria to evaluate a project have been developed. Such models vary widely in their complexity and information requirements. The examples discussed illustrate some of the different types of numeric scoring models.

Unweighted 0–1 Factor Model

A set of relevant factors is selected by management and then usually listed in a preprinted form. One or more raters score the project on each factor, depending on whether or not it qualifies for an individual criterion. The raters are chosen by senior managers, for the most part from the rolls of senior management. The criteria for choice are (1) a clear understanding of organizational goals and (2) a good knowledge of the firm's potential project *portfolio*. Exhibit 3.2 shows an example of the rating sheet for an unweighted, 0–1 factor model.

The columns of Exhibit 3.2 are summed and those projects with a sufficient number of qualifying factors may be selected. The main advantage of

EXHIBIT 3.2   Sample project evaluation form

Project _____

Rater _____   Date _____

	Qualifies	Does Not Qualify
No increase in energy requirements	x	
Potential market size, dollars	x	
Potential market share, percent	x	
No new facility required	x	
No new technical expertise required		x
No decrease in quality of final product	x	
Ability to manage project with current personnel		x
No requirement for reorganization	x	
Impact on workforce safety	x	
Impact on environmental standards	x	
Profitability		
Rate of return more than 15% after tax	x	
Estimated annual profits more than $250,000	x	
Time to break-even less than 3 years	x	
Need for external consultants		x
Consistency with current line of business		x
Impact on company image		
With customers	x	
With our industry		x
Totals	12	5

such a model is that it uses several criteria in the decision process. The major disadvantages are that it assumes all criteria are of equal importance and it allows for no gradation of the degree to which a specific project meets the various criteria.

Unweighted Factor Scoring Model

The second disadvantage of the 0–1 factor model can be dealt with by constructing a simple linear measure of the degree to which the project being evaluated meets each of the criteria contained in the list. The x marks in Exhibit 3.2 would be replaced by numbers. Often a five-point scale is used, where 5 is very good, 4 is good, 3 is fair, 2 is poor, 1 is very poor. (Three-, seven-, and ten-point scales are also common.) The second column of Exhibit 3.2 would not be needed. The column of scores is summed, and those projects with a total score exceeding some critical value are selected. A variant of this selection process might choose the highest-scoring projects (still assuming they are all above some critical score) until the estimated costs of the set of projects equaled the resource limit. However, the criticism that the criteria are all assumed to be of equal importance still holds.

The use of a discrete numeric scale to represent the degree to which a criterion is satisfied is widely accepted. To construct such measures for project evaluation, we proceed in the following manner. Select a criterion, say, "estimated annual profits in dollars." For this criterion, determine five ranges of performance so that a typical project, chosen at random, would have a roughly equal chance of being in any one of the five performance ranges. (Another way of describing this condition is: Take a large number of projects that were selected for support in the past, regardless of whether they were actually successful or not, and create five levels of predicted performance so that about one-fifth of the projects fall into each level.) This procedure will usually create unequal ranges, which may offend our sense of symmetry but need not concern us otherwise. It ensures that each criterion performance measure utilizes the full scale of possible values, a desirable characteristic for performance measures.

Consider the following two simple examples. Using the criterion just mentioned, "estimated annual profits in dollars," we might construct the following scale:

Score	Performance Level
5	Above $1,100,000
4	$750,001 to $1,100,000
3	$500,001 to $750,000
2	$200,000 to $500,000
1	Less than $200,000

As suggested, these ranges might have been chosen so that about 20 percent of the projects considered for funding would fall into each of the five ranges.

The criterion "no decrease in quality of the final product" would have to be restated to be scored on a five-point scale, perhaps as follows:

Score	Performance Level
	The quality of the final product is:
5	Significantly and visibly improved
4	Significantly improved, but not visible to buyer
3	Not significantly changed
2	Significantly lowered, but not visible to buyer
1	Significantly and visibly lowered

This scale is an example of scoring cells that represent opinion rather than objective (even if "estimated") fact, as was the case in the profit scale.

Weighted Factor Scoring Model

When numeric weights reflecting the relative importance of each individual factor are added, we have a weighted factor scoring model. In general, it takes the form

$$S_i = \sum_{j=1}^{n} s_{ij} w_j$$

where

S_i = the total score of the ith project,

s_{ij} = the score of the ith project on the jth criterion, and

w_j = the weight of the jth criterion.

The weights, w_j, may be generated by any technique that is acceptable to the organization's policy makers. There are several techniques available to generate such numbers, but the most effective and most widely used is the Delphi technique. The Delphi technique was developed by Brown and Dalkey of the RAND Corporation during the 1950s and 1960s.[10] It is a technique for developing numeric values that are equivalent to subjective, verbal measures of relative value. The method of successive comparisons (or pairwise comparisons) may also be used for the same purpose.[11]

Another popular and quite similar approach is the Analytic Hierarchy Process, developed by Saaty.[12] For an extensive example involving finance, sales, and purchasing, see pages 306–316 of Turban and Meredith.[13] This example also illustrates the use of Expert Choice®, a software package to facilitate the application of the Analytic Hierarchy Process.

When numeric weights have been generated, it is helpful (but not necessary) to scale the weights so that

$$0 \le w_j \le 1 \qquad j = 1, 2, 3, \ldots, n$$

$$\sum_{j=1}^{n} w_j = 1$$

The weight of each criterion can be interpreted as the "percent of the total weight accorded to that particular criterion."

A special caveat is in order. It is quite possible with this type of model to include a large number of criteria. It is not particularly difficult to develop scoring scales and weights, and the ease of gathering and processing the required information makes it tempting to include marginally relevant criteria along with the obviously important items. Resist this temptation! After the important factors have been weighted, there usually is little residual weight to be distributed among the remaining elements. The result is that the evaluation is simply insensitive to major differences in the scores on trivial criteria. A good rule of thumb is to discard elements with weights less than 0.02 or 0.03. (If elements are discarded, and if you wish $Sw_j = 1$, the weights must be rescaled to 1.0.) As with any linear model, the user should be aware that the elements in the model are assumed to be independent. This presents no particular problems for these scoring models because they are used to make estimates in a "steady–state" system, and we are not concerned with transitions between states.

It is useful to note that if one uses a weighted scoring model to aid in project selection, the model can also serve as an aid to project *improvement*. For any given criterion, the difference between the criterion's score and the highest possible score on that criterion, multiplied by the weight of the criterion, is a measure of the potential improvement in the project score that would result were the project's performance on that criterion sufficiently improved. It may be that such improvement is not feasible, or is more costly than the improvement warrants. On the other hand, such an analysis of each project yields a valuable statement of the comparative benefits of project improvements. Viewing a project in this way is a type of sensitivity analysis. We examine the degree to which a project's score is sensitive to attempts to improve it—usually by adding resources.

It is not particularly difficult to computerize a weighted scoring model by creating a template on Excel® or one of the other standard computer spreadsheets. The logic of using a "selection" model for the termination decision is straightforward: Given the time and resources required to take a project from its current state to completion, should we make the investment? A "Yes" answer to that question "selects" for funding the partially completed project from the set of all partially finished and not-yet-started projects.

Box 3.2

Gettin' Wheels

Rather than using an example in which actual projects are selected for funding with a weighted factor scoring model (hereafter "scoring model") that would require tediously long descriptions of the projects, we can demonstrate the use of the model in a simple, common problem that many readers will have faced—the choice of an automobile for purchase. This problem is nicely suited to use of the scoring model because the purchaser is trying to satisfy multiple objectives in making the purchase and is typically faced with several different cars from which to choose.

Our model must have the following elements:

1. A set of criteria on which to judge the value of any alternative.
2. A numeric estimate of the relative importance (i.e., the "weight") of each criterion in the set.
3. Scales by which to measure or score the performance or contribution-to-value of each alternative on each criterion.

The criteria weights and measures of performance must be numeric in form, but this does not mean that they must be either "objective" or "quantitative." Criteria weights, obviously, are subjective by their nature, being an expression of what the decision maker thinks is important. The development of performance scales is more easily dealt with in the context of our example, and we will develop them shortly.

Assume that we have chosen the criteria and weights shown in Table A to be used in our evaluations.* The weights represent the relative

TABLE A. Criteria and Weights for Automobile Purchase

Appearance	4	(.10)
Braking	3	(.07)
Comfort	7	(.17)
Cost, operating	5	(.12)
Cost, original	10	(.24)
Handling	7	(.17)
Reliability	5	(.12)
Total	41	.99

(continued)

importance of the criteria measured on a 10-point scale. The numbers in parentheses show the proportion of the total weight carried by each criterion. (They add to only .99 due to rounding.) Raw weights work just as well for decision making as their percentage counterparts, but the latter are usually preferred because they are a constant reminder to the decision maker of the impact of each of the criteria.

Prior to consideration of performance standards and sources of information for the criteria we have chosen, we must ask, "Are there any characteristics that must be present (or absent) in a candidate automobile for it to be acceptable?" Assume, for this example, that to be acceptable, an alternative must not be green, must have air conditioning, must be able to carry at least four adults, must have at least 10 cubic feet of luggage space, and must be priced less than $34,000. If an alternative violates any of these conditions, it is immediately rejected.

For each criterion, we need some way of measuring the estimated performance of each alternative. In this case, we might adopt the measures shown in Table B. Our purpose is to transform a measure of the degree to which an alternative meets a criterion into a score, the s_{ij}, that is a general measure of the utility or value of the alternative with respect to that criterion. Note that this requires us to define the criterion precisely, as well as to specify a source for the information.

Table C shows the scores for each criterion transformed to a 5-point scale, which will suffice for our ratings.

Using the performance scores shown in Table C, we can evaluate the cars we have identified as our alternatives: the Leviathan 8, the NuevoEcon, the Maxivan, the Sporticar 100, and the Ritzy 300. Each

TABLE B.   Automobile Selection Criteria, Measures and Data Sources

Appearance	Subjective judgment, personal
Braking	Distance in feet, 60–0 mph, automotive magazine[a]
Comfort	Subjective judgment, 30 min. road test
Cost, operating	Annual insurance cost plus fuel cost[b]
Cost, original	Dealer cost, auto-cost service[c]
Handling	Average speed through standard slalom, automotive magazine[a]
Reliability	Score on *Consumer Reports,* "Frequency-of-Repair" data (average of 2 previous years)

[a] Many automotive periodicals conduct standardized performance tests of new cars.
[b] Annual fuel cost is calculated as (17,500 mi/DOE ave. mpg) × $1.25/gal.
[c] There are several sources for dealer-cost data (e.g., AAA, which provides a stable data base on which to estimate the price of each alternative).

TABLE C. Performance Measures and Equivalent Scores for Selection of an Automobile

Criteria	Scores				
	1	**2**	**3**	**4**	**5**
Appearance	Ugh	Poor	Adequate	Good	WOW
Braking	>165	165–150	150–140	140–130	<130
Comfort	Bad	Poor	Adequate	Good	Excellent
Cost, operating°	>$2.5	$2.1–2.5	$1.9–2.1	$1.6–1.9	<$1.6
Cost, original°	>$32.5	$26–32.5	$21–26	$17–21	<$17
Handling	>45	45–49.5	49.5–55	55–59	<59
Reliability	Worst	Poor	Adequate	Good	Excellent

° Cost data in $1000s.

car is scored on each criterion according to the categories shown in Table C. Then each score is multiplied by the criterion weight and the result is entered into the appropriate box in Table D. Last, the results for each alternative are summed to represent the weighted score.

According to this set of measures, we prefer the Ritzy 300, but while it is a clear winner over the Leviathan 8 and the Maxivan, and scores about 8 percent better than the Sporticar, it rates only about 0.13 points or 4 percent above the NuevoEcon. Note that if we overrated the Ritzy by one point on comfort or handling, or if we underrated the NuevoEcon by one point on either of these criteria, the result would have been reversed. (We assume that the original cost data are accurate.) With the scores this close, we might want to evaluate these two cars by additional

TABLE D. Scores for Alternative Cars on Selection Criteria

Alternatives	Criteria and Weights							
	Appearance (0.10)	Braking (0.07)	Comfort (0.17)	Cost, Operating (0.12)	Cost, Original (0.24)	Handling (0.17)	Reliability (0.12)	$Es_{ij}w_j$
Leviathan 8	3 × .10 = 0.30	1 × 0.07 = 0.07	4 × 0.17 = 0.68	2 × 0.12 = 0.24	1 × 0.24 = 0.24	2 × 0.17 = 0.34	3 × 0.12 = 0.36	2.23
NuevoEcon	3 × .10 = 0.30	3 × 0.07 = 0.21	2 × 0.17 = 0.34	5 × 0.12 = 0.60	4 × 0.24 = 0.96	2 × 0.17 = 0.34	4 × 0.12 = 0.48	3.23
Maxivan	2 × .10 = 0.20	1 × 0.07 = 0.07	4 × 0.17 = 0.68	4 × 0.12 = 0.48	3 × 0.24 = 0.72	1 × 0.17 = 0.17	3 × 0.12 = 0.36	2.68
Sporticar 100	5 × .10 = 0.50	4 × 0.07 = 0.28	3 × 0.17 = 0.51	2 × 0.12 = 0.24	2 × 0.24 = 0.48	5 × 0.17 = 0.85	2 × 0.12 = 0.24	3.10
Ritzy 300	4 × .10 = 0.40	5 × 0.07 = 0.35	5 × 0.17 = 0.85	2 × 0.12 = 0.24	1 × 0.24 = 0.24	4 × 0.17 = 0.68	5 × 0.12 = 0.60	3.36

(continued)

criteria (e.g., ease of carrying children, status, safety features like dual airbags or ABS) prior to making a firm decision.

All in all, if the decision maker has well delineated objectives, and can determine how specific kinds of performance contribute to those criteria, and finally, can measure those kinds of performance for each of the alternative courses of action, then the scoring model is a powerful and flexible tool. To the extent that criteria are not carefully defined, performance is not well linked to the criteria, and is carelessly or wrongly measured, the scoring model rests on a faulty foundation and is merely a convenient path to error.

---

* The criteria and weights were picked arbitrarily for this example. Because this is typically an individual or family decision, techniques like Delphi or successive comparisons are not required.

Constrained Weighted Factor Scoring Model

The temptation to include marginal criteria can be partially overcome by allowing additional criteria to enter the model as constraints rather than weighted factors. These constraints represent project characteristics that must be present or absent in order for the project to be acceptable. In our example concerning a product, we might have specified that we would not undertake any project that would significantly lower the quality of the final product (visible to the buyer or not).

We would amend the weighted scoring model to take the form:

$$S_i = \sum_{j=1}^{n} s_{ij} w_j \prod_{k=1}^{v} c_{ik}$$

where $c_{ik} = 1$ if the ith project satisfies the kth constraint, and 0 if it does not. Other elements in the model are as defined earlier.

Although this model is analytically tidy, in practice we would not bother to evaluate projects that are so unsuitable in some ways that we would not consider supporting them regardless of their expected performance against other criteria. For example, except under extraordinary circumstances, Procter & Gamble would not consider a project to add a new consumer product or product line:

- That cannot be marketed nationally.
- That cannot be distributed through mass outlets (grocery stores, drugstores).
- That will not generate gross revenues in excess of $—million.

- For which Procter & Gamble's potential market share is not at least 50 percent.
- That does not utilize Procter & Gamble's scientific expertise, manufacturing expertise, advertising expertise, or packaging and distribution expertise.

Again, a caveat is in order. Exercise care when adopting constraints. It may seem obvious that we should not consider a project if it has no reasonable assurance of long-run profitability. Such a constraint, however, can force us to overlook a project that, though unprofitable itself, might have a strong, positive impact on the profitability of other potential projects.

Evaluating Scoring Models

As was the case with profitability models, scoring models have their own characteristic advantages and disadvantages. The advantages are:

1. These models allow multiple criteria to be used for evaluation and decision making, including profit/profitability models and both tangible and intangible criteria.
2. They are structurally simple and therefore easy to understand and use.
3. They are a direct reflection of managerial policy.
4. They are easily altered to accommodate changes in the environment or managerial policy.
5. Weighted scoring models allow for the fact that some criteria are more important than others.
6. These models allow easy sensitivity analysis. The trade-offs between the several criteria are readily observable.

The disadvantages are the following:

1. The output of a scoring model is strictly a relative measure. Project scores do not represent the value or "utility" associated with a project and thus do not directly indicate whether or not the project should be supported.
2. In general, scoring models are linear in form and the elements of such models are assumed to be independent.
3. The ease of use of these models is conducive to the inclusion of a large number of criteria, most of which have such small weights that they have little impact on the total project score.
4. Unweighted scoring models assume all criteria are of equal importance, which is almost certainly contrary to fact.
5. To the extent that profit/profitability is included as an element in the scoring model, this element has the advantages and disadvantages noted earlier for the profitability models themselves.

An interesting alternative to scoring models is an iterative rating process developed by Raz.[14] His method starts with a set of attributes that can be used to rank potential projects. He then removes all attributes that do not differentiate between the alternatives and all projects that are dominated by others. If a choice can then be made, it is made. If not, the process is repeated. In another paper, Pascale, et al. compare a weighted scoring model with an unweighted scoring model for the evaluation of innovations. They conclude that the former works well with incremental change, and the latter works better when the innovation is a "new idea."[15] They also investigate the impact of the evaluation methods on idea generation.

Choosing a Project Selection Model

Selecting the type of model to aid the evaluation/selection process depends on the philosophy and wishes of management. Liberatore and Titus[16] conducted a survey of 40 high-level staff persons from 29 *Fortune 500* firms. Eighty percent of their respondents report the use of one or more financial models for R&D project decision making. Although their sample is small and nonrandom, their findings are quite consistent with the present authors' experience. None of the respondent firms used mathematical programming techniques for project selection or resource allocation.

We strongly favor weighted scoring models for three fundamental reasons. First, they allow the multiple objectives of all organizations to be reflected in the important decision about which projects will be supported and which will be rejected. Second, scoring models are easily adapted to changes in managerial philosophy or changes in the environment. Third, they do not suffer from the bias toward the short run that is inherent in profitability models that discount future cash flows. This is not a prejudice against discounting and most certainly does not argue against the inclusion of profits/profitability as an important factor in selection, but rather *it is an argument against the exclusion of nonfinancial factors* that may require a longer-run view of the costs and benefits of a project. For a powerful statement of this point, see Hayes and Abernathy.[17]

It is also interesting to note that Liberatore and Titus[18] found that firms with a significant amount of contract research funded from outside the organization used scoring models for project screening much more frequently than firms with negligible levels of outside funding. It was also found that firms with significant levels of outside funding were much less likely to use a payback period.

The structure of a weighted scoring model is quite straightforward. Its virtues are many. Nonetheless, the actual use of scoring models is not as easy as it might seem. Decision makers are forced to make difficult choices and they are not always comfortable doing so. They are forced to reduce often vague feelings to quite specific words or numbers. Multiattribute, multiperson decision making is not simple. (For an interesting discussion of this process, see Irving and Conrath.[19])

COMMENTS ON THE INFORMATION BASE FOR SELECTION

Our bias in favor of weighted scoring models is quite clear and weighted scoring models can be simulated because both the scores and the weights are usually estimates. But irrespective of which model is chosen for project selection, a data base must be created and maintained to furnish input data for the model. Directions for the actual construction of the data base go beyond the scope of this book, but some comments about the task are in order.

The use of any project selection model assumes that the decision-making procedure takes place in a reasonably rational organizational environment. Such is not always the case. In some organizations, project selection seems to be the result of a political process, and sometimes involves questionable ethics, complete with winners and losers.[20] In others, the organization is so rigid in its approach to decision making that it attempts to reduce all decisions to an algorithmic proceeding in which predetermined programs make choices so that humans have minimal involvement—and responsibility. Here too, Saaty's[21] *Analytic Hierarchy Process* can lend rationality to a sometimes irrational process. In an interesting paper, Huber[22] examines the impact that the organizational environment has on the design of decision support systems.

The remainder of this section deals with three special problems affecting the data used in project selection models.

Accounting Data

Whether managers are familiar with accounting systems or not, they can find it useful to reflect on the methods and assumptions used in the preparation of accounting data. Among the most crucial are the following:

1. Accountants live in a linear world. With few exceptions, cost and revenue data are assumed to vary linearly with associated changes in inputs and outputs.

2. The accounting system often provides cost-revenue information that is derived from standard cost analyses and equally standardized assumptions regarding revenues. These standards may or may not be accurate representations of the cost-revenue structure of the physical system they purport to represent.

3. As noted in the previous section, the data furnished by the accounting system may or may not include overhead costs. In most cases, the decision

maker is concerned solely with cost-revenue elements that will be changed as a result of the project under consideration. Incremental analysis is called for, and great care must be exercised when using pro forma data in decision problems. Remember that the assignment of overhead cost is always arbitrary. The accounting system is the richest source of information in the organization, and it should be used—but with great care and understanding.

Measurements

It is common for those who oppose a project, for whatever reason, to complain that information supporting the project is "subjective." This epithet appears to mean that the data are biased and therefore untrustworthy.

To use the scoring methods discussed or to practice risk management in project selection, we need to *represent* though not necessarily *collect* expected project performance for each criterion in numeric form. If a performance characteristic cannot be measured directly as a number, it may be useful to characterize performance verbally and then, through a word/number equivalency scale, use the numeric equivalents of verbal characterizations as model inputs.

Subjective versus Objective

The distinction between subjective and objective is generally misunderstood. All too often the word *objective* is held to be synonymous with *fact* and *subjective* is taken to be a synonym for *opinion*—where fact = true and opinion = false. The distinction in measurement theory is quite different, referring to the location of the standard for measurement. A measurement taken by reference to an external standard is said to be "objective." Reference to a standard that is internal to the system is said to be "subjective." A yardstick, incorrectly divided into 100 divisions and labeled "meter," would be an objective but inaccurate measure. The eye of an experienced judge is a subjective measure that may be quite accurate.

Quantitative versus Qualitative

The distinction between quantitative and qualitative is also misunderstood. It is not the same as numeric and nonnumeric. Both quantity and quality may be measured numerically. The number of words on this page is a quantity. The color of a red rose is a quality, but it is also a wavelength that can be measured numerically, in terms of microns. The true distinction is that one may apply the law of addition to quantities but not to qualities.[23] Water, for example, has a volumetric measure and a density measure. The former is quantitative and the latter qualitative. Two one-gallon containers of water poured into one larger container give us two gallons, but the density of the water, before and after joining the two gallons, is still the same: 1.0.

Reliable versus Unreliable

A data source is said to be reliable if repetitions of a measurement produce results that vary from one another by less than a prespecified amount. The distinction is important when we consider the use of statistical data in our selection models.

Valid versus Invalid

Validity measures the extent to which a piece of information actually means what we believe it to mean. A measure may be reliable but not valid. Consider our mismarked 36-inch yardstick pretending to be a meter. It performs consistently, so it is reliable. It does not, however, match up accurately with other meter rules, so it would not be judged valid.

　　To be satisfactory when used in the previous project selection models, the measures may be either subjective or objective, quantitative or qualitative, but they must be numeric, reliable, and valid. Avoiding information merely because it is subjective or qualitative is an error and weakens decisions. On the other hand, including information of questionable reliability or validity in selection models, even though it may be numeric, is dangerous. It is doubly dangerous if decision makers are comfortable dealing with the selection model but are unaware of the doubtful character of some input data. A condition a colleague has referred to as GIGO—garbage in, *gospel* out—may prevail.

Uncertain Information

In the section on weighted scoring models, we noted some useful methods for finding the numeric weights and criteria scores when they take the form of verbal descriptors rather than numbers. These same methods are also useful when estimating the inputs for risk analysis models. Indeed, one of the first applications of the Delphi method[24] was technological forecasting—forecasting the time period in which some specific technological capability would be available. These methods are commonly used when a group must develop a consensus concerning such items as the importance of a technological change, an estimate of cash flows, a forecast of some economic variable, and similar uncertain future conditions or events.

PROJECT PORTFOLIO PROCESS (PPP)

Important inputs to this process are the organization's goals and strategies, and we assume here that the organization has already identified its mission, goals, and strategies—by using some formal analytic method such as SWOT analysis (strengths, weaknesses, opportunities, threats), and that these are well known throughout the organization. If this is not the case, then any attempt to tie the organization's projects to its goals is folly and the PPP will have little value.

If the goals and strategies have been well articulated, however, then the PPP can serve many purposes:

- To identify proposed projects that are not really projects and should be handled through other processes.
- To prioritize the list of available projects.
- To intentionally limit the number of overall projects being managed so the important projects get the resources and attention they need.
- To identify projects that best fit the organization's goals and strategy.
- To identify projects that support multiple organizational goals and cross-reinforce other important projects.
- To eliminate projects that incur excessive risk and/or cost.
- To eliminate projects that bypassed a formal selection process and may not provide benefits corresponding to their risks and/or costs.
- To keep from overloading the organization's resource availability.
- To balance the resources with the needs.
- To balance short-, medium-, and long-term returns.

The PPP attempts to link the organization's projects directly to the goals and strategy of the organization. This occurs not only in the project's initiation and planning phases, but also throughout the life cycle of the projects as they are managed and eventually brought to completion. Thus, the PPP is also a means for monitoring and controlling the organization's strategic projects. On occasion this will mean shutting down projects prior to their completion because their risks have become excessive, their costs have escalated out of line with their expected benefits, another (or a new) project does a better job of supporting the goals, or any variety of similar reasons.

The steps in this process generally follow those described in Longman, Sandahl, and Speir[25] and Englund and Graham.[26]

Step 1: Establish a Project Council

The main purpose of the project council is to establish and articulate a strategic direction for those projects spanning internal or external boundaries of the organization, such as cross-departmental or joint venture. Thus, senior managers must play a major role in this council. Without the commitment of senior management, the PPP will be incapable of achieving its main objectives. The council will also be responsible for allocating funds to those projects that support the organization's goals and controlling the allocation of resources and skills to the projects.

In addition to senior management, others who should be members of the project council are:

- The project managers of major projects.
- The head of the Project Management Office, if one exists.
- Particularly relevant general managers.
- Those who can identify key opportunities and risks facing the organization.
- Anyone who can derail the progress of the PPP later on in the process.

Step 2: Identify Project Categories and Criteria

In this step, various project categories are identified so the mix of projects funded by the organization will be spread appropriately across those areas making major contributions to the organization's goals. In addition, within each category criteria are established to discriminate between very good and even better projects. The criteria are also weighted to reflect their relative importance. Identifying separate categories not only facilitates achievement of multiple organizational goals (e.g., long term, short term, internal, external, tactical, strategic) but also keeps projects from competing with each other on inappropriate categories.

The first task in this step is to list the goals of each existing and proposed project—what is the mission, or purpose of this project. Relating these to the organization's goals and strategies should allow the council to identify a variety of categories that are important to achieving the organization's goals. Some of these were noted above but another way to position some of the projects (particularly product/service development projects) is in terms of their extent of product and process changes.

Wheelwright and Clark[27] have developed a matrix called the *aggregate project plan* illustrating these changes, as shown in Exhibit 3.3. Based on the extent of product change and process change, they identified four separate categories of projects:

1. *Derivative projects:* These are projects with objectives or deliverables that are only incrementally different in both product and process from existing offerings. They are often meant to replace current offerings or add an extension to current offerings (lower priced version, upscale version).

2. *Platform projects:* The planned outputs of these projects represent major departures from existing offerings in terms of either the product/service itself or the process used to make and deliver it, or both. As such, they become "platforms" for the next generation of organizational offerings, such as a new model of automobile or a new type of insurance plan. They thus

EXHIBIT 3.3   An example aggregate project plan

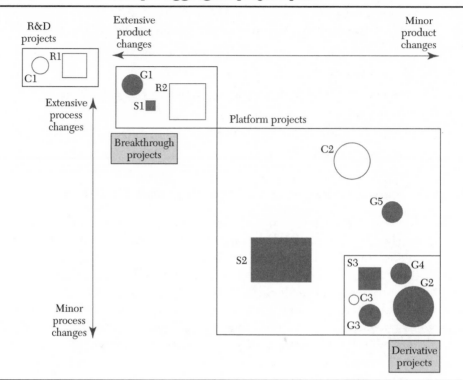

form the basis for follow-on derivative projects that attempt to extend the platform in various dimensions.

3. *Breakthrough projects:* Breakthrough projects typically involve a newer technology than platform projects. It may be a "disruptive" technology that is known to the industry or something proprietary that the organization has been developing over time. Examples here include the use of fiber-optic cables for data transmission, cash-balance pension plans, and hybrid gasoline-electric automobiles.

4. *R&D projects:* These projects are "blue-sky," visionary endeavors oriented toward using newly developed technologies, or existing technologies in a new manner. They may also be for acquiring new knowledge, or developing new technologies themselves.

The size of the projects plotted on the array indicates the size/resource needs of the project and the shape may indicate another aspect of the project (e.g., internal/external, long/medium/short term, or whatever aspect needs to be shown). The numbers indicate the order, or time frame, in which the projects are to be (or were) implemented, separated by category, if desired.

The aggregate project plan can be used for many purposes:

- To view the mix of projects within each illustrated aspect (shape).
- To analyze and adjust the mix of projects within each category or aspect.
- To assess the resource demands on the organization, indicated by the size, timing, and number of projects shown.
- To identify and adjust the gaps in the categories, aspects, sizes, and timing of the projects.
- To identify potential career paths for developing project managers, such as team member of a derivative project, then team member of a platform project, manager of a derivative project, member of a breakthrough project, and so on.

Next, the council must develop separate criteria and cost ranges for each category that determine those projects that will support the organizational strategy and goals. Example criteria might include alignment with the organization's goals/strategy, riskiness of the project, financial return, probability of success, likelihood of achieving a breakthrough in a critical offering, appeal to a large (or new) market, impact on customer satisfaction, contribution to employee development, knowledge acquisition, and availability of staff/resources.

Scales also need to be determined for each criterion to measure how different projects score on each of them. The scales on which these criteria are measured must be challenging so that the scores separate the best projects from those that are merely good. The scales should also serve as an initial screen, to start the process of winnowing out the weakest projects. Thus, they should include limits on their extremes, such as minimum rate of return (if a financial criterion is appropriate), maximum probability of technical failure given proposed budget and schedule, or minimum acceptable potential market share.

Finally, the council needs to set an importance weighting for the various criteria in each category. Note that even if the same criteria apply to multiple categories, their weights might be different. For example, if a firm needs to develop high-level, skilled project managers for their strategic projects, employee development might be more important for breakthrough projects but less important for derivative projects. Also, the weights might change depending on the life cycle stage of the project. For example, early in a project's life, strategic considerations are often most important while in the midpoint of a project, tactical considerations might be more important.

The model we have described above is a "weighted, factor scoring model," as described earlier. As noted then, there are some standard, well-known tools to help develop the weights, scales, and criteria such as the Delphi method,[28] the analytic hierarchy process (AHP),[29] a simplified version of AHP by Frame,[30] and even software such as *Expert Choice*®. For more complex situations, with large numbers of projects and or large councils, the more sophisticated approaches are often more helpful, particularly if used with software that automatically calculates the scores and ranks the projects.

Step 3: Collect Project Data

For each existing and proposed project, assemble the data appropriate to that category's criteria. Be sure to update the data for ongoing projects and not just use the data from the previous evaluation. For cost data, use "activity based costs" rather than incremental costs. Challenge and try to verify all data; get other people involved in validating the data, perhaps even customers (e.g., market benefit). Include the timing, both date and duration, for expected benefits and resource needs. Use the project plan, a schedule of project activities, past experience, expert opinion, whatever is available to get a good estimate of this data. Then document any assumptions made so that they can be checked in the future as the project progresses. If the project is new, you may want to fund only enough work on the project to verify the assumptions or determine the window-of-opportunity for the proposed product or process, holding off full funding until later. Similarly, identify any projects that can be deferred to a later time period, those that must precede or follow other projects, those that support other projects or should be done in conjunction with them, those that can be outsourced, and other such special aspects of the projects.

Next, use the criteria score limits to screen out the weaker projects: Have costs on existing projects escalated beyond the project's expected benefits? Has the benefit of a project lessened because the organization's goals have changed? Does a competitor's new entry obviate the advantages of a project? Does a new (or old) project dominate an existing or proposed project in terms of its benefits, furtherance of organizational goals, reduced costs? Also, screen *in* any projects that do not require deliberation, such as projects mandated by regulations or laws, projects that are operating or competitive necessities, projects required for environmental or personnel reasons, and so on. The fewer projects that need to be compared and analyzed, the easier the work of the council.

Step 4: Assess Resource Availability

Next, assess the availability of both internal and external resources, by type, department, and timing. Note that labor availability should be estimated conservatively, leaving time for vacations, personal needs, illness, holidays, and most important, regular functional (nonproject) work. After allowing for all of these things that limit labor availability, add a bit more, perhaps 10 percent, to allow for the well-known fact that human beings need occasional short breaks to rest or meet other human needs. Timing is particularly important, since project resource needs by type typically vary up to 100 percent over the life cycle of projects. Needing a normally plentiful resource at the same moment it is fully utilized elsewhere may doom an otherwise promising project. Eventually, the council will be trying to balance aggregate project resource needs over future periods with resource availabilities so timing is as important as the amount of maximum demand and availability.

Step 5: Reduce the Project and Criteria Set

In this step, multiple screens are employed to try to narrow down the number of competing projects. As noted earlier, the first screen is each project's support of the organization's goals. Other possible screens might be criteria such as:

- Whether the required competence exists in the organization.
- Whether there is a market for the offering.
- How profitable the offering is likely to be.
- How risky the project is.
- If there is a potential partner to help with the project.
- If the right resources are available at the right times.
- If the project is a good technological/knowledge fit with the organization.
- If the project uses the organizations strengths, or depends on its weaknesses.
- If the project is synergistic with other important projects.
- If the project is dominated by another existing or proposed project.
- If the project has slipped in its desirability since the last evaluation.

One way to evaluate the dominance of some projects over others, and at the same time eliminate nondifferentiating criteria, is by comparing the coefficients of variation of each of the criteria across the projects. This technique allows an analyst to maximize the variation within the project set across relevant criteria, eliminating similar projects that are dominated, and identifying criteria that, at least in this evaluation round, do not differentiate among the projects. See Raz [31] for an example of this approach.

The result of this step may involve canceling some ongoing projects or replacing them with new, more promising projects. Beware, however, of the tendency to look more favorably upon new, untested concepts than on current projects experiencing the natural problems and hurdles of any promising project.

Step 6: Prioritize the Projects within Categories

Apply the scores and criterion weights to rank the projects within each category. It is acceptable to hold some hard-to-measure criteria out for subjective evaluation, such as riskiness, or development of new knowledge. Subjective evaluations can be translated from verbal to numeric terms easily by the Delphi or other methods and used in the weighted factor scoring model. It must be remembered that such criteria as riskiness are usually composite measures of a set of "risks" in different areas. The same is true of criteria like "development of new knowledge."

When checking the results of this step, however, reconsider the projects in terms of their benefits first and their resource costs second. The former are commonly more difficult to assess and a reconsideration based on more familiarity with the project profiling process and other project evaluations may suggest interchanging the priority of neighboring projects. This could be especially critical around the project cutoff point. Because the projects competing around the cutoff point are typically quite close in benefit/cost scores there are usually no serious consequences resulting from "errors." This is, however, an excellent problem on which to use *sensitivity analysis.*

It is also possible at this time for the council to summarize the "returns" from the projects to the organization. However, this should be done by category, not for each project individually since different projects are offering different packages of benefits that are not comparable. For example, R&D projects will not have the expected monetary return of derivative projects; yet it would be foolish to eliminate them simply because they do not measure up on this (irrelevant, for this category) criterion.

Step 7: Select the Projects to be Funded and Held in Reserve

The first task in this step is an important one: determining the mix of projects across the various categories (and aspects, if used) and time periods. Next, be sure to leave some percent (often 10 to 15 percent) of the organization's resource capacity free for new opportunities, crises in existing projects, errors in estimates, and so on. Then allocate the categorized projects in rank order to the categories according to the mix desired. It is usually a good practice to include some speculative projects in each category to allow future options, knowledge improvement, additional experience in new areas, and such.

Overall, the focus should be on committing to fewer projects but with sufficient funding to allow project completion. Document why late projects were delayed and why some, if any, were defunded. One special type of delayed project mentioned earlier is sometimes called an "out-plan" project (in contrast to the selected "in-plan" projects).[32] Out-plan projects are those that appear promising but are awaiting further investigation before a final decision is made about their funding, which could occur in the next PPP cycle or sooner, if they warrant the use of some of the 10–15 percent funding holdout.

The result of this step (and most of the project portfolio process) is illustrated in the Plan of Record shown in Exhibit 3.4. Here, the mix across

EXHIBIT 3.4 Plans of Record

Category	Priority	Project	Resources	May	June	July	Aug	Sept	Oct
Derivative									
50% of mix	1	R	500	▬	▬				
	2	K	800	▬	▬	▬			
	3	M	300		▬	▬			
Total			1600						
Available			(1800)						
External									
20% of mix	1	S	500		▬	▬	▬		
	2	V	150						
	out-plan	LT							
Total			650						
Available			(720)						
Strategic									
30% of mix	1	A	600				▬	▬	
	2	W	370					▬	▬
	0ut-plan	SB							
Total			970						
Available			(1080)						
Aggregate Total			3220						
Unspent			380						
10% reserve			400						
Total Available			4000						

categories is listed, the priorities and resource needs of each project are given, the timing (schedule) of each project over the PPP cycle (6 months assumed here) is shown (to match resource availability), the out-plan projects, if any, are shown, and the total resource needs and availabilities are listed.

Step 8: Implement the Process

The first task in this final step is to make the results of the PPP widely known, including the documented reasons for project cancellations, deferrals, and non-selection as was mentioned earlier. Top management must now make their commitment to this project portfolio process totally clear by supporting the process and the results. This may require a PPP champion near the top of the organization. As project proposers come to understand the workings and importance of the PPP, their proposals will more closely fit the profile of the kinds of projects the organization wishes to fund. As this happens, it is important to note that the council will have to concern itself with the reliability and accuracy of proposals competing for limited funds.

Senior management must fully fund the selected projects. It is not appropriate for senior management to undermine PPP and the council as well as strategically important projects by playing a game of arbitrarily cutting X percent from project budgets. The council needs to be wary of interpersonal or interdepartmental competition entering the scene at this point also. In some organizations, individuals with their own particular agenda will ignore committees and processes (they may be heard to argue that committees never affect anything anyway) until implementation time rolls around, and then they attempt to exercise their political power to undermine the results of others' long labors. If this does occur, it is indicative of serious organizational problems and the PPP process will fail until the problems are corrected.

Of course, the process will need to be repeated on a regular basis. The council should determine how often this should be, and to some extent it depends on the speed of change in the industry the organization is in. For some industries, quarterly analysis may be best while in slow-moving industries, yearly may be fine.

Finally, the process should be flexible and improved continuously. Instinct may suggest ways that the process may be altered to better match the competitive environment, or to reflect more closely the organization's goals. The process should be changed when it is found appropriate to do so, including categories, criteria, steps, the order of tasks, and so on.

SUMMARY

This chapter initiated our discussion of the project management process by describing procedures for strategically evaluating and selecting projects. We first described the strategic objective of using projects to help achieve the organization's goals and strategy, and a project portfolio process to help achieve this. We then outlined some criteria for project selection models and then discussed the general nature of these models. The chapter then described the types of models in use and their advantages and disadvantages. Considering the degree of uncertainty associated with many projects, a section was devoted to evaluating the impact of risk and uncertainty. Concluding the discussion, some general comments were made about data requirements and the use of these models. The final section discussed the documentation of the evaluation/selection process via project proposals.

The following specific points were made in this chapter:

- The role of projects in achieving the organization's goals and strategy is critical.
- The eight-step project portfolio process is an effective way to select and manage projects that are tied to the organization's goals.
- Primary model selection criteria are realism, capability, flexibility, ease of use, and cost.
- Preparatory steps in using a model include: (1) identifying the firm's objectives; (2) weighting them relative to each other; and (3) determining the probable impacts of the project on the firm's competitive abilities.
- Project selection models can generally be classified as either numeric or nonnumeric; numeric models are further subdivided into profitability and scoring categories.
- Nonnumeric models include: (1) the sacred cow; (2) the operating necessity; (3) the competitive necessity; (4) comparative benefit; and (5) the product line extension.
- Profitability models include standard forms such as: (1) payback period; (2) average rate of return; (3) discounted cash flow; (4) internal rate of return; and (5) profitability index.
- Project management maturity measurement is a way of assessing an organization's ability to conduct projects successfully.
- Scoring models—the authors' preference—include: (1) the unweighted 0–1 factor model; (2) the unweighted factor scoring model; (3) the weighted factor scoring model; and (4) the constrained weighted factor scoring model.
- Special care should be taken with the data used in project selection models. Of concern are data taken from an accounting data base, how data are measured and conceived, and the effect of technological shock.

NOTES

1. W. E. Souder, "Utility and Perceived Acceptability of R&D Project Selection Models." *Management Science* (August 1973).

2. Booz, Allan, and Hamilton, Inc. *Management of New Products* (New York: Booz, Allen, and Hamilton, Inc., 1966).

3. K. Matzler and H. H. Hinterhuber, "How to make product development projects more successful by integrating Kano's model of customer satisfaction into quality function deployment," *Technovation* (January 1998).

4. J. Meredith, "The Implementation of Computer Based Systems," *Journal of Operations Management* (October 1981).

5. A. F. Helin and W. E. Souder, "Experimental Test of a Q-Sort Procedure for Prioritizing R&D Projects," *IEEE Transactions on Engineering Management* (November 1974).

6. See note 4.

7. R. C. Moyer, J. R. McGuigan, and W. J. Kretlow, *Contemporary Financial Management,* 7th ed. (Cincinnati, OH: South-Western, 1998).

8. S. A. Ross, R. W. Westerfield, and B. D. Jordan, *Fundamentals of Corporate Finance,* 3rd ed. (Homewood, IL: Irwin, 1995).

9. G. Githens, "Financial Models, Right Questions, Good Decision," *PM Network* (July 1998).

10. N. C. Dalkey, *The Delphi Method: An Experimental Study of Group Opinion,* RM-5888-PR (Santa Monica, CA: The RAND Corporation, June 1969).

11. R. Khorramshahgol, H. Azani, and Y. Gousty, "An Integrated Approach to Project Evaluation and Selection," *IEEE Transactions on Engineering Management* (November 1988).

12. T. S. Saaty, *Decision for Leaders: The Analytic Hierarchy Process* (Pittsburgh: University of Pittsburgh, 1990).

13. E. Turban and J. R. Meredith, *Fundamentals of Management Science,* 6th ed. (Homewood, IL: Irwin, 1994).

14. T. Raz, "An Iterative Screening Methodology for Selecting Project Alternatives," *Project Management Journal* (December 1997).

15. S. Pascale, J. W. Carland, and J. C. Carland, "A Comparative Analysis of Two Concept Evaluation Methods for New Product Development Projects," *Project Management Journal* (December 1997).

16. M. J. Liberatore and G. J. Titus, "The Practice of Management Science in R&D Project Management," *Management Science* (August 1983).

17. R. Hayes, and W. J. Abernathy, "Managing Our Way to Economic Decline," *Harvard Business Review* (July/August 1980).

18. See note 16, p. 969.

19. R. H. Irving and D. W. Conrath, "The Social Context of Multiperson, Multiattribute Decision-Making," *IEEE Transactions on Systems, Man, and Cybernetics* (May/June 1988).

20. B. Baker and R. Menon, "Politics and Project Performance: The Fourth Dimension of Project Management," *PM Network* (November 1995).

21. See note 12.

22. G. P. Huber, "The Nature of Organizational Decision Making and the Design of Decision Support Systems," *MIS Quarterly* (June 1981).

23. J. P. van Gigch, *Applied General Systems Theory,* 2nd ed. (New York: Harper & Row, 1978).

24. See note 10.

25. A. Longman, D. Sandahl, and W. Speir, "Preventing Project Proliferation," *PM Network* (July 1999).

26. R. L. Englund and R. J. Graham, "From Experience: Linking Projects to Strategy," *Journal of Product Innovation Management,* Vol. 16, No. 1 (1999).

27. S. C. Wheelwright and K. B. Clark, "Creating Project Plans to Focus Product Development," *Harvard Business Review* (March/April 1992).

28. See note 10.

29. See note 12.

30. J. D. Frame, *The New Project Management: Tools for an Age of Rapid Change, Corporate Reengineering, and Other Business Realities* (San Francisco: Jossey-Bass, 1997).

31. See note 14.

32. See note 26.

4

BUILDING THE ACTION PLAN: SCHEDULING, ESTIMATING, AND RESOURCE ALLOCATION*

Eric Verzuh

One of the marvels of a Broadway musical performance is the exuberant full-cast dance number. These action-packed scenes thrill us with precise choreography and the beauty and excitement of a full chorus. On stage, it often appears that the whole song and dance was just a spur-of-the-moment sing-along, and that's just what the producer would have us believe. The reality is hours and hours of practice to perfect the number. But what perfection! When the stage comes alive with song and dance, the exhilaration sweeps us to our feet in a cheering ovation!

The precision of the Broadway cast sets a standard few project teams will ever reach. Why? Because the cast practices day after day to get that dance number right. Once the show premiers, the cast performs that same finale night after night. In the language of management, the show is an operation, better compared to a production team than a project team. *A project is a temporary endeavor that produces a unique product.* The project team rarely gets a chance to practice, and it gets only one performance, so it had better be right the first time. Yet, many teams do get it right, and they too are a wonder to behold.

The Broadway musical has a choreographer to carefully script and rehearse the dancers. Project managers rely on detailed action plans to choreograph the team. These plans form the basis for estimating, coordination, status

---

* Significant portions of this chapter were derived from Eric Verzuh, *The Fast Forward MBA in Project Management,* (New York: Wiley, 1999).

98

reporting, communication, scope management, and many other project management functions. This chapter presents the classic project planning techniques that project managers, customers, and management use to provide a detailed plan of action. Together, these techniques answer a range of questions that enable the team to perform in choreographed harmony. The questions include:

- What work, exactly, is entailed in completing the project?
- What skills are required for this work?
- Who, specifically, performs each task?
- How many days and how much effort and expense will each task require?
- How many days and how much effort and expense for the project?
- Should the tasks be performed in a specific sequence?
- How large is the project team?

The answers to these questions can be found in network diagrams, Gantt charts, resource spreadsheets, and the work breakdown structure. All of these techniques have been used for decades. Together, they describe the schedule and cost of the project in precise detail.

DETAILED PLANS PROVIDE AN EXECUTIVE ADVANTAGE

How do executives of project-driven organizations participate in and benefit from detailed planning actions? The answers lie in the challenges of the project-driven organization.

Establishing a Standard for Project Information

Our ability to interpret data is heavily influenced by our experience with the data. Travelers often encounter this phenomenon as they move from country to country. Prices become meaningless when quoted in a new currency. Is a hotel room for 20,000 lira in Rome within the $75/day budget you set? How about the room in Liverpool for £75? The traveler must translate these prices into a common currency to make decisions. Because projects are unique, executives are often faced with this same problem. Individual project managers invent their own methods for communicating the plan or progress reports, causing confusion for management, who must translate the inconsistent data into meaningful information. As with travelers, executives need a standard currency, one that has the same meaning on every project. The planning techniques described in this chapter serve that purpose.

The planning techniques we explore have been in use for decades and are recognized around the world. Consistent rules and guidelines exist for their use, and they work the same on every kind of project, large or small, in any industry. Because of their consistency, they lead to *transparency,* a term used in finance and accounting to describe the importance of using standard accounting techniques that enable investors and loan officers to interpret the financial reports of every firm. The framework established by these techniques provides several specific benefits:

- Project estimates are created with a logical, repeatable process, which makes analyzing and validating an estimate easier. It also makes it possible to compare an estimate for a project to the actual cost and schedule results to understand why estimates are right or wrong.
- Project managers in the firm share a common language. The project-driven organization often finds relationships among its many projects. A common language is essential to understand schedule and resource interdependencies among these projects.
- These universally accepted techniques have been automated in readily available project management software tools. Because the software tools are based on these techniques, the tool reinforces correct use of each technique and, at the same time, makes it easier to apply the techniques.
- Vendors and subcontractors can be expected to adhere to these practices, which adds control during every phase, from the initial bid through project control and close-out.

Future Accounting

Managers rely on accounting information to understand the health of the organization. Routine reports on sales, expenses, orders, inventory levels, and financial data provide the facts required for both tactical and strategic decisions. That information is good to a certain extent, but it is all about the past. Nothing we do will change the profit and loss statements of the previous year. Wouldn't you like to have the same information about the future? For project-driven firms, detailed planning techniques provide at least part of the picture. These techniques are a framework for forecasting the costs of a project, the resources required, and the schedule for accomplishing the work. It is true that these forecasts are seldom precise—but they are valuable. Just as accounting reports provide the facts and data necessary for business decisions, the detailed cost and schedule plan provides a basis for rational decision making.

The importance of making project decisions based on facts and data should not be underestimated. The detailed action plan is the math that illustrates the cost-schedule-quality equilibrium of the project. Managers and executives in project-driven organizations who understand these mechanics will have more realistic expectations for their projects. They are able to do the math to calculate how many people, hours, and months it requires to meet the product specifications. They can speak the language of the estimators, project manager, and project team. If disagreements arise over cost or schedule estimates, all parties have a common framework for analyzing the project. That becomes a motivator for the project team because it perceives management to be honestly and rationally engaged in supporting the project. Finally, the detailed plan is a meaningful framework for investigating project performance, the basis for measuring progress during every step of the project.

Steering the Enterprise

Executive management's job is to marshal the resources of the firm to set and meet organizational goals. The mechanics of bottom-up planning enable management to see how the resources of the organization are being applied to the strategic goals of the firm in two ways:

1. Each goal is associated with one or more projects, so individual project progress becomes an indication of progress against strategic goals.
2. Planning methods that show resource requirements (people, money, equipment) for individual projects form a framework for forecasting the resource demands for the enterprise.

Exhibit 4.1 illustrates how this information is assembled. Strategic goals are broken into projects. Each project forecasts the resources it will require. Resource forecasts from individual projects are combined to estimate resource needs for the enterprise. This information enables the all-important capability of prioritizing projects.

Without this information, it is very common for firms to pursue more projects than they have the resources to complete. When that happens, they find that rather than finishing 6 of 10 projects, they complete 60 percent of all 10 projects—and get 100 percent completion on none of them.

Chapter 12 provides a more comprehensive description of the processes, organizational structure, and technology required to achieve an enterprise view of all projects. This chapter describes the techniques that provide the foundation of the capability.

The Six Steps of Detailed Planning

Assembling the who, what, and when of a project can be a daunting task. Even small projects can have an overwhelming amount of detail. Fortunately, project planning techniques have evolved to provide a systematic approach for breaking the project down and assembling the details in an organized, informative format.

The planning model in Exhibit 4.2 illustrates a systematic method to create an action plan. This chapter explores each step in detail. First, however, we summarize the steps:

- *Use the output of project definition.* Planning isn't the first step in initiating a project. Before detailed planning, the project manager created a statement of work that lists the purpose, scope, and deliverables of the

EXHIBIT 4.1   Detailed project plans form the basis of enterprise personnel requirements

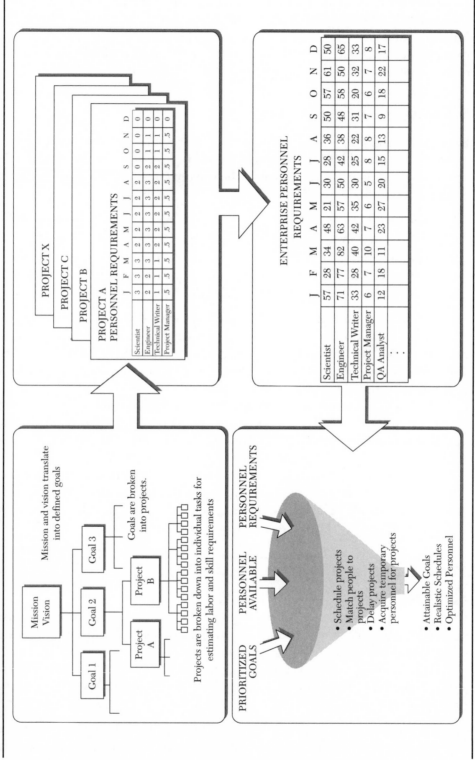

EXHIBIT 4.2   Detailed planning model

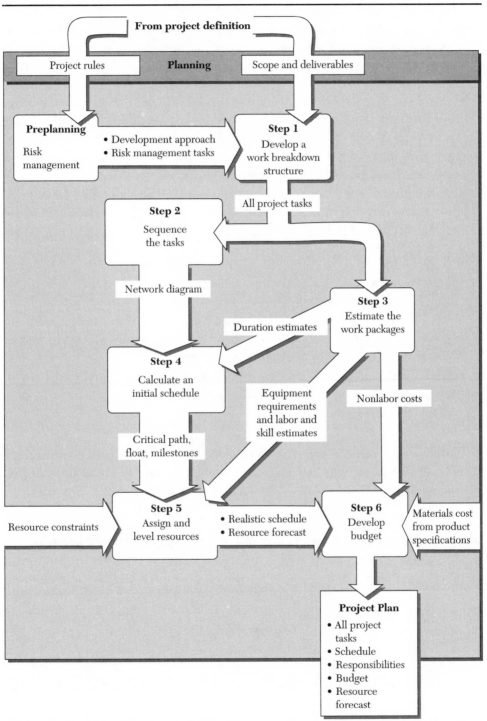

project and defines the overall responsibilities of the project team. Use this document as the launching point for detailed planning.

- *Develop a risk management strategy.* Risk management can be viewed as preplanning because risk strategies become specific tasks during the project. (See Chapter 6, "Project Risk Management," for more on the relationship of risk and detailed planning.)
- *Build a work breakdown structure (WBS) (step one).* The team identifies all the tasks required to build the specified deliverables. The scope statement and project purpose help to define the boundaries of the project.
- *Identify task relationships (step two).* The detailed tasks, known as work packages, are placed in the proper sequence.
- *Estimate work packages (step three).* Each of these detailed tasks is assigned an estimate for the amount of labor and equipment needed and for the duration of the task.
- *Calculate initial schedule (step four).* After estimating the duration of each work package and figuring in the sequence of tasks, the team calculates the total duration of the project. (This initial schedule, while useful for planning, will probably need to be revised further down the line.)
- *Assign and level resources (step five).* The team adjusts the schedule to account for resource constraints. Tasks are rescheduled to optimize the use of people and equipment used on the project.
- *Develop the budget (step six).* Combine the costs associated with materials, labor, equipment, and external services to create a detailed cost estimate and cash flow projection.

These steps generate all the information required to understand how a project will be executed. The steps are systematic, but they don't necessarily come up with the "right answer." It may take several iterations of these steps to find this answer, which is the optimal balance between cost, schedule, and quality.

PLANNING WITH PROJECT MANAGEMENT SOFTWARE

Detailed planning techniques have become synonymous with project management because many professionals first encountered these techniques when using project management software. Although great differences exist among the features and functionality of all these products, with few exceptions, they are all based on the simple six-step planning model in Exhibit 4.2. Therefore, it is always easier to use the software after you understand the six-step model. However, it must be acknowledged that using the software makes it much easier to create detailed plans. Many of the figures in this chapter were created using simple, affordable, desktop project management software. Just remember, computers manage data—you manage the project.

PLANNING STEP ONE: WORK BREAKDOWN STRUCTURE

If you take a car trip to a town less than 100 miles away, it may not take much planning. Just hop in the car, check the gas gauge, and go. But if you were going to drive from the Florida Keys to Anchorage, Alaska, you would probably spend some time looking at maps and researching your route. Somehow, you would break the big trip down into pieces. Maybe you would do this with geographic borders, such as states. Or you could plan it by how far you might go each day. Whatever approach you use, the only way to accurately plan a trip of this size is to break it down.

The same is true for projects. You may *understand* a project well enough to balance its cost-schedule-quality equilibrium, but you also need to be able to break it down—to understand the whole project by understanding its parts. The *work breakdown structure* (WBS) is the tool for breaking down a project into its component parts. It is the foundation of project planning and one of the most important techniques used in project management. If done well, it can become the secret to successful project management.

Defining the Work Breakdown Structure

The WBS identifies all the tasks in a project. In fact, a WBS is sometimes referred to simply as a *task list.* It turns one large, unique, perhaps mystifying, piece of work—the project—into many small manageable tasks. The WBS uses outputs from project definition and risk management and identifies the tasks that are the foundation for all subsequent planning (see Exhibit 4.2).

Work breakdown structures can be set up in either graphic or outline form (see Exhibits 4.3 and 4.4). Either way, they list the various tasks involved. For example, designing and putting in a new lawn with a sprinkler system, surrounded by a new fence, involves a number of different tasks. The graphic WBS paints a picture that makes it easy to understand all the parts of a project, but the outlined WBS is more practical because you can list hundreds of tasks on it—far more than can be listed using the graphic approach.

The WBS clarifies and provides necessary details for a number of project management activities. Building a WBS helps to:

- *Provide a detailed illustration of project scope.* Though the statement of work defines scope at the conceptual level, a comprehensive look at a project's scope can be accomplished only with a WBS.
- *Monitor progress.* The tasks on the WBS become the basis for monitoring progress because each is a measurable unit of work.
- *Create accurate cost and schedule estimates.* The WBS provides a detailed structure to estimate and capture costs for equipment, labor, and materials on each task.

EXHIBIT 4.3   Work breakdown structure in chart form

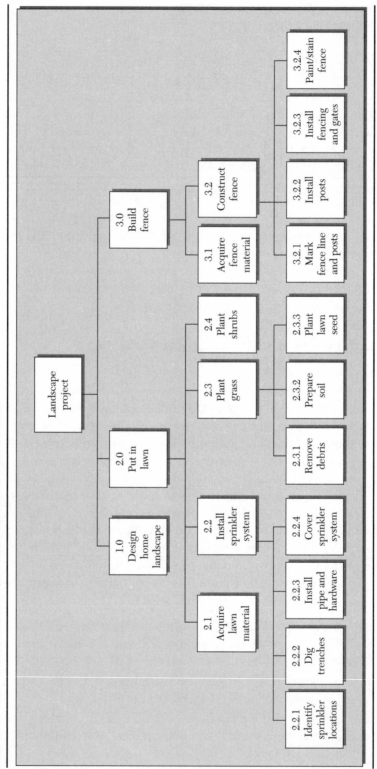

EXHIBIT 4.4 Work breakdown structure in outline form

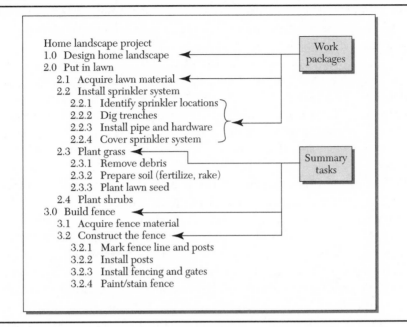

- *Build project teams.* Every team member wants clear work assignments and a sense of how his or her work fits into the overall effort. A good WBS does both. You can also increase the team's commitment to the plan by having the team participate in building the WBS.

Understanding the WBS

The WBS breaks all the work in the project into separate tasks (tasks may also be referred to as *activities*). There are two kinds of tasks on a WBS: summary tasks and work packages.

"Install the sprinkler system" for a lawn is a *summary task,* because it includes several subordinate tasks. Installing a sprinkler system might include several of these distinct, subordinate tasks, such as digging trenches or installing pipes. Each of these separate tasks is called a *work package.* By performing all these simple work packages, you accomplish a summary task (see Exhibit 4.4).

Note that a summary task is not actually executed; it is, rather, a *summarization* of the subordinate work packages. The work packages are the ones that are actually executed. Understanding the relationship between summary tasks and work packages is fundamental to building a good WBS.

Organizing the WBS for Better Communication

The WBS is the basis for communication during the project. The team, including vendors and subcontractors, refers to it at a detailed level to coordinate daily activities. Customers and management watch progress against the summary tasks and, if they need more detailed status, can drill down to look at work package problems and progress. To fully take advantage of this communication tool, we must design the WBS with our audience in mind.

After all the work packages are identified, it is possible to rearrange them in different ways. For example, it can be useful to place work packages under different summary task headings; in this case, the overall project remains the same even though the work packages are grouped differently. Exhibit 4.5 demonstrates how it is possible to have two different breakdowns of the same project tasks. The same work packages are reorganized under different summary tasks.

Different ways of organizing work packages may emphasize different aspects of a project. For example, one grouping of work packages might highlight the various components of a new product, while another arrangement might emphasize the major phases of the product's release. This kind of difference is illustrated in Exhibit 4.5, where the WBS on the top provides high-level visibility on the widget's two main components. By contrast, the WBS on the bottom provides high-level visibility on the major phases of the new release. Both may be useful when communicating with the various groups involved in the project, because the focus of each arrangement may speak to the concerns of individual stakeholders.

When organizing the WBS, remember that the sole purpose of summary tasks on the WBS is for communication, or visibility. (Recall that summary tasks are not actually executed; they are just a summarization of work packages.) Therefore, every summary task should be meaningful to some stakeholder (including the project manager). If there are summary tasks that have no audience, *erase them.* As long as the work packages remain, the scope of the project is the same.

Even though each project is different, there are often enough similarities among projects that certain standard work breakdown structures have been placed on file. Project-driven firms create WBS templates as one of the first steps when implementing project management standards. There is enormous value in having these standard templates:

- Similar projects have a common starting point when the project team begins to plan.
- The template is improved over time, capturing the experience of multiple projects and ensuring key tasks are not forgotten.
- Using templates results in every project's having the same tier one summary tasks, which makes it easier for managers and customers to understand the plans and reports of all projects.
- Consistent task breakdowns lead to consistency in estimating, and the actual performance data for each project becomes more useful as a basis for estimating.

EXHIBIT 4.5   There is more than one way to organize tasks on a project

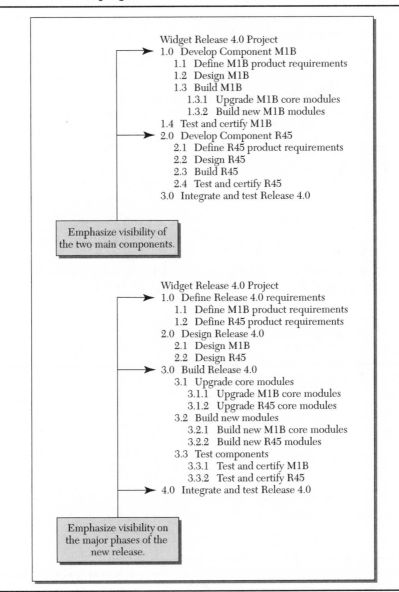

Widget Release 4.0 Project
1.0   Develop Component M1B
    1.1   Define M1B product requirements
    1.2   Design M1B
    1.3   Build M1B
        1.3.1   Upgrade M1B core modules
        1.3.2   Build new M1B modules
    1.4   Test and certify M1B
2.0   Develop Component R45
    2.1   Define R45 product requirements
    2.2   Design R45
    2.3   Build R45
    2.4   Test and certify R45
3.0   Integrate and test Release 4.0

Emphasize visibility of the two main components.

Widget Release 4.0 Project
1.0   Define Release 4.0 requirements
    1.1   Define M1B product requirements
    1.2   Define R45 product requirements
2.0   Design Release 4.0
    2.1   Design M1B
    2.2   Design R45
3.0   Build Release 4.0
    3.1   Upgrade core modules
        3.1.1   Upgrade M1B core modules
        3.1.2   Upgrade R45 core modules
    3.2   Build new modules
        3.2.1   Build new M1B core modules
        3.2.2   Build new R45 modules
    3.3   Test components
        3.3.1   Test and certify M1B
        3.3.2   Test and certify R45
4.0   Integrate and test Release 4.0

Emphasize visibility on the major phases of the new release.

Work Package Size

The most common problem with projects that are dramatically over schedule is that work packages are so large that they can spin out of control. If a task is estimated to be eight months long and 3,800 labor hours (that is, three people working full-time on the task), it's not a task, it's a subproject! This is the kind of task that is right on schedule for seven months, suddenly hits rough going in the eighth month, and ends up taking 12. The size of this task has made it unmanageable. If the entire project were to be planned in the same manner, the trouble would be multiplied many times over. To ensure that the work packages are the correct size, follow these common rules of thumb:

- *The 8/80 rule:* No task should be smaller than 8 labor hours or larger than 80. This translates into keeping your work packages between 1 and 10 days long. (This is a guideline and not an ironclad law.)
- *The reporting period rule:* No task should be longer than the distance between two status points. In other words, if you hold weekly status meetings, no task should be longer than one week. This rule is especially useful when it is time to report schedule status because you will no longer have to hear about task statuses that are 25 percent, 40 percent, or 68 percent complete. If you have followed a weekly reporting rule, tasks are reported as either complete (100 percent), started (50 percent), or not started (0 percent). No task should be at 50 percent for two status meetings in a row.
- *The "if it's useful" rule:* As you consider whether to break tasks down further, remember that there are three reasons to do so:
  1. *The task is easier to estimate.* Smaller tasks tend to have less uncertainty, leading to more accurate estimates.
  2. *The task is easier to assign.* Large tasks assigned to many people lose accountability. Breaking down the task can help to clarify who is responsible. Another potential benefit is that having smaller tasks assigned to fewer people can give you greater flexibility in scheduling the task and the resource.
  3. *The task is easier to track.* The same logic applies as in the reporting period rule. Because smaller tasks create more tangible status points, you will have more accurate progress reports.

If breaking down a task in a certain way is *not* useful—that is, if it does not make it easier to estimate, assign, or track—don't break it down.

When Very Small Tasks Make Sense

Is it possible that tasks broken down into one-hour increments would be *useful?* Talk about micromanagement! While projects spanning months probably would not benefit from such small tasks, it is common to plan to this level for complex projects of short duration. Preventive maintenance for manufacturing plants can require the entire operation to be shut down for a day or a week. To minimize the time the plant is down, these projects are often planned out in hourly increments, which allow close coordination among many people and quick identification of any behind-schedule work that could delay reopening the plant.

While many managers might balk at having to reduce a large project into relatively small increments, the results can be rewarding. Consider these examples:

- An upgrade to a municipal wastewater treatment plant had a project budget of over $500 million. In spite of the size of this project, contractors were required to plan and report work packages in units of *no more* than two weeks or $50,000. By requiring this detailed level of information, the municipal government's project office could identify any problems within a matter of weeks—no small feat for a project of this size. The project finished on time, under budget.

- In an article in *Sloan Management Review* on Microsoft, Michael Cusumano observed, "Managers generally allow team members to set their own schedules but only after the developers have analyzed tasks in detail (e.g., half-day to three-day chunks) and have agreed to commit personally to the schedules." Yet, in a company the size of Microsoft, hundreds of people may be required to develop a new product. While working with these small increments produces an enormous amount of detail, it dramatically increases the accuracy of estimating and tracking a project.[1]

Put Project Management into the WBS

You can benefit by putting project management activities into the WBS. List them under a summary task called "project management" (as shown in Exhibit 4.6). Though some of the tasks are finite, such as hiring a subcontractor, the

EXHIBIT 4.6   Project management on the WBS

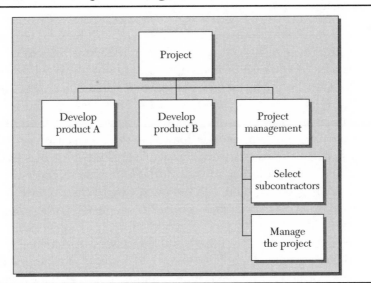

majority consists of everyday work, such as communication and problem resolution. These everyday duties may be grouped under a heading called "Managing the project." Now you have a place to assign all the time spent on project management duties.

A project can best be understood by a thorough understanding of its parts. The WBS breaks the project down into many small, manageable tasks. An accurate, descriptive WBS becomes the basis for all project communication, providing a day-to-day view of the project at the work package level and a meaningful overview of the project for executives and customers. It is the detailed description of project scope, the framework for reporting progress, and the first step of building the action plan. With this foundation in place, we move on to the next step of planning: understanding the correct sequence of the work packages.

PLANNING STEP TWO: IDENTIFY TASK RELATIONSHIPS

The sequence in which detailed tasks—work packages—are performed is determined by the relationship between the tasks. To illustrate this point, consider the following five tasks from the landscaping project described earlier. These tasks constitute a subset of that project:

1. Acquire lawn materials.
2. Remove debris.
3. Prepare soil.
4. Plant lawn seeds.
5. Plant shrubs.

As the homeowner and the teenage children who will be working on this project contemplate these tasks, the question arises: What is the proper sequence? Any time a series of tasks is performed, there are sequence constraints; that is, certain tasks must be performed before others. Sequence constraints are governed by the relationships of different tasks. For instance, the rocks, weeds, and other debris must be removed before the lawn seed can be planted. Performing these tasks in the reverse order does not make sense because the seed would be lost when the weeds were removed. Exhibit 4.7 shows both a predecessor table and a network diagram, two different ways of recording sequence constraints. A predecessor table is a common way to display task relationships (in fact, this is exactly the way most project management software records the relationships).

Notice that tasks 1 and 2 have no predecessors. Either one can be done first, or, if there are enough people, they could be done at the same time. Tasks that can be performed at the same time are known as *concurrent* tasks.

EXHIBIT 4.7   Network diagram developed from a predecessor table

Predecessor Table

Task	Predecessor	Resources
1 Acquire lawn materials		Homeowner
2 Remove debris		Teen and youth groups
3 Prepare soil	1, 2	Teens
4 Plant lawn seeds	3	Teens
5 Plant shrubs	2	Teens

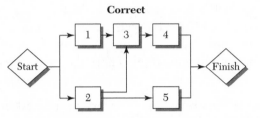

Correct

- Network diagram with milestones at the start and finish.
- This network has two *concurrent* paths.

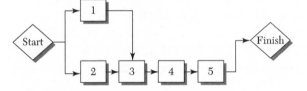

Incorrect

- The most common network diagram mistake is removing all concurrent tasks for the same resource.
- Resource constraints may prevent tasks 4 and 5 from being performed at the same time, but that shouldn't change the network. The network only represents task sequence constraints.

There are just two basic rules when graphing task relationships with a network diagram:

1. Define task relationships only between work packages. Even though a project might have hundreds of work packages and several levels of summary tasks, keep the sequence constraints at the work package level. Summary tasks, remember, are simply groups of work packages, so it would not make sense to put a task relationship between a summary task and its work package. (The only exception to this rule occurs, occasionally, on very large projects, where networks can be created to illustrate project relationships at the summary level.)

2. Task relationships should reflect only sequence constraints between work packages, not resource constraints. Changing a network diagram because

of resource constraints is the most common error in building network diagrams. The fact that there are not enough people or other resources to work on multiple tasks at the same time is irrelevant here. Regardless of resources, the tasks still have to be performed in the same order. (Exhibit 4.7 demonstrates the mistake of rearranging the network because the same resource—in this case, the teenagers—are working on tasks 4 and 5.)

Milestones Are Useful Markers

In setting up the sequence of events, many project managers find it useful to mark significant events in the life of a project. These markers—called *milestones*—are often used in work breakdown structures and network diagrams (see Exhibit 4.8). Milestones have zero duration; therefore, adding them to a project does not affect the schedule at all. There are three great reasons to use milestones:

1. Project start and finish milestones are useful anchors for the network. The milestones don't change anything on the project, but many people find it easier to read.
2. Milestones can be used to mark input from one party to another. Many projects are dependent on inputs from certain external sources (they have *external dependencies*). For example, a government agency might release an environmental impact report for an electric utility on a certain date. A project in that electric utility can use that release date as a milestone. Exhibit 4.8 shows a milestone representing an external dependency.

EXHIBIT 4.8   Milestones can show external dependencies

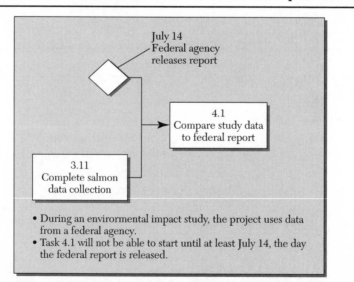

3. A milestone can represent significant events that are not already represented by a work package or summary task. For example, if a firm receives progress payments based on work accomplished, these payment points could be shown with milestones.

Milestones are useful to show major progress points, but the real progress indicators remain the detailed work packages. Every work package has specific completion criteria and a tangible result—which is the ultimate progress indicator.

Finish-to-Start Relationships

The finish-to-start relationship states that one task must be completed before its successor task can begin. The network diagrams in this chapter all follow this simple assumption because it is the most common, but there are other types of relationships. Tasks with start-to-start (SS) relationships allow the successor task to begin when the predecessor begins. Finish-to-finish (FF) tasks can start independently of each other, but the successor cannot finish until the predecessor finishes. Exhibit 4.9 shows the value of using these other types of task relationships.

PLANNING STEP THREE: ESTIMATE WORK PACKAGES

To determine the cost and duration of an entire project, it is necessary to build a cost and schedule estimate for each work package; this is called *bottom-up* estimating. A lot of information is generated in the estimating process, so it is critical to record it in a systematic manner. (Exhibit 4.10 shows the work package estimates for the home landscape project.)

The schedule estimate for a task measures the time from initiation to completion. This estimate is usually referred to as *duration* of a task. When building a schedule estimate, it is important to include *all* the time the task will span. For instance, it may take only 1 day to order materials, but if it takes 10 days for delivery, the total duration of the task is 11 days. Similarly, while a certain decision might take only two hours to make, it might be more realistic to estimate duration at five days if the decision maker is likely to be busy at that time.

Cost estimates come from four sources:

1. *Labor estimates:* These projects how much human effort will be put into a task. If three people work eight hours a day for three days, the total labor estimate is 72 hours. On small work packages, labor is estimated in hours. (At the project level, labor can be such a large item that it is sometimes expressed in years.) In addition to recording the labor estimate, you

EXHIBIT 4.9   Task relationships

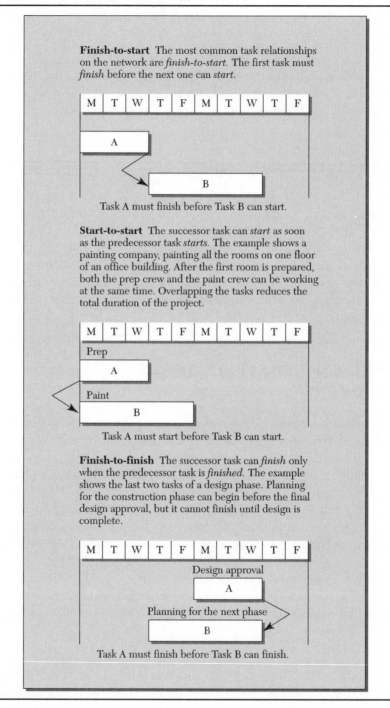

Finish-to-start The most common task relationships on the network are *finish-to-start*. The first task must *finish* before the next one can *start*.

| M | T | W | T | F | M | T | W | T | F |

A

B

Task A must finish before Task B can start.

Start-to-start The successor task can *start* as soon as the predecessor task *starts*. The example shows a painting company, painting all the rooms on one floor of an office building. After the first room is prepared, both the prep crew and the paint crew can be working at the same time. Overlapping the tasks reduces the total duration of the project.

| M | T | W | T | F | M | T | W | T | F |

Prep

A

Paint

B

Task A must start before Task B can start.

Finish-to-finish The successor task can *finish* only when the predecessor task is *finished*. The example shows the last two tasks of a design phase. Planning for the construction phase can begin before the final design approval, but it cannot finish until design is complete.

| M | T | W | T | F | M | T | W | T | F |

Design approval

A

Planning for the next phase

B

Task A must finish before Task B can finish.

EXHIBIT 4.10   Home landscape project work package estimates

ID	Task Name	Duration (Days)	Labor Hours	Resource Names
1	Design home landscape	5	80	Homeowner [0.5], teens [1.5]°
2	Put in lawn			
3	Acquire lawn materials	2	64	Homeowner, teens [3]
4	Install sprinkler system			
5	Identify sprinkler locations	1	Fixed fee, 8	Contractor, homeowner
6	Dig trenches	2	Fixed fee	Contractor
7	Install pipe and hardware	3	Fixed fee	Contractor
8	Cover sprinkler system	1	Fixed fee	Contractor
9	Plant grass			
10	Remove debris	4	256	Teens [3], youth group [5]
11	Prepare soil	4	128	Teens [3], rototiller
12	Plant lawn seed	1	16	Teens [2]
13	Plant shrubs	6	96	Teens [2]
14	Build fence			
15	Acquire fence material	2	16	Homeowner
16	Install fence			
17	Mark fence line	1	32	Homeowner, teens [3]
18	Install posts	5	80	Teens [2]
19	Install fencing and gates	6	144	Teens [3]
20	Paint/stain fence and gates	3	72	Teens [3]

° On task 1, both the homeowner and teens are working 4 hours per day.

need to record the skill requirement. For example, a task might specifically require an electrician eight hours a day for three days. If more than one skill type is required, list them all.

2. *Equipment estimates:* Equipment requirements need to be identified at the work package level. These estimates then become the basis for estimating the total equipment cost for the project. Equipment, in this case, includes the tools necessary to perform the task, from cranes to specialized software. (Don't bother to list common tools such as word processors, copy machines, or hammers.) Like labor, equipment use should be estimated in hours.

3. *Materials estimates:* Materials for the project can be a major source of project cost—or virtually nonexistent. While a construction project may have a significant portion of its total cost represented by raw materials, a project to institute new hiring guidelines will have no raw materials. Software development projects have no raw materials, but an information system project to install commercial off-the-shelf (COTS) software has to include the cost of the software. *Even though materials costs can be a major portion of the project's cost, total materials cost should be estimated from the product specifications—not estimated bottom-up using the WBS.* (See Planning Step Six later in this chapter.) Including

materials in the work package estimate helps to identify exactly when each of the materials will be needed; these schedule requirements, in turn, determine order and delivery dates.

4. *Fixed-price bids:* Fixed-estimate costs can replace the three previous cost sources. For example, a vendor or subcontractor might make a fixed-price bid that includes labor, equipment, and materials. Fixed-price bids mean that the vendor takes responsibility for costs; should there be overruns, the cost to the project will not change. (The landscape project in Exhibit 4.10 includes fixed-priced bids by the sprinkler contractor.)

Is it necessary to concentrate on costs when trying to build a realistic schedule? It is, because each cost represents a resource constraint. Costs such as hiring subcontractors and purchasing materials constrain the schedule. Later on, the schedule will be adjusted to account for these resource constraints (this is the fifth step of planning); but before adjusting the schedule, we need to identify all the resource requirements, one work package at a time.

PLANNING STEP FOUR: CALCULATE AN INITIAL SCHEDULE

Calculating a schedule may be one of the most well known, but unappreciated, of all project management techniques. It can be particularly tedious and time-consuming when done by hand for large projects. Yet, it is the key to establishing realistic schedules and meeting them. (The tedium involved is a compelling reason to use project management software.)

As mentioned earlier, program evaluation and review technique (PERT) has become synonymous with calculating schedules and is based on network diagrams. PERT relies on the method for calculating schedules that is demonstrated here.

The initial schedule is calculated by using the network diagram and the duration of each work package to determine the start and finish dates for each task and for the entire project. Exhibit 4.11 shows how the network and task duration can work together to produce an initial schedule. Schedule calculation provides a set of detailed schedule data for every work package, as shown in the following:

Early start—The earliest date a task can begin, given the tasks preceding it.

Early finish—The earliest date a task can finish, given the tasks preceding it.

Late start—The latest date a task can begin without delaying the finish date of the project.

Late finish—The latest date a task can finish without delaying the finish date of the project.

Calculating the schedule to determine these four dates is a three-step process. Referring to Exhibit 4.11 helps clarify this process.

Step One: Forward Pass

The forward pass helps you determine the early start (ES) and early finish (EF) for each task. It is so named because it involves working through a network diagram from start to finish (the next step involves the reverse—a backward pass). In Exhibit 4.11, we follow a forward pass through the diagram, step by step. Exhibit 4.12 shows another way of displaying this information. It is called a *time-scaled network* because it uses a time scale across the top and each task is laid out across the calendar. Notice that all the early start dates are the same in Exhibits 4.11 and 4.12.

Step Two: Backward Pass

The backward pass determines the late start (LS) and late finish (LF) dates. All of us have made this calculation hundreds of times—whenever we set an alarm clock. The goal of the backward pass is literally to work backward from the project finish date to determine how late any task can begin or end. The late start and late finish are calculated in Exhibit 4.11.

Step Three: Calculate Float

Some tasks have flexibility in when they can be performed in the schedule, and others have no flexibility. The term for this schedule flexibility is *float*. (Another common term is *slack*.) Float is calculated by subtracting early start from the late start. (How to calculate float is demonstrated graphically in Exhibits 4.11 and 4.13.)

Critical Path

When the initial schedule has been calculated, the project schedule begins to take shape. One of the key features of the initial schedule is the critical path. The term *critical path* is one of the most widely used—and most widely misunderstood—of all project management terms. However, the concept is simple: The critical path is defined as all of the tasks with zero or negative float. When outlined on a network diagram, the critical path is the longest path through the network. (The critical path is boldly outlined in Exhibits 4.11 and 4.13.)

The tasks that have zero float must be completed at their early finish date or the project finish will be delayed. Making sure that all critical path tasks begin and end on time is the surest way of making the project end on time. That's why you will hear a project manager motivating someone to complete a task by telling the person, "It's on the critical path!"

EXHIBIT 4.11   Calculating a schedule

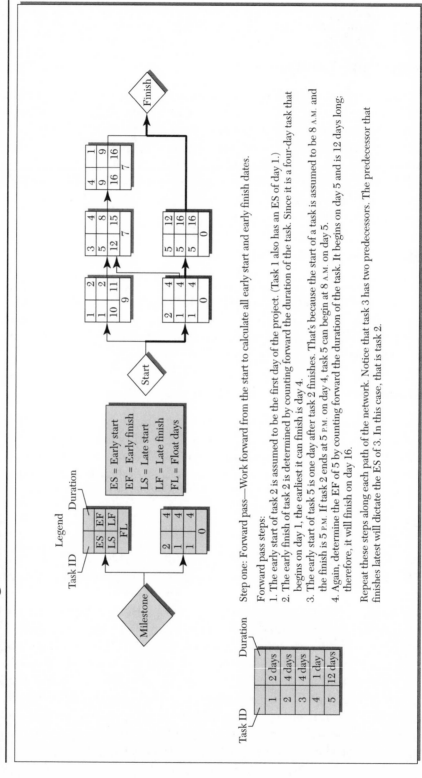

Step one: Forward pass—Work forward from the start to calculate all early start and early finish dates.

Forward pass steps:

1. The early start of task 2 is assumed to be the first day of the project. (Task 1 also has an ES of day 1.)

2. The early finish of task 2 is determined by counting forward the duration of the task. Since it is a four-day task that begins on day 1, the earliest it can finish is day 4.

3. The early start of task 5 is one day after task 2 finishes. That's because the start of a task is assumed to be 8 A.M. and the finish is 5 P.M. If task 2 ends at 5 P.M. on day 4, task 5 can begin at 8 A.M. on day 5.

4. Again, determine the EF of 5 by counting forward the duration of the task. It begins on day 5 and is 12 days long; therefore, it will finish on day 16.

Repeat these steps along each path of the network. Notice that task 3 has two predecessors. The predecessor that finishes latest will dictate the ES of 3. In this case, that is task 2.

Step two: Backward pass—Work backward from the finish to calculate all late start and late finish dates.

Backward pass steps:

1. Set the project finish date. The project's finish date can come from two places. It can be the EF of the last task on the project, or it can be an externally imposed finish date, such as April 15 for filing income tax. (An "externally imposed finish date" means that the finish date is set by someone outside the project team.) The project finish date becomes the late finish (LF) for the last task on the project, in this case, task 5.

2. Count backward the duration of the task to determine the late start (LS) for 5. The finish is day 16, so the LS is 5. That means if task 5 does not start by day 5, it will cause the project to miss the final completion deadline.

3. Work the network backward. Task 2 must be finished no later than 4 in order for task 5 to begin by day 5.

4. Repeat these steps along all paths of the network. When a task has multiple successors, its late finish must be early enough for all the successors to meet their late start time. Task 2 has multiple successor tasks. It must be finished no later than day 4 to allow task 5 to begin on time.

Step three: Calculate float and identify the critical path.

Calculating float:

Looking at the set of schedule dates for each work package, (in this Exhibit and Exhibit 4.12), it is obvious that some have the same early start and late start. Practically speaking, that means those tasks have no schedule flexibility. Float is calculated by subtracting ES from LS. Float is really the measure of schedule flexibility for a task. Notice how tasks 3 and 4 in this Exhibit have 7 days of float. These tasks have a lot of flexibility as to when they will actually be performed—task 3 can start as early as day 5 or as late as day 12.

EXHIBIT 4.12   Time-scaled network. This contains the same network information as Exhibit 4.11, but the format is different.

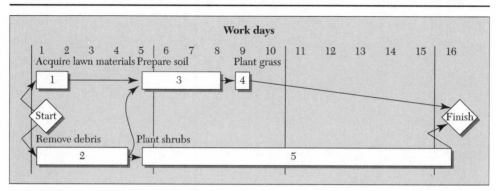

Because it is the longest path through the network (the longest path means the longest duration, not necessarily the most tasks), the critical path is one measure of schedule viability. This is because it demonstrates the *minimum* time the project will take. Sometimes it takes a network diagram with the critical path outlined to show stakeholders that their optimistic schedule estimate is unrealistic.

Shop Early and Avoid Negative Float

Not every project has a critical path. If a project has an externally imposed finish date that allows more than enough time to complete the project, all tasks will have float. A simple example is Christmas shopping. December 25 is the externally imposed finish date. Early in the year, when there are 200 shopping days until Christmas, nobody is stressed because there is still plenty of float. Like Christmas shopping, most projects with no critical path are put off until all the float is used up.

When all the float has been used up, a new term emerges to describe the situation: *negative float.* Negative float results when externally imposed finish dates are impossible to meet (such as 10 presents to buy at 6 P.M. on December 24). Exhibit 4.14, for example, shows a network diagram with a critical path that is longer than the allotted schedule. When there is negative float, it means that adjustments will have to be made to bring the schedule in line with the critical path. This is the kind of information you need when you renegotiate the cost-schedule-quality equilibrium.

Gantt Charts and Time-Scaled Networks

A picture is worth a thousand words. The network diagram is essential in calculating the schedule, but it can be terribly difficult to decipher on a large project. Thankfully, there are two very good alternatives, which display both the schedule information and the task relationships.

EXHIBIT 4.13 Home landscape project network with initial schedule data

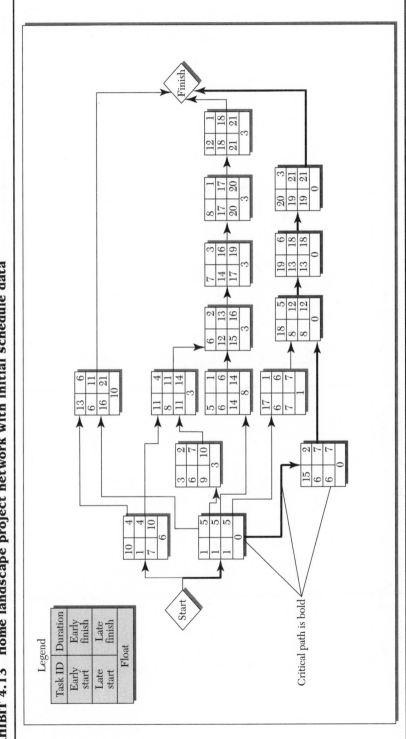

EXHIBIT 4.14 Negative float. When imposed deadlines result in negative float, that is a warning the project is out of equilibrium. The cost, schedule, or quality objectives must be revised.

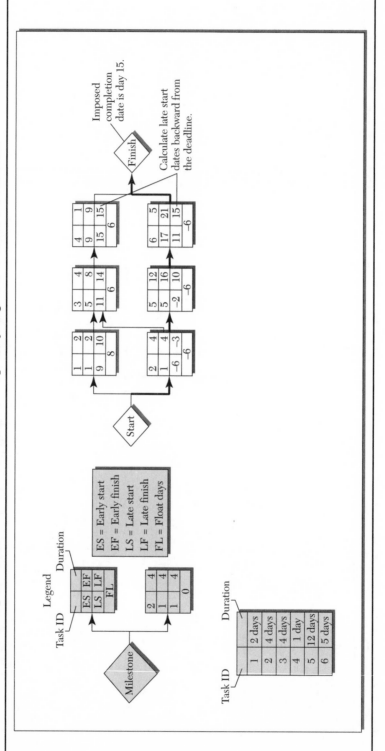

Gantt charts, named after Henry Gantt, who developed them in the early 1900s, have become the most common method for displaying a project schedule. Exhibit 4.15 is a Gantt chart for the home landscape project. It has the same schedule dates as the network in Exhibit 4.13. Notice that all the tasks are currently scheduled at their early start date—you can tell that because all non-critical tasks display float. The great advantage of the Gantt chart is its clarity. The horizontal axis shows the schedule and the vertical axis lists the WBS.

The initial schedule represents the combination of task sequence and task duration. It is called an initial schedule because it has not taken into account people and equipment limitations. The next planning step uses the initial schedule as a starting point and balances it against the resources available to the project.

PLANNING STEP FIVE: ASSIGN AND LEVEL RESOURCES

The goal of resource leveling is to optimize the use of people and equipment assigned to the project. It begins with the assumption that, when possible, it is most productive to have consistent, continuous use of the fewest resources possible. In other words, it seeks to avoid repeatedly adding and removing resources, particularly people, time and again, throughout the project. Resource leveling is the last step in creating a realistic schedule. It confronts the reality of limited people and equipment and adjusts the schedule to compensate.

Using the home landscape project as an example, we can see how resource leveling makes a project schedule more realistic. The network (Exhibit 4.13) shows, in terms of task scheduling, that it is possible to put in the lawn and build the fence at the same time. But when we consider that the family has only the three teenagers available to work on the project, that means they have just a total of 24 labor hours available per day (3 teens × 8 hours a day). Trying to put in the lawn and build the fence concurrently is unrealistic because it would require each teen to work far more than eight hours a day for more than half the project. (The resource spreadsheet on the Gantt chart in Exhibit 4.16 indicates clearly how unrealistic the schedule is.) Resource leveling will adjust the schedule to keep the teens busy at a consistent, reasonable rate. (Exhibit 4.18 shows the same project as Exhibit 4.16, but with the resources leveled.) Not only does resource leveling take unreasonable overtime out of their project, but it keeps the teens employed for a longer time at a steady rate. That is usually an advantage for any project team.

We next consider a few of the problems faced by project managers in this process of leveling resources.

Every project faces the reality of limited people and equipment. The idea is to avoid both over- and underallocation. As the home landscape project demonstrates, too many concurrent tasks can call for more resources than are

EXHIBIT 4.15 Gantt chart for home landscape project

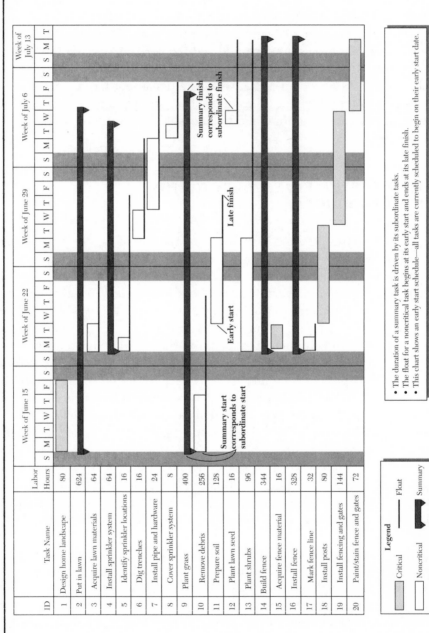

ID	Task Name	Labor Hours
1	Design home landscape	80
2	Put in lawn	624
3	Acquire lawn materials	64
4	Install sprinkler system	64
5	Identify sprinkler locations	16
6	Dig trenches	16
7	Install pipe and hardware	24
8	Cover sprinkler system	8
9	Plant grass	400
10	Remove debris	256
11	Prepare soil	128
12	Plant lawn seed	16
13	Plant shrubs	96
14	Build fence	344
15	Acquire fence material	16
16	Install fence	328
17	Mark fence line	32
18	Install posts	80
19	Install fencing and gates	144
20	Paint/stain fence and gates	72

Legend

Critical ▢ — Float

Noncritical ▢ ◣ Summary

- The duration of a summary task is driven by its subordinate tasks.
- The float for a noncritical task begins at its early start and ends at its late finish.
- This chart shows an early start schedule—all tasks are currently scheduled to begin on their early start date.

126

		Labor
ID	Task Name	Hours
1	Design home landscape	80
2	Put in lawn	624
3	Acquire lawn materials	64
4	Install sprinkler system	64
5	Identify sprinkler locations	16
6	Dig trenches	16
7	Install pipe and hardware	24
8	Cover sprinkler system	8
9	Plant grass	400
10	Remove debris	256
11	Prepare soil	128
12	Plant lawn seed	16
13	Plant shrubs	96
14	Build fence	344
15	Acquire fence material	16
16	Install fence	328
17	Mark fence line	32
18	Install posts	80
19	Install fencing and gates	144
20	Paint/stain fence and gates	72

Week of June 15 · Week of June 22 · Week of June 29 · Week of July 6 · Week of July 13

Resource assignments shown on bars:
- Design home landscape — Homeowner, teens
- Put in lawn — Homeowner, teens
- Acquire lawn materials — Homeowner, teens
- Install sprinkler system — Contractor, homeowner
- Identify sprinkler locations — Contractor
- Dig trenches — Contractor
- Plant grass — Teens, youth group
- Remove debris — Teens, rototiller
- Prepare soil — Teens
- Plant lawn seed — Teens
- Build fence — Homeowner
- Install fence — Homeowner, Teens
- Install posts — Teens
- Install fencing and gates — Teens
- Paint/stain fence and gates — Teens

(continued)

EXHIBIT 4.16 *Continued*

ID	Resource Name	S	M	T	W	T	F	S	S	M	T	W	T	F	S	S	M	T	W	T	F	S	S	M	T	W	T	F	S	S	M	T
			Week of June 15							Week of June 22							Week of June 29							Week of July 6							Week of July 13	
1	*Homeowner*		4	4	4	4	4			32	16																					
2	*Teens*		36	36	36	36	12			64	40	56	56	56			56	16	24	24	24			24	24	40	24	24			24	
3	Contractor									8								8	8	8	8			8	8							
4	Youth group		40	40	40	40																										
5	Rototiller											8	8	8			8															

Hours per day

- The resource spreadsheet shows the labor hours per day for each resource. Overallocated resources are in italics.
- The family has three teenagers working on the project, for a total of 24 hours each day (3 teens @ 8 hours).
- There is only one homeowner, who is available for 8 hours a day.
- Given this initial schedule, with all tasks beginning on their early start dates, both the homeowner and teens are overscheduled during much of the project.

Legend

Critical	——— Float
Noncritical	◄► Summary

128

available. For example, as discussed, the initial schedule had the teens working on the fence and the lawn during the same period, and this resulted in the teens' being *overallocated* during the first half of the project (they would have had to work more than eight hours a day to meet this schedule).

Project managers need to remember that whether it is teenagers to plant the lawn, bulldozers, or programmers, there are rarely many spares sitting on the shelf. This overallocation problem can become especially acute if project managers imagine that they have a large supply of a rare resource, such as the unlimited time of the only subject expert in the company. In this case, not only has the schedule become unrealistic, but the manager may have overloaded a key resource.

The other side of the problem is underallocation. If the project team is not busy on your project, it will likely be reassigned to other projects and be unavailable when the next peak comes. Or, in the worst case, during lulls in the project, some of the unassigned people may get laid off, becoming permanently unavailable and taking valuable knowledge about your project with them.

A further problem arises if people working on this project are also working on several others at the same time. If every project in the firm has wild swings in its resource requirements, it is almost impossible to move people smoothly between projects. Instead, people are yanked off one project to help another catch up, only to be thrown at another that is even further behind.

Project managers must do their best to avoid resource peaks and valleys and try to use a consistent set of people on the project at a consistent rate; this is not only more realistic, it is more efficient. This is because every upswing in resources has a cost, whether it comes from procuring additional equipment or transporting new team members to the project site. The learning costs can be the steepest. On knowledge projects, the learning curve can be so long that adding additional engineers, programmers, or graphic artists for only a few weeks can actually result in negative productivity. This is because every new team member has to be instructed both in what the project is about and in what has transpired before he or she arrived, and this instruction takes the time of an experienced team member. In addition, if the new people are on the project for only a short time, they may never get past their learning curve, which means they never actually perform productive work. The goal of resource leveling is to optimize the people and equipment assigned to the project—to plan for consistent and continuous use of the fewest resources.

The Process of Resource Leveling

It is important to remember how we are defining the term *resources*. Resources are the people, equipment, and raw materials that go into the project. Resource leveling focuses only on the people and equipment; the materials needed for the project are dictated by the specifications.

EXHIBIT 4.17 Resource histogram

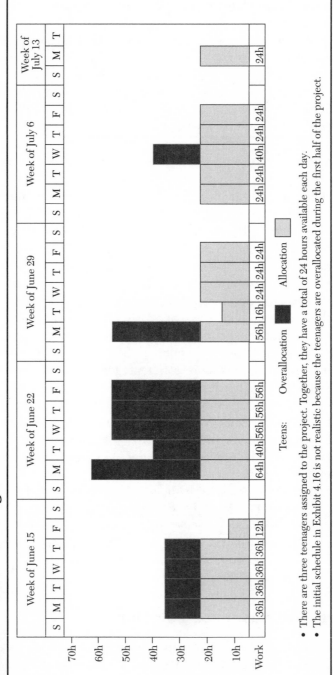

- There are three teenagers assigned to the project. Together, they have a total of 24 hours available each day.
- The initial schedule in Exhibit 4.16 is not realistic because the teenagers are overallocated during the first half of the project.

Resource leveling begins with the initial schedule and work package resource requirements (see Exhibit 4.10). The leveling follows a four-step process:

1. Forecast the resource requirements throughout the project for the initial schedule. The best tool for this process is a resource spreadsheet such as the one portrayed in Exhibit 4.16. This spreadsheet, correlated to the schedule, can forecast all the people and equipment needed on each day of the project.

2. Identify the resource peaks. Use the resource spreadsheet (Exhibit 4.16) and the resources histogram (Exhibit 4.17) to find the periods in the project where there are unrealistic or uneconomical resource amounts.

3. At each peak, delay noncritical tasks within their float. Remember that float is schedule flexibility. Tasks with float can be delayed without changing the project deadline. By delaying these tasks, you are also filling in the valleys of the resource histogram, that is, moving tasks from periods of too much work to periods when there is too little work. (A comparison of the initial schedule in Exhibit 4.16 with the leveled schedule in Exhibit 4.18 demonstrates how task 5 was delayed within its float, thus removing a resource peak for the homeowner on June 24.)

4. To eliminate the remaining peaks, reevaluate the work package estimates. (Using the project float in step 3 may not be enough to eliminate all the peaks and valleys.) For example, instead of having two or three people work together on a task, consider if just one person could do the work over a longer period of time. (Task 12 in Exhibit 4.18 was changed from two teenagers for one day to one teen for three days.)

What to Do If the Resource-Leveled Plan Is Still Unrealistic

Reestimating work packages and delaying tasks within their float can remove the worst resource peaks and valleys, but the plan might still contain unrealistic or uneconomic resource peaks. At that point, your next option is accepting a later project completion date.

On the home landscape project, the schedule had to be extended by two weeks to balance the available labor with the amount of work. This can be a difficult decision, but that's what it means to create a realistic cost-schedule-quality equilibrium.

STEP SIX: BUILDING THE DETAILED BUDGET ESTIMATE

Project budget estimates can be ballparked, calculated with parametric formulas, and determined through apportioning. While these high-level estimates are

EXHIBIT 4.18 Gantt chart with resource-leveled schedule for home landscape project

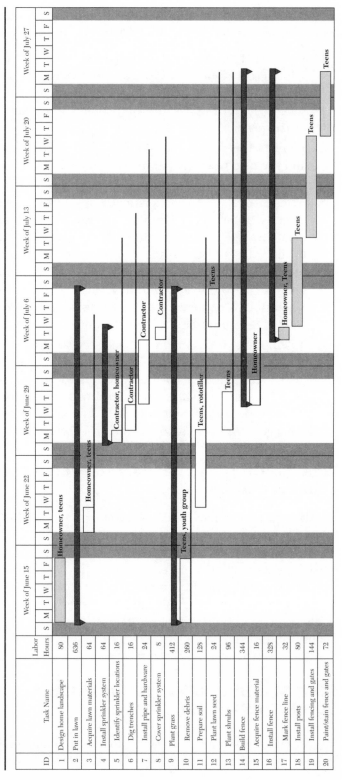

Resource leveling Gantt chart — daily hours (Hours per day) by resource and week.

ID	Resource Name	Week of June 15 (M–F)	Week of June 22	Week of June 29	Week of July 6	Week of July 13	Week of July 20	Week of July 27
1	*Homeowner*	4 4 4 4 4	8 8	8 8 8	8			
2	*Teens*	24 24 24 24	24 24 24 24	24 24 24 24	24 24 24 / 8 8	16 16 24 24 24	24 24 24 24	24
3	Contractor			8 8 8 8	8 8			
4	Youth group	40 40 40 40						
5	Rototiller		8 8 8	8				

Hours per day

Legend

Critical	—— Float
Noncritical	◤ Summary

The leveled schedule has eliminated the task overlaps, which caused unrealistic work hours for the children and homeowners.

- *Task 5*—Delayed 5 days to level homeowner while keeping the sprinkler contractor on schedule.
- *Task 10*—Reduced teens to 4 hours per day (each) so they can participate in design home landscape at the same time. (Design home landscape also calls for each teen to work 4 hours per day.) Added on additional day for the youth group to work on the task. This changed the task duration from 4 to 5 days and the total labor from 256 hours to 260.
- *Task 12*—Changed the task from two teens for one day (16 hours labor) to one teen for 3 days (24 hours labor). One teen working on the task alone won't be as efficient, but now the other two teens can work on task 18 at the same time.
- *Tasks 13, 15, and 17*—Delayed these tasks to level the project and their successor tasks were delayed as well.
- The new schedule is 10 workdays longer, but neither the teens nor the homeowner are overallocated on any day.

useful in the process of selecting projects, they are not accurate enough for managing a project. Once the project is approved, there is a need for a detailed, accurate cost estimate.

The detailed cost estimate becomes the standard for keeping costs in line. Everyone—customer, management, project manager, and team—is better served when a cost target is realistically calculated from a detailed plan. The team understands how the goal was created, and customers and management can be more confident that the project will stay within budget. Forecasting cash flow enables the project's funding to be planned and available when needed. Finally, during the course of the project, this detailed cost information will help in controlling the project, monitoring the progress, identifying problems, and finding solutions.

Sources of Data for the Detailed Budget

The actual calculation of a budget is straightforward; it involves simply adding up figures. Just about any spreadsheet program is a good tool for the total budget calculation. What is not easy is creating the numbers that go into the overall calculation. The following categories are the basis for the budget calculation. (Keep in mind that these are high-level categories. Depending on the size and nature of any project, some categories may be eliminated or may need to be broken down to be more specific.)

Internal Labor Cost

Internal labor costs represent the effort of people employed by the firm. The detailed source for all labor estimates comes from estimating the individual tasks. Including the sequence constraints and leveling the resources presents a realistic view of how many people are required. The resource projection represents the total effort. All that remains is to multiply each resource by its hourly (or daily, weekly, monthly) rate to derive the total internal labor cost for the project. Exhibit 4.19 on pages 136–137 shows the total resource projection derived from the detailed schedule, the labor rates, and the total project labor cost.

Remember that a realistic labor rate includes more than the hourly pay of the person working on the project. It includes wages, benefits, and overhead and is referred to as a *burdened labor rate.* The finance department in most firms has an established standard burdened labor rate. Use that rate in the labor cost calculation.

A big mistake—which, unfortunately, is made on a routine basis—is leaving out the cost of internal staff in the project budget. The usual justification for this folly is that "these workers are free to the project because their salary is a constant." But this statement would be true only if salaried employees had infinite hours available to work on projects. Including internal labor cost in a project budget is necessary to build the kind of realistic budget that allows management to choose among multiple project opportunities.

Internal Equipment Cost

Internal equipment costs apply to special equipment that is not routinely available. They do not apply to the kind of equipment that is standard or assumed for all workers. Technical writers, for example, are assumed to have computers with word processing software; street repair crews are assumed to have shovels. But if that street repair crew needs a backhoe, the cost for this special equipment needs to be estimated separately. This separate estimate allows the purchase and maintenance costs of the internal equipment to be passed on to the customer.

These internal equipment costs can be estimated using the same steps used in estimating internal labor costs. Exhibit 4.20 on pages 138–139 shows equipment use on the resource plan.

Estimating Equipment Used on Multiple Projects

Use a unit cost approach to estimate equipment purchased for one project but expected to be used on many others. For example, R&D engineers for an aerospace company needed an expensive computer to run complex tests. At $50,000, the computer would double the project budget, and this extra cost would probably prevent the project from being approved. However, because they could identify five other potential projects that would use the machine in the immediate future, they were able to justify the cost of the new computer by spreading its cost over the expected use for the next two years. The formula used to spread the cost across several projects gave them a unit cost (hourly rate) that they could apply to their project estimate.

External Labor and Equipment Costs

It is possible to use the same approach in estimating external labor and equipment costs as for estimating internal labor and equipment. The only differences stem from the type of contract negotiated with the external contractor or vendor. Under a cost-plus contract, the labor and equipment rates are written into the contract and the vendor bills the project for labor, equipment, and materials supplied to the project. In this case, either the project manager or the vendor can estimate the work and arrive at the total cost by using the same bottom-up method described for internal costs. In the case of a fixed bid, however, vendors estimate the total cost of labor and equipment for their part of the project and will be held to this figure (that's why it's called a *fixed* bid). In the latter case, the vendor has performed the necessary estimating; all that is needed is to add this estimate into the total labor and equipment costs.

Materials Costs

Materials are the "things" that go into a finished product. For some projects, materials represent half or more of the total costs, while for others, materials costs

EXHIBIT 4.19   Calculated labor and equipment costs using the project plan with resource spreadsheet

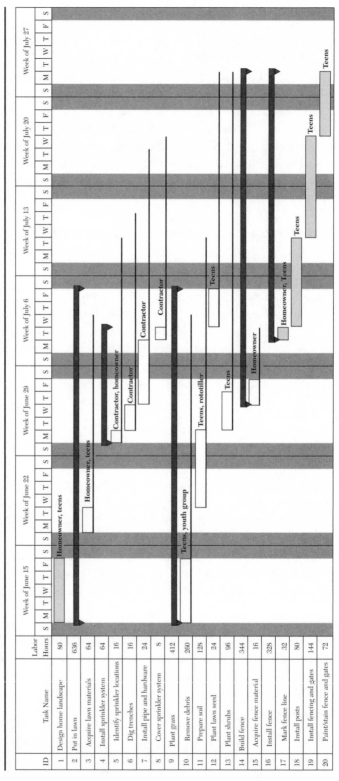

ID	Task Name	Labor Hours
1	Design home landscape	80
2	Put in lawn	636
3	Acquire lawn materials	64
4	Install sprinkler system	64
5	Identify sprinkler locations	16
6	Dig trenches	16
7	Install pipe and hardware	24
8	Cover sprinkler system	8
9	Plant grass	412
10	Remove debris	260
11	Prepare soil	128
12	Plant lawn seed	24
13	Plant shrubs	96
14	Build fence	344
15	Acquire fence material	16
16	Install fence	328
17	Mark fence line	32
18	Install posts	80
19	Install fencing and gates	144
20	Paint/stain fence and gates	72

136

Resource Spreadsheet

ID	Resource Name	Week of June 15							Week of June 22							Week of June 29							Week of July 6							Week of July 13							Week of July 20							Week of July 27						
---	---	S	M	T	W	T	F	S	S	M	T	W	T	F	S	S	M	T	W	T	F	S	S	M	T	W	T	F	S	S	M	T	W	T	F	S	S	M	T	W	T	F	S	S	M	T	W	T	F	S
1	*Homeowner*		4	4	4	4	4			8	8						8		8		8			8																										
2	*Teens*		24	24	24	24	24			24	24	24	24	24			24	24	24	24	24					24	24	24			16	16	24	24	24			24	24	24	24				24					
3	Contractor																8	8						8																										
4	Youth group		40	40	40	40	40			8							8	8	8	8				8	8																									
5	Rototiller											8	8				8																																	

Total Labor and Equipment Forecast

ID	Resource Name	Total Hours	Rate	Total Cost
1	Homeowner	68	$10	$ 680
2	Teens	704	10	7,040
3	Contractor	56	Fixed bid	2,200
4	Youth group	200	10	2,000
5	Rototiller	32	5	160

Hours per day

Legend

Critical ▭

Noncritical ▭ — Float

Summary ▰

137

EXHIBIT 4.20 Calculate a cash flow schedule using the project plan with resource spreadsheet

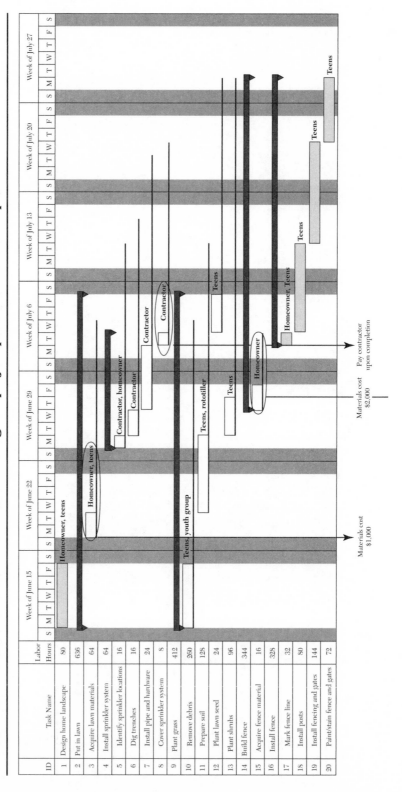

Resource Spreadsheet

Each week column below spans the days **S M T W T F S**. Hours-per-day values are shown in day order.

ID	Resource Name	Week of June 15	Week of June 22	Week of June 29	Week of July 6	Week of July 13	Week of July 20	Week of July 27
1	Homeowner	4 4 4 4 4	8 8	8 8 8 8 8	8	16 16		
2	Teens	24 24 24 24 24	24 24 24 24 24	24 24 24 24 24	24 24 24	24 24 24	24 24 24 24	24
3	Contractor			8 8 8 8 8	8 8			
4	Youth group	40 40 40 40 40		8				
5	Rototiller		8 8 8 8					

Hours per day

Cashflow Schedule

ID	Resource Name	Week 1	Week 2	Week 3	Week 4	Week 5	Week 6	Week of 7
1	Labor	$3,400	$1,360	$1,440	$1,040	$1,040	$1,200	$240
2	Contractor	0	0	0	2,200	0	0	0
3	Equipment	0	120	40	0	0	0	0
4	Materials	0	1,000	2,000	0	0	0	0
5	Weekly total	$3,400	$2,480	$3,480	$3,240	$1,040	$1,200	$240

Legend

- Critical
- Noncritical
- Float
- Summary

are inconsequential. A software development project, for example, may produce millions of lines of code, but no tangible materials are required. Materials can be *raw,* such as plywood, concrete, or welding rod, or materials can be subcomponents of your product, such as computer hardware, telephone switches, or air-conditioning units.

We have stressed the value of the WBS as the basis for identifying all costs. When it comes to materials costs, however, the WBS is relegated to second place. The first place to look is the product specification. For example, the blueprint for a building is the basis for calculating how much concrete, plywood, plumbing, or flooring to purchase. It shows the number of sinks, doors, windows, and elevators to order. Similarly, the network design determined the number of workstations, routers, hosts, and telephone switches required for a computer network.

The WBS can be used to ensure that every task that requires materials will have them. This is done by planning order and delivery tasks. Include the payment dates as tasks and you have all the information you need to build a cash flow schedule for the project.

Generating the Cash Flow Schedule

Knowing when money will be spent is almost as important as knowing how much will be spent. Companies that depend on operations to generate the cash to fund projects need to control the rate at which money goes into the project. The following operations depend on cash flow schedules:

- A small housing developer plans to build five houses, sell them, and build five more. By keeping his rate of production constant, he intends to keep all of his employees busy at a steady rate. By staggering the starting dates of all the houses, he can move crews from one house to the next, and, he hopes, sell house number one before it's time to start house number six. Timing is everything in his plan. If there are too many people on a framing crew, the job will be done too fast and the next house may not have the foundation ready for the crew. If the completed houses do not sell within his planned time frame, he will not be able to fund new houses and will have to lay off workers.

- A municipal engineering department spreads all street maintenance projects across its fiscal year to keep its use of people and equipment steady. Large engineering projects that span fiscal years are also carefully timed. The department heads make sure that they spend only the amount of budget allotted per year, but they need to stretch out this budget to the very end of the year so that a project does not have to stop and wait for the new fiscal year to begin.

Once the project's schedule and costs have been estimated, generating a cash flow projection is pretty simple. Exhibit 4.20 shows the information from the project schedule that determines the cash flow. Project management software can readily calculate cash flow from all the other data that has been entered.

SUMMARY

The detailed plan is to the project team what a map is to a traveler—a gauge to measure progress and a tool to prepare for the journey ahead. It presents options as well as obstacles. For the executive of the project-driven organization, the detailed plan is the framework for translating strategic goals into organizational accomplishment.

Through the framework of detailed planning, executives gain a clearer vision of the future. They gain a more realistic grasp of which projects can be accomplished and the resources necessary to accomplish them. In addition, the language of planning offers precise terms and meanings; that allows stakeholders with different perspectives to negotiate and problem solve when assessing individual projects.

The detailed planning techniques presented in this chapter are often downplayed as mere scheduling techniques. In reality, the six-step planning model provides an analysis method to understand how the many variables of a project can be optimized to achieve the proper balance between the resources consumed, the delivery date, and the quality and capabilities of the product. Over and over, throughout the project, the project manager, the team, and management can refer to the detailed action plan as they confront problems of coordination, scope creep, personnel shortages, changing deadlines, and the many other challenges of the project environment.

NOTE

1.   Michael A. Cusumano, "How Microsoft Makes Large Teams Work Like Small Teams," *Sloan Management Review* (Fall 1997): 13.

ACHIEVING STAKEHOLDER SATISFACTION THROUGH PROJECT CONTROL[1]

5

Eric Verzuh

The purpose of every project is to satisfy stakeholders. The ultimate judges of project success are the people who pay for, create, and use the project deliverables. Therefore, it makes sense to *plan* to satisfy these people. In Stephen Covey's *The 7 Habits of Highly Effective People*, this perspective is described as "beginning with the end in mind."[2]

In this chapter, we apply Covey's concept in two phases: first, by understanding the needs of the project stakeholders and second, by designing control systems that keep those needs visible. This process begins with stakeholder analysis—understanding who they are and their roles in the project. We secure stakeholder commitment to the project with statements of work (SOW), charters, and similar agreements. These documents establish a target for the project manager and team and form the foundation for ongoing communication. We establish the project target knowing fully that the project environment and target may change, which is the bulk of the chapter: the project control methods used to steer the project team and manage the stakeholders so that they maintain and achieve a common vision of success.

ESTABLISHING THE STAKEHOLDER FOUNDATION

To satisfy stakeholders, we must understand who they are and their stake in the project. Customers, decision makers, vendors, and employees are obviously part of this group, but, in a larger sense, anyone who participates in the project or is impacted by its result is a stakeholder.

142

Understanding stakeholders and gaining formal commitment to the project establish clear goals, which become the targets against which we measure our performance. Together, these form the foundation for project success. All managers in a project-driven organization contribute to effective stakeholder management, which contains the following elements:[3]

- *Stakeholder identification and analysis:* Finding and understanding the people who have an interest, either real or perceived, in what the project produces and how the project will be performed.
- *Securing stakeholder commitment:* Actually writing down the goals, constraints, and responsibilities agreed on by stakeholders. These agreements form the basis for project activity and measuring performance.
- *Leading stakeholders:* Fostering and maintaining relationships with stakeholders, holding them to their commitments, and ensuring the project continues to meet their expectations.

Sifting through the people and interests at the beginning of a project requires a balance of perseverance, directness, and tact from the project manager. Executives, too, play an important role during this early phase of the project, contributing two crucial elements:

1. *Clearly visible support for the authority of the project manager:* The trick is to be visibly supportive without usurping the project manager's authority. During early meetings with project stakeholders, allow the project manager to run the meeting and lead discussions. Defer questions to the project manager. Most important, issue a project charter, a formal declaration of the project manager's authority on the project. (The charter is described in detail later in this chapter.)
2. *Insistence that stakeholder commitments are documented:* It is common sense to get these formal agreements, but it is also human nature to skip the formalities in the rush to get the project rolling. Management's job here is to hold the project manager accountable for the formal agreements. (The methods for documenting commitment are described later in this chapter.)

As the project manager does the footwork to identify stakeholders and build relationships, the support of his or her management can make the difference between an uphill battle and a downhill ride.

STAKEHOLDER IDENTIFICATION AND ANALYSIS

It is not enough to deliver on the customer's demands; successful projects have to meet *all* stakeholder expectations. This is a tough target because each stakeholder has a different idea of what constitutes success on the project. In addition, they often pop up later in the project with new demands and requirements. That's why it is critical for project managers to know who the stakeholders are and what they want from the start.

While project managers must satisfy each stakeholder, they also receive valuable contributions from each one. All parties involved in a project have a vital interest in the project's success, and each has an essential contribution to make. Whether it is authority, funding, or expertise in product requirements, all these contributions are needed to ensure success. Some stakeholders are obvious; others are a surprise. Project management author David Cleland divides stakeholders into two categories: primary and secondary.[4] Exhibit 5.1 illustrates these two categories in relation to the project team.

Secondary stakeholders often create our unexpected surprises. Secondary stakeholders can have a large impact on the project, but they are classified as *secondary* because they do not conduct transactions with the project. To find them, the project team should ask "Who else will be impacted by or care about what we do on this project?" The answer often includes other people in your organization who are the *customers of your customers*. This is particularly true in information technology projects where a change in one system can ripple through a dozen more.

EXHIBIT 5.1 Project stakeholders

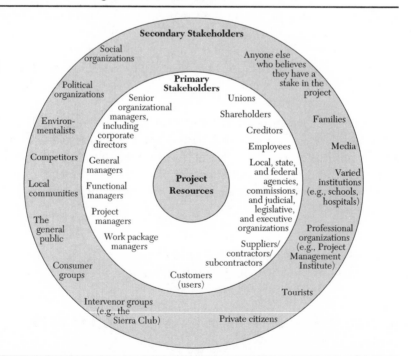

From the chapter by David Cleland entitled "Stakeholder Management," published in *The Project Management Handbook,* Jeffrey K. Pinto, editor. Copyright 1998 by Jossey-Bass, Inc. Reprinted by permission of John Wiley & Sons, Inc.

Another way to find secondary stakeholders is to play the devil's advocate. You know why your project is valuable. But take the opposing view. Why is your project harmful? For example, every airport expansion project has its share of opponents. Whether these opponents are right or wrong is a matter of perspective. What is certain is that without planning for secondary stakeholders, they will arise and do their best to derail the project.

Secondary stakeholder analysis is a form of risk management (see Chapter 6). As with all risks, an ounce of prevention is worth a pound of cure. Because risks can be managed only after they are identified, invest some critical thinking in finding secondary stakeholders and trying to understand their perspectives.

Primary stakeholder analysis should be less mysterious, but it still requires diligence. According to Cleland, primary stakeholders, such as project owner, members of the project team, customers, and suppliers, are legally bound to the project and conduct transactions with it. For example, whenever a project exists, somebody pays for it. Whoever pays usually gets the first and last word on product description, budget, and success criteria. This sounds simple enough, but in reality, determining the true customer can be much more complex. Consider a project to upgrade the operating system on all desktop computers at a company: The system allows many configuration options. Who should decide which options to install? Should the 500 people who use the computers chime in on the decision? Is this group the customer? Or is it the president of the company, who is funding the project? In this case, the project manager must go beyond the question "Who is the customer?" Instead, the project manager should ask "What process should I use to determine the requirements?" and "Which stakeholders should I involve in the process?" These two questions are central to the identification of any stakeholder, not just customers. Here are some guidelines:

- The project manager must distinguish between the people with final authority over the project, those who must be consulted as the project is developed, and those who simply need to be informed of what the project is or what product it will produce. (The responsibility matrix, discussed later in this chapter, is a good tool for managing this challenge.)
- One of the responsibilities of upper management is to make timely decisions based on the facts provided by the project team. However, identifying the right managers can be tricky. Start with the obvious ones:
  —Managers whose operations will be affected by the outcome of the project.
  —Managers representing other stakeholders, such as the customer.
  —The manager to whom the project manager reports.
- For each of these managers, keep in mind why they are interested in the project and which decisions they will influence.
- In the case of industries whose products have many customers (automobiles, software, appliances, etc.), the project manager must ascertain

which departments should be included as stakeholders. In companies like these, there are so many end customers that the project must develop alternate "customer representatives." Marketing departments often fill this role, but other departments may also want to be included.

- Regulators are stakeholders. Regulators can be government agencies, banks, and auditors. You can also include support people who can veto project decisions, such as a purchasing manager.

- The people who perform the work on the project are stakeholders. The core team, suppliers, subcontractors, support staff, and the project manager have expectations about the way the project will be performed. If your workforce is represented by unions, you had better know their role in the project, too.

Both primary and secondary stakeholders will emerge throughout the project, but the sooner you find them, the better you will be able to prepare for their interests. This issue justifies early attention. Time devoted by the project manager, sponsor, and team members in stakeholder analysis pays off in fewer disagreements, less rework, and overall better relationships. The following are some helpful questions to get started identifying stakeholders:[5]

- Who are the primary and secondary stakeholders?
- How will they be satisfied? (Can they ever be satisfied?)
- How will they affect the day-to-day work of the project team?
- How is the project responsible or obligated to each stakeholder?
- If certain stakeholders are adversarial to the project, what are their strengths and weaknesses? How will they attack the project?
- Who can significantly influence the outcome of the project?
- How can the project team prepare for and manage the challenges presented by each stakeholder?
- Can the project team determine whether it is managing stakeholders effectively? How will it know?

Figuring out who your stakeholders are is important because these are the people your project must satisfy. Some will actually sign off on agreements; some will carry out the work. Others will remain silent until their interests come into conflict with the project.

Securing Stakeholder Commitment

Any time people play a game—whether it's soccer, chess, or Crazy 8s—they must understand and agree on the rules before the game begins. As long as everybody understands the rules and that rules apply equally to everyone, we play the game and have fun. Projects need the same kind of agreement for the same reasons, so we create a statement of work (SOW), project charter, and a communications plan. I like to refer to this early documentation as establishing "the rules of the project." We may have gained an understanding of who the stakeholders are and what they want, but we are not really ready for action unless we have achieved a clear, documented agreement.

Project Charter

Because projects are unique and temporary, a project manager's position and authority are temporary. When a project begins, most of the people necessary for its success don't even know it exists. Without formal recognition, the project operates much like Tom Cruise in the movie *Mission: Impossible*—mysteriously and without supervision, but with far less spectacular results. That is why a project charter is so important; it brings the key players out in the open where everyone can see them.

A project charter announces that a new project has begun. The purpose of the charter is to demonstrate management support for the project and the project manager. It is a simple, powerful tool, but it is not necessarily complex. As an announcement, it can take the form of a memo, a letter, or an e-mail. It contains the name and purpose of the project, the project manager's name, and a statement of support from the issuer. The charter is sent to everyone who may be associated with the project, reaching as wide an audience as practical because its intent is to give notice of the new project and the new project manager.

Statement of Work

Clearly documented and accepted expectations begin with the SOW. It lists the goals, constraints, and success criteria for the project. The project manager writes the SOW. It is then subject to negotiation and modification by the various stakeholders. After they formally agree to its content, it becomes the rules for the project.

This is one control document that, though widely used, is called by many names. Many firms use *statement of work* as it is defined in this book. But watch for other terminologies: Some firms use *charter* instead of *statement of work*. This can be confusing because, as we have seen, this term has another common use in the project management vocabulary.

The term that an organization may use to describe the statement of work is ultimately unimportant. It is the content that matters, and this content must establish clear expectations among all stakeholders.

The SOW is meant to document the goals and constraints of a project. However, it cannot and should not attempt to document *every* agreement about the project. There are other control documents for this purpose, such as requirements, specifications, and customer acceptance tests. The SOW should record the goals and constraints for *managing* the project. While that can contain a wide range of information, the minimum content listed here gives you an idea of what belongs in the SOW:

1. *Purpose statement:* A clear, succinct description of *why* we are doing this project.
2. *Scope statement:* A description of the major activities of the project in such a way that it will be absolutely clear if extra work is added later on.
3. *Deliverables:* A list of outputs the project will produce, including intermediate deliverables, end deliverables, and deliverables related to project management.
4. *Cost and schedule estimates:* In addition to a budget and a deadline, a description of how flexible the budget is and the rationale behind the deadline.
5. *Project objectives:* The specific, *measurable* goals of the project.
6. *Chain of command:* An organization chart that spells out who makes decisions and to which superior problems will be reported. It is often a good idea to include the organization chart of the customer, as well.

The SOW is a tool for managing expectations and dealing with change. When disagreements arise after the project has started, they can sometimes be solved by simply reviewing the original SOW. However, it is also true that the original agreements and assumptions may change during the course of a project. In this case, all stakeholders must understand and agree to these changes, and the project manager must write them into the SOW. The SOW that remains at the end of the project may be very different from the original document. The amount of this difference is not important; what is important is that everyone has been kept up to date and has agreed to the changes.

Responsibility Matrix

The responsibility matrix precisely details the responsibilities of each group involved in the project. The importance of this document is growing as corporations reengineer themselves and form partnerships and virtual companies. In these kinds of environments, many groups that otherwise might have nothing to do with one another are brought together to work on projects.

A responsibility matrix is ideal for showing cross-organizational interaction. For example, when a truck manufacturer creates a new cab style, it requires changes in tooling for the supplier as well as on the assembly line. The inevitable questions then arise: Who makes design decisions? Will the supplier have a voice in these decisions? When does each group need to get involved? Who is responsible for each part of this project? The responsibility matrix is designed to answer such questions. Exhibit 5.2 shows a template with possible responsibility codes. After the document is accepted, it becomes part of the rules for the project, just as the SOW does. All future changes must be approved by those who approved the original version.

EXHIBIT 5.2 Responsibility matrix template

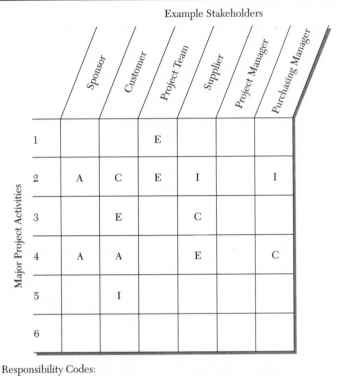

Responsibility Codes:
E- Responsible for task execution   I - Must be informed of decisions
C- Must be consulted about decisions   A - Final approval for decisions

Communications Plan

One of the largest contributing factors to project failure is lack of communication with stakeholders. When communication is limited to periodic reports, stakeholders can be in the dark when a project begins to slip. That is, they are in the dark until it slips to the point where the project manager must finally bring it to their attention. For stakeholders in this scenario, there are only two states for the project: "Everything's fine" and "The end is near!" This leads stakeholders to mistrust the project manager and project team, making correcting the problem even more difficult.

The remedy is consistent, frequent, and candid communication. The project manager uses plans, agreements, and status reports to communicate with stakeholders and manage their expectations. In addition, as with everything on a project, a solid plan improves the probability of success. Every project should have a communication plan, a written strategy for getting the right information to the right people at the right time. The stakeholders identified in the SOW and responsibility matrix are the audience for most project communication.

However, on every project, stakeholders participate in different ways and all have different requirements for information. If everyone has all the information needed, schedule slippages and cost overruns do not come as a surprise. In fact, because good communication means that stakeholders are more aware of project status, they can actually help the project manager get things back on track. Guidelines for developing a communication plan include:

- *Use short, concise status reports.* Obese reports are overwhelming for a busy audience. Determine what should go into a status report by asking the audience what they care about. Different customers may want status on separate factors in the project.

- *Have an escalation procedure.* These are guidelines for elevating a problem to higher management. (See discussion of this later in this chapter.)

- *Make the information timely.* Executive sponsors may need reports less frequently than your immediate manager.

- *Make sure regular status meetings are included in the plan.* Many stakeholders want to have status meetings only as needed, meaning only when there is a big problem. By including the scheduled meetings in the communication plan, customers and higher level managers are agreeing to be more informed about the project—which helps to avoid unpleasant surprises later in the project.

- *Be consistent with other projects.* As much as possible, your project documentation should have the same look and content as other projects in your organization. If there are standards, use them. If not, find good examples from other projects *that have the same stakeholders.*

- *Use multiple channels of communication.* Web sites, newsletters, and project bulletin boards can be used to post information of interest to all stakeholders. These communication mediums complement status reports because they can provide a wider scope of information. Finally, realize what you say in the written report may come across differently when you present it verbally, so consciously include face to face meetings in your communication plan.

Projects don't fail from overcommunication. However, they can suffer when subject to unorganized, unfocused blasts of project data. Thoughtful, conscious communication is essential to maintaining a unified direction.

Leading the Stakeholders

Project managers have a paradoxical relationship with stakeholders. The project manager is supposed to satisfy the stakeholders. Stakeholders make the big decisions on the project; they set the cost-schedule-quality equilibrium. At the same time, though, the project manager must *lead* this disparate group. Customers, management, vendors, and all the other stakeholders need focus and direction to play their parts well. We explore many techniques for controlling the project later in this chapter.

We conclude this section on stakeholder management with three principles for the project manager:

1. *Manage stakeholder expectations.* All of the tools of project management can be employed to communicate clearly what is possible and what will be done.

2. *Control who becomes a stakeholder.* Among managers and customers, there is no shortage of people eager to influence the project. However, if they don't have the right to this influence, push back.

3. *Manage upward.* Many of the stakeholders, including the sponsor, functional managers, and customers, have more formal authority than the project manager. But the project manager must actually lead *them.* They need the project manager to ask the hard questions, provide feasible alternatives, confront them with facts, and continually motivate them toward action with persistence and enthusiasm.

PROJECT CONTROL LEADS TO STAKEHOLDER SATISFACTION

> The best laid schemes o' mice and men
> Gang aft a-gley,
> And leave us naught but grief and pain
> For promised joy.
>
> —Robert Burns, "To a Mouse"

> No battle plan survives first contact with the enemy.
> —Field Marshal Helmuth von Moltke

We know what our stakeholders want; we've written it down in our SOW. We think we know how to achieve these goals. It is written in our detailed action plans, responsibility matrix, and communication plan. We manage the gap between writing our goals and achieving them with project control.

Think of controlling activities as akin to driving a car: You monitor progress, you change course to avoid obstacles, and sometimes you even change your destination.

The remainder of this chapter is dedicated to the techniques used to control the project to satisfy our stakeholders. It is organized into four major topics:

1. Developing a control plan.
2. Measuring progress, including the use of earned value analysis.
3. Corrective action options.
4. Pitfalls and dangers of project control.

DEVELOPING A CONTROL PLAN

Some projects need little or no monitoring, while others must be measured every step of the way. Therefore, when developing a control plan, consider how much monitoring and control is necessary. The amount of effort devoted to monitoring and control should be decided during the planning phase, before the project starts. Exhibit 5.3 illustrates how project size and complexity dictate the appropriate amount of control. Knowing the difference between a project that merely needs to be planned and scheduled and a project that requires regular monitoring and corrective action is a skill gained primarily through experience with prior projects. As a rule, project controls should be established when regular monitoring of the project can result in changes to any of the following in the project plan:

- *Project and task duration:* The time that future tasks will take and the impact of any changes on the entire project.
- *Resource allocation:* The way that resources—people, capital, and raw materials—are allocated to tasks.
- *Task sequence:* Changes to the order in which tasks are completed.
- *Objectives*: Changes to the scope or objectives of the entire project.

EXHIBIT 5.3   Assess the control requirements

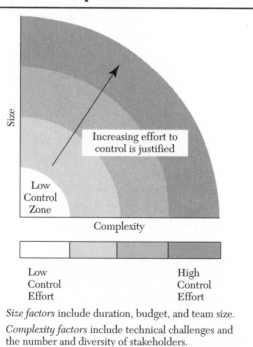

Size factors include duration, budget, and team size.

Complexity factors include technical challenges and the number and diversity of stakeholders.

Simply monitoring a project can become a project in itself. With limited time and resources, project control comes down to a question of emphasis, according to author James Snyder:

> It is important to know where to put the emphasis in the monitoring and control phases of any project. If no actions will be taken as a result of collecting information about project status, or if the knowledge of the real-world happenings cannot be applied to future projects, then the use of resources to monitor and evaluate project status may not be justified.[6]

The Control Process

The project control process is designed to spot problems early, while they are still small enough to correct. It is an iterative feedback loop in which the project manager uses measurement and testing to evaluate deviations from the plan as to cost, schedule, quality, and risk. These deviations may or may not result in corrective action. The key is to monitor closely enough and often enough to spot such deviations before they get out of control. There are five steps in the project control process:[7]

1. *Define what will be measured and/or tested and how often.* This should incorporate business requirements, cost constraints, technical specifications, and deadlines, along with a preliminary schedule for monitoring that includes who is responsible for it.
2. *Monitor progress and evaluate deviations from the plan.* During each reporting period, two kinds of information are collected:
   - Actual project data, which include time, budget, and resources used, along with completion status of current tasks.
   - Unanticipated changes, which include changes to budget, schedule, or scope that are not results of project performance. For example, heavy rain may delay the completion of a housing project.

     Earned value analysis, described later in this chapter, is a useful method for evaluating cost and schedule deviations.
3. *Report progress.* Keep reports succinct and timely. Do not delay a report until after a problem is "fixed" to make the report look better. Likewise, avoid lengthy reports that delay the dissemination of important information to others in the organization.
4. *Analyze the report.* Look for trends in the data. Avoid trying to "fix" every deviation. If there is no trend to the deviation, it likely does not require corrective action at this time.
5. *Take action where necessary.* This includes updating the project plan and notifying any stakeholders who are affected by the changes. If the changes are big enough, they will require stakeholder approval in advance.

Project control mirrors W. Edwards Deming's *Plan-Do-Study-Act* cycle and is intuitive in this respect. (See Chapter 7 for more on Deming.) Other guidelines for establishing this process that are born of experience are discussed in the following section.

Stakeholders Influence Project Control

The factors that a project manager monitors and reports on to stakeholders depend on who the stakeholders are. For example, consider a major upgrade to computer systems at an international airport. Stakeholders on this project include the Federal Aviation Administration and several major airlines. The FAA is concerned most with safety and wants to see data that show the project is meeting objectives to prevent computer system failure in the future. The airlines are also concerned about safety, but they are equally concerned about the amount of airport downtime during the project because they want to minimize the amount of time their planes stay on the ground. The project manager must monitor both safety, which is the primary objective of the project, and airport downtime, which occurs because of the project itself.

Another example of the influence stakeholders have on project reporting is determining reporting periods. Reporting periods define the frequency that progress is formally monitored and a status report is produced. The size, speed, and complexity of the project influences length of a reporting period, but so do stakeholders. Consider these factors:

- *The need for information at the executive level:* This information usually relates to big picture questions such as "Will we deliver on time?" or "Are we on budget and on schedule?" Project managers demand and use monitoring information more frequently than executives, but knowing when their superiors expect accurate updates will affect the monitoring cycle.

- *New information about activities or schedule:* The project schedule will change. As the project progresses, the project team gets a better picture of what is required to complete the project and can, therefore, improve its original estimates. If stakeholders dictate an aggressive schedule, more frequent reporting will uncover significant deviations sooner. Because trends are more useful for understanding a project's trajectory, frequent reporting periods provide earlier warnings that schedule targets may be missed.

- *Resource mix:* Changes in the quality or quantity of resources assigned to a project can have dire consequences on the team's ability to complete it on time and on budget. The monitoring plan can allow you to stay on top of getting the right people, materials, and equipment to the right place at the right time.

- *Major events:* Whether positive or negative, major events can change the assumptions on which the project objectives are based. Many major events that will affect the project are known in advance. These can include the end of a project phase, selection of a major subcontractor, and external events such as political elections. You know the event is important to the project, so schedule time to assess the impact.

Cost and Schedule Baselines

Baselines are used to track the progress of the project against cost and schedule goals. Cost and schedule baselines represent the original project plan, as approved by the stakeholders. Ideally, a project should never vary from its original plan; therefore, a comparison between actual performance and the baseline should show no variance. In reality, this zero variance never happens. Even though everything may not happen according to plan, however, many projects do meet original cost and schedule goals. Keeping the baseline cost and schedule goals visible is one way of holding the focus on the original goals, even when changes start to happen.

It's a virtual certainty that the cost and schedule baseline developed in the planning phase will be inaccurate. How can we expect the project team to meet cost and schedule goals when we know from the start that they are wrong? Author Harvey A. Levine points out the importance of keeping the baseline realistic:

> It is my belief that a project baseline is managed, rather than frozen. . . . If the participants realize that the baseline is suspect or invalid, then how can we demand that they diligently manage the project to achieve baseline values? If the project team is experiencing rampant changes in the measurement base, perhaps 20 percent to 50 percent of original values, how can we ask them to then manage the project to stay within, say, 10 percent of the baseline? The process becomes a farce, and support for that process goes down the drain.[8]

There is tension surrounding setting baselines. We need to hold people accountable, but we also know that even the best plans will not be completely accurate. Often, after planning is over and the project begins, we find that:

- Vital tasks and deliverables have been left out of the plan.
- The way we will do the work has changed.
- Estimates for cost, schedule, and resources are shown to be wrong.
- One or more stakeholders have asked for increases or decreases to project scope.

All of these are valid reasons to change a project baseline early in the project. In fact, a good way to handle this is to allow such changes for the first couple of reporting periods after the project begins, then freeze the baseline for the remainder of the project. Keep in mind that changes to project scope require sufficient justification, planning, and approval from all stakeholders. According to Levine, a good policy for maintaining a valid baseline includes the following:

- An initial baseline is developed that estimates the necessary costs, schedule, resources, and people. A baseline "freeze date" should be set at this time.

- Changes to this initial baseline may be made early in the project, until the baseline is frozen.

- Additions to scope after the freeze date must go through a thorough change control process, including full definition and approval, before the baseline is altered.

- Changes to the baseline are not made just because the work is not going according to plan.

Says Levine:

> We do not make changes to the baseline to accommodate poor performance. Rather, we maintain the baseline so that incidences of poor performance are disclosed.[9]

Phased Baselining

Perhaps the biggest key to the effective use of baselines is knowing the limitation of our planning horizon. A planning horizon is the distance you can accurately look into the future. For instance, if I think I want to build a house for my family, there is not much point in setting cost and schedule baselines before I purchase the property. I may have schedule goals and cost constraints, but to commit too early to a baseline for moving into the house is pointless. Common sense? Yes, but the many information technology (IT) projects that finish 100 percent over cost and schedule baselines are probably guilty of this error. Far too many IT projects are baselined in the name of project control before they have nailed down system requirements or design. This does not mean we abandon baselining entirely. Rather, we update the baseline as phases of the project are completed, when more information is available to make good estimates. This can be done by setting up the work breakdown structure (WBS) in phases, so that while we are tracking the project, we have:

- An original baseline.
- A modified baseline for the entire project after each phase that reflects what we have learned so far.

This technique is also described as "rolling wave planning" or a "sliding planning window." Each new baseline should be rigorously examined and approved by stakeholders. Remember, the purpose for updating the baseline is to provide the most realistic estimates for cost and schedule, not to hide or make up for poor performance.

The baseline is more than just a starting point; it also represents the accepted cost-schedule-quality equilibrium on the project. The project team is committed to meeting the baseline and should assume it will continue to be held to the baseline, unless otherwise directed by the project manager. At some point early in the project, the baseline is typically frozen. Changing the baseline is a big deal because it represents a new equilibrium. This new equilibrium requires approval from all the stakeholders. If the justification for the change is good enough, meeting the new baseline might even be considered as success. Other times, however, it simply represents accepting a new reality. If all the evidence suggests that the project will miss the original cost and schedule goals, it probably makes sense to change them. Maintaining unrealistic goals is rarely motivating. At the same time, however, the baseline must be changed cautiously and honestly, because it also affects motivation if the baseline is changed repeatedly. The new baseline should be as realistic as possible, reflecting the level of performance that led to the baseline change.

Planning Stakeholder Communication

Constant, effective communication among all stakeholders is integral to project control. While status reports and other regular communication are specified in the communication plan, there are several instances where the project manager must plan for more active stakeholder participation. These are the change control process, escalation thresholds, configuration management, and issues management.

Change Control Process

Every kind of project faces changes. During a kitchen remodel, the customers might change their minds about appliances, or a certain type of window might be unavailable. During a software development project, the competition might release a product with some exciting new features, forcing the development team to add these features as well. The specific change management process should fit the size and complexity of the project, with special attention paid to the number and diversity of stakeholders. However, every change process is based on the same fundamental model. Change management planning—establishing how the process of change will take place—occurs during the project definition stage. Any good change control procedure includes the following:

1. A set process for changing scope, including how to submit a change request and the frequency of change request evaluations.
2. Creation of a change review board and specification of escalation thresholds. (Both are discussed later.)
3. A rigorous examination of each proposed change, including the tasks, where they fit into the WBS, and impact to cost and schedule.
4. Identification of how the change will be funded.
5. A central record for all scope changes that is managed by a project team member.

A change board is assembled at the time the SOW is signed. Its purpose is to represent all the stakeholders affected by the cost-schedule-quality equilibrium. Approving changes through this body takes time and may seem bureaucratic and inefficient, but in reality, it saves time and money because without this board, a change request from one stakeholder might be quickly implemented only to find it in direct conflict with the interests of another. At a minimum, the change board should include representation from the project team, the customer, and groups with related products. For example, the change board for a redesign of a truck fender should include engineers responsible for other parts of the truck's cab.

Escalation Thresholds

While the project team has the authority to solve certain problems, others need to be escalated to higher management or may even demand the direct attention of senior management. The determining factors for who handles a problem or approves a solution are its cost and schedule impacts. Escalation thresholds represent preset variances that signal the severity of a problem; these thresholds are set during the planning process. Thresholds accomplish several important functions:

- Change management thresholds separate the types of changes the project team can approve from those the change control board must approve.
- Problem resolution thresholds bring the proper level of attention to specific problems. When a problem is encountered that threatens project cost and schedule goals, it needs to be identified and raised to the proper level immediately, skipping the normal project status process. Any single problem that is big enough to cross an escalation threshold is big enough to demand immediate attention; passing the problem from one level of management to the next using the normal status process of weekly or monthly status meetings would take much too long. The threshold shows exactly who needs to be involved in solving the problem.

Overall project progress thresholds signal upper management that it is time to become actively involved in the project. The project may have fallen behind a little at a time, and the trend may have been apparent over several status periods; but at a certain point in this decline, the escalation threshold will be crossed. This is the signal that management either needs to intervene to solve the problems or must be willing to set new cost and schedule goals. Exhibit 5.4 is an example of setting escalation thresholds using cost and schedule variance.

Configuration Management

Configuration management limits changes to control documents and other project deliverables to prevent confusion over changes to the project plan. For

EXHIBIT 5.4   Escalation thresholds

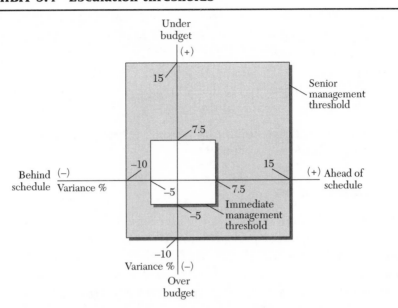

- Problems and changes beneath the immediate management threshold are left to the team to resolve.
- Any problem that can potentially cause a –10 percent cost or schedule variance will be immediately escalated to senior management.
- Changes that result in extremely positive variances will also be quickly escalated.
- Both midlevel and senior management will monitor the project on a routine basis while it is below their escalation thresholds, but they are less likely to actively intervene.

example, on a housing project, when the fifth revision is made to the blueprints, the electricians may still be working from the third version and the roofers may still be working from the first version. At this point, someone is bound to notice that the chimney and the fireplace are on different sides of the house. Configuration management prevents problems like these to ensure that everyone is "reading from the same sheet of music."

The U.S. Department of Defense originally began this process to track replacement parts for advanced technical equipment. Today, it is a vital process in any software project.[10] Any deliverable or product that might have multiple versions during the project should be monitored and controlled under configuration management. These include:

- *Control documents:* Product specifications and requirements documents are examples of control documents, because once they are formally accepted (signed by stakeholders) these documents become the basis for project action; in other words, these documents control our activities. Any document that records a decision by project stakeholders must be under configuration management.

- *Products or files that are stored electronically:* These can be easily changed without the knowledge of other groups in the project.
- *Prototypes or product mock-ups:* They are upgraded and changed many times during a project.
- *Test environments:* These are designed to simulate real-life product behavior. They are costly to create and might lead to incorrect test results if untracked changes are introduced.

Configuration management processes and responsibilities are established during project definition and planning.

Issues Management

Throughout the life of the project, problems arise that are beyond the control of the project manager and project team. We call these *issues*. Every project needs a process to track these problems to make sure they are all resolved before they actually have a negative effect on cost, schedule, or quality. The process need not be complex, but it should contain the following:

- A regularly scheduled review of open issues. It is common to have this review at project status meetings.
- A log of the issues that have been identified. For each issue, there must be:
  —A description of the problem.
  —The date it was logged.
  —How it affects the project.
  —When it begins to affect the project ("needs resolution by" date).
  —The person on the team responsible for getting resolution.
  —Current actions being pursued.
- After the issue is resolved, the solution should be documented and the status changed to "closed."

Issue management is an early warning system, alerting the team and its management of problems before cost and schedule deviations occur. It can also be used to manage customers and higher level management because it puts them on notice when they become responsible for solving project problems. The savvy project sponsor makes sure this process is in place and monitors it to continually seek out and resolve issues.

MEASURING PROGRESS

The key to finishing a project on time and on budget is to start out that way and stay on track throughout the project. When projects start with challenging schedules, if they fall behind, even by a little, they spend the rest of the project trying to catch up. Other projects, however, seem to have a self-correcting process built into them; if they fall behind a little, the problem is quickly identified and dealt with immediately. Progress measurements are the tools we use to identify problems when they are small and there is still time to catch up. Because cost and schedule progress comprise two-thirds of the cost-schedule-quality equilibrium, they are the primary focus of progress measurement.

During each reporting period, the project team records actual start and completion dates for each task in the WBS, along with the actual cost incurred by each. This data is then compared to the cost and schedule baseline to evaluate project team performance against the plan.

The primary tool for illustrating a schedule is also good for displaying schedule status. Exhibit 5.5 is a Gantt chart showing schedule progress. Exhibit 5.6 is a summary-only Gantt, useful for reporting schedule progress to high-level management or customers who are not interested in all the details. Notice that the focus here is on displaying schedule status. To get actual task completion status, the project manager must communicate with those working on the task.

The truth about cost and schedule status is often elusive because it is hard to pin down what portion of a task or project is really complete. Many a project has fallen into the trap of subjective assessment of progress. Subjective assessments—a gut feeling from the project manager or team members—tend to be overly optimistic early in the project. Even as the project passes the halfway

EXHIBIT 5.5 Gantt chart with schedule progress bars. All progress bars are behind the current date, showing the project is behind schedule.

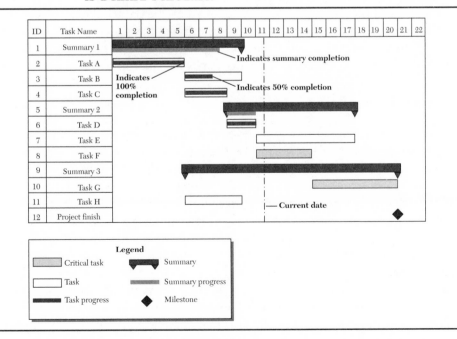

EXHIBIT 5.6   Progress displayed at the summary level only

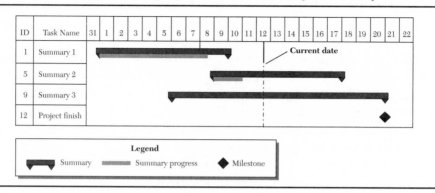

point in the schedule, if we rely on intuition or how we "feel" about the project, the assessment often turns out to have little relationship to reality.

Few organizations admit to running their project by the project manager's "gut feeling," but their assessment methods are far from objective. Project managers may be asked to give a project a rating of "green, yellow, or red" to indicate their confidence or need for executive involvement. This subjectivity multiplies when considering a portfolio of projects. As manager of 10 or 100 projects, how do you really know the status of each one? If you have a subjective assessment of how your projects are going, how do you compare one project to another for making decisions on your project portfolio?

The alternative to subjective judgments of "percent complete" is to derive the overall project progress from analysis of the detailed plan. It's entirely possible for a project manager to replace the subjective "feels good" to the precise "3 percent ahead of schedule and 2 percent over budget." That type of precision is achieved using earned value analysis, the topic of the next section.

Earned Value Analysis

The project management industry developed earned value analysis (EVA) with the encouragement of U.S. government agencies such as the Department of Energy and the Department of Defense. In fact, the Department of Defense has required this approach on all major project contracts since 1967.[11] This analysis method is appropriate for all projects, from the enormous, technically complex projects at NASA, to relatively simple home remodeling jobs. It does not require project management experts or brainy calculations and can be used to measure cost performance, schedule performance, or both at the same time. One very important caveat: EVA requires a valid baseline to work. Without a valid baseline, the variances calculated through EVA are meaningless.

EVA uses costs and task completion data to create a complete picture of a project's performance against the plan. For example, projects can be ahead of schedule (good), but over budget (bad). Or they can be ahead of schedule and under budget (really good). Project managers should always track both cost and schedule to get a complete picture. Analyzing only one of the two tells just half of the story.

At the center of EVA is a concept called *earned value,* the monetary value of work performed at a given point, according to the baseline plan. The foundation of using EVA is a good work breakdown structure (WBS) with clearly defined tasks, each of which has been assigned a cost. For example, the project in Exhibit 5.7 has 12 finite tasks (each task has well-defined completion criteria), and each task has been assigned a cost estimate. With this baseline in place, we are prepared to compare both schedule and cost variance.

EXHIBIT 5.7   Earned value analysis

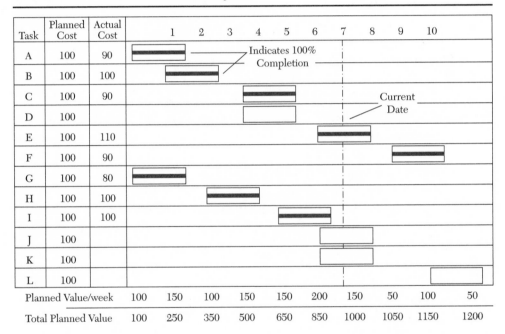

Task	Planned Cost	Actual Cost	1	2	3	4	5	6	7	8	9	10
A	100	90										
B	100	100										
C	100	90										
D	100											
E	100	110										
F	100	90										
G	100	80										
H	100	100										
I	100	100										
J	100											
K	100											
L	100											
Planned Value/week			100	150	100	150	150	200	150	50	100	50
Total Planned Value			100	250	350	500	650	850	1000	1050	1150	1200

After six weeks, some tasks are ahead of schedule while others are behind.

Total Actual Cost = 760   Earned Value = 800   Planned Value = 850

$$SV\% = \frac{EV - PV}{PV} \qquad CV\% = \frac{EV - AC}{EV}$$

$$SV\% = \frac{800 - 850}{850} \qquad CV\% = \frac{800 - 760}{800}$$

SV% = –0.0588 or 5.88% behind schedule   CV% = .05 or 5% under budget

New estimate at completion = Total Planned Value × (AC/EV)
EAC = 1200 × (760/800)
EAC = 1140

EVA is simple in concept and practice, but it requires familiarity with several new terms. A discussion of schedule variance and cost variance follows.

Measuring Schedule Variance

Is the project on schedule? This is a question that all stakeholders want answered at regular intervals. The question becomes even more difficult to answer on large projects when there are many concurrent tasks. If some tasks are behind schedule while others are ahead, what is the real truth about schedule progress? With EVA, a project manager compares the amount of work that has been done to the amount of work that was supposed be done in a given period to compute schedule variance. Tracking schedule with EVA requires an understanding of the following terms:

- *Planned value (PV):* The planned (budgeted) cost of work that should have been completed to date (also called *budgeted cost of work scheduled,* or BCWS). In Exhibit 5.7, the project had planned to accomplish $850 worth of work by the end of week 6.
- *Earned value (EV):* The planned (budgeted) cost of tasks that are complete. This is also known as the *budgeted cost of work performed* (BCWP) for the project, because it is the value of the work that has been completed. In Exhibit 5.7, the project has actually accomplished $800 worth of work by the end of week 6.
- *Schedule variance (SV):* The schedule variance is the difference between the value of the work that was planned for completion and the value of the work that was actually completed. It uses *cost* values to measure *schedule* performance. SV = EV − PV (negative = behind schedule).
- *Schedule variance percent (SV percent):* The schedule variance divided by planned cost to date. A positive SV percent is good; it means more work has been performed to date than originally planned. A negative SV percent is bad because it means less work has been completed than the plan called for. SV percent = SV/PV. This calculation allows us to report we are "5.88 percent behind schedule" in Exhibits 5.7 and 5.8.
- *Schedule performance index (SPI):* Earned value/planned value (SPI > 1.0 = ahead of schedule, SPI < 1.0 = behind schedule).

Given these formulas, a clearly defined baseline, and accurate task status, we can confidently report overall progress in precise, objective terms.

Even using EVA, we can fall into the trap of subjective assessment as we report partial progress on detailed tasks. One popular alternative for reporting partial completion on a task is to apply the 0-50-100 rule of progress:

- *0 percent complete:* The task has not begun.
- *50 percent complete:* The task has been started but not finished.
- *100 percent complete:* The task is complete.

EXHIBIT 5.8 Graphing cost and schedule variance using EVA

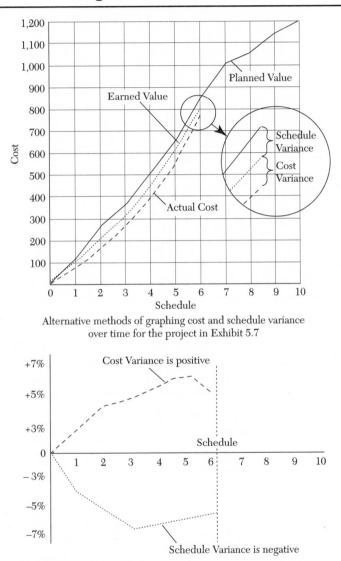

Alternative methods of graphing cost and schedule variance
over time for the project in Exhibit 5.7

For this approach to work, the actual work packages on the project must be broken down into small units. The planning guideline that is the corollary to this monitoring guideline is to break tasks down until they are no longer than one reporting period. This combination of small tasks and 0-50-100 percent status means that no task should be "in progress" for more than one status point. When it comes to assessing schedule progress at the task level, you really know only two things: whether it is started and whether it is finished. Therefore, the greater the detail in your WBS, the greater the accuracy of your schedule progress.

Measuring Cost Variance

Project managers and managers responsible for multiple projects have two primary concerns with cost:

1. Can our funding rate match our spending rate (cash flow)?
2. Will we complete the project within the budgeted amount?

The detailed planning techniques in Chapter 4 describe how to forecast the rate of spending over the weeks and months of the project. Comparing the actual expenses per reporting period with the plan will reveal deviations. While the details of cash flow management are outside the scope of this book, it should be obvious that even a fully funded project may not have its entire budget available up front. This is particularly true for long, expensive projects. Keeping an eye on the rate of spending can prevent temporary project shutdowns that result from getting ahead of the funding schedule.

Comparing planned cash flow with actual cash flow has its uses, but it does not tell you whether the project is under or over budget. EVA compares budgeted costs to actual costs for all work accomplished to date, providing a measurement of cost performance. Calculating cost variance uses some of the same terms as schedule variance:

-   *Planned cost:* The planned (budgeted) cost of any or all tasks.
-   *Earned value (EV):* The planned (budgeted) cost of tasks that are complete (also called *budgeted cost of work performed,* or BCWP).
-   *Actual cost (AC):* The actual cost of tasks that have been completed (also called *actual cost of work performed,* or ACWP).
-   *Cost variance (CV):* The difference between planned and actual costs for completed work. CV = earned value – actual cost (negative = over budget).
-   *Cost variance percent (CV percent):* Cost variance divided by the planned cost. A positive CV percent is good; it means the work was performed under budget. A negative CV percent is bad, because it means the work was over budget. CV percent = cost variance / earned value. This calculation is the basis for status of "5 percent under budget" in Exhibits 5.7 and 5.8.
-   *Cost performance index (CPI):* Earned value / actual cost (CPI > 1.0 = under budget, CPI < 1.0 = over budget).
-   *Budget at completion (BAC):* The budget, or planned value, at the end of the project.
-   *Estimate at completion (EAC):* This is a reestimate of the total project budget. The original budget is multiplied by the actual cost and divided by the earned value. It is a way of saying that if the current cost performance trends continue, the final cost can be predicted (EAC = BAC × CPI).
-   *Estimate to complete (ETC):* The budget amount needed to finish the project, based on the current CPI (EAC – AC).

EXHIBIT 5.9   A portfolio view

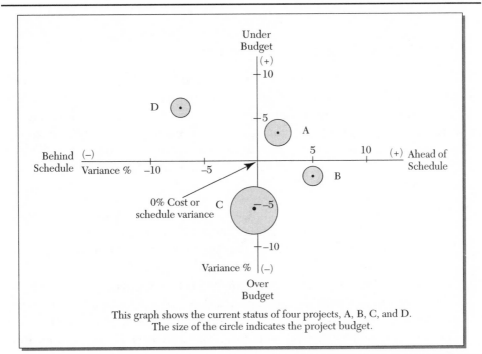

This graph shows the current status of four projects, A, B, C, and D.
The size of the circle indicates the project budget.

- *Variance at completion (VAC):* The estimated difference, at the end of the project, between the budget and actual cost of the project (BAC – EAC).

The cost variance for the overall project washes out the positive and negative variance seen on individual tasks. Analyzing cost trends gives us an early indicator of whether the actual cost of the project is close to the budget. Exhibit 5.8 demonstrates two common methods of displaying cost and schedule variance.

By applying EVA to all projects in a portfolio, managers can "compare apples to apples" in assessing the status of each project. Using a graph such as the one in Exhibit 5.9, managers can quickly ascertain which projects are going well and which require immediate attention.

OPTIONS FOR CORRECTIVE ACTION

For experienced managers, developing valid baselines and tracking cost and schedule variance are the easy part. The hard part is deciding when to take corrective action and selecting an action to take when a correction is necessary. The right thing to do depends on the situation and the industry. However, when the skies darken and rain begins to fall, consider the strategies discussed in the following sections.

Re-Baseline with Better Estimates

Shortly after the project begins, the project manager realizes that even though the team is working hard and making the best use of its time, it will come up short against cost and schedule goals. This is a case where poor estimating, not poor performance, is the reason for significant negative cost and schedule variance. Reevaluating the baseline to improve the estimates within it is the best course of action. It involves checking original assumptions in the SOW and work package estimates:

> *Trade-off:* In this case, developing a more accurate baseline means lengthening project duration or adding resources that increase cost. As a result, the business case for the project may no longer be valid because the estimated financial benefit of the project will not be achieved.

> *Impact on risk:* More accurate estimates and an updated plan should reduce the risks of missing cost and schedule goals. The real risk here is to the business case. A delayed finish date or increased budget may threaten the overall goals of the project. Still, the sooner we have accurate forecasts for cost and schedule, the better our business decisions are.

Crash the Schedule

At the midway point of a large project, EVA figures indicate that the project team is significantly behind schedule and will not catch up in time to meet a firm deadline. The project manager can increase the rate of work to meet the deadline by "crashing" or compressing the schedule to shorten the duration of the project.

In short, crashing the schedule trades money for time. Reducing the duration of tasks can be done in several ways, including adding people, adding resources, increasing the productivity of existing workers, and working overtime. Crashing can be expensive, but when faced with a deadline that cannot be moved, it is sometimes a project manager's best option. The critical path dictates which individual tasks that, when reduced, have an impact on overall project duration.

In crashing a schedule, a project manager should:

1. Focus only on the critical path.
2. Develop a *crash estimate* for each task being considered for compression. The crash estimate is the fastest the task could be performed and the cost of that speedy performance. By definition, a task cannot be completed in less time than its crash estimate.

EXHIBIT 5.10   Using a crash table to evaluate the cost of compressing the schedule

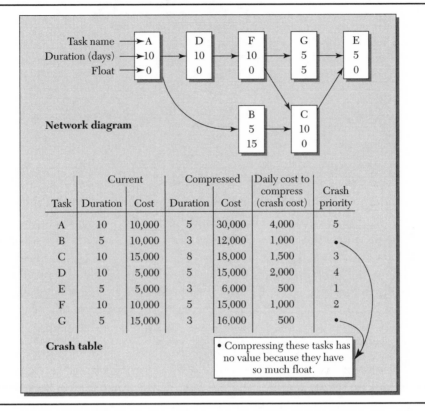

Crash table

Task	Current Duration	Current Cost	Compressed Duration	Compressed Cost	Daily cost to compress (crash cost)	Crash priority
A	10	10,000	5	30,000	4,000	5
B	5	10,000	3	12,000	1,000	•
C	10	15,000	8	18,000	1,500	3
D	10	5,000	5	15,000	2,000	4
E	5	5,000	3	6,000	500	1
F	10	10,000	5	15,000	1,000	2
G	5	15,000	3	16,000	500	•

• Compressing these tasks has no value because they have so much float.

3. Build a table to analyze which tasks to crash. The table in Exhibit 5.10 points out the tasks that provide the best schedule compression per dollar.

While it is important to recognize that only those tasks on the critical path are candidates for crashing, it is not necessary to crash all of the activities; rather, crash only enough tasks so that the deadline can be met. The objective of this time-cost trade-off is to find those tasks that, when shortened, reduce project duration enough to meet the deadline at the lowest possible increase to project cost. It is best to first focus on crashing tasks that occur in the near term. There is little point in reducing the duration of tasks in the distant future; when the time comes, you may find you do not need to reduce their durations after all. Second, focus on tasks with longer durations. Reducing a 10-day task by 40 percent, or four days, has a greater impact than completely eliminating a one-day task. During your crash analysis, remember that compressing tasks on the critical path may actually result in a new critical path. If that happens, you can repeat the analysis to find new schedule savings:

EXHIBIT 5.11 Crashing a schedule increases schedule risk

Projects with multiple critical paths have increased schedule risk. If each path in the network below is critical, and each path has a 0.9 probability of on-time completion, the probability that the project will finish on time is only 0.72.

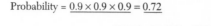

Probability = $\underline{0.9 \times 0.9 \times 0.9 = 0.72}$

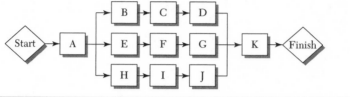

Trade-off: Crashing increases project cost to decrease project duration.

Impact on risk: Crashing the schedule increases risk significantly because it means managing more people, more concurrent activities, or both. Moreover, if crashing a schedule results in multiple critical paths on the project, the probability of meeting schedule goals decreases. When investing in crashing the schedule, if the schedule probability of each path in the network diagram does not increase, the project manager is also investing in schedule risk. Exhibit 5.11 illustrates what happens to schedule probability with multiple critical paths.

Adding people is the most obvious way to reduce the schedule because the project team can increase either the number of tasks that can be done simultaneously or the number of people working on each task. But beware. Pouring more people onto the project may appear to shorten the schedule, but it increases the cost of coordination and communication. Even the most competent people need some time to ramp-up. Further, in most cases, you actually need well-qualified people if they are going to make a positive difference. Unfortunately, many project managers have asked for more people only to have the most available people (which usually means least competent) sent to their projects. Weighing the project down with unskilled workers can create such a drag on productivity that it is almost certain to drive up both cost and schedule.

Increase Productivity by Using Experts from within the Firm

It is no secret that some people are more productive than others. Every industry has people who are simply more capable than their counterparts. So why not get as many of them as you can on your project? High performers have technical competence, problem-solving skills, and positive attitudes. Adding them to a project means meeting or beating cost and schedule goals. High performers not only deliver the best possible schedule performance but also are cost effective. They might double the production of the average team member, but it is rare that they will be paid twice as much for doing so. In addition, their expertise is likely to produce a better product.

On the other hand, this is an inefficient strategy for the firm as a whole. Putting all these stars on one project means that they'll probably be doing work that's well below their ability levels—something a junior staff member could do as well, even if not as fast. Moreover, when other projects begin to suffer, the stars are reassigned and the stellar project falters.

Top people are spread around many projects so that their ability and expertise can make other people more productive. Getting the optimal mix of average and star players requires three steps:

1. Work to create experts on each team. As much as possible, assign related tasks to a team member and thereby build his or her in-depth understanding of that area of the project. Over time, you will develop some team members into subject matter experts, if not outright stars.

2. Using the WBS, network diagrams, and work package estimates, identify the tasks that benefit most from top talent. Three indicators are:

   • *Cost:* The most complex tasks produce the highest returns from top performers. These are the kinds of tasks that produce productivity ratios of 10:1.

   • *Schedule:* Put the top performers on critical path tasks, where their speed translates to a shorter overall project schedule.

   • *Quality:* Top performers make good technical leads, by making major design decisions and spending time discussing work with junior team members.

3. Involve top performers in project management activities such as risk management, estimating, and effective assignment of personnel:

   Trade-off: Bringing stars onto one project means that other projects may not be as successful.

   Impact on risk: This action reduces cost and schedule risk on the project because of the superior expertise and productivity each star brings. It increases risk for other projects in the organization, which do not now have as much "star power."

Increase Productivity by Using Experts from Outside the Firm

The same logic from the previous alternative applies here, except that this option seeks to pull in the best people from outside the firm. Whether you hire individual people as contract labor or engage a firm to perform specialized tasks, the process is similar: Use the WBS to identify the best application of their talents and manage them as part of the team.

Some work is so specialized and sporadic that it doesn't pay to have qualified people on staff to do it. The additional costs incurred by hiring the outside experts will be more than offset by the speed and quality of their work. Just as with the experts from within the firm, assign them the time- or quality-critical tasks to get the most leverage from their work.

Hiring outside experts is useful when it appears that their specialized skills will move the project along faster. Expect these experts to attend team meetings and participate in product development discussions; do not let them become islands, working alone and avoiding interaction with long-term employees. Like the inside experts, they should be included in project management and other high-leverage activities. And, before they leave the project, whatever they produce should be tested and documented.

Trade-off: The added productivity that outside resources bring to the project must outweigh the cost of the effort to find and hire them. The ideal situation is to have a long-term relationship with a special services firm, whose employees have demonstrated their expertise on past projects.

In addition, every contract laborer or subcontractor who walks out the door at the end of the project takes some knowledge along, and this problem intensifies if the work is "brain work." In this case, the project manager needs to make sure that work has been properly recorded and documented.

Impact on risk: Bringing an outsider into the project introduces additional uncertainty. Unfortunately, not every expert delivers; he or she may not live up to the promises. By the time you find out your expert isn't productive, you may find, in spite of the added costs, that the project is behind schedule. In addition, finding a qualified vendor or contract employee can be time-consuming; if it takes too much time, it can become a bottleneck in the schedule.

Outsource the Entire Project or a Significant Portion of It

This corrective action involves carving out a portion of the project and handing to an external firm to manage and complete. This option is especially attractive if this portion of the project requires specialized skills not possessed by internal workers. This moves a large portion of the work to experts whose skills should result in greater productivity and a shortened schedule.

Trade-off: This shifting of responsibility means the project manager will have less control over the progress of the work, and, if the outside specialists prove to be less than competent, it may be too late to "switch horses." Even if it succeeds, an outside firm leaves little of its expertise with your firm at the end of the project.

Impact on risk: Outsourcing is at the high end of the risk/return spectrum. When it works, it can be a miracle of modern business methods; when it doesn't, it can result in real catastrophes. The keys to successful outsourcing are finding qualified vendors and coming to clear agreements before the work begins.

Shift Project Work to the Owner or Customer

If the project is short on people or long on cost, it is often fruitful to identify tasks that customers can perform themselves. Homeowners frequently use this method to reduce costs on home improvement projects. For example, to reduce the cost of a kitchen remodel, a homeowner might remove the old cabinets himself or herself instead of paying the contractor to do it. On large projects, a customer might take on the responsibility for ordering equipment and materials or delivering end-user training.

The most promising places to look for customer involvement are in administrative or low-expertise tasks. Another place to look is at the beginning or the end of a project, when there are various tasks requiring cooperation between the customer and the project team. In addition, the work package estimates and responsibility matrix show areas of the project where the owner/customer is already involved and could possibly take on a greater role. Finally, the list of people and skill types required on the project highlight any employees with special skill sets that the customer may have on its staff—and might loan to the project.

Trade-off: The project cost is lowered because the owner/customer pays its employees to do some of the work at a lower rate than they would pay the project team.

Impact on risk: It depends on the tasks being considered. If the owner/customer has experience with these tasks, risk impact could be minimal. Either way, more cooperation is required between the project team and customer, which may increase coordination risk.

Reduce the Product Scope

If the goals of the project will take too long to accomplish or cost too much, the first step is to scale down the objectives, or product scope. The result of this alternative is to reduce the functionality of the end product. Perhaps an aircraft will carry less weight, a software product will have fewer features, or a building will have fewer square feet or less expensive wood paneling. (Remember the difference between product scope and project scope: Product scope describes the functionality and performance of the product, project scope is all the work required to deliver the product scope.)

The key to reducing a product's scope without reducing its value is to reevaluate the true requirements for the business case. Many a product has been over budget because it was overbuilt. Quality has best been defined as "conformance to requirements." Therefore, reducing product scope so that the requirements are met more accurately actually improves the value of the product because it is produced more quickly and for a lower cost.

Trade-off: When a product's functionality is reduced, its value is reduced. If the airplane won't carry as much weight, will the customer still want it? If a software product has fewer features, will it stand up to competition? A smaller office building with less expensive wood paneling may not attract high enough rents to justify the project.

Impact on risk: Reducing scope usually means reducing risk because fewer things can go wrong. However, the risk that the product will not succeed because it does not meet requirements increases. Essentially, reducing scope means eliminating several smaller risks (such as being over budget or behind schedule) for one large one: that the product will not succeed at all.

Fixed-Phase Scheduling

During the early days of a product development life cycle, it is difficult to pin down the cost, schedule, or product quality. But some projects, for very important reasons, need to complete by a specific date. When fixed-phase scheduling is employed, the project phases are apportioned from the top down and scheduled according to the required completion date. At the end of each phase, the scope of the project is reevaluated (functionality is added or removed) to fit the remaining schedule. Because functionality can be added as well as removed, the project will meet the schedule with the best possible product because it was consciously rescoped several times. Quality (product performance) remains high with this method, because quality-oriented tasks will not be sacrificed at the last minute to meet the schedule.

Products whose delivery date is set and whose products can be scaled up or down during development without compromising design lend themselves best to this method. Software (including information systems) is probably the best candidate for fixed-phase estimating because most software designs are modular. In addition, it is critical that these products meet their delivery dates because their market success often depends on beating a competitor to the punch.

Trade-off: Fixed-phase scheduling prioritizes schedule goals over functionality goals. The project manager must be prepared to present hard choices to the customer and other stakeholders several times during the project. This also increases the cost of communication and coordination.

Impact on risk: Not every product lends itself to functionality changes several times during the life cycle. The design for many products is holistic, encompassing all the functions. For these products, changing the functions may cause design rework and additional costs. For example, a sports stadium may have an aggressive schedule so that it can be ready for opening day of the season. That still doesn't make it realistic to modify the scope of the building.

Phased Product Delivery

In a situation where the project cannot deliver the complete product by the deadline, there is still the possibility that it might deliver some useful part of it. Information systems projects composed of several subsystems, for example, often implement one subsystem at a time. Tenants can move into some floors in a new office building while there is active construction on other floors, and sections of a new freeway are opened as they are completed rather than waiting for the entire freeway to be complete. Phased delivery has several benefits:

- Something useful is delivered as soon as possible.
- Often, as in the case of information systems, phased delivery is actually preferred because the changes introduced by the new system happen a little at a time. This longer time frame can reduce the negative impacts to ongoing business operations.
- Feedback on the delivered product is used to improve the products still in development.
- By delivering over a longer period, the size of the project team can be reduced; a smaller team can lead to lower communication and coordination costs. In addition, because the people are working for a longer time on the project, project-specific expertise grows. These factors should lead to increased productivity in subsequent project phases and to an overall lower cost for the project.
- Phased delivery allows for phased payment. By spreading the cost of the project over a longer time, a larger budget might be more feasible.

Modularized products, whose components can operate independently, can be delivered in phases. To determine how to phase a product delivery, you need to look for the core functionality—the part of the product that the other pieces rely on—and implement that first. The same criteria may be used in identifying the second and third most important components. When multiple components are equally good candidates, they can be prioritized according to business requirements.

Although some consumer products such as automobiles do not appear to be good candidates for phased delivery ("You'll be getting the windshield in January and the bumpers should arrive in early March . . ."), a limited amount of phased delivery is possible for others. For example, software products can be upgraded cheaply and effectively over time by using the Internet, and current customers can download product updates directly onto their computers from company sites on the World Wide Web.

Trade-off: Phased implementation increases functionality at the expense of schedule. If the approach requires old methods to run concurrently with new methods, it could also temporarily lead to higher operating costs.

Impact on risk: When components of a solution are delivered over time, the connections, or interfaces, become high risk. For information systems, that could mean corrupted data. For highway projects, that could mean more accidents.

DANGERS IN CONTROL

Even with a sound project control system in place, there exist dangers and pitfalls that must be avoided to ensure success. Use these guidelines to fine-tune your project control strategy:

Take completion criteria seriously. Every work package is supposed to have completion criteria and should not be considered 100-percent complete until it meets these criteria. Project managers must be rigid about this; if tasks are consistently allowed to register as complete before all the final details are taken care of, the project might fall far behind, even though the official status reports it as being on schedule. Likewise, progress cannot be monitored if completion criteria and milestones are not recognizable or are undefined.

Schedule performance measures accomplishment, not effort. Just because you have used up 50 percent of the labor budget doesn't mean you have accomplished 50 percent of the project. Schedule status measures whether you have accomplished as much to date as planned.

The danger of management by exception. Management by exception is a seductive method for keeping the project on schedule, which, in many cases, can actually increase schedule problems. Management by exception focuses on keeping critical path tasks on schedule, while ignoring noncritical tasks that fall behind their scheduled start or end dates. This strategy holds that if a task is not critical, it doesn't matter if it falls behind. Eventually, all tasks become critical; therefore, all tasks eventually get management attention. The fallacy with this logic is that these delays can lead to a resource crisis at the end of the project—which is the worst time to try to get extra work accomplished. The people poured onto the project at the end will have had little or no experience with the project. In addition, you will have increased your schedule risk because a late completion of any one of the critical tasks can delay the project finish.

Accounting lag times reduce cost variance accuracy. Accounting lag times can make cost information arrive months late. This kind of delay means that a project's cost performance might appear to be excellent all the way through the project. However, after completion, the bills just keep coming in. Even if you are using an EVA system, large accounting lag time means you'll never know enough about cost to control it. When setting up your control system, find out how costs are attributed and, if necessary, create your own method for getting actual costs in a timely manner.

Watch out for large work packages. The size of work packages plays a big role in calculating schedule variance accurately. The 0-50-100 method described earlier in this chapter results in accurate schedule variance calculations if the work packages are small. If the work packages are large, the variance becomes skewed, either positively or negatively, from week to week.

Beware of change when using shared resources. When the project schedule is based on resources that are shared with other projects, change becomes risky, particularly if there are outside vendors and subcontractors involved. In this situation, a minor delay of a few days can turn into a delay of weeks as the shared resources are rescheduled against their other commitments.

THE EXECUTIVE'S ROLE IN STAKEHOLDER SATISFACTION

The purpose of projects is to satisfy stakeholders. Magnify that for the manager or executive responsible for many projects. Project managers often cite timely decisions, sufficient staffing, participation in customer status meetings, and visibility to the team as signs of management support. Yet, maintaining active involvement and oversight for a range of independent projects seems nearly impossible. A manager with a schedule full of customer and project meetings can feel more like a bottleneck than a productivity multiplier.

The only way to effectively support multiple projects *and* devote your time to the projects that need it the most is to monitor and control your portfolio using the project control systems described in this chapter. Managers of multiple projects have no choice; they must use SOW, regular status reports, issue logs, and the other control tools to sufficiently understand their project portfolios.

Project managers say that their best bosses understand the language of project management. This language allows them to speak precisely about problems and progress. Decisions are made based on facts and rational analysis. When the organization adopts consistent formats for the project management tools, the communication between projects and management becomes even clearer.

The advantage of clear communication in the language of project management extends to customers, support staff, and other stakeholders. More than anything else, clear expectations and consistent, honest communication form the foundation of successful, long-term stakeholder relationships. After a department in a large organization begins to use the communication tools described in this chapter, its customers begin to adopt these techniques on their own projects.

The only disadvantage to project managers and their management team is that using consistent project controls makes it hard to hide problems. Everybody, particularly the team, knows the truth about whether the goals are realistic and whether they will reach them. Or maybe this is the biggest advantage.

NOTES

1. Portions of this chapter were excerpted from Eric Verzuh, *The Fast Forward MBA in Project Management* (New York: Wiley, 1999).

2. Stephen R. Covey, *The 7 Habits of Highly Effective People* (New York: Simon & Schuster, 1989).

3. David I. Cleland and Jeffrey K. Pinto, eds., *Project Management Handbook* (New York: Wiley, 1998), p. 56.

4. See note 3, pp. 59–72.

5. See note 3, p. 64.

6. James R. Snyder and David I. Cleland, eds., *Field Guide to Project Management* (New York: Wiley, 1998), p. 301.

7. Deborah S. Kezsbom and Katherine A. Edward, *The New Dynamic Project Management: Winning through the Competitive Advantage* (New York: Wiley, 2001), pp. 316–320.

8. Harvey A. Levine, *Practical Project Management: Tips, Tactics and Tools* (New York: Wiley, 2002), pp. 226–228.

9. See note 8, p. 224.

10. See note 7, p. 342.

11. See note 7, p. 330.

6 PROJECT RISK MANAGEMENT*

Eric Verzuh

Two hundred years ago, the Corps of Discovery, led by Meriwether Lewis and William Clark, left St. Louis on a journey of scientific and geographic discovery. Their historic journey to open up the continent's western lands to further exploration and settlement still ranks high among great American achievements. Along the way, they would travel on unmapped waterways, discover and record unknown animals and plants, and pass among the native peoples, some whom they feared would be hostile. In short, the expedition held the prospect of enormous benefit to the young United States, but faced tremendous risks.

From the time the expedition was launched by President Jefferson in 1803 until they actually set off up the Missouri River in May 1804, Lewis and Clark analyzed their undertaking from every perspective and their preparations reflected the breadth of their risks. In their boats, they brought upwards of 10 tons of supplies that included dried food, candles, axes, knives, and cooking utensils. They packed beads, fishhooks, and other goods for trading. For hunting and self-defense they obtained rifles from the army, gun powder, and lead for making bullets. Their crew of approximately forty men contained a blacksmith, expert hunters, a gunsmith, and men who knew the Missouri River and western Indian languages. Lewis and Clark spent the winter of 1803–1804 camped north of St. Louis with the men they had recruited for their corps, judging who among them had the character and skills necessary for the hardship and adventure ahead. Their courage in leading this expedition

---

* Significant portions of this chapter were derived from Eric Verzuh, *The Fast Forward MBA in Project Management*, (New York: Wiley, 1999).

is universally acknowledged; their thorough preparations were equally essential to their survival and success.[1]

Lewis and Clark prepared to the utmost of their capability for the unknown. Today, in the opening years of the twenty-first century, project managers and executives can profitably imitate these legendary explorers. Every project, by definition, is unique. Every project contains risks—dangers—both known and unknown. Project risk management contains the disciplined practices we use to plan for and react to the uncertainty inherent in every project.

Consider the following scenarios:

- A Silicon Valley software company subcontracts part of a product development effort to a software shop in Los Angeles. How will the project manager in San Jose make sure the subcontractor produces the right product on time?

- To reduce administration costs and streamline admissions, a hospital is considering reengineering its process for creating and storing patient records. How can hospital administrators budget for the unpredictable costs associated with culture and process change?

- In the design to build a completely new fighter aircraft, a defense contractor specifies lightweight composite materials. How can the contractor be sure the new materials will hold up under the pressures a fighter jet endures?

In these projects, there is uncertainty about the schedule, the costs, and the quality of the end product. How can this uncertainty be managed?

Risk management is the means by which uncertainty is systematically managed to increase the likelihood of meeting project objectives. The key word is *systematic,* because the more disciplined the approach, the more we are able to control and reduce the risks. This chapter presents a framework for identifying risks and developing strategies for managing them.

THE RISK MANAGEMENT ADVANTAGE

All projects experience the unexpected; but some project managers are ready for it. Impossible? The language of project risk management explains this phenomenon:

- Known-unknowns represent identified potential problems, such as the possibility of a strike when a labor contract expires or enough rain to stall a construction project during winter in Seattle. We don't know exactly what will happen, but we do know it has a potential to damage our project and we can prepare for it.

- Unknown-unknowns are the problems that arrive unexpectedly. These are the ones you honestly couldn't have seen coming. But seasoned project managers do expect them, because they know something unexpected always happens.

The risk management advantage is that fewer problems catch the project team off-guard. For every surprise thundershower, the project manager just happens to have an umbrella handy.

The ability to prepare for and reduce uncertainty is well illustrated within the insurance industry, where risk management has become a sophisticated science. Actuaries are constantly researching the probabilities of various calamites and this research helps them set insurance premiums. But not only do insurance companies charge us for assuming risks, they actively try to avoid risks by encouraging their policyholders to avoid risky behavior. Premiums are reduced for nonsmokers and for automobile owners with good driving records. The insurers even send representatives into businesses to advise them how to avoid accidents—and reduce the clients' premiums when they follow the advice.

The insurance industry's systematic effort to understand and account for risk and to look for opportunities to reduce risk is a worthy example for projects and project-driven organizations. Project risk management practices, when systematically implemented and given support from all levels of management, provide similar benefits: increased predictability, lower incidence of failure, and overall lower project costs.

RELATIONSHIP OF RISK MANAGEMENT TO OTHER PROJECT MANAGEMENT FUNCTIONS

Systematic project risk management techniques are complimentary to all project management functions. Exhibit 6.1 demonstrates the relationship of risk management to the primary functions of definition, planning, and control. As previously discussed in Chapter 1, these primary functions are performed by the project manager and project team throughout the life of the project. Definition produces decisions and documents that are used within planning; planning produces updates to the definition documents as well as outcomes used during control; control functions require the outputs of definition and planning and produce changes that cause definition and planning to be repeated. Risk management activities are repeated within each of these primary functions.

Definition

The first risks surface as the project is conceived, the business case is constructed, and the goals for cost, schedule, and product scope are developed. Initially, these risks may be listed as assumptions, but as it becomes clear that they represent specific uncertain factors or events they become the first documented risks. While Exhibit 6.1 indicates that detailed risk planning occurs after project definition, some of the most important risk management occurs during initial development of the business case because that is where budget reserves are allocated to accommodate the risks of the project. The diagram

EXHIBIT 6.1 Relationship of risk management to the primary project management functions

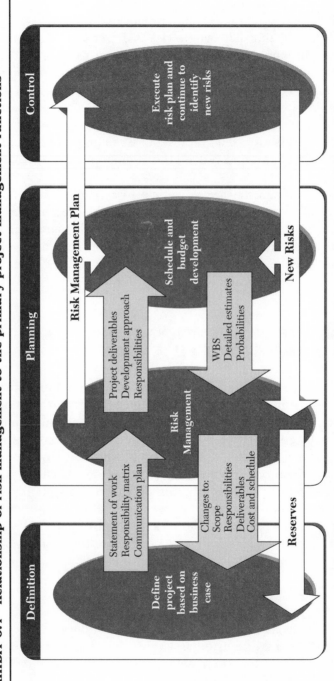

represents this as the business case risk coming out of *Definition* and the *Reserves* that feed back from risk planning.

For example, a real estate developer may choose to purchase property to develop apartments. In the initial business case for the project, any known risks (such as the difficulty of getting a permit) would be listed and additional funds would be designated within the budget for *all* risks—both known and unknown. This high level information is used during risk planning and, as shown in Exhibit 6.1, the outcome of risk planning is likely to be refinement of original assumptions about scope, responsibilities, cost, schedule, and the budget reserves for risk.

Planning

Exhibit 6.1 shows the function of planning as having two major components: risk planning and schedule and budget development. Schedule and budget development are the detailed plans required for day-to-day management of the project. Techniques for creating these detailed plans are described in Chapter 4. Risk planning represents the formal, conscious activities of the project manager and team to identify risks and to formulate strategies for managing the risks. It cannot be over-emphasized that risk planning happens repeatedly through the project. In the same way that the project schedule is updated and adjusted throughout the project, the risk management plan is continuously updated. Inputs to risk planning are, initially, the outputs of the definition process: the goals, scope, and vision for the project. As the project team analyzes these high-level parameters, they identify risks and develop strategies for neutralizing the risks. Those strategies, in turn, will affect the detailed action plan and may require changes to the statement of work, responsibility matrix, or communication plan.

A significant way risk planning affects schedule and budget development is illustrated with risk strategies and the work breakdown structure. Risk reduction strategies can show up as specific tasks on the WBS or, in some cases, actually influence all the tasks on the WBS. For instance, when a project team identified *uncertain user requirements* as a risk, they chose a prototyping approach to develop the product. As a result, the entire work breakdown structure reflected this risk reduction strategy.

To fully appreciate the integration of risk management on planning, visualize the two components of planning as being iterated two to four times before project execution begins. With each iteration the assumptions are more fully exposed and the risk management plan and the detailed schedule and budget become a more accurate reflection of reality.

Control

Recall that the control function consists of the activities performed by the project manager to keep the team coordinated and progress on track. (Control activities are discussed in greater detail in Chapters 1 and 5.) Execution of the risk management plan requires control activities similar to execution of the project schedule, and therefore the risk control activities can be blended in with the overall project control activities. As the project is monitored for progress, known risks are watched and new risks are identified. Risks that don't materialize are removed from the risk plan, new risks are added, and the process of risk planning is repeated. All of these activities result in updates to the statement of work, budget reserves, progress reports, work breakdown structure, and the many other project management deliverables.

Good Risk Management Improves Product Quality

The practices that ensure the correct product is produced and that it works as specified work hand in hand with risk management. For instance, during risk identification a common question to ask is, "are requirements clearly documented and stable?" Decisions about the development approach, whether to outsource particular sections of the project or testing methods, are directly influenced by risk planning. The descriptions of risk identification and response development later in this chapter expand on this relationship.

THE ROLE OF EXECUTIVE MANAGEMENT IN PROJECT RISK MANAGEMENT

Executive management plays a crucial role in every project's success. The primary responsibility for carrying out risk management activities lies with the project manager and the project team, but they cannot do it alone. The project sponsor and the executives responsible for project selection and portfolio oversight make four essential contributions to risk management:

- Maintain both a contingency and a reserve within the project budget. Contingency accounts for known risks and the possible cost of dealing with them if they arise. Reserve accounts for the unknown-unknowns. The method of establishing these amounts within the budget is discussed in greater detail later in this chapter.

- Hold the project manager and team accountable for the risk management deliverables, and allow for the time it takes to create them. Ben Franklin's adage, "An ounce of prevention is worth a pound of cure" applies to risk management; project executives must pay for and demand the ounce.

- Promote a climate that recognizes the value of risk management. Strange as it may seem, many project managers are criticized for identifying risks and developing contingency plans: they are accused of pessimism or planning to fail. These project managers should receive praise rather than criticism because they are investing in avoiding obstacles, solving problems before they arise; the ultimate act of proactive management.

- Never forget the relationship between cost, schedule, quality, and risk. The so-called *triple constraint* is well known in project management: cost, schedule, and quality are related because it takes time and money to produce a product. Risk is an inherent, though often unrecognized, factor in that relationship. Most strategies to cut schedule and cost increase risk. When an executive asks a project team to produce a more aggressive schedule (i.e., cut some time off the team's proposed schedule) or to sharpen their pencil to reduce the budget estimate, that executive is asking the team to add risk.

Business Risk versus Project Risk

The City of Seattle acquired a beautiful new office tower in the early 1990s after the lender foreclosed on the original developers. The city government was able to buy the building at a huge discount because so much of it was vacant. The developers had taken a risk in building the tower, and when the downtown office market hit a slump, they began to lose money. There was no evidence of cost overruns during construction; demand for office space simply didn't materialize.

This is an example of a successful project (a beautiful building, on time and on budget) that turned out to be an unsuccessful business venture. Business risk is inherent in all business activities, but it is seldom the project manager's job to manage it; that responsibility lies with the owner of the project. *Selecting the right project is business risk. Managing uncertainty to meet the stakeholders' objectives is project risk.*

Reducing business risk is beyond the scope of this chapter, but not beyond the scope of this book. Chapter 3 presents a full discussion of project selection and Chapter 11 presents a specific method of risk reduction when developing new products.

Risk Management Framework

The purpose of project risk management is depicted in Exhibit 6.2: throughout the project continue to identify the unknowns on the project and reduce the potential for damage. Although we can plan for both the known-unknowns and unknown-unknowns, we are much better at accounting for specific, recognized risks. The process illustrated in Exhibit 6.3 provides a structured, repeatable method for identifying and managing risk continuously from concept through completion. The remainder of this chapter describes each of the four processes in detail, but we will begin with an overview of the process.

EXHIBIT 6.2 Risk identification reduces unknown risks

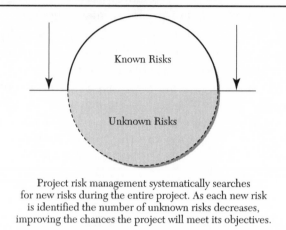

Project risk management systematically searches
for new risks during the entire project. As each new risk
is identified the number of unknown risks decreases,
improving the chances the project will meet its objectives.

Identify Risks

The beginning of proactive planning is to look for all the possible problems you will encounter during the project. *All the possible problems* is a very large number, even on a simple project, so it is also necessary to sift and prioritize them so you can focus on those most likely to cause the greatest damage.

Develop Response Plans

Understanding a problem is the first step in solving it, so clearly understanding each risk is the first step in risk response development. Defining a risk consists of describing specifically what problem might occur and the potential negative impact of the problem. Notice that in defining risk we use terms such as *might occur* and *potential impact* because we are forecasting the future. So another element of risk definition is quantifying the probability that the risk event will actually take place. The combination of the probability of the risk and the damage it will cause helps to prioritize the risks and to determine how much we are willing to spend to avoid or reduce the risk. Every risk response attempts to reduce the probability and/or impact. The primary outcome of developing response plans is a risk log. The risk log is the full list of risks the project team will actively manage and contains the specific tasks associated with managing each risk.

Establish Reserves

Ideally, some reserves have already been allocated in the project's budget for responding to risks. However, once detailed risk planning has been performed we will have a much more accurate assessment of how much money to set aside for responding to known risks and unknown risks. Contingency reserves are allocated for known risks. Management reserve is allocated for unknown risks.

EXHIBIT 6.3   Project risk management

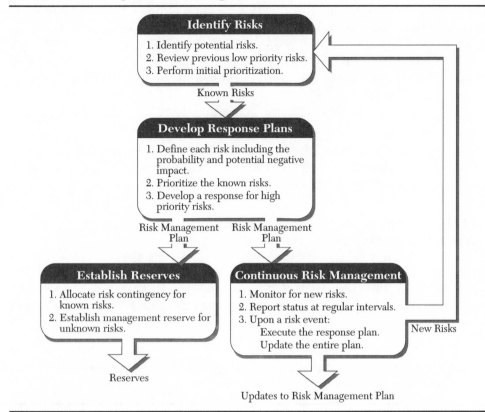

Continuous Risk Management

If it is smart to proactively plan for risk at the beginning of a project, it is even smarter to continuously plan for risk during the project. Continuous risk management is a conscious repetition of risk identification, response development, and carrying out the risk plans. At regular intervals the known risks are reassessed and the team vigorously searches for new risks. The risk plan is updated to record whether the risks actually occurred and whether the response strategy actually worked. Reports to management include updates on the status of high profile risks and the amount of contingency and reserve expended to date.

IDENTIFY RISKS

One of the scenarios at the beginning of this chapter involved defense contractors that were concerned about the strength of the new material they were building into fighter planes. In this example, the first critical step of risk management was performed: The risk was identified. Identifying risk is both science and art: the science uses the lessons of the past to systematically predict the future while the art blends the historical data with the intuition and insights of project stakeholders. Both art and science demand knowledge of project management and an understanding of the technology of the project. For example, schedule and resource risks can be identified by analyzing a network diagram; the risks associated with using lightweight composite materials in an aircraft design are understood by the engineers because of their technical knowledge.

There are many techniques for identifying risks, but they fall into four major categories: asking the stakeholders; checking against a list of possible risks (a risk profile); learning from similar past projects; and analyzing the schedule and budget. This chapter will look at each of these methods in detail, along with tips for making them work better.

Getting Information about Risk from Stakeholders

If you want to know what could possibly go wrong on a project, just ask the people on the team—they've probably been making their own lists since they were assigned to the project. Here are two ways to involve the team in identifying project risks:

1. *Brainstorming sessions:* Everyone's favorite method for generating ideas works well for identifying risks. Gather the stakeholders and any others involved in the project and follow basic brainstorming rules:

   a. Generate as big a list of potential risks as possible. Don't try to evaluate the risks as they are named; let the creativity of the group flow.

   b. After generating a list of potential risks, combine similar risks and order them all by magnitude and probability. Risks that have little chance of affecting the project can be crossed off.

   Don't try to solve all the risks at the meeting. If there are easy answers, be sure and capture them, but keep the session focused on *risk identification, not response development.*

2. *Interviewing:* Interviewing individuals about risk requires a more structured approach than brainstorming. Using a risk profile with specific questions will help stimulate the person being interviewed to think about all aspects of the project.

Murphy's Risk Management Law

The art of identifying risk begins with a critical attitude. Because we are trying to find problems before they emerge, it is appropriate at first to adopt the attitude that "anything that can go wrong, will go wrong." Later, after we've developed solid strategies for managing the risks, we can be optimistic again. There is, however, a big difference between a critical examination of the project to identify risks and plain old griping. It's up to the project manager to set the tone.

People bring different perspectives to the project depending on their project role. Be sure to include customers, sponsors, team members, subcontractors, functional management, and people who've worked on similar projects. They all have a stake in the project and they'll gladly take this chance to help ensure its success.

Using a Risk Profile

One of the best ways to ensure the success of a project is to apply the lessons learned from past projects. This is done by using a risk profile. A risk profile is a list of questions that address traditional areas of uncertainty on projects (see Exhibit 6.4). These questions have been gathered and refined from previous, similar projects. Creating a risk profile is an ongoing process: At the end of this project, what has been learned will be incorporated into the profile.

EXHIBIT 6.4   Example: Risk profile questions

Project Team
1. How many people are on the team?
2. What percent of the team is fully dedicated to the project?
3. Which team members will spend 20 percent or less of their time working on this project?
4. What is the experience level of the team?
5. Have team members worked together before?
6. Is the team spread out geographically?

Customer
1. Will the customer change current processes to use the product? (No) (Minor changes) (Major changes)
2. Will the project require the customer to reorganize? (No) (Minor changes) (Major changes)
3. Are the customers in different departments? Companies?

Technology
1. Will there be technology that is new to the development team?
2. Will there be technology that is new to the users or customers?
3. Is there any new or leading-edge technology in the project?
4. Are the product requirements clearly documented and signed by all the necessary stakeholders?
5. Are the product requirements stable?

Executive Support
1. Is there a known project sponsor who is actively involved in the project?
2. Is there sufficient recognition, support, and involvement from all senior management required for the success of the project?
3. Is senior management setting deadlines or budget limitations independent of the project manager's schedule and budget estimations? If so, are these constraints realistic?

- Develop categories of risk, then list several questions for each category.
- Each question probes at a possible weakness.
- Add new categories and questions over time.

Good risk profiles follow these basic guidelines:

- *They are industry-specific.* For example, building an information system is different from building a shopping mall.
- *They are organization-specific.* While industry-specific profiles are a good place to start, the profiles are even better when they address risks specific to a company or department.
- *They address both product and management risks.* Risks associated with using and developing new technology are product risks. Management risk addresses project management issues, such as whether the team is geographically dispersed. Exhibit 6.4 has examples of both product and management risks.
- *They predict the magnitude of each risk.* Even simple, subjective indicators of risk such as "high—medium—low" contribute to a clearer assessment of specific risk factors. More specific quantitative indicators offer the opportunity for greater refinement and accuracy over many projects.

Risk profiles are generated and maintained by a person or group independent of individual projects. The keeper of the risk profile participates in postproject reviews to learn how well the risk profile worked and to identify new risks that need to be added to the profile. These profiles, when kept up to date, become a powerful predictor of project success. The combined experience of the firm's past projects lives in their questions.

It is even possible to buy good risk profiles. Consulting firms will sell them as part of their project management services. The Software Engineering Institute offers a detailed list of questions for evaluating risk on software projects in its *Continuous Risk Management Guidebook.*[2]

Historical Records

History continues to be the best predictor of the future. In addition to the history incorporated in the risk profile, a project manager can investigate what happened on similar projects in the past. There may be useful risk-related information already written down that you can tap into, such as:

- Planned and actual performance records that indicate how accurate the cost and schedule estimates were.
- Problem logs that portray the unexpected challenges and relate how they were overcome.
- Postproject reviews that generate the lessons learned from the project. Find out what a similar project team did right and wrong, and learn from their experience.
- Customer satisfaction records. Records like these are increasingly available in our service-oriented economy. You can mine them for the pitfalls or triumphs of your predecessors, particularly when a previous project

generated either glowing praise or mountains of complaints from the customer.

Be Your Own Historian

You can be your own source of historical records in the future. Organize project documentation in such a way that it will be easy to reference long after the project has been finished.

Estimating Schedules and Budgets

Risk management contributes to detailed planning, but detailed planning is also an opportunity to discover risks. As part of the plan, each low-level task will require a cost and schedule estimate. When you are involved in this process, watch for those tasks that are difficult to estimate; this usually means that there is some uncertainty associated with it. Treat these individual tasks the same way you would any other risk: Identify the reason for the uncertainty and create a strategy for managing it.

The risks identified during scheduling and budgeting usually affect smaller parts of the project, but are important just the same. Managing the small risks as well as the big ones means that little things are less likely to trip you up.

Recognizing detailed planning as a risk management opportunity further emphasizes the iterative and unbreakable relationship between risk planning and schedule development.

Prioritize the Risks

If performed energetically, these risk identification activities will have created a long list of potential risks. However, many of these risks won't be worth managing—they'll have a low impact, low probability, or both. Without bothering to perform detailed analysis on these risks the project manager and team will still be able to use their intuition to quickly sort through the list to winnow out the risks it doesn't pay to worry about. That means the outcome of the risk identification process is a list of known risks that are worth studying and planning for.

DEVELOP RESPONSE PLANS

Not every risk will jeopardize a project. Some are no more than pebbles in a pond; they cause a ripple that quickly subsides. But others resemble an underwater earthquake that causes a tidal wave. Project managers must recognize the difference between the two. They must know how to discern the magnitude of the risk *and* how to develop an appropriate strategy to deal with it. This strategy is called *response development* and it has three components:

1. Defining the risk, including the severity of the negative impact.
2. Assigning a probability to the risk. How likely is it that this problem will occur?
3. Developing a strategy to reduce possible damage. This strategy will be based on the severity and probability of the risk.

Defining the Risk

Being able to concisely describe the risk is essential to understanding it. The Software Engineering Institute offers this simple but effective format for recording a risk.[3]

Condition: A brief statement describing the situation that is causing concern or uncertainty.

Consequence: A brief statement describing the possible negative outcomes that may be caused by the condition.

The more clearly the condition can be described, the more accurately the impact can be predicted—and the better chance there will be of effectively managing the risk. Here's an example of a poorly defined risk:

The project requires the use of technology that is new to the project team.

This statement doesn't give any clues to how badly the cost and schedule might be affected. The new technology should be named, and why it is causing uncertainty should be explained.

Here's a statement that does it better:

The state agency requires that all diagrams be developed using a software tool that our technical writers have not used before. In addition, the only boring machine that can handle the soil conditions is a complex product that has been used only a few times by our company.

Now that's getting more specific. In fact, we see that there are two separate risks associated with new technology. Each should be addressed separately. That will also make it easier to assess the impact, or consequences, that attempting to use the new technologies could have on the project.

After you have successfully defined the risks, you need to record the consequence of these risks in terms of cost, schedule, and possible damage to the project. Cost and schedule effects are tangible and can be matched against the original cost/benefit analysis, while damage refers to the intangible negative affect of a risk. Exhibit 6.5 and 6.6 are examples of risk statements in which the condition and the consequence have been clearly defined.

Just as the first rule of problem solving is to thoroughly understand the problem, the first rule of risk analysis is to thoroughly describe the risk.

EXHIBIT 6.5   Risk analysis example 1

Definition

Condition: The soil conditions in the area where the pipeline crosses the river require a complex boring machine with which we have little experience.

Consequence: Incorrectly operating the machine will damage it and/or the riverbank. Damage to the machine could cost from $50,000 to $250,000 in repairs and 2 to 4 weeks in lost time. Damaging the riverbank may result in landowners or environmental groups trying to prevent us from obtaining permits for future pipelines.

Probability

Probability of $75K equipment damage—20%

Probability of $200K equipment damage—20%

Probability of no equipment damage—60%

Probable cost of equipment damage—$55K

Probability of riverbank damage—25%

Strategy

The equipment provider will supply an operator for an estimated cost of $10,000. Using their operator reduces the chance of equipment damage to less than 5% and they will bear the cost of repair. The probability of riverbank damage is also reduced to 5%.

- The probability was determined from the experience of this company and interviews with two other companies who use the product.
- Probable cost of damage = ($75K × 20%) + ($200K × 20%)
- The strategy add $10,000 to the project cost but reduces the risk of cost damage to zero and the schedule risk to less than 5%. The risk of intangible cost because of riverbank damage is also reduced.
- The strategy is described in two project management tools:
  1. Communication plan—Includes increased monitoring and coordination activities with the equipment vendor.
  2. Project plan—Shows the equipment vendor as the resource on the task and the additional $10,000 in labor.
- This risk strategy is referred to as "risk transfer" because the project paid the equipment operator to take the risk.

Using Probability Theory in Risk Management

What are the chances of getting a six when rolling a single die? The math is pretty simple. There are six sides and all have an equal chance of being on top, so the probability is one out of six, or 0.167. How many houses in a specific area are likely to have flood damage in a year? An insurance company will count the number of houses in the area that have had flood damage in the past to predict flood damage in the future. What are the chances of falling behind on your project because a subcontractor didn't come through? That's a little bit harder to quantify, but it's part of our job when we're analyzing risk.

EXHIBIT 6.6   Risk analysis example 2

Definition

Condition: The state agency requires that all diagrams be developed using a software tool that our technical writers have not used before.

Consequence: All diagram generation and document management tasks will take longer. Limitations of the tool will cause rework.

Probability

On average, the slower work and the rework will add up to 25% more effort on documentation tasks.

Probable labor cost: $1.25 \times 20 = 25$ labor months

Probable schedule: 1.25×4 months $= 5$ months

Strategy

Send all the technical writers to a 2-day course on the new tool. The training cost is $2,200. This will reduce the productivity factor to 1.1.

Make one of the technical writers the tool expert. It will be his or her job to spend an average of 1 day each week to exercise the tool to find its limitations and to create standards and templates to build on its strengths. This will bring the productivity factor down to 1.0.

The tool expert will spend 5 labor days to create document management strategies that ensure a smooth production process and eliminate rework.

- The probability is a subjective estimate based on the average normal productivity of a junior technical writer versus a senior technical writer. Since all writers will be new to the tool, all are assigned the junior productivity factor.

- The normal cost for the required documentation is 20 labor months and the normal duration is 4 months.

- The strategy is to shorten the learning curve. It will cost 2 days of training (duration) and the time spent by the tool expert on experimentation adds a cost of 21 days (1 day a week for 4 months plus 5 days). So the new tool's duration consequence is cut to 5 days and the cost consequence is 21 days labor plus the cost of training.

- The strategy is described in the project documentation: Project plan—Shows the cost and duration of training and who will attend. Tasks are added for experimenting with the tool and developing tool standards. These additional tasks result in increased labor costs.

Predicting the likelihood that a problem will occur contains the same difficulties as making any estimate. Many of the same rules apply to both. Looking at historical data will generally give the best indication of possible problems. But even when experienced project managers use all the tools at their disposal, assigning probabilities to a risk remains as much an art as a science. The sheer number of possible problems, including those that are intangible and impossible to quantify, requires that a project manager use creativity and intuition as well as knowledge and experience in assessing risks.

There is a temptation to flee from the hard work of developing a probability estimate for each risk. Often times the hard data that makes statistical analysis possible just doesn't exist. Why worry about the infinite number of possible problems your project could encounter? That is exactly the point: because there are an infinite number of possible risks to your project it is necessary to quantify the known risks in order to prioritize them and establish a budget for managing them.

Assigning a probability to the risk helps to assess the consequences of the risk. If you multiply the probability of a risk by the negative consequences you will begin to see how bad the risk really is. This is often referred to as the *expected value* of the risk:

Probability × Impact = Expected value

The example in Exhibit 6.5 defines probability in terms of percentages to predict the probable cost of the damages. That means the expected value of the risk is $55,000. Understanding the expected value will influence the amount spent reducing the risk.

Even when there is absolutely no hard data available about a risk, the project manager can distill the intuition of the team to provide useful assessments of probability and impact. A common method (illustrated in Exhibit 6.7) is to use a consistent probability and impact matrix throughout the project. It uses subjective assessments to place risks in one of nine quadrants. Key components of using this subjective assessment are:

- The same matrix must be used throughout the project since the method relies on subjective judgment. This allows team members to adjust their thinking to a consistent reference point.
- It is okay to make a larger matrix. Again, make sure the same matrix is used throughout the project.

**EXHIBIT 6.7   Assign probability and
impact to known risks**

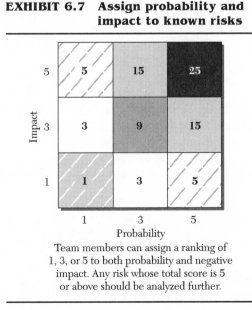

Team members can assign a ranking of
1, 3, or 5 to both probability and negative
impact. Any risk whose total score is 5
or above should be analyzed further.

- Continue to use objective data to quantify both probability and impact whenever possible, then place that risk in one of the quadrants. Using objective data for reference points makes the subjective judgments more consistent.

- Have a diverse group of project stakeholders assess the risks then merge their assessments. If only the project manager is rating probability and impact, the ratings will be skewed by his or her unique perspective and risk tolerance.

Some risks have less to do with a specific event and more to do with the project's environment and its effect on productivity. For instance, the entire risk profile developed by the Software Engineering Institute addresses environmental risk factors such as the possible changes in requirements for a project, how skilled the project team may be, and the diversity of the user community.[4]

Assigning a probability to risks from the project's environment again relies on intuition and experience. You need to ask the right questions: How good are the team's skills and how much faster or slower will it make them? How strong is the business case for the project and how many major changes in requirements will happen? Because these factors are intangible, they are hard to assess, but if risk management is practiced systematically on all projects, at least there will be a record of how skillfully a manager used his or her intuition. This feedback will aid in making future risk assignments more accurate.

The combination of subjective and objective assessments of known risks enables the team to produce a new ranked list. The risks at the top will receive attention first and the risks at the bottom of the list will be addressed later. Some low priority risks may even be removed from the *actively managed* list (also known as the *risk log*, which will be discussed in the next section) (Exhibit 6.9).

How to Reduce Risk

Up to now, we have concentrated on assessing and quantifying the risks to a project's success. The time has come to develop strategies for dealing with these risks. This is the difficult part because there are as many ways to reduce risks as there are potential risks.

What is the best way to reduce a risk? The answer lies in the method we have discussed for assessing a risk: reduce the impact, probability, or both. For instance:

- If an event is out of my control but I can prepare for that event, then I have reduced the impact (Exhibit 6.8). That is why I take a first aid kit on a camping trip.

- In risk example in Exhibit 6.5, hiring an expert to operate a complex machine reduces the probability of an accident.

EXHIBIT 6.8   Risk beyond the project's control

Definition

   Condition: The product design calls for a computer operating system that is yet to be released, and the manufacturer has a reputation for releasing unreliable products late.

   Consequence: If the product doesn't meet specifications, custom software will have to be written. If the product is late, the entire project will be delayed.

Probability

Probability of the product having defects that affect the project is 15%.

Probability of the product being 1 month late (enough to negatively impact our project) is 30%.

Strategy

1. **Avoid:**   Choose a new design that relies on stable technology.
2. **Monitor:**   Get on the beta test team to have early access to the software and thoroughly test the features that affect the project. Two months prior to the planned product release, assess the probability of the risk and have an alternative design ready.

Two possible strategies are listed. Each results in changes to project documentation:

1. Avoid
   - Project plan—Shows the new design and development tasks and the associated increase in cost and schedule.
   - Product requirements—Document any changes in the product's capability.

2. Monitor
   - Communication plan—Includes monitoring the beta test results and reporting them.
   - Project plan—Shows the additional activities for the beta test and development of the contingency design.

    There are basically five categories of classic risk reduction strategies: accepting, avoiding, monitoring, transferring, and mitigating the risk. Let's look at these in detail.

1.   Accepting the Risk

Accepting the risk means you understand the risk, its consequences, and probability, and you choose to do nothing about it. If the risk occurs, the project team will react. This is a common strategy when the consequences or probability that a problem will occur are minimal. As long as the consequences are cheaper than the cure, this strategy makes sense.

2.   Avoid the Risk

You can avoid a risk by choosing not to do part of the project. This deletion of part of the project could affect more than the project—the business risk could also be affected. Changing the scope of the project might change the business case as well, because a scaled-down product could have smaller revenue or cost-saving opportunities (see Exhibit 6.8). "Risk/return" is a popular expression in finance—if you want a high return on an investment, you'll probably have to take more risk. Avoiding risks on projects can have the same effect— low risk, low return.

3. Monitor the Risk and Prepare Contingency Plans

Monitor a risk by choosing some predictive indicator to watch as the project nears the risk point. For example, if you are concerned about a subcontractor's performance, set frequent status update points early in the project and inspect his or her progress. The risk strategy in Exhibit 6.8 is to monitor the risk by being part of the test team.

Contingency plans are alternative courses of action prepared before the risk event occurs. The most common contingency plan is to set aside extra money, a *contingency fund,* to draw on in the event of unforeseen cost overruns. It's important to make sure that this fund is used only for unforeseen cost overruns—not to make up for underestimating or substandard performance. Exhibit 6.8 contains an example of a contingency—the project team is betting on a new technology, but they are also creating an alternative design that uses more stable technology. If it looks like the new technology isn't going to be workable, the team will have an alternative in place. It's important to note here that creating the alternative design probably costs a substantial amount. Contingency plans can be looked on as a kind of insurance and, like insurance policies, they can be expensive.

When using this *monitor-and-be-prepared-to-act* strategy, two factors should be included in the risk response plan: detectability and trigger events:

- A tricky factor in monitoring a risk is the ability to detect the risk in time to respond. For example, hurricane response procedures rely on the fact that most hurricanes can be tracked for several days as they develop over the ocean. Knowing the speed and intensity of the storm gives authorities time to broadcast instructions to local residents. Conversely, a tornado can form, touch down, and wreak havoc virtually without notice. For a known risk within the project, the team should assess the *detectability* using a subjective scale (such as 1–5 where 5 is very difficult to detect). The effort invested in monitoring the risk will reflect the probability, impact, and ability to detect. If a risk is particularly difficult to detect and the impact and probability is large, it probably justifies plenty of mitigation as well as contingency preparation.

- Trigger events define the line we cross between monitoring the risk and implementing the contingency plan. Trigger events are described as objectively as possible, so it is clear when we've arrived at one. The reason for trigger events is illustrated in a well-known story: If a frog jumps into a pan of boiling water, it will immediately jump out. But if a frog is sitting in a cool pan of water that is placed on a stove it will stay in the water until it is boiled to death. Trigger events help us recognize when the water in our project is *too hot* and we need to take action. The monitoring strategy in Exhibit 6.8 has a *trigger date* set to monitor the risk and make a decision about whether to implement the contingency.

4. Transfer the Risk

Even though paying for insurance may be expensive, assuming all the risks yourself could cost a great deal more. Many large projects purchase insurance for a variety of risks, ranging from theft to fire. By doing this, they have effectively *transferred risk* to the insurance company in that, if a disaster should occur, the insurance company will pay for it.

While purchasing insurance is the most direct method of transferring risk, there are others. For example, hiring an expert to do the work can also transfer risk. In one example (see Exhibit 6.5) the project manager was concerned that a piece of heavy equipment operated by the project team would be damaged—or would damage the job site. Her solution was to hire an operator from the company leasing the equipment. Because this operator works for the equipment leasing company, the leasing company would pay for any damage to the equipment or to the site.

Another way to transfer risk is to use a contract for service, in this case, a *fixed-price contract.* A fixed-price contract states that the work will be done for an amount specified before the work begins. Fixed schedules may also be added to such a contract, with penalties for overruns. With fixed-price contracts, project managers know exactly what the cost of this part of a project will be. They have effectively transferred the cost and schedule risks from the project to the subcontracting firm; any overruns will be the responsibility of the subcontractor. (The only downside to this scenario is that the subcontractor, knowing it will be held to the original bid, will probably make the bid higher to make up for the risk it is assuming.)

Another type of contract for service is called a *reimbursable,* or *cost-plus,* contract. Reimbursable contracts pay subcontractors based on the labor, equipment, and materials they use on a project.[5] The risk of cost and schedule overruns is borne completely by the project on these contracts. The project is not able to transfer risk with this kind of contract, but when the work to be performed is poorly defined, or the type of service is open-ended, a reimbursable contract is the only type a subcontractor will sign.

Clearly, transferring risk to another party has advantages but also introduces new risks. A major component of this strategy is effective contracting and subcontractor management—topics beyond the scope of this chapter.

5. Mitigate the Risk

Mitigate is jargon for "work hard at reducing the risk." The risk strategy in Exhibit 6.6 includes several ways to mitigate, or reduce, the productivity loss associated with using a new software tool. Mitigation covers nearly all the actions the project team can take to overcome risks from the project environment.

TIPS FOR DEVELOPING RISK STRATEGIES

The first step in determining a response to a possible problem is to identify those risks that are within the control of the project team—and those that are not. Here are a few examples of each kind of risk:

- Federal laws and regulations that affect your project are beyond your control. Labor disputes that cause some or all of your team to walk off the job are up to the company to handle. Who controls the weather? When the risk is beyond your control you generally have two options: Avoid it or monitor it and prepare a contingency plan.
- The behavior of the project team is within the team's control. For example, a breakdown in communication can be solved by changing the way the team communicates. Other challenges such as design or staffing problems can also be overcome by changing the way the team works.

Beware that for each risk problem solved, a new risk might appear. For instance, if you contract out specialized work, this can reduce risk by transferring it the subcontractor. But subcontracting can reduce control over the project and increase communication difficulties. In addition, you will need to develop a strategy for managing the subcontractor. What all this means is that you need to weigh the advantages and disadvantages of each proposed risk strategy very carefully.

PRODUCE A RISK MANAGEMENT PLAN

The analysis and strategies generated during risk identification and response development must be recorded. The most common method is to produce a risk management plan that has four primary components:

1. *Risk log:* This is the list of actively managed risks (see Exhibit 6.9) in order of priority. You'll notice that the information in the risk log is a summary of the analysis performed on the high priority risks. That analysis should be maintained in a way that makes it easy to retrieve should any risk need to be re-evaluated or if a contingency plan needs to be executed.
2. *Low-priority risk list:* These are risks that have been identified in the past but were judged as having too low an impact or probability to further analyze. We keep this list because it is re-evaluated during future risk identification activities.

3. *Schedule for risk management activities;* These are the ongoing risk management activities we'll perform throughout the project. See the next section on continuous risk management for more detail.

4. *Risk summary report:* This is the information you'll be passing upward to your management team during the project. It typically lists the near-term risks, risks needing executive action, the current contingency and reserve amounts, and recently retired risks.

In addition to the risk management plan, it is important to remember that risk management strategies affect other project management documents (see Exhibit 6.1). For instance, shifting responsibilities among stakeholders to reduce a risk should be reflected in the responsibility matrix. Risk mitigation activities such as the strategy of developing two product designs, described in Exhibit 6.8, result in additional tasks that will be added to the work breakdown structure, project schedule, and performance budget. Since the statement of work contains the overall project goals and constraints, it is also likely to be changed as a result of some risk management strategies.

ESTABLISH CONTINGENCY AND RESERVE

The notion of a rainy day fund is an old one. On a regular basis we set aside money—usually a small amount—in a sugar bowl or bank account, earmarked for that rainy day when things go wrong. When the car suddenly needs a new transmission, the refrigerator dies, or some other unpredictable malady strikes, we have the funds available to handle it. Some consider it the act of a cautious person; others maintain it is just common sense—something any responsible person would do. In project risk management terms these are called contingency and reserve funds and it is absolutely the responsibility of the project manager and the sponsor to establish these accounts.

We have established that the risks recorded in our risk log are known-unknowns; we know about them but we can't predict with certainty what will happen to them. To prepare for these risks we have several strategies available, some of which call for preparing a contingency plan—a plan that we will execute if the risk materializes. It makes sense that these contingency plans must be funded in advance, but it is not clear how much money should be set aside—after all, it is statistically unlikely that every contingency plan will be executed. Here are four steps you can follow to produce a reasonable contingency budget:

1. Identify all the risks in the risk log where your strategy is to monitor the risk and prepare a contingency plan.

2. For each of these risks, estimate the additional cost of executing the contingency plan. If you total the cost of all the contingency plans, that is the amount you'd set aside if the probability for each of these risks was 100

EXHIBIT 6.9   Monitor risks using a risk log

Risk ID	Priority	Date Found	Responsible Person	Description	Strategy	Current Status (As of 6/12)
7	1	5/12	J. Daniels	The product design calls for a computer operating system that is yet to be released, and the manufacturer has a reputation for releasing unreliable products late.	1. Get on the beta test team. Test features affecting the project. 2. Assess the probability of the risk on 7/14. 3. Have an alternate design ready.	1. Beta versions are very unpredictable. New beta due 6/15. **Risk: High.** 2. Meeting scheduled. 3. Have identified alternative software. Design will be ready on 7/14.
2	2	5/7	F. Oak	The state agency requires that all diagrams be developed using a software tool that our technical writers have not used before.	1. Send all technical writers to training. 2. F. Oak is creating standards and templates to build on its strengths. 3. F. Oak will create document management strategies.	1. Completed 6/2. Improving learning curve. 2. Completed 6/10. Templates and standards are effective. 3. Having trouble with document merging. Working with product representative to solve. **Risk: Medium.**
12	3	7/7	J. Barnes	Soil conditions require a complex boring machine that we are likely to damage.	The equipment provider will supply an operator for an estimated cost of $10,000.	Operator and equipment are contracted and scheduled. **Risk: Low.**

202

percent. But the probability for each risk isn't 100 percent, so derive an expected value of the contingency for each risk by multiplying the probability the risk will occur times the cost of the contingency plan (Expected value of contingency = Cost of contingency × Probability of risk event).

3. Sum the expected value of contingency for each of these risks. That will produce a number that executive management will choke on because nobody could conceive of so many things going wrong on a project. This is where the negotiation begins.

4. There is no good guy or bad guy in this negotiation. Set aside too much money, and you are denying funds to other legitimate projects from which the firm could benefit. Set aside too little money and when known risks materialize you won't be able to fund a response. All parties to this negotiation should have the same goal in mind—to prepare for the known risks. All parties face the same challenge—they are forecasting the future.

Contingency reserves account for identified risks, known-unknowns. Management reserve accounts for the unknown-unknowns. As we've said before, the unknown-unknowns are the events that we didn't see coming. No project, no matter how diligent the risk identification actions, will avoid the unknown-unknowns. Therefore, like our rainy day fund, we set aside a specific amount, earmarked to be spent on reacting to unforeseeable obstacles that arise during the project. How much do you budget for the unknown? Firms that consistently establish a management reserve for projects will tell you that over time a certain percentage of the performance budget (the budget based on the work breakdown structure) emerges as the right amount. High risk industries such as software development may add as much as 30 percent to the budget. More predictable projects will use an amount closer to 5 percent of the performance budget. The key to establishing management reserve is to do it consistently for every project and at the end of the project to determine how much was spent. Over multiple similar projects an acceptable range will appear.

Management and contingency reserves add to the total budget for the project. That means the original business case should be re-evaluated, particularly if there was no allocation for risk in the original estimates. If the numbers still hold up, the probability that the project can meet financial goals just increased.

CONTINUOUS RISK MANAGEMENT

No matter how rigorous, thorough, and diligent the initial risk planning activities, it is the ongoing risk management activities that ultimately put the plans in motion and produce the results. The continuous risk management activities fall into three categories: ongoing risk planning, performance of specific risk response plans, and reporting risk status to management. This section explores each of these activities in detail.

Ongoing Risk Planning

Our risk plan is based on the best information available when the project began. As the project is performed, new information emerges—some favorable and some unfavorable. From a risk management perspective, we want to know how that affects our known risks and whether any new risks emerge. Therefore, the project team should schedule the following activities on a regular basis:

- *Monitor known risks.* Each known risk has a probability and expected time frame. Since there is a person responsible for each risk, we can ask that person to stay aware of the factors affecting the probability of the risk, particularly as the time frame for the risk event nears. Each risk in the risk log can simply be updated before every project status meeting to reflect the most recent information—even if that means no change.
- *Check for new risks at regular status meetings.* Add a standing item to the project team meeting to ask for new risks. This activity won't have the same level of thoroughness that the first risk identification activities had, but by routinely asking for new risks the project develops a climate of risk awareness. When team members do sense a risk they'll know where to report it.
- *Repeat the major risk identification activities at preplanned milestones within the project.* These can be temporal, such as every six to nine weeks, or at the beginning of a new phase. The key is that these are planned in advance and that they are actually performed, otherwise it isn't likely to happen. If there is reluctance on the part of project team members to repeat these activities during the project, remember that investing in risk identification is the ounce of prevention. During these activities you will look for new risks and revisit the list of low-priority risks that were previously identified to see if their probability or impact has risen.
- When new risks are identified, prepare response plans and check whether sufficient contingency or management reserve exists.

Perform Risk Response Plans

It almost goes without saying that you have to implement the risk response strategy, but there are a few guidelines worth noting:

- Whether the response was mitigation, monitoring, transfer, or avoidance, it resulted in some specific tasks that can be tied to the work breakdown structure and/or project schedule. By tying the response plan into the project schedule, you increase the likelihood the plan will be executed.

- When a risk event occurs, invoke the contingency plan. Make sure that the additional costs associated with reacting to the risk are drawn from the contingency reserve.
- Some risks don't materialize. When that happens, retire them from the risk log but be sure to record why they didn't materialize—was it good luck or good risk management?

Reporting Risk Status

Involving management in the project is always a good idea. The more they know about the project, the better able they are to support the project team. So add some risk management information to your regular status report or produce a risk summary report with the following information:

- *Near-term risks.* The team will confront these in the next two reporting periods. By including these, the project manager ensures his or her management won't be caught off guard if one of these risks occur.
- *Risks needing executive action.* If management has the capability to reduce the probability or impact of a risk, make sure that is clearly communicated.
- *The current contingency and management reserve amounts.* If the project is using more or less contingency or management reserve than planned, management may want to either increase the reserves or take some of that reserve and allocate it to other uses.
- *Recently retired or experienced risks.* Management will want to know what happened to the risks that were near term on the last few reports.

Continuous risk management is essentially the practice of repeating the major risk management processes throughout the life of the project. Through constant vigilance we continuously find problems before they find us.

SUMMARY

When Meriwether Lewis and William Clark led their Corps of Discovery up the Missouri River, they did not know what they would find, or to be more precise, they did not know *exactly* what they would find. So, they prepared as best they could for all the eventualities they imagined. As they traveled westward they never ceased to query the travelers they met or the native peoples they encountered to learn more about the journey ahead.

Modern day project managers and the executives of project-driven organizations can benefit from the same risk management attitude displayed by Lewis and Clark. We must confront risk as a reality of the project environment; yet we do not let risks deter us from our goal. Systematic assessment of possible problems and reasoned responses are common sense and the epitome of proactive, success-oriented leadership.

NOTES

1. Barbara Fifer and Vicky Soderberg, *Along the Trail with Lewis and Clark* (Great Falls, MT: Montana Magazine, 1998).

2. Software Engineering Institute, *Continuous Risk Management Guidebook* (Pittsburgh, PA: Software Engineering Institute, 1996), pp. 439–442.

3. See note 2.

4. See note 2.

5. R. Max Wideman, ed., *Project and Program Risk Management* (Newtown Square, PA: Project Management Institute, 1992).

7 QUALITY, QUALITY MANAGEMENT, AND PROJECT MANAGEMENT

Ned Hamson

Project managers, quality managers, CEOs, in fact, all managers have questions that wake them up in the middle of the night in a cold sweat:

Are we doing the right thing?

Are we doing the right thing, right—correctly?

Are we getting any better, can we get better?

Can we be the leader? Can we leapfrog the pack?

Am I doing the right things—right for my customers, my employees, my stockholders, my career?

Not you? Then perhaps you recognize yourself or your firm in one or more of the following statements. If you've run into any of these or similar problems, quality management has much to offer you and your projects:

We delivered a knock-their-socks-off product but were completely surprised when the customer blew his stack. *You delivered what he asked for but not what he needed.*

A reputation for getting the job done always won business for you in the past. *Now, however, competitors, are winning* your contracts *on the strength of their processes.*

The weak link in your organization was small in comparison to the whole project. *However, that small, weak link brought a huge project to a dead stop.*

Your engineers are constantly frustrated because they want to build the absolute best (complex, finely tuned, and "worth" the added cost). *Sales and marketing keep saying: "To our customers, quality means simpler and less expensive."*

If you recognized your organization or some of your own project manager experience in one of these statements, you are now ready to see what quality management can do for you.

This chapter demonstrates how quality management (which, like project management, is a well-established discipline) will help you by improving your ability to manage the processes that enable you to meet your customers' requirements within the time and budgets allotted. This chapter is divided into six sections. The first section discusses why quality management is critical to project management; the second section covers the overarching principles and perspectives of quality management as encapsulated by its gurus and then distilled into global standards. The final four sections address specific components of quality management and their application in the project environment. The four components of quality management are:

1. Establishing customer requirements.
2. Designing and managing systems and processes.
3. Continuously improving processes and systems in a cost-effective manner.
4. Innovating—creating new ways to satisfy customers.

Given quality management's broad scope, we have selected a set of field-tested and robust techniques—some larger and more complex, others simple to understand and apply—that are most applicable as means to overcoming the most common project management challenges.

WHAT IS QUALITY MANAGEMENT?

Many people associate quality improvement and quality management with continuous or repetitive manufacturing or service processes and products. Companies and products that come to mind include Shell, Exxon, Dodge Trucks, Honda, BMW, Sony Walkman, Phillips, Gold Star TVs, Gateway, Macintosh, Dell, Burger King, Coors, Pepsi, and Taco Bell. The work takes place on an assembly line, in a steel mill, in a bank, at a hotel, or at a fast-food drive through.

The early quality management adopters in the United States (Ford: "Quality Is Job One") began their quality journeys during the early 1980s in response to Japan's (and the other Asian Tigers—Taiwan, South Korea, etc.) taking significant market share or dominating the markets of the Big Three Detroit automakers, Pittsburgh Steel, and coast-to-coast producers of high-end consumer technology products (cameras, watches, televisions, radios, stereos, tape decks, and VCRs). The masters of the "new game" of high quality, high productivity, and low cost were (and to a great extent still are) Toyota, Nissan, Canon, Nikon, Minolta, Panasonic, Honda, Gold Star, Daewoo, and Mitsubishi.

How do these firms, all in mass production, relate to project management? All these firms are as good at the project management part of their businesses as they are at cranking out hundreds of thousands of production units. The projects, or project management, in which they excel range from research and design, to product development activities, planning and building new assembly lines, to thousands of quality improvement projects. And they all excel in the first and most important step in project management and production management—determining with great precision the end-use customer's requirements and the requirements of other stakeholders.

Quality management has had fad phases in the same way as other advances in modern management such as industrial engineering, customer satisfaction research, human resources management, and project management. The firms noted as quality leaders and firms similar to them have neither "dropped" nor discarded quality management; they have incorporated quality management into how they manage success. Even though quality managed firms have their ups and downs in how well they apply these principles and techniques, they consider quality management as basic to staying in business today and tomorrow.

Quality management can help you be a better project manager, leader, or company in the same manner as it vaulted Toyota, Mitsubishi, and Sony into world-class status for three specific reasons:

1. Quality management enables you to be globally competitive. Global competition really is global and reaches into your local or regional market. Firms that pioneered applying modern quality methods to reach world-class status are also involved in project-based work and products. Kawasaki, Mitsubishi, Hyundai, and Samsung compete globally as both mass production and project-based organizations. Three of the *Forbes* Top Ten Companies in the world—BP, Royal Dutch/Shell Group, and Nippon Tel & Tel—are heavily involved in either selling or buying project management services. All of these firms count on quality management to fuel their productivity and quality, as well as that of their suppliers. The long and short of answering whether quality and quality management should be of concern to you is this: Whether you manage and work on projects in your firm or your firm is a project-based firm, your current and future competitors are using quality and quality management to gain and maintain a competitive edge.

2. Quality management enables you to match the competition from those certified as being quality competent. If your competitor is saying: "We are better at project management (a better buy and a better completed project) than you are because we are registered to the world quality management standard, ISO 9000–2000" (see Box 7.2 for an explanation of ISO 9000–2000), and some of your present customers are ready to leave because they want that assurance or security, quality management is not just important, it is a requirement to stay

in business. More than 500,000 firms are now registered as meeting ISO 9000–2000 (or one of its industry-specific variants—telecommunications, aerospace, and finance). If your firm is in a supply chain in which the supply chain leader requires all suppliers to meet corporate or group quality standards, your success as a project leader and manager is based in part on your knowledge and experience with quality management. Just two years ago, Boeing restructured its quality management system and informed its suppliers: "All Boeing sites shall have a quality management system compliant to the new standard . . . ISO 9000 as supplemented by SAE AS9100."[1]

3. Quality management can help you solve chronic project management problems. Quality management offers tools and approaches to better address and, in many cases, overcome common and chronic project management headaches. Quality management offers specific methods to determine customers' requirements, specify how to meet those requirements, manage systems and processes to produce those requirements, solve problems that crop up, improve your processes as your project proceeds to final delivery, and help you better manage reinventing or innovating on your offer to the market as a project-based firm.

Quality management's offer to a project manager can be summarized in three points:

1. It can improve your ability to specify and meet customer requirements.
2. It can make your job easier. Using quality methods helps reduce errors, waste, and rework, which makes you more productive and improves work satisfaction by reducing significant "hassle" factors in your work environment.
3. It can increase your marketability. Using quality methods improves your ability to manage and improve project performance.

AN OVERVIEW OF QUALITY MANAGEMENT

Each field has its leaders and gurus. There are seemingly endless discussions about who is a leader and who isn't. The quality management field is no different. There are, however, the vital few, those whom most quality management professionals would list if asked to name the top four who have most influenced the practice of quality management. In addition, there are leaders whose influence and perspective gave form to the default global quality management standard—ISO 9000–2000. The vital few quality management leaders are W. Edwards Deming, Phil Crosby, Armand V. Feigenbaum, and Joseph Juran.

A brief sketch of each leader's contribution follows, along with a ready reference chart of each one's quality management system is shown in Box 7.1.

In addition to these four quality giants, a number of others have had significant impact on quality management, especially as applied in manufacturing.

Box 7.1

Deming, Crosby, Feigenbaum, and Juran Compared

W. Edwards Deming

Quality is continuous improvement through reduced variation.

Deming's Five Principles

1. The central problem in lack of quality is the failure of management to understand variation. (Everything varies. Statistics help us to predict how much variation there will be.)
2. It is management's responsibility to know whether the problems are in the system or in the behavior of the people.
3. Teamwork should be based on knowledge, design, redesign. Constant improvement is management's responsibility. Most causes of low quality and productivity belong to the system.
4. Train people until they are achieving as much as they can (within the limits of the system you are using).
5. It is management's responsibility to give detailed specifications.

Deming's 14 Points

1. Create constancy of purpose toward improvement of product and service with a plan to stay in business and to provide jobs.
2. Adopt a new philosophy. We can no longer live with commonly accepted levels of delays, mistakes, defective materials, and defective workmanship.
3. Cease dependence on mass inspection. Require statistical evidence that quality is built in.
4. End the practice of awarding business based on price tag alone.
5. Improve constantly and forever the system of production and service. It is management's job to work continually on the system.
6. Institute a vigorous program of education and retraining.
7. Adopt and institute leadership. The responsibility of supervision must be changed from sheer numbers to quality. Improvement of quality automatically improves productivity.
8. Drive out fear so that everyone may work effectively for the company.

(continued)

9. Break down barriers between departments. People must work as a team to foresee problems of production that may be encountered with various materials and specifications.

10. Eliminate numerical goals, posters, and slogans that ask for new levels of productivity without providing new methods.

11. Eliminate work standards that prescribe numerical quotas.

12. Remove barriers that stand between the hourly worker and his or her right to pride of workmanship.

13. Encourage education and self-improvement for everyone.

14. Create a structure in top management that pushes every day on the previous 13 points.

Philip B. Crosby

Quality is conformance to requirements.

The Four Absolutes of Quality Management

1. The definition of quality is conformance to requirements.
2. The system of quality is prevention.
3. The performance standard is zero defects.
4. The measurement of quality is the price of nonconformance.

14-Step Quality Improvement Plan

1. Management commitment is defined, created, and exhibited.
2. Quality improvement team is formed.
3. Measurement to determine areas for improvement.
4. Cost of quality measures is developed as a stimulus.
5. Quality awareness is created in everyone.
6. Corrective action is taken on problems previously identified.
7. Zero defects planning.
8. Education of all employees in the company.
9. Zero-defects day is held to let all employees know there has been a change.
10. Goal setting for individuals and groups.
11. Error cause removal by employees sharing with management the obstacles they face in attaining goals.
12. Recognition for those who participated.
13. Quality councils to communicate regularly.
14. Do it all again to emphasize quality improvement never ends.

Armand V. Feigenbaum

Quality is what the buyer wants and needs to satisfy his or her requirements for use, not what the manufacturer wants (to accommodate some internal operating purpose or need).

Five Steps to Excellence in Product Development

1. Make quality a full and equal partner with innovation from the beginning of product development.
2. Focus on customer inputs as the fundamental basis for specifications.
3. Emphasize getting high-quality product design and process matches upstream.
4. Make full-service component suppliers a quality partner at the beginning of design rather than a quality surveillance problem later.
5. Make the acceleration of new product introduction a primary measure of the effectiveness of a quality program.

Joseph M. Juran

Quality is fitness for use.

The Quality Trilogy

1. Quality improvement.
2. Quality planning.
3. Quality control.

Ten Steps in the Quality Improvement Process

1. Build awareness of the need and opportunity for improvement.
2. Set goals for improvement.
3. Organize to reach the goals.
4. Provide training throughout the organization.
5. Carry out projects to solve problems.
6. Report progress.
7. Give recognition.
8. Communicate results.
9. Keep score.
10. Maintain momentum by making annual improvement part of the regular systems and processes of the company.

Source: Adapted from "Three Paths, One Journey," Steve Gibbons—The Principal Financial Group, *Journal for Quality and Participation* (October/November 1994); articles by Armand V. Feigenbaum in *Journal for Quality and Participation* (1988–1996).

They and their tools or contributions are noted where appropriate in the discussion of each of the four components later in the chapter.

THE GIANTS OF QUALITY MANAGEMENT

W. Edwards Deming

Americans became concerned with *quality* when it became obvious, after the 1970s oil shortage crisis, that American automakers were not losing market share to Japanese automakers just because Japan's autos were fuel efficient and inexpensive. The Big Three were being challenged by price, fuel efficiency, and noticeably higher average "fit and finish" quality, which customers noticed and cared about.

Dr. Deming, as most people addressed him, became known as *the* quality expert after NBC televised a special titled, "If Japan Can, Why Can't We?" on June 24, 1980. The program featured Deming as the American who introduced quality to Japan, and it showed how his quality approach fueled Japan's remarkable recovery from the devastation of World War II. As a result of that television program and Deming's work with Ford and General Motors, thousands of quality control engineers and technicians were introduced to quality management, and managers from many areas of specialty with an interest in improved productivity or reducing waste and errors were introduced to the concept of statistical quality control—variation—an elegantly simple decision-making/problem-solving method *Plan, Do, Study/Check, Act* known as *PDSA* by Deming purists and *PDCA* by many others. In addition, Deming introduced his 14 points of quality management. Deming's students and enthusiasts then introduced his system to thousands of organizations in the United States with varying degrees of success. Following his death in 1993, students and supporters of his approach established the Deming Institute, founded to carry on dissemination of his approaches to quality improvement.

Phillip B. Crosby

Phil Crosby entered the quality scene in 1979 with his best-selling book *Quality Is Free*. In a number of talks with Crosby, I learned that his work with the military, via the Pershing missile project at Martin Marietta Corp., and his work for the conglomerate ITT were the biggest influences on his approaches to not only improving quality but imbedding it into a firm's management system, rather than considering it an add-on activity. His Quality College trained more than 20,000 GM managers in the 1980s. His definition of quality—conformance to requirements—not only turns focus to the customer, but it is sufficiently strategic that ISO adopted it as its definition for quality in 1994. Crosby's concept of *Zero Defects* is one of the major points in Boeing's

1999/2000 Quality-First Environment ("Simplify and supplement the design engineering and manufacturing processes into a zero-defects paradigm").

Armand V. Feigenbaum

Dr. Armand V. Feigenbaum is a leading exponent of seeing the firm as a whole system—the responsibility for quality extends well beyond the manufacturing department. From 1958 to 1968, Feigenbaum was worldwide director of manufacturing operations and quality control at General Electric Company before becoming president of General Systems Company Inc. Feigenbaum's idea that every function in the organization is responsible for quality became known as total quality control (TQC).

Joseph M. Juran

Dr. Joseph M. Juran began his work and interest in quality in 1924, when he joined the inspection department at Bell Telephone's Hawthorne Works. Working in the Bell System, Juran was personally involved in applying statistical approaches in the production of telephone equipment. Juran visited Japan in 1954 and assisted Japanese leaders in taking charge of restructuring their industries for exporting to world markets. He helped the Japanese adapt the quality concepts and tools designed primarily for the factory into a series of concepts that would become the basis for an overall management process.

Each of these leaders' systems has separately and together influenced how thousands of organizations implemented quality management systems from the 1950s through the late 1980s. During the mid-1980s, leaders of standards organizations around the world began discussing whether an international quality management standard would benefit the world economy and how they would construct a standard that could be applied in virtually any organizational setting. Their process was to distill the thought and practice of the leaders into a manageable set of principles. ISO 9000–2000 is version two of that distillation; the first version was released in 1994.

As you read the principles that make up the ISO 9000–2000 "generic" quality management map (Box 7.2), you should be able to see or hear the voices of each of these leaders in the ISO 9000 system for quality management. We have further distilled this set of quality principles into the four overarching activities of quality management: determining customer requirements, designing and managing systems and processes, continuously improving systems and processes, and innovating.

What Is Quality?

The most used definition of quality is derived from Dr. Juran's "fitness for use," Phil Crosby's "conformance to requirements," Dr. Feigenbaum's "Quality is

---

Box 7.2

What Is ISO 9000–2000?

The ISO 9000–2000 standard is the current international standard for quality management. The standard was developed and is maintained by the International Organization for Standardization (ISO), which is a worldwide federation of more than 140 national standards bodies. Its work results in international agreements, which are published as International Standards (www.iso.ch). Variants of ISO 9000–2000 (TL 9000, AS 9000, and FS9000) were developed to meet industry-specific needs of the telecommunications, aerospace, and financial services industries. Additional standards related to the ISO 9000 family that may apply to your firm's business activities or processes are the ISO 10006 for project management, ISO 10007 for configuration management, ISO 10012 for measurement systems, ISO 10013 for quality documentation, ISO/TR 10014 for managing the economics of quality, ISO 10015 for training, ISO/TS 16949 for automotive suppliers, and ISO 19011 for auditing.

ISO 9000–2000 principles form what is now the default expectation of what is involved in managing quality in any type of endeavor. These principles are derived from the practice of the leaders or giants of quality.

ISO 9000–2000 Quality Management System

Principle 1   Customer Focus

Organizations must determine, understand, and meet the current (and future) customer requirements. Typical action steps are:
- Researching and understanding customer needs and expectations.
- Linking organization objectives to customer needs and expectations.
- Communicating agreed-on customer needs/expectations throughout your organization.
- Measuring customer satisfaction and acting on the results.
- Systematically managing customer relationships.

Principle 2   Leadership

Leaders establish unity of purpose and direction of the organization. They should also create and maintain an organizational environment that enables people to be fully involved in achieving the organization's objectives. Typical action steps are:
- Ascertaining and balancing the needs of customers, owners, employees, suppliers, financiers, local communities, and society as a whole.
- Establishing a clear vision of the organization's future.

- Setting challenging goals and targets.
- Creating and sustaining shared values at all levels of the organization.
- Establishing trust and eliminating fear.
- Providing people with the required resources, training, and freedom to act with responsibility and accountability.

Principle 3   Involvement and Support of People

Full involvement and support of employees enable them to fully contribute to their continuous improvement and success as well as that of their work groups and organization. Typical action steps are:

- People understanding the importance of their contribution to the organization.
- People evaluating performance, their own and others, against their individual, team, group, and organizationwide goals and objectives.
- People sharing knowledge, experience, and openly discussing problems and issues.

Principle 4   Process Approach

A desired result is achieved more efficiently when activities and related resources are managed as a process. Typical action steps are:

- Analyzing and measuring of the capability of key activities.
- Identifying the interfaces of key activities within and across functions of the organization.
- Focusing on factors such as resources, methods, and materials to improve key activities of the organization.
- Evaluating risks and intended and unintended consequences of decisions and activities on customers, suppliers, and other interested parties.

Principle 5   Systems-Oriented Management

Identifying, understanding, and managing interrelated processes as a system enhances the organization's ability to its objectives. Typical action steps are:

- Structuring a system to achieve the organization's objectives in the most effective and efficient way.
- Understanding the interdependencies between the processes of the organizational system.
- Continuously improving the system through measurement and evaluation.

(continued)

Principle 6   Continuous Improvement

Continuous improvement of the organization's overall performance is not just an ongoing objective; it is a requisite for survival and meeting customer requirements in the future—not yet expressed. Typical action steps are:

- Employing a consistent organizationwide approach to continuous improvement of the organization's performance.
- Providing people with training in the methods and tools of continuous improvement.
- Making continuous improvement of products, processes, and systems an objective for every individual in the organization.

Principle 7   Factual Approach to Decision Making

Effective decisions are based on the analysis of data and information. Typical action steps are:

- Ensuring that data and information are sufficiently accurate and reliable.
- Making data accessible to those who need it.
- Making decisions and taking action based on factual analysis, balanced with experience and intuition.

Principle 8   Mutually Beneficial Supplier Relationships

An organization and its suppliers are interdependent, and a mutually beneficial relationship enhances the ability of both to create value. Typical action steps are:

- Pooling of expertise and resources with partners.
- Identifying and selecting key suppliers.
- Sharing information and future plans.
- Establishing joint development and improvement activities.

Source: Adapted from "World Quality Management Principles According to the International Standards Organization (ISO)" (www.iso.ch), Geneva, Switzerland.

what the buyer wants and needs to satisfy his or her requirements for use," and embedded in ISO 9000s definition: "Quality is meeting customer requirements." Deming's continuous improvement goal also indicates clearly that efficiency or productivity is an assumed aim or part of quality.

There is, however, another aspect of quality: *unexpressed customer requirements.*

Perhaps the most valuable example of how quality management affects a project's success is illustrated in Exhibit 7.1. Here, John Guaspari shows us

EXHIBIT 7.1 Project management and customer interaction quality

Functions	Interaction with Customer Performance Criteria	Interaction Features	Customer Action Assessment	
Marketing	I never heard about the company. Too little information in ad. Too much information in ad.	The ad was clear and informative. Ad was in a magazine I read (on a Web site I visit). I got it in a timely way.	I found out about the database design firm.	
I called (e-mailed) for more information Customer Service	They put me on hold. The e-form was too small to write on. I got 3 answers, all the same, all asking me for more information. I called (e-mailed) again, they never heard of me. They told me I would be called.	All it took was one call. They sent clear, timely information. I got detailed e-mail, they called to be sure my questions were answer satisfactorily.	"Let's get started on Acme B-100e!"	I think our money was very well spent.
Design I	I had to call back; their design person didn't call me. They called but had my name and model wrong. I was put on hold 3 times during the call.	An experienced designer called me within 60 minutes. Done in 1 hour and I got a detailed confirmation.	I placed the initial design order.	
Design II	I had to call (e-mail) 6 times to find out where my order was in process. They said they sent prototype as e-mail attachment. I did not receive it. They sent the wrong database.	They sent the prototype database via e-mail and called to be sure I got it and it worked. I previewed the prototype online; refinement details were noted/confirmed in real time.	Final design consultation was flawless. I approved it!	
Design III	I had to call several times to see if my order would be on time. They called central office. They had "lost" my number and e-mail.	I previewed the final product and documentation online. Everything was perfect!	Produce, deliver, and install it!	
Delivery/ Installation	A "new" person had brought the wrong package. I had to "walk" them through the installation.	The design engineer. I had been dealing with arrived on time; we were up and running in less than one hour!	I got it! It worked!	
Accounting	The amount was wrong. My name was misspelled. The bill got to my office; the software did not.	The invoice was accurate. It was clear.	I paid for it.	
Bad		Overall Rating		Good

Source: John Guaspari designed this flow chart as a means to demonstrate how the customer has numerous transactions, or interactions with different parts of an organization as his or her single purchase "flows" through the firm. It demonstrates that at each interaction, or transaction point, customer requirements are well met or not well met. The "sum" of the customer experience at each point affects the final judgment of whether his or her total requirements have been met. (Guaspari, John, "So That's What We'd Better Be Building," *Journal for Quality and Participation*, September 1990.)

that quality—conformance to requirements—is not measured just by the technical requirements of the finished product or service; a high-quality project must meet the customer's unexpressed social or human interaction requirements (expectations) as well. Guaspari's chart demonstrates how two firms can produce the same product yet create two completely different customer satisfaction experiences.

Two important points to note are:

1. At each step, or with each interaction, your organization may or may not satisfactorily meet the customer's transactional expressed or unexpressed requirements; therefore, you risk *keeping* or *losing* the customer at each step.

2. You may hold on to the customer until the product, project, or service is delivered. You may deliver 100 percent on the customer's expressed and contracted-for requirements. You will be paid, but you may have lost forever any repeat or reference business because of the customer's *experience* during the project.

Quality is conformance to technical requirements *and* conformance to unexpressed social or human interaction requirements. The chief difference between the two is that:

- Technical quality is measured by the customer when the product is delivered and used.

- Customer service, experience, and interactions are *produced and consumed/used* throughout the *entire transaction* process—during each interaction between buyer and seller.

The important point for a project manager's list of quality management do's is this: *Define, track, and improve on both the customer's expressed/contracted requirements and the customer's unexpressed requirements.*

With this understanding of "conforming to customer requirements"—whether technical or experience-oriented—we now examine specific quality management concepts and techniques that apply to the project environment.

ESTABLISHING CUSTOMER REQUIREMENTS

> We delivered a knock-their-socks-off product but were completely surprised when the customer blew his stack. *You delivered what he asked for but not what he needed.*

Project managers and quality managers know that their starting point to success is establishing all of their customers' requirements for the products/services that they and their organizations have agreed to deliver. This is an extension of Principle 1 of ISO 9000–2000.

So, why do projects and project managers still stumble in this area? Managers of all sorts, not just project managers, will tell you about times they got "stuck" or "hammered" because either they or their team members assumed they knew what the customer meant, or that because the customer said nothing about a specific feature, it was being left to their "expert" judgment.

Getting customer requirements correct and complete is critical to the success of any project or project manager. In quality, or quality management, it is the step that sets up success in the other basic steps or factors of quality: designing and measuring quality, improving your quality, and innovating.

In this section, we discuss two topics that are essential to getting the customer's requirements right the first time:

1. The distinction between customer (or business) requirements and technical (product/service) requirements.

2. A technique for structuring the conversation with the customer toward specifying and prioritizing his or her requirements to be sure we give customers the best deal they can get.

J. Davidson Frame makes the useful distinction between business and technical requirements:

> Business requirements define business conditions that the deliverable must achieve. . . . Technical requirements describe what the deliverable should look like and what it should do.[2]

At the most basic level, we think of business/customer requirements describing the *what* of the product or service, while the technical requirement describes the *how*. A business requirement for an airplane describes how much weight or how many passengers the aircraft must be able to carry. That's really what the customer wants to buy. The aircraft engineers and designers translate that *what* into *how* as they create requirements for the wings and propulsion systems.

Why make the distinction? Because successfully delivering on technical requirements does not always guarantee we will meet the original business— or customer—requirement. The problem arises when we focus on technical requirements—product features and specifications—before clearly articulating the original driving business requirement. You can probably name half a dozen such examples yourself.

We get into this problem because project teams are usually composed of expert technicians, people skilled in some discipline that enables them to build solutions. However, if these same people are not skilled in listening to the customer—and to what the customer really wants to accomplish—our experts are likely to build the product they themselves value most in this situation. And it isn't just our technically advanced project teams who create this problem; many customers are guilty of wanting someone else to help them solve problems they don't understand themselves.

This problem has occurred in many industries over many, many years. In the past decade, a new approach has emerged to overcome this problem—Quality Function Deployment (QFD). In addition to discerning and distinguishing between customer/business requirements and technical requirements, QFD enables the team and the customer to prioritize both types of requirements, including a comparison of the cost and difficulty of implementing solutions for these requirements.

QFD was designed, as Dr. Deming might put it, to reduce variation in the process employed to determine your customer's requirements—to improve the quality of determining customer requirements. Correctly determining the customer's requirements is the first step to assuring that you can deliver quality—"conforming to requirements."

QFD was developed in Japan over a 15-year time span by Yoji Akao and others to improve a firm's ability to more accurately determine customer requirements earlier in the design and production process. It became available in the late 1980s and early 1990s.

The aim of QFD is to improve how you determine the customer's business and technical requirements and transform them into product and/or service requirements and processes, which then can be carried through each stage of the production process.

QFD is best explained with its graphic depiction that has become known as the "House of Quality," illustrated in Exhibit 7.2.

The following is a description of what might be involved in a basic QFD session. It is basic in the sense that as the systems and/or needs grow in complexity, the QFD tool may make use of additional subtools to aid the overall process.

EXHIBIT 7.2   QFD "House of Quality" format

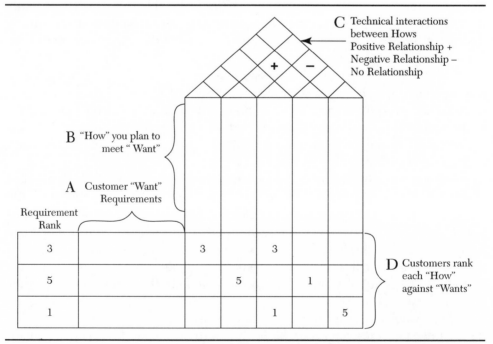

Step-by-Step QFD Session

Step One: QFD begins with defining what customers want and expect from the products and services your organization provides. These are your customer's requirements, following Phil Crosby's definition of quality as "conformance to requirements." Begin with a face–to–face meeting with the customer/stakeholders to determine the *Whats*—what the customer wants (see A in Exhibit 7.2):

1. Elicit and list the customer's requirements in the customer's terms.
2. Come to an agreement and understanding on each requirement.
3. As customers, we want many things from the products and services we buy. Some things are much more important than others, however. Ask the customer to weigh and rank requirements according to their importance: 5 if high, 3 if medium importance, and 1 if low importance.

Step Two: Establishing the *Hows*—how you are going to deliver/produce what the customer wants. These are design features and functions (see B in Exhibit 7.2).

Step Three: The roof of the House of Quality (see C in Exhibit 7.2). The roof provides early notice of problems, synergies, or trade-off points of concern to both customer and supplier. The design team rates each *How* for interactions between it and other *Hows*. A plus sign indicates a positive correlation; as one design feature is maximized, the other design feature is also maximized. Too many positive interactions suggest potential redundancies in product requirements/technical characteristics. A minus sign indicates a negative correlation; one design feature is maximized at the expense of the other design feature. Here, consider product concepts or technology to overcome these potential trade-offs or the trade-offs when establishing target values to be attained for the feature. No mark indicates that the design feature does not interact with other design features.

Step Four: Ask customers to assign weights to the *Hows* using a scale of 1 = little correlation; 3 = some correlation; 5 = high correlation (see D in Exhibit 7.2). By comparing these values with the customer's ranking of each *Want*, you quickly see whether your design even begins to meet the customer's requirements.

Using QFD to Design Apartments[3]

To demonstrate how you might use QFD to determine your customer's requirements, we look at how a QFD application improved the design (and appeal) of apartment complexes during their design phase. The goal in this case was to better understand what potential customers would want that would increase the speed of sales when the apartments went on the market. The basic layout of each unit includes two bedrooms, two bathrooms, one living/dining room, kitchen, laundry, and balcony. (We limit our examination to a subset of the 30 design features that were actually evaluated.)

The QFD objectives:

1. Define design specifications for residential apartments that meet the highest level possible of customer requirements (business requirement).

2. Ensure consistency between customer requirements and measurable product characteristics such as dimensions and features of rooms and finish materials used in the construction work (technical requirements).

3. Ensure consistency between the design phase and the construction work to minimize constructability and rework problems that often arise when moving from design to construction phases (technical/functional requirements).

4. Optimize how customers' requirements might affect return on investment (ROI) elements such as construction cost, speed of sales, schedule, and cash flow. Reduce the time to produce quality features throughout product development (business requirement/need).

What Do Customers Want in an Apartment?

WHATS

	Customer Requirement	Degree of Importance
Entrance	Social entrance—another for Kitchen	4
	One Kitchen entrance	4
Kitchen	Large counter top—durable material	1
	Space for full-size appliances	5

The *Whats,* or customer requirements, that correspond to area A in the generic House of Quality in Exhibit 7.2 were developed using a focus group, made up of potential apartment buyers, owners of similar apartments, real estate agents, architects, and engineers. The group was asked to evaluate some 30 features of the proposed design and to compare them with competitors' offerings or with previous apartment owners' experience.

Focus group members were asked, for example:

- What do you like in the design of this apartment?
- What do you dislike in the design of this apartment?
- What do you think the most important features in the kitchen of this apartment are? Why? Choose three features.

The group was given drawings and basic information on materials used on other projects. The features compared and evaluated included, for example, dimensions of rooms, finishing materials, and kitchen layout.

The features selected by focus group members as important included:

- At least two entrances for the apartment—living room and kitchen.
- A large counter top in the kitchen—more space for food preparation or other tasks.
- Floor easy to clean in the kitchen and bathroom.

After selecting changes in features and materials, or different layouts, the focus group then rated the degree of importance of their design preferences. Our example shows only the requirements for the entry room and the kitchen. Space for full-size appliances was rated as one of the most important design requirements/changes.

Not all preferences are rated equally. For example, the large kitchen counter top was selected as a customer preference (requirement), a feature already planned for by the developer. The QFD ranking indicated that it was not nearly as important as the location of an outside entrance to the kitchen and space for full-size kitchen appliances. Without this ranking, a project developer could have decided to "save" expenses by offering a larger, more luxurious counter top, in lieu of a more expensive expansion of the kitchen, or an additional entry point to the apartment. The ranking exercise of the QFD process helps the developer avoid what could have been a costly construction savings.

How Will We Meet the Customer's Requirements?

HOWS

One social entrance separated from kitchen entrance—no change.
One kitchen entrance separated from living/dining room—change.
Large marble or granite counter top in the kitchen—no change.
More space in the kitchen for full-size appliances—change.

The *Hows,* or technical requirements, correspond to area B in the generic House of Quality in Exhibit 7.2. The apartment design team, with the focus group's preferences and rankings in hand, used a brainstorming session to develop the apartment's technical requirements. Changes from the original design were identified and then inserted into the Technical Requirements Matrix. The illustration shows only the *Hows* selected for the entrance and kitchen. At this point in the QFD process, the design team could specify movement or change/no change and indicate the direction of change from the original apartment plan target values (technical specifications). After the project design team determined what changes were needed in their technical solution, they could determine specific target values for each technical solution.

The QFD Correlation Matrix, which corresponds to Area D in the generic House of Quality in Exhibit 7.2, establishes the correlation between the customer requirements (Whats) and technical requirements (Hows) and indicates the strength of the relationship and its impact on the customer requirement.

The developer and design team further manipulated that data to produce an importance weight and relative weight of the technical requirements, which enabled them to further refine their understanding of the level of importance of the design requirements. With those results, the design team could prioritize and implement the new layout solutions and new features in the specification and design of the apartment unit.

The House of Quality creates a dramatically different home. The Before and After QFD design comparison (Exhibit 7.3) dramatically illustrates the difference QFD made in the developer's offer to the market.

We can see how QFD improves our ability to hear the voice of the customer. The ranking of requirements and correlation of their ranking with how we intend to fulfill those requirements enables us to hear in numbers: "I really, really want this feature!" "You missed the mark but not by much." "Home run; you got it!"

Where else is QFD working? Two brief descriptions of projects that used QFD to improve determining customer requirements and importance of those requirements follow:

1. Fusion UV Systems produces ultraviolet (UV) curing systems and UV-based, custom-engineered process solutions for applications in printing, coating wood and metal products, and so on. While developing a new product for off-the-shelf use, they used a QFD process to guide customers through a preview of the product in early development. Dwight Delgado, Fusion UV Systems, later reported in a presentation at the thirteenth annual QFD Institute Symposium: "We were surprised at what they told us during our QFD-guided customer visits. . . . To avoid disaster, we had to rethink our strategy and redesign a more successful product line."[4]

2. Although MD Robotics had no previous experience with theme park attractions or dinosaur robots, it accepted the challenge to combine talents with Universal Creative and Hall Train Studios to provide life-like, large-scale, highly realistic animals brought back from extinction. The conceptual design scope of the work document, used to drive the QFD study, specified that the outcome should include specifications such as degrees of freedom of movement, maximum velocity, range of motion, skin characteristics, and so on. The May 1999 opening of the new Triceratops Encounter at Universal Studio's Jurassic Park attraction prompted *U.S. News & World Report* to write "These three creatures snort, stomp their feet. . . . Ask the 'keeper' if you can pet them. It's up to him or her to decide."[5]

The best news about QFD, even though at first glance it may seem daunting, is that there is readily available QFD software designed to make using QFD easier. And both QFD and software to aid in its use have been specifically developed for software development (SQFD). There are also numerous sources

EXHIBIT 7.3   Before and after QFD design comparison

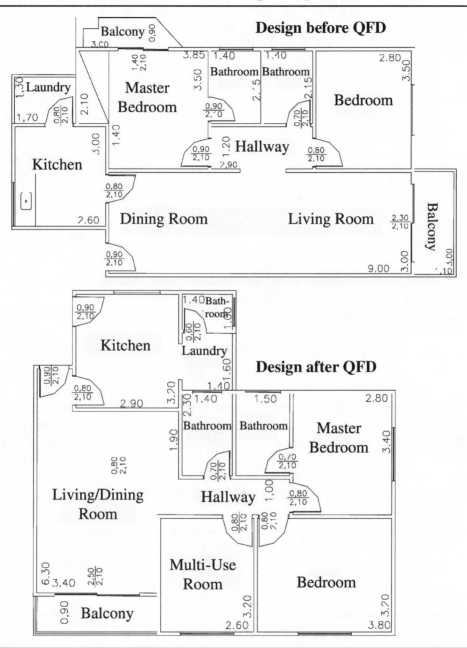

on the Internet to help with QFD—even one that allows you to outline your project online and see how you might use QFD.

Glenn Mazur, director of the QFD Institute, when asked what he might say to a project manager about QFD, said:

> When the iron triangle of schedule, budget, and content seem to be crushing the life out of the project manager, it is essential that content not be sacrificed to the needs of the other two. Because the project manager is responsible for schedule and budget, content is at risk. Yet, if content or quality is reduced, the impact on customer satisfaction can be severe.[6]

He notes that when time is very short, he recommends using what he calls "blitz QFD" to protect the most critical customer requirements and "schedule deployment" to reduce the negative impact of multitasking.

Determining customer requirements is one of the most important steps to improving the quality of managing projects. Managing systems and processes to reduce variation is the next step.

DESIGNING AND MANAGING SYSTEMS AND PROCESSES

> A reputation for "getting the job done" always won business for you in the past. *Now, however, competitors are winning "your contracts" on the strength of their processes.*

Managing your process is an increasingly common phrase in the business environment. What process management means from a practical, project management standpoint is getting the processes and procedures that highly skilled and experienced people carry around in their heads out into the open so they can be documented, standardized, and improved for everyone's benefit. The concepts in this section embody the ISO 9000–2000 Principles 4 and 5, process and systems-oriented management.

The macro-quality management principles for designing and managing systems and processes that have the greatest use for project management are:

- Visibility.
- Documentation.
- Standardization.
- Traceability to customer/stakeholder requirement(s).

These principles are derived from a systems and process approach to complying with requirements. The simplest view of a system is outlined here:

Inputs to the system are customer requirements.

The *transformation* process (the project) is made up of techniques/ methods, steps, tasks, systems, and processes that acquire and manipulate material, human, fiscal, technological, and information resources into system outputs.

The *output* of the system is a product that consists of specific technical and social products and services that conform to the customer's requirements (see Exhibit 7.4).

Visibility: Do we know and can we plainly see what techniques, methods, steps, systems, and processes are involved in creating the output desired by the customer? Do we know the sequence of these steps and the relationship between steps?

Documentation: Have we specified and *recorded* the sequential order and a measure for conformance of each of the techniques, methods, steps, systems, and processes involved in creating the output desired by the customer?

Standardization: Have we created methods and processes to *control variation* in the techniques, methods, steps, systems, and processes involved in creating the output desired by the customer?

In the following project examples, we demonstrate how using these principles can improve your ability to assure that your project conforms to your customer's/stakeholder's requirements:

Project: Setting up a 500-exhibit booth area for a trade show.

Business requirement: The exhibit area opens to the public at the 9 A.M. opening event. (There is a contractual penalty for any booth not ready at 9 A.M.)

Challenge: At 10 P.M. on the evening before the 9 A.M. opening, the exhibits setup manager is told three electrical contractor crews are "no shows." Replacement crews have been located and report to the exhibits setup manager at midnight for a briefing and work assignments. They have less than 9 hours to "get up to speed" and complete tasks that had been budgeted for 10 hours.

This would be "sweating bullets" time for many project-based organizations, but this one had been using quality management principles to improve their processes for several years. Instead of having to problem solve on the fly or hire six crews to get the work done on time, the setup manager simply had

EXHIBIT 7.4   Simple system model

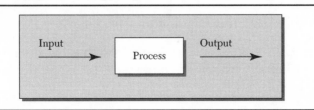

to show the crew chief of the replacement crew the booth setup system and briefly explain the process he and his crews would follow. The system and processes represent two years of continuously improving common processes (adaptable to the unique needs of each show).

The setup manager's instructions to the replacement crew's chief were:

> Your crews are assigned aisles 349, 350, and 351. We are supplying each worker with a work kit containing the tools needed for the types of work that can be ordered for each booth.
>
> Yellow is the color we are using for electrical work.
>
> Each crew should begin at the north end of its assigned aisle, then go to the first booth with a yellow dot on its banner.
>
> At the foot of the banner is a yellow supply tub with a yellow worksheet in the clear plastic envelope on top of the tub.
>
> The worksheet is the crew's guide for the work ordered and a check-off control sheet is provided (as an item is finished, the worker marks it done on the worksheet). The materials list is on the back of the sheet at that booth. (If any materials are missing or the work order is unclear, the worker should call for assistance on the two-way.)
>
> When a booth is done, the worker should check the worksheet to see that everything has been checked off, sign it, and hang it in its envelope on the banner pole.
>
> Then the crew should move on to the next booth in the aisle color coded for electrical work, complete the work in the same manner, and so on, until finished with the assigned aisle.
>
> When one of my aisle coordinators sees a yellow worksheet hung on the bannered pole, he or she goes to the booth, uses the worksheet to conduct a quick visual check of the work, and if complete, removes the yellow dot from the banner (we can see that from up here, so we can note it in the database and on the table model) so everyone knows the electrical work is done. A banner with no dots, by the way, is ready for the opening.

Visibility, documentation, standardization, and traceability to customer requirements have been designed into the overall process of making the hall "exhibitor and visitor ready."

This organization standardized, documented, and made visible the processes of knowing:

- Which booths did or did not require electrical work.
- Which booths were done—exhibitor and visitor ready or still needed work.
- What specific work was required for each booth.

They standardized, documented, and made visible the process of checking/measuring whether customer requirements for a specific booth were met, as well as for the entire hall.

They standardized, documented, and made available a process for communicating and correcting unacceptable variation of materials, documentation, and standards (the two-way radios).

It is also clear that other processes were similarly designed. The process that controlled or "mapped" getting the specific and correct worksheet and materials tub to each booth was planned, standardized, documented, made visible, and integrated into the process of making the exhibit hall exhibitor- and visitor-ready by the agreed-on time.

A standardized, documented, and plainly visible process enables you to focus on the particular task, get it done, and move on to the next one. When the process of marking work done is standardized, you *see* it and do not have to run around trying to find out if you can begin work on your part of the overall process.

The next example demonstrates, again, how standardization contributes to controlling variation (less time needed to decide how to complete common tasks) and to both productivity and quality by "creating" time to focus on and address uncommon, or special, tasks:

> *Project:* A one-time, unique project to convert a military logistics system from one mainframe computer operating system to another.
>
> *Business requirement:* Reduce complexity and maintenance and improve productivity by using a better operating system.
>
> *Challenge:* Reduce the probability of error and need for rework in converting thousands of programs and, at the same time, increase productivity.

The first of Deming's Five Principles of Quality Management ("The central problem in lack of quality is the failure of management to understand variation") helps us focus on processes that if made visible, documented, and standardized, could improve quality or, in Deming's terms, continuously improve the system by reducing variation.

With more than 100 programmers each evaluating, modifying, and then certifying thousands of existing programs, there were numerous opportunities to apply systems and process management principles to improving program performance.

Deming's advice on variation leads us to ask: "Will each of the programmers use the same or a substantially similar procedure or collection of steps to evaluate, modify, and certify the computer programs assigned to him or her for conversion?"

If there is no agreement or protocol to follow when evaluating, modifying, or certifying the work, you can expect variation in how the programmers:

- Set up their daily work.
- Select what methods, tools, and so on each would use to evaluate, modify, and then certify the program as workable on the new system.

Improving the quality of managing the work processes of this one-time project begins with determining whether standardizing similar work processes (evaluating, modifying, and certifying) will reduce variation in how the work is done as well as reduce the time it takes to complete the tasks involved in working with each specific program.

To improve productivity and reduce variation, this organization attempted to create standardized processes. Before attacking the thousands of programs to be converted, a core team:

- Set up a checklist of the most common modifications.
- Brainstormed a list of common modifications.
- Prepared standard code and tests (procedures) for these changes.

Once established, these standard procedures enabled the 100-plus programmers to buzz through the common changes, which then enabled each to focus more effort on time-consuming uncommon changes. In addition, as the project progressed, programmers were encouraged to identify additional commonly required modifications, create standard code, and test those modifications.

These process improvements documented procedures, which could then be checked as used or not and as a "work done" signal—in short, the procedure became a quality control process that could be tracked and measured for additional continuous improvement.

As a standard work instruction, it enhanced productivity twice because it reduced the amount of time it would take someone new to the project to get up to speed.

The first two examples demonstrate a systems and process approach within a project. The next example shows how a project-based organization may apply similar process analysis and standardization to many projects.

The project-based organization was a 15-person engineering group that developed computer hardware for managing networks:

Project: Improve the productivity of a project-based firm that designs hardware for managing computer networks.

Business requirement: Improve ability/capacity to manage an increased workload created by the past success and growth.

Challenge: Identify and/or create opportunities for productivity improvements.

Because of past company success, the workload for each engineer had been growing, even as the firm added more people to handle the work. There were three pressing problems:

1. The firm had outgrown the "one engineer, one project" work model.
2. It was becoming increasingly difficult for the manager to assess progress of the 10 to 15 projects the firm was responsible for at any one time because the engineers were running their projects "in their heads."

3. Handoffs between engineers were a source of failure—key information was often passed on orally or sometimes even forgotten.

To solve these problems, the engineers applied process management principles to create a common work breakdown structure (WBS) in a facilitated, four-hour session. Using a three-stage process:

1. They agreed on the six major steps that each of their projects passed through.
2. They broke into smaller teams, each of which agreed on and listed four to six minor steps within one or two of the major steps.
3. The entire group then merged the detailed steps from the subteams into one standard, two-tiered WBS.

The standard, two-tiered WBS gave them a common language, or process, for reporting project progress. To further reduce communication errors, they assigned each engineer a few of the detailed tasks to be formalized using the input-process-test-output model.

Initial resistance to "bureaucratizing" their work washed away because each engineer had experienced frustration or rework caused by miscommunication in the past.

The standardization used here gave those involved a visual map of the work processes that facilitated communication. When someone said, for example, "Here's our status on Xxx," those involved knew what was being referred to because it called up a mental picture of that map.

There are two valuable lessons to draw from this example:

1. The processes we are discussing already exist and are in use—they are in people's heads; it's their way of making decisions, accomplishing tasks, and so on. Your challenge is to get them out of people's heads—externalize them and make them visible—to enable you and others to determine: "Does the process work?" "Is it one that others should use?" "Can it, if combined with or modified by other people's process for doing the same thing, become a standard?"
2. The WBS chart (Chapter 4) is a tool that you can use directly or adapt to map your processes and then determine which are good candidates for standardization (will help reduce variation, improve productivity, etc.).

Mapping processes to make them standardized and visible can be done in a variety of ways. In the project environment, several techniques used to plan the project may also be used to map and analyze processes:

- The WBS (described in Chapter 4), as shown in the previous example, lists activities with expected outputs.
- The WBS also provides a visible, traceable link to customer requirements, because every function in the product is represented by one or more tasks on the WBS.

- We can create checklists or flowcharts for any particularly complex tasks on the WBS, thereby providing a detailed description of the proper steps in a task.
- The Network Diagram (also discussed in Chapter 4), maps the sequence between tasks.

These examples show the benefits project managers can derive from managing processes with the concepts of visibility, documentation, standardization, and traceability to customer requirements. All of these rely on and improve upon our first principle, understanding customer requirements. In the next section, we take our visible, standard processes and improve upon them.

CONTINUOUS IMPROVEMENT

The weak link in your organization was small, in comparison to the whole project. However, that small, weak link brought a huge project to a dead stop.

Despite our best efforts to get the requirements correct and to design processes and systems that reduce variation (errors) and optimize productivity, the opportunity to improve never ends.

The continuous improvement topics in this section embody the ISO 9000–2000 Principles 6 and 7 (continuous improvement and a factual approach to decision making). In the manufacturing world of repetitive and continuous processes, these principles are exemplified by the small and large projects initiated to improve production on assembly lines, oil rigs, or fast-food counters.

In the project environment, where even similar projects are unique, continuous improvement occurs at two levels:

1. Continuous improvement spawns projects. From problem recognition and selection to problem solution, you have a project—sometimes a series of projects. This perspective encourages project managers and project-based organizations to use the concepts in this section as they launch improvement projects.
2. Continuous improvement can happen in a project. Project managers can apply the tools and methods in this section to seek out productivity improvement opportunities and solve the inevitable problems that occur on every project.

In this section, we address continuous improvement in two steps:

1. Reducing "garbage in" to prevent "garbage out."
2. The best solutions to process problems come from fact-based decision making.

Reducing "Garbage In" to Prevent "Garbage Out"

Toyota does not refer to the "garbage in—garbage out" rule, but they do begin their quality journey with policies, processes, and methods that help to ensure there is little or no "garbage in" at the front end of their manufacturing system. Toyota, as well as Honda, Nissan, and others, works with its suppliers to help them deliver only goods and services that meet technical specifications derived from their end-use customer's requirements. However, if 100-percent inspection is found to be necessary to prevent parts with unacceptable variances from coming into the system, Toyota inspects 100 percent until they determine the processes and systems that produce those parts are again in control. Such 100-percent inspections could be triggered by a worker or floor supervisor who discovers that, despite best efforts, several parts are defective and stops the line. The 100-percent inspection may well be just on those parts required for that shift, but notice goes quickly back up the system to determine where, how, and what is causing the variance.

On projects, we get one chance to do it right. Finding an error downstream results in rework that is rarely within the budget. This concept is clear, but we now look at three specific ways to improve our chances of getting it right upstream.

We previously examined how the QFD process can help us get our customer requirements clear and correctly prioritized—a good example in itself. Translating the customer requirements to a product design is another opportunity for incorporating customer needs—but this time the customer is our downstream coworkers. Invite those people who will build and maintain the product to the product design activities. It makes sense that the production engineers and assembly workers will see ways to shave production costs that the design engineers never considered. Any time you've struggled to perform some basic maintenance on your car because the spark plug, oil filter, or water pump was tucked far out of reach, you see the failure of this principle at work.

In many industries, finished work must be inspected before it can be certified for use. Passing inspection is a vital step in the construction process of many different types of devices, structures, and components. When inspections are performed at multiple steps in the process, errors are found early, rather than only at the end when the cost of rework could be exorbitant. It makes sense and exemplifies good process management. Quality management takes us one step better: Inspection and measurement of conforming to requirements is done at the level of the work before performance. For example:

> A roofer is installing new roofs on several old and interconnected buildings. The building inspector is invited to the site to approve or assist the roofer in determining if the methods and actual construction in process are conforming to building code requirements rather than merely hope his processes are correct when the finished work is inspected.

Moving the inspection forward, before the work is performed, makes sense in the project world because every job is different. The roofer in our example had an unusual situation, so he received approval on the approach as well as the finished product.

One particularly disappointing source of garbage in is *improvements* to the product or the process that have unforeseen negative impacts on other parts of the product or project. You may think that your improvement will automatically improve the whole process/system, that it affects only your area, or that it has no impact on conforming to requirements. However, you may be creating a project stopper downstream. For example:

> A firm initiated a project to redesign work processes and data management systems to give employees faster access to product and customer data while serving customers online. The purpose of the project was to enable the sales force and customer service personnel to better serve the customers through better access to customer and product information. However, the IT security group decided independently to add several layers of complex security steps/procedures as its "improvements" to the new system. These unrequested improvements actually restricted the access of the customer service associates, reducing their ability to sell new products to existing customers.

There are several approaches to designing in prevention of downstreaming problems through improvements. The first is to maintain a system and process view of the work. The project, any work for that matter, is composed of many parts, all of which are designed to work in harmony to conform to customer requirements.

Another method for making sure our improvements do not result in a problem for someone else is to play the devil's advocate with every improvement idea. This perspective is vital because a common project management problem is that we assess only the benefits of solutions. It doesn't have a special name—call it an *implication review*—it's simple, yet powerful.

Here is how it works: After you have selected a solution or identified an improvement, tested it, and are ready to implement, stop. Gather several people together, and run this exercise:

1. Write the solution on a white board and ask: "If we do this, what might then happen? How will others react to it?" Say, "Please use the self-stick notes in front of you, and write down five positive and five negative possible reactions to or impacts arising from this decision. Stick your notes up on the board as you finish them."

2. When all the notes are up, check for duplicates and arrange them in categories.

3. Use the same process to identify secondary implications or reactions that result from this first set of implications. You'll get a diagram similar to a decision tree illustrated in Exhibit 7.5.

EXHIBIT 7.5   Implication review diagram

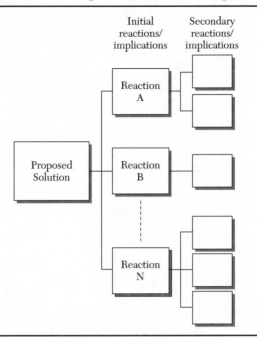

4. Assess the probability. Assign a weight (1 = unlikely, 3 = likely, 5 = very likely) to each reaction or impact on each branch. Even if the first reaction is judged a collective "1," if it did take place, would the secondary reaction be more likely, or not?

Who should attend such a session? Again, think upstream and downstream, cross-functional, and even cross-corporate. If necessary, bring suppliers and marketing partners in.

This type of review takes you beyond the factors that you may usually consider. It can point you to even greater improvements, or it can help you to avoid outright downstream disaster. For instance, a positive improvement could lead to demand that totally outstrips your estimates. By the time you catch up, customers may have decided you were unreliable. Joel Barker has developed this type of analysis into a robust and adaptable tool called the *Implications Wheel.* Sound too complex? Just keep in mind Ben Franklin's advice: An ounce of prevention is worth a pound of cure!

QUALITY MANAGEMENT PRINCIPLES FOR SOLVING PROBLEMS

Of all the quality management methods and techniques commonly used in the workplace, problem-solving tools are probably the most widely recognized. As mentioned earlier, you can apply these tools at the macro level to generate a project or at the micro level to solve problems within the project. The remainder of this section is an introduction to some of the most valuable problem-solving tools and concepts that apply to the project environment.

The principles and methods we discuss in this section are:

- Involving those who work directly with the process to continuously improve the process and solve problems in the process.
- The Shewhart-Deming Plan-Do-Study-Act Cycle for problem solving.
- Six Sigma.
- Lessons learned sessions.

Involving Those Directly Involved with the Process

If there is a general management principle for continuous improvement and problem solving, it is this:

> The more you involve those who are directly involved in the variances to be reduced, the improvement process/project to redesign the system or process, and the corrective action process, the higher the probability of success. Not doing so reduces the probability of your success.

The following example illustrates problem solving of a problem that is often a *problem* only to those directly involved with the work. If this type of involvement in problem solving is not part of your organization's quality management approach, you are missing an opportunity to save money and time, improve safety, and boost pride in workmanship.

The $1.79 solution to a $50,000 per year problem:

Project: Installing underground utilities at new commercial and residential construction sites.

Business requirement: Consistent productivity and safety are critical stakeholder requirements.

Challenge: Rework, unnecessary costs, and safety hazards caused by heavy equipment driving over finished utility boxes.

A Memphis Light, Gas, and Water (MLGW) work team, responsible for installing and repairing underground utility boxes at residential and commercial construction sites, wanted to reduce rework and improve safety by reducing breakage of finished and buried utility boxes for electricity, gas, and water service. Their rework and safety problem was being caused, they determined with simple observation and use of a checksheet, by heavy construction equipment driving over installed utility boxes to the tune of $50,000 of rework a year.

The team's solution was one that only those closest to the work are likely to have come up with. The team determined that plainly marking the location of the finished box and informing heavy equipment drivers what the marking meant would solve the problem by preventing it from happening. To implement the solution, the team purchased a $1.79 spray can of "day glow" orange paint, painted three-foot lengths of onsite waste PVC pipe and then "planted" their "Careful—Buried Utility Box Here" signs next to their utility boxes. Problem solved, problems prevented, quickly at the level of the work, at a low cost with an annual return of $50,000 cost avoidance.

Related to this concept of involving those closest to the problem is ISO 9000–2000 Principle 8: Mutually beneficial supplier relationships. When your firm has truly achieved mutually beneficial relationships with suppliers, it becomes natural to include them, rather than exclude them because you fear they will only take advantage of the situation to increase their own profit.

The Shewhart-Deming Plan-Do-Study-Act (PDSA) Cycle for Problem Solving

The PDSA model for decision making and problem solving was developed by Dr. Deming's mentor, Dr. Walter Shewhart, and popularized by Dr. Deming. Applying PDSA can be as simple and direct as using it as a process guide when dealing with problems that require an immediate decision (see Exhibit 7.6):

- Evaluate what is happening.
- Think of several solutions.
- Consider/weigh their consequences and probability for success.
- Take action.
- Monitor it for refinement when more time is available.

EXHIBIT 7.6   Shewhart-Deming PDSA cycle

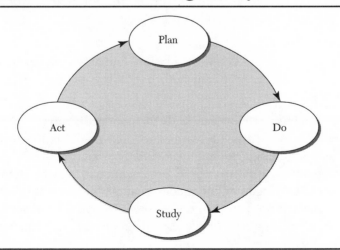

It is also a rigorous step-by-step process for decision making and problem solving. The following generic description comes from literally hundreds of organizations that use PDSA as the standard framework for their step-by-step problem-solving process:

An Eight-Step Improvement and Problem-Solving Approach Using the PDSA (Plan-Do-Study-Act) Pattern as a Guide

PLAN 1. Identify the problem.

Select the problem to be analyzed, clearly define it and establish a precise problem statement, set a measurable goal for the problem-solving effort, and establish a process for coordinating with (and when necessary, gaining approval of) leadership.

PLAN 2. Study the current situation.

Analyze the problem, identify processes that impact the problem and select one, list the steps in the process as it currently exists, map the process, validate the process map, and identify potential causes of the problem. Set goals and targets for the improvement.

PLAN 3. Find root causes.

Using the data collected in Step 2, collect and analyze data related to the problem, verify or revise the original problem statement, identify root causes of the problem, and collect additional data if needed to verify root causes.

DO 4. Choose solution.

Develop solution(s), establish criteria for selecting a solution, generate potential solutions that address the root cause(s) of the problem, select a solution, plan the solution.

DO 5. Develop and carry out an action plan or pilot solution.

Develop an action plan for putting the solution to work; implement the chosen solution on a trial or pilot basis.

STUDY 6. Study/check results.

Compare the collected data before and after the action to see if the planned steps were accomplished and if the planned/expected results were achieved.

ACT 7. Establish reliable methods for standardization.

Develop clear procedures and reliable methods to ensure the solution(s) is maintained; communicate information about the procedure to those responsible for the overall organizational improvement process, or ISO 9000–2000 documentation coordination. The new procedure may become a standard used throughout an organization for the same, or similar, processes. Plan ongoing monitoring of the solution for future improvement opportunities.

ACT 8. Review.

Review the process used in solving the problem; identify any remaining problems and lessons learned from the problem-solving process and project.

Six Sigma

Six Sigma is a term used to describe an expert-driven approach to process improvement. It uses a variety of process analysis tools and methods as means to significantly improve an organization's quality performance—to a level at which errors occur at a rate of 3.4 errors per million parts (Six Sigma) or less. Six Sigma is similar to other "programic" approaches to process improvement such as total quality management (TQM), continuous quality improvement (CQI), and so on.

Six Sigma is often used to focus on systems or processes that flow across a number of organizational boundaries. Generally, a small number of managers (Six Sigma Black Belts) are given training in the common problem-solving tools and a variety of statistical analysis methods, as well as QFD, as their tool kit. The problem-solving process is similar to PDSA. The Six Sigma performance improvement model is known as Define-Measure-Analyze-Improve-Control (DMAIC).

At General Electric Appliances in Louisville, Kentucky, the process is summarized as:

- Defining the goals of the improvement activity.
- Measuring the process output of the existing system.
- Analyzing the process inputs for criticality (bottlenecks, long setup times, wait or hold times, etc.).
- Improving the process by modifying inputs (project and other planning management tools may be applied). Statistical methods are used to validate the improvement.
- Controlling the process by controlling the appropriate input.

Lessons Learned

After-action reviews are used on most projects as a learning and continuous improvement process, but many projects could benefit from a sharing of experience and learning while they are in process. If the project is scheduled to take more than a week to complete, improvement activities will be enhanced if you create the time, space, and structure for lessons learned sessions.

Lessons learned sessions can be once a week, 30-minute discussions, or perhaps longer if the project is months long. Topics or questions might be: What's working? What isn't working? Who solved a tough problem this week?

What have been the biggest hassles this week? Who's had a great week and why? Discussion themes can spark improvements and the sharing of ideas and solutions, which could apply elsewhere in the project.

An ongoing quality improvement and problem-solving database, accessible to everyone involved in the project, pairs up well with these sessions. Many projects have had the experience of inventing the same or similar solution to a problem, simply because no one knew the problem had been solved. At the same time, this database supports using solutions that people have used in past projects.

INNOVATING

When customers begin their search for a *quality* project-based organization, one of the first questions asked of the marketplace is "What's new?" or "Who has a totally new process or offer?" The final challenge that quality management can help you with as leader of a project-based organization is designing and managing your organization's innovation processes.

Getting to *totally new* is not a natural act or easy. If it were either, we would see innovations as radical as the airplane or the telephone every day. Getting to totally new takes discipline—and a good innovation process. After you get to totally new in concept or approach, your product development processes, which have been enhanced by using quality management, take over.

Getting to totally new begins with rethinking continuous improvement and thinking about innovation as being the result of a *discontinuous improvement,* which kills an existing market or reinvents a market, product, or significant aspect of the customer transaction. Xerox's plain paper copier killed the market for NCR's market-leading and high-quality carbonless copy paper.

Leading your company toward *totally new* or discontinuous improvement begins with using the involvement principle to establish an innovation process in which everyone in the organization has a stake and potentially a role to play. The most robust, adaptable process, I know of is called *scouting.* I have been involved in its development with Robert Holder.

Scouting involves scanning the social economic system for emergent commercial, technology, lifestyle, and cultural trends that impact people's expectations or needs in significant ways and using the resulting information to create "possible futures." Scouting, in general, involves six steps or stages that track Deming's PDSA model.

Scouting Steps

PLAN 1. Define the scouting purpose.

Macro scouting is used to identify and seek to understand relationships among emergent commercial, technology, lifestyle, and cultural trends that affect stakeholder attitudes and behavior and, therefore, have an impact on the organization. Micro scouting focuses on discovering specific short-range trends, issues, and information that affects or contributes to the firm's operations.

PLAN 2. Select scouting information sources.

These resources may include public and private Internet-based databases, direct observation, newspapers, magazines, journals, e-mail listservs, associations, plant tours, conferences, conference proceedings, peer networks, and surveys.

PLAN AND DO 3. Create scouting processes and structures.

There is no set way, or best way, to create a scouting process or structure for your organization. The scouting examples that follow and as described in other scouting steps will give you some ideas, which may be adapted for your use. (The book *Global Innovation,* written by Bob Holder and me, contains a number of additional scouting process and structure examples.) Scouting process and structure examples include:

—NEC has a committee composed of middle managers and executives who scout a variety of marketing and technological data to discover new product concepts.

—Great Plains Software's scouting system involves customers, partners, employees, and members of user groups in surveys and scouting visits. Great Plains has 10,000 to 15,000 active suggestions to work with at any given time. Associates and managers are supported in continuously transforming their operations based on this information.

DO 4. Conduct scouting (scanning).

Core questions during scanning are "What is and is not happening?" Scanning involves collecting data and information. Go out and watch customers and people shopping and using products and services.

STUDY 5. Transform scouting information and data into knowledge and intelligence.

The core question is "What can be done with this knowledge?" The U.S. Army's After Action Review and Center for Lessons Learned (CALL) gathers troops and their officers together for intense reviews of what did and did not happen and what can be done to improve performance. When forces face uncertainty and new missions, CALL teams push useful knowledge to them. They also have developed lessons learned libraries that can be accessed by commanders and planners.

ACT 6. Meet to create action plans based on scouting reports.

Action planning's questions include: What is our aim (desired outcome or mission)? What is our concept? What steps need to be taken to enact our intent and concept? What resources do we possess and/or require? What are the measures of success? All these activities may be managed or coordinated by your product development group and lead management team.

Neither scouting nor any other planned innovation activity guarantees innovations on a predictable basis. It has no consistent return on investment. That's the nature of innovation; it is like prospecting for gold. However, like prospecting, innovation has one guarantee: If you don't look for it, you are almost certain not to find it.

THE LEADER'S ROLE IN QUALITY MANAGEMENT IN A PROJECT-BASED ORGANIZATION

The leader's role is always tempered by his or her knowledge that people watch your feet and not your lips. "Walking your talk" is the advice of every approach to improving organizational performance.

We have the same advice here, but it is presented through the lens of complete customer focus.

As the leader of a project-based organization, you must understand and be the constant advocate of quality management and using customer focus to drive organizational success. Taking that one step further to include all customers/stakeholders, consider how you might use Phil Crosby's advice in a 1992 article on twenty-first century leadership.[7] He was writing about the complete organization and the complete leader. His leadership principles of completeness are to make employees successful, make suppliers successful, and make customers successful:

1. In talking with stakeholders, their requirements are first on your mind. Your job is to make them successful.
2. When talking with employees, their requirements as customers should also guide your actions. They need to be trained, not blamed for everything that goes wrong. The work system should be designed to facilitate their focusing on task, conforming to customer requirements, and being actively involved in improving the system and not having to fight the system to do their jobs. Your job is to make them successful.
3. When talking and working with suppliers, their requirements as customers should also guide your actions. Work with suppliers on quality management issues, as well as require it of them. Your job is to make them successful.
4. When designing how you are going to conform to your customer's requirements, you are asking those involved how they are designing quality and continuous improvement into the system that enables the organization to conform to their requirements.
5. When problems arise, your questions come from the customer's perspective first, and facts are asked for first, second, and third. When

time is short with little or no time for PDSA, the guide is: With the facts we do have at hand, this is what we are going to do. Then we immediately begin to track or measure how well the decision is working and work on an improvement.

One final note on the leader's role. My experience with project management is based on 18 years of events management, about the same number of years observing project-based NASA suppliers and NASA itself, and working with a variety of firms that ran thousands of quality improvement projects. The best leaders took an active role in the improvement process itself. The president of Lockheed Electronics taught the course on quality leadership that his managers had to take—and he taught them on Saturdays. A number of senior executives that I have known also participated directly in some quality improvement activity that involved their own work or their work with their direct reports. Therefore, they could not only talk about the methods and nod approvingly during reports, but also they could say, "When I was using QFD, or a Pareto chart, on our problem, I . . ."

QFD RESOURCES

"Improving the Design of Adequate Combat Systems for U.S. DOD," Kirk Kirkpatrick, Lockheed Martin Missiles and Fire Control; Maj. Shel Jones, U.S. Army; Glenn Mazur, Japan Business Consultants, Ltd.

Brown, Mark Graham, "Defining Customer Requirements Service Quality Deployment," *Journal for Quality and Participation* (March 1990).

Mizuno, Shigeru, and Yoji Akao (eds.), *QFD: The Customer Driven Approach to Quality Planning and Deployment,* APO, 365 pp., 1993, ISBN 92-833-1122-1.

Quality Function Deployment Institute. http://www.qfdi.org.

Reid, Robert P. and Margaret J. Hermann, "QFD: The Voice of the Customer," *Journal for Quality and Participation* (December 1989).

NOTES

1. Boeing Quality Management System (BQMS), ELS/RSS Supplier Conference (March 2000).

2. J. Davidson Frame and Joan Knuston, eds., *Project Management for Business Professionals* (New York: Wiley, 2001).

3. Luiz Antonio Gargione, "Using Quality Function Deployment (QFD) in the Design Phase of an Apartment Construction Project," Proceedings IGLC-7 357.

4. QFD Killed My Pet (Project)—Using QFD to Confirm Market Needs for New Technology by Dwight Delgado, Fusion UV Systems; Glenn Mazur, Japan.

5. "Jurassic QFD: Integrating Service and Product"; Andrew Business Consultants. Ltd., Symposium Proceedings 2001: 13th Symposium on Bolt, MD, Robotics,

Canada; Glenn H. Mazur, Japan Business QFD, Baltimore, MD, November 6–9, 2001 (ISBN1-889477-13-3); Consultants, Ltd.; The Eleventh Symposium on Quality Function Deployment, Novi, MI (June 1999).

6.   From an e-mail conversation between Mazur and Hamson, October 8, 2002.

7.   Philip B. Crosby, "Getting from Here to There, 21st Century Leadership," *Journal for Quality and Participation,* (July/August 1992, Association for Quality and Participation, Cincinnati, OH).

PART THREE

BUILDING A HIGH-PERFORMANCE PROJECT TEAM

People get projects done. From start to finish, people perform the work. With all the attention we give project objectives, risk management, detailed schedules and budgets, progress reports, and project management information systems, we must never forget that these are all designed to serve the people who accomplish the work.

Decades of management thinking have gone into understanding how people function in the work environment. We want to understand how to achieve that ultimate win-win formula: the environment that attracts talented people and, at the same time, generates the maximum sustainable productivity.

Project managers strive to master this formula because we often need projects to deliver high performance: We ask project teams to generate new products, solve pressing problems, and accomplish what ordinary functional units can't. Clear goals and solid plans are definitely part of the answer. But the science of project management is not enough. The human factor demands that project managers pay attention to the project culture and environment. Part Three of this book addresses these factors from three different perspectives: (1) the characteristics of a high-performing team; (2) using the science of project management as the foundation for the art of weaving the project team together; and (3) the factors necessary on virtual teams.

Chapter 8 analyzes the components of a high-performance team. Ironically, projects inherently contain many obstacles to high performance. Because every project is temporary and unique, project managers and teams face a consistent set of problems:

- High-performing teams exhibit high trust and strong personal relationships, yet projects formed to accomplish unique goals often assemble unique teams. If it takes too long for the team to bond, the project begins to slip behind schedule—underperformance begins to eat away at morale in a negative spiral.

- The culture required by the project may be in contrast to the culture of the enterprise. A heavily-regulated utility, for instance, may find it difficult to form a nimble, responsive team to explore a new product idea.

- Many projects begin with aggressive cost and schedule targets. As a result, any unexpected problem can put the project up against the wall. When that happens, the people on the team often take up the slack, working long days and too many weekends. The people who survive the project move on to the next one weary and wary. Whether they created it or not, project managers carry the baggage of past projects.

- The unwritten rules of any workplace take time to learn. On a project team, the unwritten rules lead to confusion. It could be as simple as recording decisions during a meeting and distributing meeting minutes, but if there are no stated guidelines, it just doesn't get done.

- Project teams solve problems. That means there are decisions to be made and conflict is sure to arise.

The biggest challenge, however, is that project teams are made up of people, and people require special handling. We thrive with proper guidelines and clear communication. We work better with people whom we trust and who will rise to a challenge. We want to be recognized for our contributions and know that we play a valuable role. Recognizing these obstacles is the first step in overcoming them. We realize it takes conscious, purposeful actions to create a productive environment for our teams. In Chapter 8, Elaine Biech describes 10 specific components of a high-performing team that you, as a project manager, can build into your project.

In Chapter 9, Neil Whitten presents the unifying role of discipline within a project. He illustrates how the science of project management forms the framework for a successful project and how the people bring it to life. Through his examples, we see that neither the people nor the science are sufficient on their own, but it is in weaving them together that we create the magic of cohesive, highly productive teams.

The technology boom in the past decade has dramatically improved productivity in many ways, particularly as a tool for communication.

Better communication is usually good news for project teams, but this progress has presented a new challenge: the virtual team. Virtual teams are not defined by physical or organizational boundaries. Instead, they are defined by a common goal and mutual reliance on each other. To some degree, this definition is true for all project teams, but the looseness with which virtual teams are formed pushes the difficulties to new levels and requires the virtual team leader to be even more conscious of the team's environment. In Chapter 10, authors Deborah Duarte and Nancy Tennant Snyder provide seven factors that will strengthen the performance of a virtual team.

Every chapter in Part Three presents a different perspective on building a positive, productive environment. Notice that in each chapter there exists strong ties to the project management discipline presented in Part Two. Clear goals, for instance, are one of Biech's 10 essential components, and a project's work breakdown structure and statement of work are two specific methods of establishing clear goals. Together, these three chapters speak to our intuitive awareness that project management is an art and a science. The art is using the science to bring the team to life; building an environment where the people reach further, accomplish more, and create an experience they want to repeat on every project.

8 A MODEL FOR BUILDING TEAMWORK

Elaine Biech

Have you ever been a member of a high-performing, smoothly running team? If you have been, it's an experience that you are not likely to forget. Probably people trusted one another, worked cooperatively, enjoyed the task, and achieved goals higher than anyone may have imagined. Experts agree that effective, successful, high-performance teams have several similar characteristics. What are they? The 10 main characteristics are described below.

TEN CHARACTERISTICS OF SUCCESSFUL TEAMS

Exhibit 8.1 provides a visual model of the characteristics that exist within most successful teams. We hope this information will provide a starting point for you to begin to build a stronger team.

The blocks shown in the model were not assigned random positions. Each has been placed in its respective spot for a reason. The blocks at the bottom (*clear goals, defined roles, open and clear communication,* and *effective decision making*) are the *foundation.* They must be strong and be in place early. The items in the second row (*balanced participation, valued diversity,* and *managed conflict*) are a step above the base and also required early in the team's formation. The third row contains characteristics that make working on a team personally satisfying and rewarding, but these are not imperative to completing the task. However, most team members will tell you that a *positive atmosphere* and *cooperative relationships* are the ultimate goals of teamwork.

251

EXHIBIT 8.1   Ten characteristics of a high-performance team

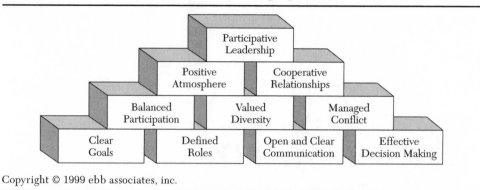

The *participative leadership* block is the only one that can be removed without disturbing any of the other blocks. What does this tell you? Perhaps that one single leader is not always necessary. The position of the block, however, also suggests that participative leadership will generally emerge later in a team's formation. Let's examine each of these blocks required to build a team.

The bottom row of blocks serves as the foundation: clear goals, defined roles, open and clear communication, and effective decision making. What makes these so valuable to a team?

Clear Goals

Clearly defined goals are essential so that everyone understands the purpose and vision of the team. You might be surprised at how many people do not know the reason they are doing the tasks that make up their jobs, much less what their team is doing. Everyone must be pulling in the same direction and be aware of the end goals.

Clear goals help team members understand where the team is going. Clear goals help a team know when it has been successful by defining exactly what the team is doing and what it wants to accomplish. This makes it easier for members to work together—and more likely to be successful.

Clear goals create ownership. Team members are more likely to "own" goals and work toward them if they have been involved in establishing them as a team. In addition, the ownership is longer lasting if members perceive that other team members support the same efforts.

Clear goals foster team unity, whereas unclear goals foster confusion— or sometimes individualism. If team members don't agree on the meaning of the team goals, they will work alone to accomplish their individual interpretations of the goals. They may also protect their own goals, even at the expense of the team.

How can a team ensure that its goals are clear and understood by everyone? A good test is to have each team member list the team's goals, then compare differences and similarities and agree on the final goals. Final goals should be written and distributed to each team member, then reviewed periodically.

Defined Roles

If a team's roles are clearly defined, all team members know what their jobs are, but defining roles goes beyond that. It means that we recognize individuals' talent and tap into the expertise of each member—both job-related and innate skills each person brings to the team, such as organization, creative, or team-building skills.

Clearly defined roles help team members understand why they are on a team. When the members experience conflict, it may be related to their roles. Team members often can manage this conflict by identifying, clarifying, and agreeing on their individual responsibilities so that they all gain a clear understanding of how they will accomplish the team's goals.

Once team members are comfortable with their primary roles on the team, they can identify the roles they play during team meetings. There are two kinds of roles that are essential in team meetings.

Task Roles

Task roles contribute to getting the work of the team done. People in these roles supply the information, ideas, and energy necessary for the group to accomplish its goals. Task roles generate, organize, and complete the work and include roles such as the proposer, the coordinator, and the procedurer.

Maintenance Roles

Maintenance roles contribute to group cohesion and effectiveness. People in these roles establish and maintain interpersonal relationships and a group-centered atmosphere. Maintenance roles address people and atmosphere issues and include specific roles, such as the reconciler, the motivator, and the relaxer.

All team members have responsibility for both task and maintenance roles. These roles are flexible, with members pitching in as needed to fill any void that occurs. Recognize that team members have different strengths in carrying out these roles. Accept these differences. Encourage team members to use their strengths, but also encourage them to "try on" new roles as part of their development.

Open and Clear Communication

The importance of *open and clear communication* cannot be stressed enough. This is probably the most important characteristic for high-performance teams. Most problems of all kinds can be traced back to poor communication or lack of communication skills, such as listening well or providing constructive feedback.

Enough books have been written about communication to fill a library. That makes it difficult to identify only a few key points in this area. Excellent communication is the key to keeping a team informed, focused, and moving forward. Team members must feel free to express their thoughts and opinions at any time. Yet, even as they are expressing themselves, they must make certain they are doing so in a clear and concise manner.

Unfortunately, most of us are not very good listeners. Most of us could improve our communication if we just started to listen better—to listen with an open mind, to hear the entire message before forming conclusions, and to work toward mutual understanding with the speaker. We allow distractions to prevent us from giving our full attention to the speaker. We allow our minds to wander instead of focusing on the speaker. We allow our biases and prejudices to form the basis for our understanding. Instead, we should allow the new information we are hearing to form the basis for our understanding.

Many benefits exist for working toward improving communication for your team. Consider those listed in Exhibit 8.2.

If team members attend to no other high-performing team characteristic, working to improve their communication with other team members will increase trust, decrease problems and rework, and build healthy interpersonal relationships. Invest in improved communication; it will pay off!

Effective Decision Making

Decision making is *effective* when the team is aware of and uses many methods to arrive at decisions. Consensus is often touted as the best way to make decisions—and it is an excellent method and probably not used often enough. But the team should also use majority rule, expert decision, authority rule with discussion, and other methods.

EXHIBIT 8.2 Benefits of good team communication

There are many benefits for improving communication on your team:

- Open communication encourages team members to express their points of view and to offer all the information they can to make the team more effective.
- Clear communication ensures that team messages are understood by speakers and listeners.
- Two-way communication increases the likelihood that all team members hear the same message.
- Good listening skills ensure that both the speaker's content (words) and the intent are heard.
- Attention to nonverbal communication helps further identify feelings and hidden messages that may get in the way of teamwork.

The team members should discuss the method they want to use and should use tools to assist them, such as force-field analysis, pair-wise ranking matrices, or some of the multivoting techniques.

Effective decision making is essential to a team's progress; ideally, teams that are asked to solve problems should also have the power and authority to implement solutions. They must have a grasp of various decision-making methods, their advantages and disadvantages, and when and how to use each. Teams that choose the right decision-making methods at the right time will not only save time, but they will also most often make the best decisions.

This completes the four basic foundation characteristics: clear goals, defined roles, open and clear communication, and effective decision making. The next three blocks in the model build on their foundation.

Balanced Participation

If communication is the most important team characteristic, participation is the second most important. Without participation, you don't have a team; you have a group of bodies.

Balanced participation ensures that everyone on the team is fully involved. It does *not* mean that if you have five people each is speaking 20 percent of the time. Talking is not necessarily a measure of participation. We all know people who talk a lot and say nothing. It does mean that each individual is contributing when it's appropriate. The more a team involves *all* of its members in its activities, the more likely that team is to experience a high level of commitment and synergy.

Balanced participation means that each team member joins the discussion when his or her contribution is pertinent to the team assignment. It also means that everyone's opinions are sought and valued by others on the team.

Participation is everyone's responsibility. As a team moves from a forming stage to more mature stages of group development, team members must make certain that everyone is an active participant. If you have team members who did not participate early in the formation of the team, they will withdraw even more as the going becomes more difficult. To achieve the best participation, a team might start by asking some of the questions found in Exhibit 8.3.

EXHIBIT 8.3   Question to ask for increased participation

- Did everyone on the team give his or her point of view when we established the ground rules?
- Did everyone have input into our goals?
- When we solve problems, do we make sure everyone has spoken before we decide?
- Do we consistently ask the shy members of our team what we think?
- Do we seek opposing points of view?
- Do we ask all team members what they want?

Two important things influence team participation: the leader's behavior and the participants' expectations.

Leader's Behavior

A *leader's behavior* comes as much from attitude as from anything. Leaders who are effective in obtaining participation see their roles as being a coach and mentor, not the expert in the situation. Leaders will get more participation from team members if they can admit to needing help, not power. Leaders should also specify the kind of participation they want right from the start. Will everyone share their own ideas and then decide what to do or will the group discuss the pros and cons of the leader's idea? If everyone knows the answer, then there are no lingering questions.

Leaders need to create a participative climate. They must make it a practice to speak last to avoid influencing others. Often a leader may put an idea on the table "just to get things started." But what happens? Everyone jumps on the idea and stops thinking. People may feel, "Well, if that's what she wants, that's it."

Leaders need to reward risk taking. Those "half-baked" partial ideas that people bring up may be just what gets the team moving toward a solution, idea, or new opportunity. Leaders must always protect the minority views. Anyone can think like everyone else. It takes courage to think and speak differently.

Leaders need input from everyone, but usually some team members have been selected for their expertise and experience. To ask for input, the leader must recognize those people for their expertise and/or experience, direct questions to them, and lead the discussion that results so that everyone is included. That's what participation is all about.

Participants' Expectations

Participants must volunteer information willingly rather than force someone to drag it out of them. They should encourage others' participation as well by asking question of others, especially those who have been quiet for a while.

Participants can assist the leader by suggesting techniques that encourage everyone to speak, for example, a round robin. To conduct a round robin, someone directs all members to state their opinions or ideas about the topic under discussion. Members go around the group, in order, and one person at a time says what's on his or her mind. During this time, no one else in the group can disagree, ask questions, or discuss how the idea might work or not work, be good or not good.

Only after everyone has had an opportunity to hear others and to be heard him- or herself, a discussion occurs. This discussion may focus on pros and cons, on clarifying, on similarities and differences, or on trying to reach consensus.

Participants can also encourage participation by establishing relationships with other team members between meetings. Another thing they can do is to call people by name. We all like to hear our names used by others—especially in positive ways!

Remember that each and every member of a team has responsibility not only to participate, but also to ensure that everyone else is given the opportunity to participate.

Valued Diversity

Valued diversity is at the heart of building a team. Thus, the box is at the center of the model. It means, put simply, that team members are valued for the unique contributions that they bring to the team.

Diversity goes far beyond gender and race. It also includes how people think, what experience they bring, and their styles. A diversity of thinking, ideas, methods, experiences, and opinions helps to create a high-performing team.

Sometimes team members may realize that they do not have the kind of variety they need. They will note this, discuss it, and then do what is necessary to become more diverse. In the short term, the team may tap into expertise from another department for a specific project. In the long term, the team may identify the specific requirements it is missing so that the next person they bring in can fill the gaps.

Whether individuals are creative or logical, fast or methodical, the effective team recognizes the strengths each person brings to the team. Sometimes these differences are perceived by individuals as *wrong*. The high-performing team member sees these differences as imperative for the success of the team and respects the diverse points of view brought by others.

Yes, it is more difficult to manage a highly diverse team, but the benefits will show up in the end. It takes work and a very special group of people to encourage the differences that each brings to the team. Flexibility and sensitivity are key.

Managed Conflict

Conflict is essential to a team's creativity and productivity. Because most people dislike conflict, they often assume that effective teams do not have it. In fact, both effective and ineffective teams experience conflict. The difference is that effective teams manage it constructively. In fact, effective teams see conflict as positive.

Managed conflict ensures that problems are not swept under the rug. It means that the team has discussed members' points of view about an issue and has come to see well-managed conflict as a healthy way to bring out new ideas and to solve whatever seems to be unsolvable. Here are some benefits of healthy conflict:

- Conflict forces a team to find productive ways to communicate differences, seek common goals, and gain consensus.
- Conflict encourages a team to look at all points of view, then adopt the best ideas from each.
- Conflict increases creativity by forcing the team to look beyond current assumptions and parameters.
- Conflict increases the quality of team decisions. If team members are allowed to disagree, they are more likely to look for solutions that meet everyone's objectives. Thus, the final solution will most likely be better than any of the original solutions that were offered.
- Conflict allows team members to express their emotions, preventing feelings about unresolved issues from becoming obstacles to the team's progress.
- Managed conflict encourages participation. When team members feel they can openly and constructively disagree, they are more likely to participate in the discussion. On the other hand, if conflict is discouraged, they withdraw.

Teams can benefit tremendously from the conflict they experience. Make it a point to maintain an environment in which conflict is not only managed, but encouraged.

Positive Atmosphere

To be truly successful, a team must have a climate of trust and openness, that is, a *positive atmosphere.* A positive atmosphere indicates that members of the team are committed and involved. It means that people are comfortable enough with one another to be creative, take risks, and make mistakes. It also means that you may hear plenty of laughter, and research shows that people who are enjoying themselves are more productive than those who dislike what they are doing.

Trust is by far the most important ingredient of a positive atmosphere. How do team members reach a point where they can trust one another? What are the characteristics that make some people seem more trustworthy than others? Trust and credibility can be described behaviorally. They can be seen in a more logical way than you might think. Consider for a minute. What do people need to do to build trust with you?

Did you think about honesty? Dependability? Sincerity? Open-mindedness? You've just identified some of the characteristics and behaviors that build trust. It's important to keep in mind that what one person sees as trustworthy is not necessarily what another sees. We each have different values. So when you want to build trust and credibility with others, it's as important to know what those individuals value as it is to know what is already your strong suit.

Let's examine some characteristics and behaviors that build trust:

- To build trust with some people, you will need to be *honest* and *candid.* The messages this sends are: "I say what I mean." "You will always know where I stand." "You can be straight with me."
- To build trust with some people, you will need to be *accessible* and *open.* The messages this sends are: "I'll tell you what works best for me." "Tell me what works for you." "Let's not work with hidden agendas."
- To build trust with some people, you will need to be *approving* and *accepting.* The messages this sends are: "I value people and diverse perspectives." "You can count on being heard without judgment or criticism."
- To build trust with some people, you will need to be *dependable* and *trustworthy.* The messages this sends are: "I do what I say I will do." "I keep my promises." "You can count on me."

Interestingly, these seem to be very strong, positive messages. But some people may perceive them differently. Like everything that involves human beings, there is not one clear way. Generally, to build trusting relationships with others, people must also provide credible evidence. There are two types of evidence: objective and subjective.

Objective evidence includes facts and figures or other measured and quantified data. *Subjective* evidence includes the opinions of others who are highly regarded (friends, family, or competent colleagues) and perceived as relevant resources and knowledgeable about the subject.

Of course, trust is not built overnight. Individuals have their own requirements for how long it takes to build trust with them, including these four:

1. *One time or until you prove otherwise:* "I guess you might call me optimistic. I tend to start with a clean slate."
2. *A number of times:* "I need some history. I tend to let my guard down after a few positive interactions with people or after people have demonstrated their trustworthiness."
3. *A period of time:* "I need some history, too, but I tend to prefer a period of time to a specific number of times before I am comfortable placing trust in people."
4. *Each time:* "I value consistency. Call me pessimistic if you like, but I think I'm just being realistic. I guess I can be hard to convince."

Building trust on a team will be one of your greatest challenges. If a team you work with has done a good job of building trust, the other aspects of a positive atmosphere will come more easily. Those aspects include: individuals who are committed to the team's goals; an atmosphere that encourages creativity and risk taking; people who are not devastated if they make mistakes; and team members who genuinely enjoy being on the team. A positive atmosphere is one of the characteristics of a mature team.

Cooperative Relationships

Directly related to having a positive atmosphere are *cooperative relationships*. Team members know that they need one another's skills, knowledge, and expertise to produce something together that they could not do as well alone. There is a sense of belonging and a willingness to make things work for the good of the whole team. The atmosphere is informal, comfortable, and relaxed. Team members are allowed to be themselves. They are involved and interested.

Cooperative relationships are the hallmark of top performing teams. These top teams demonstrate not only cooperative relationships between team members, but also cooperative working relationships elsewhere in the organization.

Although it takes more than a list of ideas to build positive, cooperative relationships, there are several actions you can take. Teams can be made aware of the following areas:

- Recognize and value the different strengths that each member brings to the team. Focus on each person and on why he or she is on the team. The team should be certain to utilize each person's unique strengths.

- Provide a forum in which team members can give and receive constructive feedback. One of the best measures of a positive, cooperative relationship is whether people are honestly providing feedback to one another.

- Conduct self-evaluations as a part of normal business. Individuals can evaluate themselves as well as the team. Remember that it is everyone's responsibility to encourage growth and learning.

- Build an environment of trust and cooperation. Trust is the linchpin between a positive atmosphere and cooperative relationships. It's like the chicken and the egg. It's difficult to tell which came first. The team members should demonstrate a team spirit that values cooperative relationships outside the team as well.

- Celebrate the team's successes. Most teams are very task-oriented and forget to celebrate their successes. Don't forget to reward yourself as a team. Some ways could include going out to lunch together, having a picnic, or publicly announcing an achievement to the rest of the organization.

Completing assignments brings closure to the task aspect of teamwork. Celebrating team accomplishments brings closure to the interpersonal aspect of teamwork. To maintain the highest possible performance on a team, all team members should be responsible for relationship building.

Participative Leadership

The *participative leadership* block is not at the top of the model because it is the most important. It is at the top because it is the only block that can be removed without disturbing the rest. *Participative leadership* means that leaders share the responsibility and the glory, are supportive and fair, create a climate of trust and openness, and are good coaches and teachers.

In general, it means that leaders are good role models and that the leadership shifts at various times. In the most productive teams, it is difficult to identify a leader during a casual observation.

In conclusion, a high-performing team can accomplish more together than all the individuals can apart.

LEARNING TO BE A TEAM

Remember, too, that there is often learning that must occur for everyone on the team. But learning isn't enough. People's behaviors must change as well. Behavioral change can be the most difficult part of teamwork, and it may be quite uncomfortable at first.

Try this experiment. Cross your arms. Now look at how your arms are crossed. Which one is on top? Now cross them the other way—with the other arm on top. Keep them crossed and read on. Keep them crossed as long as you can. How does it feel? Uncomfortable? Awkward? Strange? Keep them crossed! Keep reading! Having a hard time concentrating? Wish you could uncross them? Well go ahead, uncross your arms.

It was uncomfortable to cross your arms the other way (not the *wrong* way). Crossing your arms is a very simple task, yet when you tried to do it differently, it felt uncomfortable. In fact, for some of you, it may have been so uncomfortable that you couldn't even concentrate as you continued to read.

Yet, if you wanted (for whatever reason) to change the way you cross your arms and you continued to cross your arms the new way for six months, what do you think would happen? Eventually, it would become comfortable and the natural way to cross your arms.

Would you ever slip back to crossing your arms the other way? Yes. Especially when you were under the stresses of short time lines or were facing problems.

Will the team members you work with ever slip back to working more as individuals than as team members? Yes. Especially when time is short, problems pop up, or the discussion or task becomes difficult. Let's think about that. When do team members need teamwork the most? When time is short, problems pop up, or something becomes difficult. Think about the implications. When teamwork is needed the most, teams are most likely to slip back to working as individuals.

Recognize that dedicating yourself to building high-performance teams requires you to encourage team members to do *many* things differently. It is not nearly so easy as learning to cross your arms differently. It takes practice and patience on the part of every team member. Teams don't start off great. They *learn* to be great.

9 DISCIPLINE: THE GLUE THAT HOLDS IT ALL TOGETHER*
Neal Whitten

All leaders want to run a tight ship, but not at the expense of their project personnel's creativity, sense of commitment and ownership, and willingness to take risks. If a leader is too strict or rigid, a level of bureaucracy can evolve that actually has a stifling affect on employee productivity and motivation. On the other hand, if a leader is too permissive, a project can be robbed of the crucial management support and order that is so vital in maintaining a well-run, consistently productive organization. Somewhere, between these extremes of rigidity and permissiveness, is a desirable balance that offers the most in achieving and maintaining a healthy organization. Within this scale, where would you position your leadership abilities?

> **Lesson: The single greatest factor that can make or break a software development project is the degree of discipline that the project's leadership exercises.**

Briefly stated, *discipline* is the act of encouraging a desired pattern of behavior. Discipline is the glue that holds it all together. Most projects that do not meet their schedule, budget, quality, or function fail because the level of discipline exhibited across the organization is deficient.

---

* This chapter was originally written for software project managers, but its contents apply to project managers in every industry.

This chapter discusses the important subjects of:

- The need for discipline.
- How to recognize the disciplined organization.
- How to establish and maintain discipline.
- Attributes of the successful leader.

This chapter is primarily, but not exclusively, for the leaders in a project. These leaders might direct a team of two or an organization of 1,000 and include technical, administrative, financial, and project leaders. Project leaders include both managers and nonmanagers. This chapter also should be of interest to those aspiring to be leaders.

PROJECT TALES

The short scenarios presented in this section illustrate situations to be avoided. They demonstrate situations where discipline is weak, misguided, or missing. Can you recognize the problems? Have you seen them before?

A new department has been created in a busy and expanding development organization. At the first department meeting, the manager, Ralph Nettle, looks over his employees and sets some ground rules for the operation of the department. Weeks later those at the meeting recall that Nettle's most notable statement was: "Do as I say, not as I do."

In the meeting, Nettle announces that he will meet with employees individually to determine their role and degree of progress in the current project. He arranges to meet with each person for 30 minutes over the better part of two days. The first meeting takes 40 minutes; the next, one hour. At the end of two days, six employees have yet to be seen. He reschedules them for the next day but finds time to meet with only one. He apologizes to the other five and reschedules again—and again. Two weeks later he has met with everyone. During each meeting Nettle has committed to get personally involved with each employee on specific problem areas. He sets dates to get back with each of them. After one month has passed, only 25 percent of his commitments have been fulfilled.

The department manager, Matt Holstein, feels really in tune with what's going on in the project. He has been a manager for just under one year. However, Holstein is no newcomer to software development projects. He has held several leadership roles on past projects. He feels he has learned the "right" way to do things and wants the best possible performance from his department. To obtain this goal, he feels he must take an active role in all primary decisions and many lesser ones. He believes that no one in his department can do most tasks as well as he can. He also feels that no one seems to be as self-motivated as he believes they should be. If this department was a separate company, and he was to leave, he just knows that the company would fold. He acknowledges there are people in his department who have potential, and he is determined to bring that potential to the surface.

As a manager, Holstein feels he is a natural leader and can guide his department to excellence in everything he does. To this end, he has defined himself as the focal point for all activities. He initiates and performs most planning exercises. He thoroughly reviews all his department's documents and deliverables before he will allow them to be distributed outside his department. He also, and just as thoroughly, reviews all documents generated by other departments that are for his department's review. He consolidates any comments from within his department and personally creates the response memo for his signature. He not only attends the more important meetings within his department, he runs them. Almost nothing happens within his department without his personal participation.

With all the care and attention he gives to his employees' assignments, Holstein cannot understand why everybody else seems unwilling or unable to make decisions on their own. He notices he is usually the only one working overtime. He does not look forward to being out of the office because, when he returns, he is sure there will be too much work to catch up on and, possibly, from which to recover.

A new project has just started. The staffing occurred almost immediately, with programmers transferred from other projects. The new project is small by some standards, with 20 programmers. The project leader, Erin Springer, sees an opportunity to achieve great things with this newly assembled talented crew and proceeds to declare the schedules that must be met. These schedules are over a one-year period. The project members quickly recognize the difficulty in achieving such aggressive schedules. The generally held view is that aggressive schedules are good business as long as they are achievable. An attempt is made to put more realistic schedules in place but Springer holds firm. She states that the schedules have been committed to higher management and, therefore, must happen. Not much is known about Springer's past leadership experiences. In an attempt to be fair, the project members give her the benefit of the doubt and hope she has an "ace up her sleeve." A month passes and the new schedule is one week behind. The next month sees another week lost. At this rate, the project will be late by 25 percent of the schedule's length, yet Springer is unwilling to adjust the schedule. She attempts to compensate by mandating overtime and adding people to the project. Four months into the project, progress is more than one month behind schedule. Hope is rapidly fading that an ace will appear.

The project is four months old, with at least two years to go. The number of people involved in the project has grown rapidly. Several of the earlier people to come on board have been given the more critical lead roles. These people do not appear to be particularly experienced, skilled, or gifted, but they are recognized as being loyal to June Pritchard, the project head. The project is proving to be a challenge in many ways, not the least of which are its technical complexity and sheer size. As is to be expected with any project of this magnitude, daily problems arise and compete for attention. The people Pritchard has assigned to take the critical lead roles are having difficulty extinguishing fires as fast as they flare up. Small problems fester through neglect and grow into serious problems. Many decisions are made and then remade days or weeks later, causing much rework and consternation among the employees affected. Communication across the project is suffering severely. Commitments are being made without consulting the people who must carry them out. Many believe that the people assigned to the project's more critical lead roles are not qualified. Pritchard discounts this notion. She asserts that the project leadership is as it should be. Her view is that the major problem lies in the large number of relatively inexperienced, uncommitted, and unmotivated employees throughout the organization.

Michelle Barret, a hardworking employee, feels frustrated. She graduated as class valedictorian from a prominent university and went on to earn, with honors, a master's degree in computer science and a minor in business. She has worked for one company since finishing college four years ago. At that time, it was her belief that two types of successful companies exist: those that hire their lead people from other companies, and those that grow and groom their leaders from within. She favored working for a company that placed a premium on developing its own people. She felt that this type of company would best prepare her for an executive position.

Barret's views about successful companies have not changed, but her views about her own company have. The lead people in this organization have done little to coach, counsel, or inspire her or any other of the project personnel. She actually feels the opposite happens. People are reprimanded publicly for taking on risks that fail. Those who complete their assignments on schedule and with superior quality are all but ignored. It is next to impossible to receive any personal recognition for a job well done. Barret regularly observes the project leaders she works with reacting to people and situations without listening to the facts. Inconsistent decisions are commonplace. Advancement is significantly slower than is generally expected within companies in the same industry. Today Barret has, with personal regret, submitted her resignation.

These scenarios depict situations that hurt the people involved, the project, and the company. Yet action can be taken to avoid replays of these stories and numerous others like them.

The remainder of this chapter offers some ways to recognize and maintain a properly disciplined organization and to understand the numerous benefits of such an organization. Also presented are the attributes that are characteristic of successful leaders—*self-disciplined* leaders. After you have read this chapter, you might find it useful to revisit the scenarios to identify their problems—and to determine how they could have been avoided.

THE NEED FOR DISCIPLINE

> Discipline is the soul of an army. It makes small numbers formidable, procures success to the weak, and esteem to all.
>
> —George Washington

Lesson: All people want and need to know the acceptable pattern of behavior that is expected of them.

Everyone wants discipline. Everyone wants to work in an environment where people know what to expect. Again, discipline is the glue that holds a project together. It is *the* tool for managing change—and change is essential for progress. The processes and methodologies employed within a project cannot be sustained without the necessary, underlying discipline. A project needs discipline to achieve the desired level of accomplishment for each of its major parameters. These major project parameters are listed in Exhibit 9.1.

The following sections offer insight on the impact that discipline can have on these major project parameters.

Employee Morale

Lesson: Projects run their best when employee morale is high.

While great human achievements typically are not accomplished on morale alone, history seems to show that strong morale has added to the effectiveness of many great achievers. Obviously high employee morale offers great value to a project. Good morale can have a positive affect on every major project parameter. However, discipline from the project's leadership is essential for achieving high morale within an organization.

EXHIBIT 9.1   Major project parameters

- Employee morale
- Productivity
- Quality
- Schedules
- Cost

For example, project members want and need to:

- Know what their mission is.
- Understand their assignments.
- Understand how they are measured against their performance.
- Know that they will be recognized and rewarded for their achievements.
- Know what to expect from their leaders.
- Believe that project leaders make a genuine effort to understand their people and maintain good, two-way communications.
- Believe that project leaders will make the best decisions for the success of the project.

When project leaders exhibit discipline in insisting on an environment that satisfies these wants and needs from the project's personnel, then almost anything can be accomplished. Significant accomplishment, however, is impossible when the project's management fails to exercise the necessary level of discipline that is needed to create and sustain such an environment—an environment that *encourages* high employee morale.

Productivity

Lesson: Employee productivity is at its highest when employees know what to do, how to do it—and do it!

Employee productivity is at its best when project processes are defined, measurable, and enforced—and project members are educated about their roles. Discipline within the project is required to make these things happen. Consider an example.

In every software development process, the product passes through phases as it is being developed. Some typical phases are:

- Product definition.
- Product design.
- Code.

Each of the project's phases can, in turn, be defined in more detail. For example, *product specifications* falls within the phase *product definition*. The product specifications activity could be divided into five smaller activities:

- Product specifications preparation.
- Product specifications review.
- Product specifications update.
- Product specifications approval.
- Product specifications refresh.

Each of these activities can be defined further in terms of entry, implementation, and exit conditions.

After the project's processes to be followed are defined to a level at which the participants can measure their adherence, the project members then must be properly trained and educated to understand those processes fully. Finally, those processes must be fully supported and enforced by the project leaders. To make all this happen, the project's leadership must demonstrate discipline.

Quality

Lesson: Quality will suffer without deliberate discipline.

Quality is another major project parameter that will suffer without discipline. It seems that many people have their own definition of quality. (See Chapter 7 for more on planning for quality.) Regardless of the definition used, however, there is always a great need to define and follow processes that will yield the desired product quality. While quality often is associated with the "worker bee" in the trenches doing the designing, coding, or testing, the project's leadership must first exhibit the discipline that leads to a quality-producing work environment. There is a real temptation to sacrifice quality first—whenever a project falls behind schedule. But quality actually should be the last parameter to be sacrificed, if ever. Sheer discipline from the project's leadership is required to avoid the let's-lower-the-quality trap. The following saying holds true for too many projects—perhaps even yours.

We never have enough time to do it right, but we always find time to do it over.

Schedules

Lesson: The need for continuous discipline is perhaps most evident when managing a project's schedules.

This saying leads into the next reason for discipline—schedules. How many projects do you know about that actually finished under the same schedule they began? For those projects that changed their schedules, how much of a contributing factor was the lack of project discipline by the project leaders?

Earlier it was mentioned that change is essential to progress. When a project's schedules are defined and approved early in the software development process, many assumptions and dependencies are identified. As times passes and some activities complete and many more begin, the project personnel who participated in the creation and approval of the schedules become more knowledgeable. For example, a certain document that was estimated to take four weeks to write might now require six weeks because the expected dependencies were late or because the effort simply was underestimated.

What is happening is that *change* is being introduced into the project equation. In order to maintain the overall schedules, the discipline required to manage this ongoing change must be alive and active. Software development projects are not static. They are extremely lively and in constant need of attention. Discipline from project leaders is vital to maintain the overall, committed project schedules.

Cost

Cost is another major project parameter at the mercy of discipline. Budgets are affected by such factors as the number of programmers involved, the number of computer workstations available, the tools employed, office space, furniture, and so on. The list can be extensive. Even the timing chosen by a project's leaders to begin moving people from one project into another can be quite costly. The opportunity to spend beyond the budget can be too tempting. "Borrowing from Peter to pay Paul" only defers pain into the future. Rationalizing a multitude of ways to recover costs can become easy. Of course, when recovery plans are implemented later, many turn out to have looked better on paper. Here again, discipline by project leaders is essential—essential in routinely controlling budgets so costs can be contained.

> **Lesson: A great deal of discipline is required to manage the constant change that is common to all software development projects.**

All of the major project parameters—employee morale, productivity, quality, schedules, and cost—influence each other to some degree. For example, if morale is low, then quality and productivity will suffer. This will cause schedules to be extended, which, in turn, will increase costs. But no matter which parameters are used to show this domino effect, any parameter that "goes south" can pull the overall project with it. Again, the management of change is critical to the success of the project. And critical to the management of change is the discipline required to hold all parameters of a project together.

RECOGNIZING THE DISCIPLINED ORGANIZATION

Have you ever noticed that some organizations seem to be more successful than others? That the energy level of the people involved seems to be higher? That these people generally seem to have better attitudes about themselves and the work they are doing? That more things just seem to go right? Also, have you noticed that these organizations seem to be able to attract the most interest from employees in sister organizations who desire to join?

> **Lesson: The better managed projects manage discipline better.**

What is so unique about these seemingly "magnetic" organizations that attract good fortune at most turns? The general answer is that they are managed better. The specific answer is *discipline* exercised by project leaders in both *what* they do and *how* they do it. Discipline comes in many flavors, but only the discipline that supports the project's mission is desirable. This is the discipline that supports the pattern of productive behavior needed in and wanted by project personnel. This is the discipline that should be encouraged. This is called positive discipline. Positive discipline is what this chapter is all about.

Before venturing further into this topic, it can help to take a brief look at negative discipline. Remember, discipline is the act of encouraging a desired pattern of behavior. If the leader of a group trains the group's members to follow a certain pattern of behavior, and that behavior is not productive to achieving the group's mission, then the discipline exercised is negative discipline. As an example, consider an organization that needs its employees to take more risk in accepting responsibility. Now consider a leader within that organization who continually punishes each risk taker who meets with failure. This leader would be displaying negative discipline because the discipline works against the project's mission. The scenarios at the beginning of this chapter provide additional examples of negative discipline.

IMPLEMENTING DISCIPLINE

Now consider positive discipline once again, focusing on the discipline that project leaders demonstrate in both *what* they do and *how* they do it. Exhibit 9.2 shows the four essential traits that are the *what* of the well-disciplined organization. This is a good point to examine these traits closer and discuss *how* they need to be addressed.

EXHIBIT 9.2   Traits of the well-disciplined organization

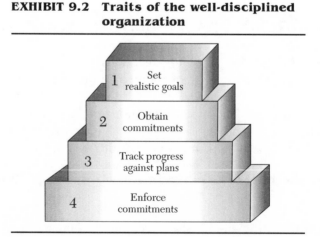

1 Set realistic goals

2 Obtain commitments

3 Track progress against plans

4 Enforce commitments

Trait One: Set Realistic Goals

Every organization needs goals. How else can success be measured? Goals must be:

- Simply stated.
- Understood by all.
- Measurable.

Lesson: Discipline begins by setting realistic goals.

To "do good" is not a goal. To build a defect-free product is a goal. However, to expect a defect-free product might not be realistic. If your product will have 1 million lines of code, and your measure of success is to prove that it is 100 percent defect-free, then you will likely go out of business. Why? Because the tremendous cost to develop 1 million lines of code that is defect-free would likely extend schedules and raise the product price to a point that would reduce its competitiveness significantly. However, if your goal is to deliver this product with no more than one defect for every 10,000 lines of code, and technology is within reach to make this happen, then your goal is realistic. (In this example, assume that the customer accepts this defect rate. Also assume that the frequency and effect of the defects discovered by the customer are manageable—for instance, the defect is encountered only once during the start of leap year and will not lead to disaster.)

How do goals (that are theoretically achievable) happen? They happen when the project's leadership establishes and maintains a productive environment. The leaders must make it easy for people to do their jobs and must create a work environment that sets people up for success, not failure. In creating a productive environment, project leaders should strive to:

- Provide the necessary training, processes, and tools.
- Offer a sense of accomplishment.
- Foster teamwork.
- Encourage risk-taking.

Now take a closer look at these elements.

Provide training, processes, and tools. A goal is not realistic if the people expected to make it happen have not been trained properly, processes have not been defined and implemented, and the necessary tools have not been made available. The project's leadership is responsible for making these things happen. In the 1-million-lines-of-code program example, project personnel will not know if they have achieved the acceptable defect rate unless a rigorous software development process has been defined and implemented to track and measure product defects carefully.

Offer a sense of accomplishment. People achieve their best when they are "stretched"—when their skills are used and their potential is tapped. When these things happen, people sense they are valued as members of the team. Project leaders should not hold back in providing people with assignments that are challenging but achievable. A project's goals are closer to being realistic when the project's members are happy about their work.

Foster teamwork. Fostering teamwork involves encouraging the participation of *all* project members. Great human achievements are possible when people work as a team. Whether the project is to harness the great energy of the atom, to walk on the moon, or to build a large complex software program, teamwork draws on individual accomplishments. These individual accomplishments are collected in a fashion that allows greatness to be achieved at a level far beyond the abilities of any one person. Everyone has something to offer to a team. The more participation is encouraged, the greater the likelihood that the project's goals will be met.

Encourage risk-taking. Taking risks is the difference between *doing* the unthinkable and only *dreaming* about it. Establishing a risk-supportive environment can allow the imagined to become reality. It may be *the* ingredient that allows the estimated 1-million-lines-of-code program to be done with 25 percent less code. Or it may simply make the difference between delivering a product on schedule or much later. An environment that encourages risk and rewards success but does not penalize failure is an organization to be reckoned with. The movers of tomorrow are taking risks today.

Trait Two: Obtain Commitments

The last section, "Trait One: Set Realistic Goals," stresses that a well-disciplined organization defines realistic project goals in a manner that is simply stated, is understood by all, and is measurable. Furthermore, all project players understand their individual assignments and roles in making the bigger picture happen. A second trait of a well-disciplined organization is the obtainment of commitments from *each* person in the organization.

Lesson: Everyone must feel personally committed for discipline to have its greatest impact.

A committed plan does not exist until *everyone* has made a personal commitment. This means from the very top gun to the troops in the trenches, managers and nonmanagers alike. People will take more pride in their work when they have a personally committed stake, when they sense they have responsibility and accountability. No greater tool exists for motivating people to do their job than getting their personal commitment to making it happen. Giving people the opportunity to participate in developing product, content, processes, and schedules is not only beneficial, it is a must.

Trait Three: Track Progress against Plans

At this point, the organization has a realistic project plan (trait one) to which all members of the project have committed (trait two). So far, so good. The third trait is the tracking of each activity against the plan. (Techniques for tracking plans are discussed in detail in Chapter 5.)

> **Lesson: It is not enough to plan your work; discipline requires that you also ensure that you are working your plan.**

Remember that discipline is the act of encouraging a desired pattern of behavior. Now that a plan for the project is in place, how can the project's leadership be sure that the plan is being followed continually? More important, how will the leadership know when problems arise and where resources should be redeployed to help solve problems and protect the planned schedules? Discipline is required to track the plan on a regular and frequent basis. Tracking the plan also involves recording new problems and ensuring that current problems are being solved satisfactorily.

> Scenario: Consider the plight of a person walking through a desert. Without sophisticated navigation tools, it is highly improbable that this person could walk a straight line through the desert. (For this example, assume it is physically possible to track to a straight route, free of obstacles.) In this analogy, the start and end points of the person's journey represent the start and end points of a project. The straight line, which is the shortest route through the desert, is symbolic of the shortest project schedules possible. Now picture this person veering a little more off course each week. For any given week, the deviation doesn't represent a major alteration of the final destination. However, as the weeks pass, these minor off-course excursions collectively could spell disaster. That is, the final destination would not be reached anywhere near the planned date. If, however, this person's direction could be reset each week, problems could be addressed close to the time they occur, so that the final destination's targeted arrival date has a much higher chance of being achieved.

The desert example is simplistic but nevertheless provides insight into the need to track against a project plan at frequent, regular intervals. Often just the act of tracking the plan is a form of preventive maintenance. People are more apt to meet a checkpoint if they are being tracked regularly and frequently than if they are tracked infrequently.

Trait Four: Enforce Commitments

You may want to read this section twice. The reason is simple: If everything mentioned up to now has been done—setting realistic goals, obtaining commitments, tracking progress against plans—but this final, fourth trait of the well-disciplined organization is not made to happen, then all bets are off. Enforcing commitment is an absolute must. This is not a strong arm tactic.

Rather, the enforcement of commitments represents a statement of support from the project's leadership to the project's participants.

Most software development projects will encounter several severe problems along the way. (A severe problem is defined here as one that potentially can cause a delay in the final delivery of the product.) Moreover, many severe problems are not totally solvable by the specific group that is experiencing the problem. An example is the team that falls behind schedule in writing test scripts. The people are all working overtime but still may not be able to complete the activity on schedule. The person leading this team has no other resource to add to this effort. The project's leadership, however, can choose to redeploy people from other areas of the project to shore up the development activity of the test scripts.

Therefore, one useful approach project leaders can employ to ensure that commitments are met is *management of priorities*. Priorities requiring attention often will vary from week to week. As a result, management of priorities requires discipline to ensure that the proper activities are getting the needed resources and focus. Often it is more fun and easier to deal with some problems ahead of others. However, this temptation should be resisted. Instead, it is better to understand problems and take action on resolving them according to priorities that best serve the organization.

Another important action to take in enforcing commitments can be called "making it happen now." This is a tightly held philosophy of leaders who have a reputation for getting things done. Whereas, management of priorities ensures that resources within the organization are being diverted dynamically for the good of the total plan, "making things happen now" is the act of dealing swiftly with problems before they fester and grow out (or further out) of control. This is considered to be a strong positive act of support for the people in the organization.

Lesson: People need to be rewarded regularly for demonstrating the desired behavior.

Reward those who meet or beat their commitments. Whether the reward is expressed privately or publicly, stated on paper, made with money, or made through some other means, it is important to provide feedback to individuals and to the organization. Let people know when their behavior contributes to the project's goals.

Lesson: Everyone looks to the project's leadership to provide a work environment that encourages success.

By the same token, proceed cautiously before reprimanding failure. Be firm but fair. Maintain a sense of justice and fair treatment. Most people don't fail intentionally. Could it be that the project's leadership did not provide the proper work environment to facilitate the employee's success? If it is clear that a person is performing unsatisfactorily, don't ignore this. Help the person to develop an acceptable level of performance. If, after a reasonable energy expenditure, the person still is not showing the needed improvement, then find a job that fits this person's skills or remove him or her from the company. *Do not do nothing.* All eyes are on the project's leadership to take proper action before the situation deteriorates further.

ATTRIBUTES OF THE SUCCESSFUL LEADER

> Leadership is action, not position.
> —Donald H. McGannon, American broadcasting executive

This section is devoted to the role of the leader and contains what I believe to be among the most important leadership philosophies, or tenets, that have been shared with me over the years or that I have shared with others. These leadership tenets have worked for me and I have seen them work for others. Being a leader carries a lot of responsibility, but it also can be a lonely, stressful job if you allow the role to control you rather than you taking charge of your own emotions.

Earlier sections have discussed the need for discipline within the organization and have explained how to recognize a disciplined organization. Now is a good point to focus candidly on *self-discipline* for the leader. First, consider some definitions of a leader. A leader:

- Is the principal player within a team, the human "glue" that holds the team together.
- Inspires and guides a team toward a common goal.
- Exhibits integrity.
- Is a continual source of energy.
- Encourages desired behavior from others.
- Sets an example for others.
- Is accountable.
- Achieves results.

Lesson: The importance of leadership in creating and nurturing a successful organization cannot be overstated.

This is certainly not an exhaustive list of what being a leader is all about. However, it is sufficiently complete to point out the importance of a leader in creating and nurturing a successful organization.

Exhibit 9.3 lists the attributes of the successful leader. Let's take a closer look at each of these attributes.

EXHIBIT 9.3   Attributes of the successful leader

The ability to:

- Create and nurture a vision
- Not fear failure
- Expect and accept criticism
- Take risks
- Empower others
- Be decisive
- Be persistent
- Be happy
- Laugh
- Leave your ego behind
- Think before acting—do not criticize hastily
- Meet commitments
- Coach your team—be a role model
- Maintain a winning attitude
- Believe in yourself

The Ability to Create and Nurture a Vision

As a leader, it is important to create and nurture a vision—a far-reaching purpose—that you can share with your entire team and that the team can think about all day long, all week long, all project long. This vision will translate into the team purpose. Having a purpose has a powerful effect on the positive outcome of the team's mission. Not only does a purpose channel the energies of the team into a single focus, it helps to ensure that the trade-offs and compromises made along the way fully support the vision.

Note, however, that creating a vision requires you to know where you want to go. This is essential if you plan to lead others to that destination. Only then can you be sure that the journey followed will result in victory. Great accomplishments are made possible by great visions.

The Ability to Not Fear Failure

> Failure is, in a sense, the highway to success, inasmuch as every discovery of what is false leads us to seek earnestly after what is true.
>
> —John Keats, English poet

We all fail at things—all the time. It is natural and expected. It is the way we learn. You could not walk the first time you tried. Or talk. Or type. Or ride a bike. Or play that video game. And so on. When we were very young, we simply got up, dusted ourselves off, and tried again and again until we mastered our goal. But something happened to some of us as we "matured." We began to fear failing and therefore shunned opportunities that we believed increased our chances for failing.

What a shame. You see, life is full of paradoxes. The person who is no stranger to failure is often the person who is *most likely to succeed.* Every failure offers a lesson and from every lesson comes strength. If you learn from each failure, you get a little stronger. And after a while, you can even amaze yourself at the progress you have made.

Of course, all this is made more possible if you don't fear failure. Fear can perpetuate failure and encourages you to "quit." Think of those around you who fear failure. Most likely they are not leaders, are content with complacency, and seek so-called safety by maintaining the status quo wherever they may be. They literally withdraw from many of life's opportunities.

Now look at those whose failures seem to be visible, yet from each fall they rise to prepare for the next challenge. If failure means growth and opportunity, then it should never be feared. The only real failures are the experiences we don't learn from. The most successful leaders have learned to view failures as the positive force they are, that is, as the necessary steps in enabling us to grow and to achieve those things that are important to us.

The Ability to Expect and Accept Criticism

> Criticism is something we can avoid easily—by saying nothing, doing nothing, and being nothing.
>
> —Aristotle, Greek philosopher and scientist

If you expect criticism, you will seldom be disappointed when you receive it. However, note that there are two types of criticism: *constructive* and *destructive.* Of course, you should welcome constructive criticism, which is well-meaning and useful feedback. Constructive criticism should leave you feeling that you have been helped. This type of feedback can help you to learn about yourself and the impact you are having as a result of your actions. It is information you can use to help make choices for yourself and to help you grow in the direction of your personal goals.

Destructive criticism is input you receive that might be maliciously rooted and offers little, if any, real value for your learning and growth. However, what often may appear to be destructive criticism might, in fact, just be an unfortunate and ineffective attempt to offer some useful information—but from a person who does not know how best to communicate the information. Be aware that some well-intended criticism might come your way awkwardly masked in destructive garb.

You will always find those who disapprove of your behavior or your decisions. Even the people you love, and who love you, will, at times, disapprove of your actions. When people criticize you, remember it is only their opinion. If you allow the absence of their approval to immobilize you, then you are allowing others to control you. You are, in effect, saying that what other people think about you is more important than what you think about yourself. Instead, you should ask yourself if there is something to be learned from the criticism. If there is, then, by all means, learn! If there is nothing to be learned, then forget the experience and go about fulfilling your dreams.

The Ability to Take Risks

Great deeds are usually wrought at great risks.

—Herodotus, Greek historian

Risk—that simple yet mighty four-letter word. The willingness to take risks is what changed the perception of a flat world to round, gave humans wings to fly, and gives people the ability to understand their own capabilities. If you want to achieve the extraordinary, you *must* take risks. Risk-taking can occur on a small scale, such as driving a new route home from work, speaking out when you disagree with an issue, or volunteering to take on an additional assignment. If you practice becoming comfortable with smaller risks, you will find yourself much more prepared to recognize a larger risk and much more willing to take it on.

If you increasingly take on more risk, you will find an unexpected benefit—the recognition that your level of energy and enthusiasm grow in proportion to the risk that you take. Often assignments that are the riskiest are later viewed as the assignments that were the most enjoyable, memorable, and career-building. There is nothing wrong with gradually expanding your risk-taking abilities. Only you can decide what your limitations are and what level of risk is suitable for you. The leaders of tomorrow are taking risks today.

The Ability to Empower Others

No man will make a great leader who wants to do it all himself, or to get all the credit for doing it.

—Andrew Carnegie, American industrialist and philanthropist

It is common for new leaders not to give up some of their "power" by empowering others—to give them full responsibility and accountability for key tasks. The reasons include a belief that they can do the job better or faster than another or even the fear of giving others too much work. Another reason: They allow society's work ethic—being independent and self-reliant—to interfere with their duties as a leader of others. Resist these attitudes and transfer some of your tasks, your key tasks.

A successful leader knows he or she achieves goals through the dedication, skill, and efforts of others. You must learn to trust and work with others in ways that allows them to grow and achieve their dreams. After all, you appreciated the opportunities that others gave you to learn. Give others their chance as well. It is good for you and good for your team members. It frees you to lead and frees them to learn. Everybody will win.

The Ability to Be Decisive

> Once the WHAT is decided, the HOW always follows. We must not make the HOW an excuse for not facing and accepting the WHAT.
>
> —Pearl S. Buck, American novelist

Your organization will react to your actions. When you delay in making crucial decisions, you also are delaying the time that will be needed to implement those decisions. Many organizations have the capacity to increase their productivity and effectiveness. By putting off decision making, you are not driving your organization efficiently. If you delay your own decision making, you also are preventing the next tier of decisions from being made. This *decision queue* can build to a point where progress within the organization is seriously impacted. The result is an uncontrollable sluggishness that spreads throughout the organization and that only the project leader can correct.

It is better to make decisions early—when their pain and cost to the organization are relatively minor, yet when their long-term impact can have a major positive effect. Some decisions will, in hindsight, prove to be less than the best. However, if you wait until absolutely no risk remains before taking a position on a problem, then you will lose all competitiveness.

The Ability to Be Persistent

> Great works are performed not by strength, but by perseverance.
>
> —Dr. Samuel Johnson, English poet, critic, essayist, and lexicographer

Perseverance is a universal characteristic of successful leaders. This attribute can propel a so-called common person to achieve uncommon feats. Perseverance pushes a chemist to try that 10,000th mixture that finally succeeds, an athlete to achieve an Olympic-class victory, an artist to create a masterpiece, and the medical biologist to locate a disease-causing gene. Perhaps, however, the most inspiring effect of perseverance can be seen in a person who overcomes a major physical handicap and goes on to accomplish a feat that would be difficult for even a fully functioning person to achieve.

Intellectual and physical capabilities vary widely among people. However, it is encouraging to know that we all have the innate ability to exercise perseverance and determination in achieving those goals that are important to us. Being persistent can make all the difference between dreaming and seeing the dream blossom into reality. Act as if it is impossible for you to fail. You can achieve nearly anything you set out to make happen if you are persistent in following your dreams.

The Ability to Be Happy

> Everything you need to be totally fulfilled you already have . . .
>
> —Dr. Wayne Dyer, American psychologist and author

Be happy. Feel good about yourself. Being happy is the cornerstone of your continued effectiveness. Don't *strive* to be happy. Don't set goals and then tell yourself that once those goals are reached you will be happy. Putting off happiness until some external event occurs will guarantee that your happiness will continue to be elusive.

You have everything you need today to be happy. You don't need a promotion, award, new car, vacation, retirement, or whatever, to be happy. Happiness is an attitude. It is something that comes from within—not from external events or things. It is an acceptance of what is. It is something that no one can take away from you. You can lose all your material possessions and still be happy.

This does not mean you should stop working for self-improvement or improvement to your family, job, company, world, or whatever is important to you. It means that you must not allow external factors to control you to the point at which your actual happiness is no longer within your own control. However you define success for yourself, you will improve your likelihood of attaining your goals significantly if you recognize and exercise your ability to be and remain happy.

The Ability to Laugh

> It is my belief, you cannot deal with the most serious things in the world unless you understand the most amusing.
>
> —Sir Winston Churchill

Consider this scenario: A meeting has just been called to settle a dispute between two parties. As people are assembling in the meeting room, an uncomfortable silence is felt. Everyone has arrived and the meeting is about to start. There is an instability in the air, a feeling of tension that one wrong word or action could ignite into an emotional explosion. The first words are spoken and strike everyone in the meeting with the same response—a round of heavy uncontrollable laughter fills the room.

Can you relate to this scenario? Most of us can. That well-timed bit of humor was sorely needed. All too often we take the moment much too seriously. We fail to loosen up and find the humor in our situation and ourselves. How terribly depressing for an organization to resist expressing the lighter side of the daily problems we face. As a leader, support a healthy dose of humor in the organization. Displaying a sense of humor also helps you to remain cool under pressure and to keep problems in perspective.

Caution: Don't use sarcasm in your humor. While many people may view your comment as amusing, it may leave others feeling uncomfortable and unsettled. Sarcasm also can hurt the trust you have developed with others. People appreciate benevolent humor better than sarcastic humor. If you have a hard time initiating this welcomed variety of humor, then at least show appreciation when others are amusing. While humor has been shown to preserve the health of people, it also adds value to the health of the total organization.

The Ability to Leave Your Ego Behind

We all have an ego. For some, the ego can cause a paralysis, inhibiting their quest for growth and opportunity. Here is another paradox: Often the person who insists on attention is the one least likely to receive the type or amount of attention desired. An overactive ego does not help win the recognition, admiration, and approval that the egotist seeks. Instead, it has a repelling effect that encourages others to want to limit their association with the egotist. Furthermore, it leads others to question the real value and substance that exist behind all the verbal arm waving.

An oversized ego also can interfere with recognizing others for their contributions. And it can bias decisions being made, favoring who is right rather than what is right. You probably have seen leaders with large egos. Having an exaggerated ego doesn't mean you will never get to be a leader. It means that fewer people will trust you or want to work for and with you. It means that you will make your job harder and less effective than it needs to be. An unbridled ego is a haunting liability. The less approval you demand from others, the more you are likely to receive.

The Ability to Think before Acting— Do Not Criticize Hastily

Resist the temptation to criticize hastily. When you suspect poor work, ask questions and carefully listen to the answers. Once a wrong or regrettable word is spoken, it cannot be taken back. After you understand the reason behind a problem, attack the problem, not the person.

Give others the same courtesy that you would like for yourself. Take this opportunity to not only help someone resolve a problem, but to help him or her benefit from the experience. Also, work at increasing the bond and trust between you and the project member. If you demonstrate constructive behavior and resist attacking the person, you may find yourself with a more loyal and dedicated project member.

The Ability to Meet Commitments

When you make a commitment, it is a personal statement about yourself. It is a statement that says that you can be depended on, that you will do everything within your abilities to honor the pledge that you have given another.

The success of any organization depends on its ability to meet its commitments. As the saying goes, a chain is only as strong as its weakest link. The project structure, represented as a chain, can break quickly when one or more commitments are broken.

Make no commitments lightly. Commit only to that which you believe you can achieve. To commit unconditionally to more is to be distrustful, for if your commitment is weak, so too are those commitments that depend on you. Pull your own weight and do as you say you will.

When you meet your commitments, you will be recognized as a greater value to the organization. You also may find that you will be given the option to assume greater responsibilities as well as be exposed to increased opportunities. People will prefer to have you on their team or will want to be on your team. You also will find that you will be given greater freedom to manage your activities as you choose.

The Ability to Coach Your Team—Be a Role Model

We all learn the easiest and fastest by observing others—by having an example to mimic. As a leader, others look to you—and rightly so—for that example. They look to you for strength, for wisdom, for caring, for attention. They also look to you for your honesty with being human and having human frailties. For example, the integrity that you demonstrate when you make a mistake, admit it, recover, and continue on can have a profound positive impact on those around you.

Teach what you have learned. Impart your knowledge and experience. Prepare others to take on more responsibility. You know what you want from your leaders; work to provide the same to your subordinates and peers, and even back up to your leaders. Work continuously to build a stronger organization this month than the one that existed last month. When you come across a problem, fix the problem—then fix the process that caused the problem. The greatest leader is the one who leads by example. Practice what you expect from others. Show you care, offer your support, be there to make it happen.

The Ability to Maintain a Winning Attitude

> The quality of work is affected as much by one's attitude as by one's skill.
>
> —Anonymous

Attitude is the disposition, manner, or approach that you bring to everything you do. One of the most admired traits you can have is a good attitude, or positive attitude. A positive attitude actually can bring pleasure to performance of a tedious or difficult task. A positive attitude can make a long day seem short and even can improve the productivity and quality of the work being performed. People who consistently maintain positive attitudes tend to have higher energy levels than those who are less positive. These people look for something positive—and they find it—in every chore they tackle. You have probably observed a situation where two people are being considered for the same assignment and the person chosen is the one who appears to have somewhat less experience or knowledge. Yet this person was chosen because of his or her positive attitude.

As a revealing anonymous quote states: "A pessimist finds difficulty in every opportunity; an optimist finds opportunity in every difficulty." People can take great liberties in choosing how to think. A glass of water can be half filled or half empty. How a person thinks does not change the fact that the glass has 50 percent of its capacity *used up* by water. But how a person chooses to think does have an affect on the efficiency with which a task is completed and on the enjoyment the person derives from accomplishing that task.

As a leader, you want the people whom you are leading to demonstrate good attitudes in every endeavor that you assign them. People who exhibit these upbeat attitudes are considerably easier to manage and more enjoyable to be around than less positive people. In order for a winning attitude to permeate your team, you must demonstrate and encourage that characteristic. As a leader, the manner in which you approach your work is also the manner most likely to be adopted by those who work under, alongside, and above you. Adopt a winning attitude in the tasks that you undertake, and you also will create winning people and winning products in the process.

The Ability to Believe in Yourself

> Always bear in mind that your own resolution to succeed is more important than any one thing.
>
> —Abraham Lincoln

The most successful leaders have learned to *believe* in their ability to make something happen—to follow their dreams and transform those dreams into reality. They draw from an inner strength that they have chosen to acknowledge is there to work for them. An inner strength that no one can take away—unless they allow it. You *must* believe in yourself if you expect to be and remain a successful leader, and if you expect others to believe in you. In fact, the belief in one's own capabilities magnifies the contribution from all the other attributes that we have discussed.

If you believe you can—you will. If you believe you can't—you won't. These pearls of wisdom have been around at least as long as recorded history. They are as true and as real as the mountains and oceans themselves. And the great news is that no one has a monopoly on these words. They apply to you as much as they do anyone.

Lesson: You are what you perceive yourself to be. Your vision of yourself becomes your reality.

You deserve to be what you choose to be and work at becoming—regardless of your age, race, sex, religion, current wealth, whatever. You are what you perceive yourself to be. Your vision of yourself becomes your reality. As a leader, you must believe in your ability to get the job done, to achieve the desired results. If people took on only those jobs where they knew all the answers and had no chance for conflict or failure, there would be no leaders. A successful leader knows that no one person holds the answer to every problem, but with the proper balance of time, energy, and talent, no problem escapes being solved.

It is almost always true that our greatest obstacle to becoming what we truly want is ourselves. If it is truly important to you then never, never, *never* give up. As Henry David Thoreau, American writer, philosopher, and naturalist, said:

> If one advances confidently in the direction of his dreams and endeavors to live the life he has imagined, he will meet with a success unexpected in common hours.

I believe that everyone has the capability to be a successful leader. Everyone! There is room for many more leaders, millions more. Although some are more effective than others, or rise to greater heights, this does not diminish the great opportunities for turning your visions into realities. All the attributes can be learned if you choose to learn them.

CHECKING THE ORGANIZATION'S PULSE

If you follow this chapter's advice up to this point, how can you tell if it is working for you and your organization? The external signs should be quite evident. For example, the status of the project plan would be known at regular and frequent intervals, schedules should be tracking to plan, and any exceptions would have recovery plans. Problems would be logged, assigned an owner, and target dates for closure committed. But what about the internal signs? What do the individual project members really feel about their organization and how it is being run?

Managers can use many methods to test the effectiveness of the discipline exercised across a project. Some of these methods are listed in Exhibit 9.4. Let's take a closer look at each method listed.

Random walks through work areas have the greatest immediate payback because listening to project members' spontaneous opinions offers the best opportunity to learn. These walks can build a closer and more trusting working

---

EXHIBIT 9.4   Methods to check the organization's pulse

- Random walks through work areas
- Scheduled one-on-one interviews
- Scheduled group round tables
- Formal group surveys
- Quality improvement teams

relationship between managers and nonmanagers. Understanding problems at the point where pain is felt the most also adds valuable insight into providing the support needed. These walks are most effective if they can take place for at least 30 to 60 minutes each day at least two to three times per week. Surveying the members less frequently is still, however, a valuable method for gaining insight into the way a project is running, but it will be more difficult to maintain a personal bond with project members.

Scheduling chats with project members for 30 to 60 minutes per person is also a useful way to get feedback. These *one-on-one interviews* can be scheduled once or twice a week with a different person from a different group each time. The person can be given up to a week's notice. The meeting should be set at a convenient time for the invited member. The actual interview should first focus on any questions or thoughts that the member wants to pursue. Then the manager might ask a few general questions of the project member.

Roundtables are a productive way to meet the most people in the least amount of time. Roundtables typically involve a gathering of five to 15 people from across the organization. These sessions may occur once every one or two weeks and may last up to two hours. Such meetings are not only informative tools for the manager, they also are team-building techniques for roundtable members.

Formal opinion surveys typically are administered on paper or through a computer workstation. The anonymous survey may ask a few or many questions, most of which would be answered by rating the participant's views from "very satisfied" to "very unsatisfied." This is an effective tool for medium- to long-range planning.

Quality improvement teams are another effective way to understand the problems that can stifle parts or all of an organization. Quality improvement teams are mentioned here due to their considerable benefit in encouraging participation of project members from across the organization. These teams can candidly assess any discipline-related problems that may exist and can offer creative recommendations that have the added benefit of being sponsored from the bottom up rather than from the top down.

THE DESIRE FOR DISCIPLINE

Lesson: As a project leader, your actions always will speak louder than your words.

You must want discipline in order to make it happen. Discipline cannot and will not happen without your support. If you say you want discipline, but your actions tell another story, the entire organization will read you like a book. Vague policies and permissive attitudes convey the impression that unproductive (destructive) behavior is acceptable.

Lesson: As a manager, you are accountable for the well-being of your organization; it cannot be delegated.

You hold the keys to building a poor, ordinary, or extraordinary organization. You are the boss. You can initiate change whenever and wherever you want. Most problems are not as large as they appear. What is large is the fear or hesitancy to deal with problems head-on—when they first appear. This is not to say that all problems are easy to solve or can be solved in a short time. Problems that compete for resources or time need to be prioritized according to the needs of the organization. Then these priorities need to be managed with the urgency they deserve.

Lesson: Discipline—the glue that holds it all together.

Discipline is an everyday thing. It is not occasional. Discipline is the glue that holds it all together. Everyone wants positive discipline. Exercising discipline has great value to each project participant, to the organization as a whole, and to the products that are developed by the organization. Everyone wins. Can you afford to have your project fail, to be less than it needs to be? Be a winner!

10 VIRTUAL TEAM CRITICAL SUCCESS FACTORS

Deborah L. Duarte and
Nancy Tennant Snyder

In today's business environment, organizations adapt quickly or die. Gaining competitive advantage in a global environment means continually reshaping the organization to maximize strengths, address threats, and increase speed.[1] The use of teams has become a common way of doing this.[2] The formation of teams can draw talent quickly from different functions, locations, and organizations. The goal is to leverage intellectual capital and apply it as quickly as possible. The methods that organizations use to manage this process can mean the difference between success and failure.

Consider the example of a team in a global firm that produces durable goods. This product-development team, with members from around the world, had just completed the development of a new product. When the team unveiled the product to the senior staff of the organization, it included a description of the way the team worked. The presentation showed an icon of an airplane with the entire team of 22 people traveling from country to country. The team members had continually moved from site to site for activities, such as status reviews, design meetings, and prototyping sessions. The cost of the travel was tremendous, not only for hotels and airline tickets, but also in terms of the human cost of being away from home and the lost work time and productivity.

Contrast this with the experiences of teams in organizations such as Hewlett Packard, the National Aeronautics and Space Administration (NASA), John Brown Engineers & Construction, DEC, and Rank Hovis.[3] These organizations also form world-class teams to quickly address customer problems, develop products, and deliver services, but these teams often operate virtually, without the physical limitations of distance, time, and organizational boundaries. They use electronic collaboration technologies and other techniques to lower travel and facility costs, reduce project schedules, and improve decision-making time and communication.[4] For many teams, traveling and having continual face-to-face meetings is not the most efficient or effective way of working.

Organizations that do not use virtual teams effectively may be fighting an uphill battle in a global, competitive, and rapidly changing environment. Organizations that will succeed in the next millennium have found new ways of working across boundaries through systems, processes, technology, and people.

Understanding how to work in or lead a virtual team is becoming a fundamental competence for people in many organizations. Virtual teams often are formed as a reaction to a business requirement or as a result of programs, such as telecommuting, that introduce new ways of working.[5]

It is not uncommon to talk with people who lead or work in virtual teams who do not have a great deal of experience working on teams in a colocated environment. Most of the large consulting firms (Accenture, formerly Andersen Consulting, is one primary example) do a large majority of their work virtually. Consultants who join these firms may never have the opportunity to work in or lead a traditional team in a colocated environment. They are immediately placed in situations that are more virtual than traditional. IBM has an entire unit in which employees telecommute, so new hires may never have a chance to work in a traditional office setting.[6]

People who lead and work in virtual teams need to have special skills, including an understanding of human dynamics, knowledge of how to manage across functional areas and national cultures, and the ability to use communication technologies as their primary means of communicating and collaborating.

HOW BEING VIRTUAL ADDS COMPLEXITY

It is easy to characterize the types of virtual teams using the same categories as traditional teams. They can, however, be much more complex. The two primary categories of variables that make virtual teams more complex are: (1) they cross boundaries related to time, distance (geography), and organization; and (2) they communicate (share information) and collaborate (work together to produce a product) using technology. (We use the term *technology* to denote electronic communication and collaboration technology.)

As the distance between team members increases, so do differences in time zones. This makes communicating and collaborating at the same time problematic. Working across national boundaries complicates the situation because differences in language, culture, and access to technology impede effective communication and collaboration.

As members from different organizations join a virtual team, integration of work methods, organizational cultures, technologies, and goals make communication and collaboration more difficult. Partners and suppliers often have conflicting goals and organizational cultures. This even holds true when team members come from different functional areas within the same organization. For example, people from functional areas, such as marketing and human resources, frequently operate with a different set of processes than those from more technical areas, such as engineering and information systems.

Finally, complexity is increased by the number of different choices for team interaction. Traditional teams typically interact face to face at least some of the time. Virtual team interactions, however, are almost always mediated by electronic communication and collaboration technology. Interactions fall into four categories: (1) same time, same place (like face-to-face meetings); (2) same time, different place (such as an audio conference or video conference); (3) different time, same place (such as using a chat room or a shared file on a network); and (4) different time, different place (such as exchange of e-mail or voice mail messages).[7] The selection of technology and choice of interaction vary according to factors such as the type of team, the nature of its task, and the members' access to technology.[8]

CRITICAL SUCCESS FACTORS FOR VIRTUAL TEAMS

The business justification for virtual teams is strong.[9] They increase speed and agility and leverage expertise and vertical integration between organizations to make resources readily available. Virtual teams also lessen the disruption of people's lives because the people do not have to travel to meet. Team members can broaden their careers and perspectives by working across organizations and cultures and on a variety of projects and tasks.

Although the effective use of electronic communication and collaboration technologies is fundamental to the success of a virtual team, virtual teams entail much more than technology and computers. When virtual teams and their leaders are asked about successes and failures, they rarely mention technology as a primary reason for either.[10] Bill Davidow, a former executive with Intel and Hewlett Packard, comments: "Information and communication technology provides an infrastructure for the corporation to communicate with customers and deliver information necessary for decision making. . . . If management insists on maintaining a purely functional organization or does not empower workers, information systems will add little value."[11]

There are seven critical success factors for virtual teams, of which technology is only one. Others are human resource policies, training and development for team leaders and team members, standard organizational and team processes, organizational culture, leadership, and leader and member competencies. These are discussed in more detail later in this chapter.

Of course, all the critical success factors do not have to be in place for virtual teams to succeed. The implementation of virtual teams within an organization can actually push toward the attainment of critical success factors. Successful virtual teams seem to demand certain conditions, and the existence of the teams will, over time, help to create the infrastructure conditions that make them work.

NORTEL's Information Systems Group implemented virtual teams before it had attained many of the critical success factors. The teams immediately recognized that they needed certain things to succeed, such as high levels of autonomy to do their jobs, standard team-initiation processes, structured communication plans, and appropriate electronic communication and collaboration technologies for all team members. They also recognized that they needed to reeducate their customers about what to expect from a virtual team work environment.

The leaders of the virtual teams independently created team processes and standards, communication plans, and empowerment guidelines for team members. They put together customer-education packages. The training organization created a virtual team Web site and collected and placed the processes and lessons learned on the intranet for new virtual team leaders and members. Over time, NORTEL took a more deliberate approach to moving toward an infrastructure that would support virtual teams. Many of the processes it formally institutionalized got their start through the *bootstrap* approach of its first virtual teams.

This chapter is not specifically about preparing the organization for virtual teams. Its focus is on tools and techniques for team leaders and team members. However, team leaders and members influence the implementation of critical success factors that are associated with team success.

The next part of this chapter outlines a set of critical success factors for organizations. Complete the diagnostic tool found in Exhibit 10.1 prior to reading about the factors. Your results on the diagnostic tool can direct your attention to the categories of success factors that affect your situation. Although you may not be able to influence all of them, the results can serve to direct your actions when it is possible or help you to develop a case to present to management for virtual team resources.

Seven Critical Success Factors

Seven factors affect the probability of a virtual team's success:

1. Human resource policies.
2. Training and on-the-job education and development.
3. Standard organizational and team processes.
4. Use of electronic collaboration and communication technology.
5. Organizational culture.
6. Leadership support of virtual teams.
7. Team-leader and team-member competencies.

The following discussion describes the seven factors and tells how team leaders can help to create the conditions that lead to success.

EXHIBIT 10.1 Assessing critical success factors

Instructions: Check the response that best matches your organization on each item.

Section One: Human Resource Policies	Strongly Disagree 1	Disagree 2	Neither Agree nor Disagree 3	Agree 4	Strongly Agree 5
1. Career-development systems address the needs of virtual team members.					
2. Reward systems reward/ recognize working across boundaries and working virtually.					
3. Results are what is rewarded.					
4. Nontraditional work arrangements, such as telecommuting, are actively supported.					
Section Two: Training and Development					
5. There is good access to technical training.					
6. There is access to training in working across cultures.					
7. There are methods available for continual and just-in-time learning, such as Web-based training.					
8. There are mechanisms, such as lessons-learned databases, for sharing across boundaries.					

(continued)

EXHIBIT 10.1 *Continued*

Section Three: Standard Organizational Processes	Strongly Disagree 1	Disagree 2	Neither Agree nor Disagree 3	Agree 4	Strongly Agree 5
9. There are standard and agreed-on technical team processes used throughout the organization and with partners.					
10. There are standard and agreed-on "soft" team processes used throughout the organization and with partners.					
11. Adaptation of processes is encouraged when necessary.					
12. The culture supports shared ways of doing business across teams and partners.					
Section Four: Electronic Communication and Collaboration Technology					
13. There are consistent standards for electronic communication and collaboration tools across the organization.					
14. There are ample resources to buy and support state-of-the-art electronic communication and collaboration technology.					
15. People from all functional areas have equal access to, and are skilled in using, electronic communication and collaboration technology.					
16. People from all geographic areas have equal access to, and are skilled in using, electronic communication and collaboration technology.					

EXHIBIT 10.1   *Continued*

Section Five: Organizational Culture	Strongly Disagree 1	Disagree 2	Neither Agree nor Disagree 3	Agree 4	Strongly Agree 5
17. The culture can be described as "high trust."					
18. There is high trust between this organization and its suppliers and partners.					
19. Teamwork and collaboration are the norm.					
20. People from different cultures are valued here.					
Section Six: Leadership					
21. Leaders set high expectations for virtual team performance.					
22. Leaders help gain the support of customers and other stakeholders.					
23. Leaders allocate resources for the training and technology associated with virtual teams.					
24. Leaders model behaviors, such as working across boundaries and using technology effectively.					

(continued)

EXHIBIT 10.1   *Continued*

Section Seven: Competence	Strongly Disagree 1	Disagree 2	Neither Agree nor Disagree 3	Agree 4	Strongly Agree 5
25. Team leaders are experienced in working in virtual environments.					
26. Team members are experienced in working in virtual environments.					
27. Team leaders are experienced in working across organizational and cultural boundaries.					
28. Team members are experienced in working across organizational and cultural boundaries.					

Analyzing Your Results
Average your scores in each of the seven areas:

Critical Success Category	Average score in this category (add total and divide by 4):
Human resource policies	
Training and development	
Standard organizational processes	
Electronic communication and collaboration technology	
Organizational culture	
Leadership	
Competence	
Overall average (total divided by 28):	

An overall score of 4.0 to 5.0 in any one category and as an average of all categories is excellent. Moderate scores are in the 2.5 to 3.99 range, and low scores fall between 0 and 2.49.

Low scores in specific areas may indicate some of the challenges you face as virtual team leader. Scoring low in technology, for example, may tell you that all your team members may not have equal access to electronic collaboration technology. In this case, you may need to make a case for funding for groupware. The text provides an explanation of each category and actions to attain success criteria.

Human Resource Policies

Human resource policies should support working virtually. Systems must be integrated and aligned to recognize, support, and reward the people who work in and lead virtual teams.

Career-Development Systems. Team leaders can help to support virtual team members by providing career opportunities and assignments that are comparable to those in traditional team settings. Applying promotion and career-development policies and actions fairly to people who work in virtual settings helps to reinforce the perception that working virtually is an accepted career option. Virtual team members often mention that they fear that they will be looked over for promotional opportunities because they are not seen every day. This fear is not unfounded. Managers who lose visual and verbal proximity to their employees often put up the strongest resistance to alternative work and team arrangements.[12] Virtual team leaders must ensure that the members of virtual teams have the same career-development opportunities as the members of traditional teams.

Rewarding Cross-Boundary Work and Results. Organizational reward and recognition systems often favor individual and functional work. Virtual team members, however, frequently operate in a cross-functional and/or cross-organizational environment. Changes must be made in the ways in which people are recognized and rewarded. Leaders must develop performance objectives for team members that include working across boundaries and sharing information to support virtual teamwork.

In addition, performance measures must be adapted to reward results. In a traditional office environment, where people are seen putting in effort every day, it is relatively easy to at least partially reward people for effort as well as for results. In a virtual environment, effort is more difficult to discern. When IBM went to a virtual environment, a shift to a reward structure that was based more on results than effort was a major part of the transition.[13]

The use of formal and informal public recognition of virtual teamwork through "on the spot" awards, bonuses, and other mechanisms can reinforce the perception that working virtually is valued. You can use Web-based technology, such as setting up a site for virtual team "best practices" and advertising team successes and performance, as a way to publicly recognize people in a virtual setting. You also can use examples of your virtual team's success in speeches, presentations, and discussions with other team leaders and with management.

Providing Resources and Support for Working Virtually. Create and support policies that provide your team with technical support for working remotely. All team members should have equal and immediate access to electronic communication and collaboration technology, training, and technical support.

Many virtual team leaders set a standard for technology and make certain that everyone has access to the same hardware, intranet and Internet connections, and applications. They ask the information systems group to assist in the implementation. NORTEL helps virtual team members who are telecommuters to set up "home bases" to ensure that they have access to the best and latest technology.

Training and On-the-Job Education and Development

Formal training in using technology is vital for success. For example, team leaders at the World Bank believed that underfunded technological training for team leaders and team members was one reason that their efforts to implement groupware did not fully succeed. Money was spent on the technology—machines, applications, and compatibility—but not on teaching people how to effectively utilize it.[14]

In addition to a formal training curriculum, make certain that the team members have access to continual online training and technical support. Ask your training department about the feasibility of creating and implementing these types of systems. For example, Federal Express provides many of its technical and leadership classes through its intranet, so people can select where they want to learn. NASA provides a Web site for its project managers so that they can receive help in learning how to select, access, and use the appropriate electronic communication and collaboration tools. In both cases, the training, tools, and support are upgraded on a regular basis to ensure that they are state of the art.

Learning how to use technology is not enough to guarantee success. Team leaders should make certain that they get the training and support they need to be adept at facilitating meetings using technical and nontechnical methods. Training in facilitation skills should be an integral part of a development curriculum for team leaders and team members.

Provide training and support for your team in working collaboratively across organizational, cultural, and functional boundaries. Many organizations provide direct consulting support and training to virtual teams in this area. Johnson & Johnson's Learning Services offers support to virtual team leaders in enhancing collaboration skills in cross-cultural and functional interactions, using what it calls the Team Performance Series. See if your organization offers similar services.

Create and implement systems for sharing knowledge across functions, projects, and organizations. Shared lessons, databases, knowledge repositories, and chat rooms are used in organizations that embrace virtual teamwork. NASA's Web site for project managers contains a place where "lessons learned" are stored. It also has a bulletin board where project managers can ask questions and receive suggestions from other project managers. In many cases, these knowledge-sharing projects were created by virtual teams themselves.

Standard Organizational and Team Processes

Consider developing and implementing standard team processes. The use of standard processes reduces the time needed for team startup and may eliminate the need for unnecessary reinvention of operating practices each time a team is chartered. Practices need to be flexible, however, to promote adaptation to a particular virtual team's situation. Common standard technical processes include:

- Definitions of requirements.
- Estimates of costs.
- Procurement.
- Team charters.
- Project planning.
- Documentation.
- Reporting.
- Controlling.

It is also a good idea to define the preferred software for each of these major processes. Many organizations use standard project-management software packages so that any team, virtual or colocated, is familiar with and trained in using that package. Also have agreed-on team processes in "soft" areas, such as the establishment of team norms, conflict-resolution procedures, and communication protocols. Experienced virtual teams prepare team charters that delineate suggested team norms and communication standards. They use these as starting points to create processes suitable for their unique situations. Reinforce and expect the use of both technical and soft processes from the team.

Electronic Collaboration and Communication Technology

As a virtual team leader, you will need to select electronic collaboration and communication technology that meets the needs of your team. You also will need to ensure that the organization is ready to support your technical needs. Introducing the electronic communication and collaboration technology needed for virtual teamwork, such as desktop video conferencing or groupware, requires that three primary organizational conditions be in place:[15]

1. The organization has a well-funded, respected, and established information systems staff, whose members are experienced in installing and supporting electronic collaboration technologies in many different locations.
2. There is commitment by the organization to keep personal computer systems as up to date as possible, regardless of a person's title or duties. When systems fall behind, the costs of upgrades and the time to introduce

them mounts quickly. Productivity also may fall as people spend time attempting to fix their equipment or work around it.

3. The organization has a well-maintained corporate network that has room to expand to meet the needs of more complex systems and users.

If your organization is lacking in any of these three areas, you might consider adopting a less complex suite of technology than if they are in place. In either case, it is important to select a reasonable set of standards for your team in electronic communication and collaboration technology. Standards should meet the business needs of the team and match its mission and strategy.[16] A global team that needs to communicate and work collaboratively, for example, must have a minimum set of standards for technology. For communication, this includes touch tone telephones, audio conferencing equipment, voice mail, fax capability, and access to a common e-mail system that allows people to send messages and exchange files. Video conferencing, scheduling, real-time data conferencing, electronic meeting systems, collaborative writing tools, and whiteboards can be added if the strategy calls for intensive collaborative work or if sufficient information systems resources exist to make the technology work reliably. Make certain that external partners and suppliers have access to compatible communication and collaboration technologies if they are considered part of the team.

Ensure that skill in using the electronic communication and collaboration technology is equally distributed among team members from different functional areas, geographic locations, and partner organizations. Often skill in, access to, and use of electronic communication and collaboration technology is more prevalent in technical functions, such as engineering and information systems, than in less technical areas, such as marketing, human resources, and finance. If this is the case, there is a risk that team members from less technical areas, if they are not able to use the technologies well, may be perceived by other teammates as having less status.

Ensure that the technology used by each virtual team is available to all team members, wherever they are located. One team leader ran into trouble when some of her team members in China did not have access to touch tone telephones and their word-processing software was outdated. The Chinese managers were using technology to signify status and intentionally did not upgrade the team members' equipment. Of course, these actions put the team members at a disadvantage relative to their teammates and decreased productivity.

Finally, factor electronic collaboration hardware and software directly into the team's budget. It is important to recognize that the benefits of technology grow over time. Virtual teams do reduce costs, but often there is an up-front and long-term investment for technology and training to make them work effectively. The more people and teams work virtually, the more quickly these business practices will translate into savings.

Organizational Culture

Organizational culture includes norms regarding the free flow of information, shared leadership, and cross-boundary collaboration. It helps to create organizational norms and values that focus on collaboration, respecting, and working with people from all cultures, keeping criticism constructive, and sharing information. The organization's culture sets the standard for how virtual team members work together. An adaptive, technologically advanced, and nonhierarchical organization is more likely to succeed with virtual teams than is a highly structured, control-oriented organization.[17]

The success of virtual teams is related to how the organization fosters or impedes trust between itself and its external partners. Treating partners as less than equal, hoarding information, forgetting to share data or results in a timely manner, and using competitive or proprietary information inappropriately can erode trust quickly. For example, many Australian firms report that they have abandoned virtual partnering structures because of issues of trust and control.[18]

If the organization is multinational or global, norms must honor different ways of doing business if they are to be effective. Create policies about how to do business in different cultures. Be aware that legal issues, such as who owns the copyright to product designs, can become murky when teams are working across national boundaries.[19]

Many virtual team leaders cannot affect organizational culture with the same clout as can senior managers. It is possible, however, to create a "microclimate" that supports effective norms and values. Team leaders who act in a conscious manner to build trust across boundaries and to share information and power create environments in which this type of culture can grow from the ground up.

Leadership

For virtual teams to succeed, the organization's leadership must establish a culture that values teamwork, communication, learning, and capitalizing on diversity. The key to establishing an organizational culture that promotes virtual teamwork is that managers and virtual team leaders at all levels must be open to change and must support virtual teamwork. Richard Karl Goeltz, vice chairman and chief financial officer of American Express, notes, "It's important to have a multifunction team of [senior] managers promoting and supporting a virtual office initiative right from the start."[20]

Virtual team leaders and members can help managers to develop supportive behaviors. They can offer specific suggestions to management regarding the four categories of leadership behaviors that encourage virtual team performance: communicating, establishing expectations, allocating resources, and modeling desired behaviors.

First, it is critically important to communicate throughout the organization that working across time and distance and with organizational partners is not just a temporary fad but a new way of doing business, one that leverages knowledge and skills and capitalizes on diversity. This includes assigning virtual teams important and high-visibility tasks and projects and reporting the benefits and results of their work so that virtual teamwork is respected in the organization.

Second, it is important to establish clear expectations about how virtual teams work. Procedures and goals must be clear, so that virtual team members know how they are to work and what their objectives are. With all the new things they must learn about operating in a virtual team, the team members need clear guidelines and objectives to steer by. The other members of the organization also need to understand how virtual teams operate, and that the teams' end goals are aligned with organizational objectives and are, in effect, the same as those of colocated teams. Setting high expectations for performance also strengthens the perception that virtual teams deliver results.

It also is important to gain the support of customers and other important stakeholders by helping them to see the benefits of virtual teamwork. This includes establishing expectations about the virtual work environment and how virtual teamwork is going to affect their contacts with team members. Leaders must stress the benefits, such as lower costs and what the stakeholders have to gain, and find ways to make customers part of the change. One practice is to invite external customers who work with virtual teams to team kickoff sessions in which norms and communication plans are discussed. Customers and other stakeholders also can be offered training in team technology. Customers can be provided with software to "sit in" on team meetings. This helps customers who are unsure of the virtual team approach to become more comfortable with it.

Leaders also can work with stakeholders, such as leaders and managers from other functions or suppliers who interface with the teams, to help them understand and support the virtual team concept. They can make it clear to peers and to other managers in the organization that virtual teams work as hard and as productively as colocated teams. Leaders can become adept at providing evidence, including schedule and cost data, to sway more skeptical stakeholders. Finally, they can help to establish reasonable expectations about the time it takes to realize a return on the investment. The paradox is that the complexities of working across time and distance can, in the short run, lead to increased costs and longer cycle times because of difficulties with operating procedures and startup issues.[21]

Third, leaders who allocate resources for training, technology, and travel send strong signals that bolster the message that virtual teams are important. Chartering virtual teams to work in an underfunded environment is a prescription for failure. Time and money must be allocated for training for virtual team members in areas such as cross-cultural work, project management, and technology. Time and money must be allocated for team leaders to travel for face-to-face meetings with team members at the beginning of the team's life and then when necessary. Resources also must be dedicated to acquiring and maintaining the technology needed to facilitate the team's work.

Fourth, and most important, effective leaders model the behaviors they expect. They align cross-functional and regional goals and objectives. They work with other managers across geographic and cultural boundaries. They solicit team members' input and demonstrate trust in their judgment, particularly in the members' functional areas of expertise. Effective team leaders show flexibility, changing as business conditions dictate. They do not expect behaviors from others that they do not engage in themselves.

Team-Leader Competencies

The challenges that virtual team leaders face are immense. Many report that they feel as if they are the "glue" that holds their teams together. They have to establish trust in an environment with little or no face-to-face contact or feedback. These challenges necessitate the development of an additional set of competencies that complement the skills for leading traditional teams. These competencies are as follows:

1. Coaching and managing performance without traditional forms of feedback.
2. Selecting and appropriately using electronic communication and collaboration technologies.
3. Leading in a cross-cultural environment.
4. Helping to develop and transition team members.
5. Building and maintaining trust.
6. Networking across hierarchical and organizational boundaries.
7. Developing and adapting organizational processes to meet the demands of the team.

Team leaders can champion their own development by deliberately undertaking training and on-the-job assignments that build competence in these areas.

Team-Member Competencies

The people who work as virtual team members have to develop their own competencies. First, virtual teamwork is not for everyone. Serving on a virtual team may seem too transitory for some individuals who need face-to-face interaction and stability in a work environment. Without the structure of a colocated setting and day-to-day contact with team members, they may feel lonely or left out.

All members of traditional and virtual teams need solid grounding in their respective disciplines. However, virtual team members need new competencies.

EXHIBIT 10.2 Leadership behaviors that support virtual team success

Communicating	Establishing Expectations	Allocating Resources	Modeling Behaviors
Communicate the business necessity of virtual teams.	Define how virtual teams work and set clear procedures and goals.	Allocate time and money for training for virtual team leaders and members.	Align cross-functional and regional goals and objectives.
Communicate that virtual teamwork is respected.	Set high standards for virtual team performance.	Allocate time and money for travel for team leaders for face-to-face meetings.	Work together on management team across geographic and cultural boundaries.
Discuss the value of diversity and of leveraging skills.	Establish expectations of customers and other important stakeholders.	Dedicate resources for technology.	Solicit input from and display trust in team members.
Communicate the benefits and results of working virtually.	Factor in startup costs and times.		Show flexibility.

Team leaders can help to facilitate competence development by working with team members to create learning plans that use training and on-the-job assignments. The definitions of team-member competencies will vary, depending on the team's type, mission, and composition. There is, however, a relatively stable set of six critical competencies:

1. Project management techniques.
2. Networking across functional, hierarchical, and organizational boundaries.
3. Using electronic communication and collaboration technologies effectively.
4. Setting personal boundaries and managing time.
5. Working across cultural and functional boundaries.
6. Using interpersonal awareness.

Over time, most people can develop the competencies that are needed to work virtually. Adequate training, education, and leadership support and feedback can speed development.

IMPLEMENTING PILOT PROJECTS

A pilot project is a good idea in an organization in which virtual teamwork is new and untried. If you do decide to create your own pilot test with your team or to orchestrate a larger pilot project, you may use the guidelines offered here.

First, select a problem to work on that is highly visible and difficult to solve traditionally.[22] Set expectations that the pilot will take extra time and attention from management, staff, consultants, and information systems. It will include some expenses for equipment, software, and travel. Ask for executive sponsorship; find an upper-level manager who has a vested interest in the pilot and ask him or her to help in obtaining resources and stakeholder support.

Second, don't make it overly complicated. Begin the pilot with two or three teams in a function or area that makes sense, such as sales, telemarketing, project engineering, or consulting.[23] Most employees in these functions already are used to working remotely. For example, American Express began its pilot project in 1993 with virtual sales teams that were accustomed to working on the road.[24]

Third, check on the team leader's and team members' progress on a regular basis. Make sure that they understand the performance objectives and the ways in which results will be measured. Most people who work in a colocated team can meet with their teammates or leader in impromptu moments and ask for advice. Plan new ways for team members to exchange information and receive feedback in order to ensure that they are receiving the support they need to perform well. These ways might include mandatory Monday-morning telephone conferences to discuss performance or documentation of interim deliverables with feedback from the customer and the team leader.

Fourth, assign a dedicated (not necessarily full-time) member of the information system staff to assist the team with equipment, software, and operations.

Fifth, evaluate the effort with multiple measures. "Hard" measures include the costs of equipment, software, travel, and consultant time. "Soft" measures include how people feel about the arrangement, the problems they encounter, and the feeling of cohesiveness on the team.

NOTES

1. J. B. Quinn, *Intelligent Enterprise: A Knowledge and Service Based Paradigm for Industry* (New York: Free Press, 1992).

2. D. J. Grimshaw and F. T. S. Kwok, "The Business Benefits of the Virtual Organization," *The Virtual Workplace,* eds. M. Igbaria and M. Tan (Hershey, PA: Idea Group Publishing, 1998).

3. See note 2.

4. M. Apgar IV, "The Alternative Workplace: Changing Where and How People Work," *Harvard Business Review* (May/June 1998): 121–139. See note 2.

5. See note 4, Apgar.

6. See note 4, Apgar.

7. D. D. Mittleman and B. O. Briggs, "Communication Technology for Teams: Electronic Collaboration," *Supporting Work Team Effectiveness: Best Practices for Fostering High-Performance,* eds. E. Sunderstrom and Associates (San Francisco: Jossey-Bass, 1998).

8. See note 7.

9. See note 2.

10. J. F. Nunamaker Jr., B. O. Briggs, N. Romano Jr., and D. D. Mittleman, "The Virtual Office Work Space: GroupSystems Web and Case Studies," *GroupWare:*

Collaborative Strategies for Corporate LANs and Intranets, ed. D. Coleman (Upper Saddle River, NJ: Prentice Hall, 1997).

11. R. Pastore, "A Virtual Visionary," *CIO* (July 1993): 46.

12. See note 4, Apgar.

13. See note 4, Apgar.

14. G. O'Dwyer, A. Giser, and E. Lovett, "GroupWare and Reengineering: The Human Side of Change," *GroupWare: Collaborative Strategies for Corporate LANs and Intranets,* ed. D. Coleman (Upper Saddle River, NJ: Prentice Hall, 1997).

15. C. Perey, "Desktop Videoconferencing," *GroupWare: Collaborative Strategies for Corporate LANs and Intranets,* ed. D. Coleman (Upper Saddle River, NJ: Prentice Hall, 1997).

16. See note 15.

17. See note 4, Apgar.

18. Bureau of Industry Economic, *Beyond the Firm* (Canberra: Australian Government Publishing Service, 1995).

19. See note 2.

20. See note 4, Apgar.

21. See note 2.

22. See note 10.

23. See note 4, Apgar.

24. See note 4, Apgar.

PART FOUR

MANAGING THE PROJECT-BASED ORGANIZATION

Managing a single project presents many challenges: estimating cost and schedule, coordinating cross-functional personnel, building cohesive temporary teams, maintaining a balance between producing what is needed and when it must be delivered, and so on. Now multiply those challenges by the number of projects in your organization, and the need for a conscious, consistent approach to managing the project-based organization is obvious.

Before the late 1990s, any discussion of managing multiple projects was classified as *program* management, using the definition that a program was a collection of related projects. Year 2000 (Y2K) computer projects often fit this description, with the Y2K program manager or program management team coordinating the work of many related teams. On the very largest scale, such as a program to develop a new Boeing commercial airliner, the program management team coordinated thousands of personnel over a period of years. Because all of the projects are related to the same goal, program management can leverage the project management techniques described in Part Two to create a structure for control and communication. Program management in this context is really just project management on a very large scale. I am not suggesting that program management is a lark. Large-scale program management is a difficult challenge that few firms have mastered. But we must distinguish program management from managing a project-based organization.

The project-based organization is managing many projects, only some of which are related. IT departments, construction firms, and

305

software product companies are just a few examples of firms that have 20 percent or more of their budget/revenue devoted to projects, but the projects may have unrelated goals or customers. The additional challenges—on top of the classic project management challenges—are selecting the right combination of projects and deploying limited resources among these projects.

The basic nature of projects—that they are temporary and unique—is a major source of the problems. How do we staff our organization for a constantly changing workload? How can we have optimal organizational structure, one that facilitates communication and proper authority, when so many projects end up being cross-functional?

Part One of this book presented the reasons that organizations are formalizing their project management processes and reorganizing to optimize project performance. Parts Two and Three presented the discipline of project management, the factors that must be present on every project. In Part Four, we examine the processes required *above* the project level—the processes and organizations that provide a foundation for excellence on every project. We see that the power of the project management methods described in Part Two can be either energized and magnified or diluted by the overall processes and structure of the organization.

The purpose of project management techniques is to *manage*—to improve the performance and productivity of the resources applied to meet the project goal through better communication, coordination, and planning. As valuable as project management techniques are, they are insufficient to manage the overall organization. Part Four adds the other processes that make the project-based organization complete and provides guidance for achieving the organizational changes.

Many projects are undertaken to introduce new products to customers. Project managers can apply all the techniques for managing scope, schedule, and cost and still produce a product that flops in the marketplace. That's because nowhere in the project management discipline is there a method for discerning what combination of cost, schedule, and quality will make the product successful. Robert Cooper has spent years researching successful new product development efforts and is the acknowledged authority on this topic; in Chapter 11, he details a process for bringing a concept or idea through full development to market. This Stage-Gate™ process is essential for project-based organizations to understand regardless of what they produce, because it demonstrates the need and the methods for managing the business case for the project. The multiple phases of a full product development process can be managed as a series of projects—each phase becoming one or more projects. This perspective is essential to reducing the risk of managing any concept-to-delivery efforts, and the need for it is magnified for organizations that manage many of these initiatives at the same time.

Project management maturity is a phrase that is increasingly used to describe the sophistication of an organization's project management processes. In Chapter 12, Denis Couture applies his firm's experience to describe exactly what processes, organization structure, and accompanying information technology infrastructure are necessary for the project-based organization. Firms seeking to improve their maturity will be able to use Couture's enterprise project management model as a benchmark or target on their own journey to improving their project management capability. In describing his model, Couture makes the important point that implementing just some of the processes or structure is not enough; just as a three-legged stool requires all its legs, an enterprise project management system requires all the functions described in this chapter to be effective.

A few project management experts in the organization can put their heads together and in a relatively short time design the project management standards, organizational structures, and information technology infrastructure necessary for effective management of the project-based organization. Why, then, does it often take years to fully deploy these designs? Why do firms abandon the journey to formalize their project management structures? Because implementing new standards requires more than new software in our computers; it requires new values and thought processes in our hearts and minds. In Chapter 13, authors Graham and Englund propose a seven-step path to achieve cultural, organization, and process changes. It should be no surprise that change begins with visible commitment from top management. Their advice guides the human side of the transition.

Project-based firms ultimately do *not* measure their success by the maturity of their project management processes. They measure their success by the *results* of their projects. Shareholders of publicly owned companies do not prize project management maturity; they value the growth of revenue and profits. Therefore, true project management maturity occurs when the captains of the enterprise can ignore the mechanics of portfolio, program, and project management and return their focus to corporate strategy. To achieve this final level of maturity, project management processes must mesh seamlessly with the other essential operations of the enterprise. As the transmission in my car is useful only to the extent it complements the rest of the vehicle, my project management systems must fit into the overall context of the project-based organization. Chapter 14 raises our perspective to the enterprise level to see how the project management systems we have focused on fit into their environment. We explore the reality of merging project-focused standards into organizations where as much as 80 percent of the work is *not* project-based, including adjusting the design and functions of the project management office.

More than any other part of this book, the chapters in Part Four offer insights and guidance on the leading edge of managing the project-based organizations. The prescriptions and concepts contained in these chapters are neither simple to grasp nor simple to follow. Neither are they beyond the reach of most organizations. As with all endeavors related to project management, persistence and dedication are major success factors.

STAGE-GATE™ NEW PRODUCT DEVELOPMENT PROCESSES: A GAME PLAN FROM IDEA TO LAUNCH

11

Robert G. Cooper

Facing increased pressure to reduce the cycle time yet improve their new product success rates, companies look to new product processes, or Stage-Gate™ systems,[1] to manage, direct, and accelerate their product innovation efforts.[2] This chapter outlines what the Stage-Gate or phase-gate process is, why it is important, and how it has been modified to handle different types of development projects. The chapter concludes with some steps on how to design and implement this process in the company.

WHAT IS A STAGE-GATE™ PROCESS?

A Stage-Gate process is a *conceptual and operational road map* for moving a new product project from idea to launch—a blueprint for managing the new product process to improve effectiveness and efficiency.[3] Stage-Gate breaks the innovation process into a predetermined set of stages. Each stage defines a set of prescribed, cross-functional, and parallel activities to be undertaken by the project team, much the way a *playbook* defines the actions to be taken by a football team (see Exhibit 11.1). Management then builds into these stages best practices and critical success factors.

The entrance to each stage is a gate: These gates are analogous to huddles in a football game. Gates are meetings that control the process and serve as the

EXHIBIT 11.1 An Overview of a typical Stage-Gate™ process

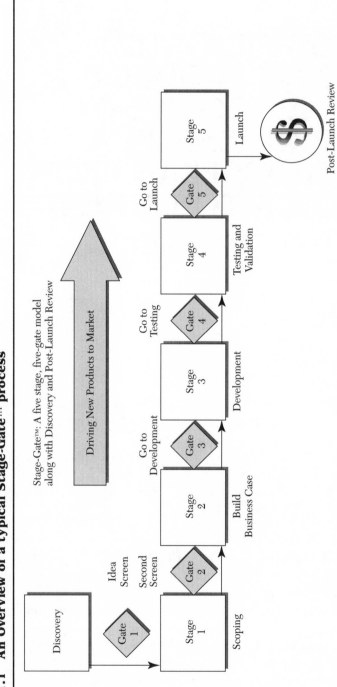

Stage-Gate™: A five stage, five-gate model along with Discovery and Post-Launch Review

Driving New Products to Market

quality control and "go/kill" checkpoints. At these gate meetings, the project is scrutinized by senior management: They review the progress of the project; determine whether the criteria necessary to move forward have been met; and either approve the task and resources for the next stage (go), ask for more information (recycle), or stop the project (kill or hold).

This stage-and-gate format leads to the name *Stage-Gate process.* Other names include *phase-gate* and *phase review* processes.

WHY HAVE A FORMAL NEW PRODUCT PROCESS AT ALL?

Dealing with High Failure Rates

New products have an alarming failure rate. Of every ten product concepts, only one becomes a commercial success, according to a Product Development & Management Association (PDMA) study.[4] A review of many studies suggests that one-third of new products fail at launch, even after all the product tests, customer trials, and even test markets. Another investigation reveals that 46 percent of companies' resources spent on new product development (NPD) go to unsuccessful ventures.[5]

Why do so many new products fail, and why do the majority of businesses underperform in NPD? The reasons for failure or poor performance have been widely studied; some of the more important ones include:[6]

- Lack of understanding of the market and customer—market potential, customer needs and wants, competitive situation.
- Failure to commit the necessary resources to product development (or to the project team)—people assigned to the project are simply stretched too thinly, so they cut corners and execute in haste.
- Lack of solid upfront homework before development begins—a "ready, fire, aim" approach to NPD.
- Lack of a discipline to the new product process and paying lip service to quality of execution—things simply don't happen as they should, when they should, or as well as they should in NPD projects.
- Lack of good new product ideas as feedstock to the process.
- Moving targets—unstable product requirements and project scope creep.
- Lack of senior management commitment to and engagement in NPD.

The existence of these and other recurring reasons for new product failure has caused many firms to rethink the way they go about conceiving, developing, and launching new products. The result has been systematic new product processes that overcome these deficiencies and failure points.

The Top Three Drivers of Performance

Having a high-quality and systematic new product process was one of the top three drivers of NPD performance uncovered in a major benchmarking study into NPD practices (see Exhibit 11.2).[7] This study probed multiple measures of new product performance, including percentage of sales by new products, success rates, impact on the business, and overall profitability of the business's total new product efforts.

The top three drivers of performance—what really separates the best performers from the rest—in order, are:

1. *A high-quality new product process:* A stage-and-gate process that demands upfront homework, sharp and early product definition, tough go/kill decision points, and quality of execution and thoroughness, yet provides flexibility.

2. *A defined new product strategy for the business:* One where there are new product goals for the business, where areas of focus are delineated, where the role of new products is clearly communicated, and where there is a longer term thrust.

3. *Adequate resources (people and money):* Where senior management commits the necessary resources, provides the needed people (and frees up their time for projects), and resources the effort with adequate R&D funding.

EXHIBIT 11.2   Three key factors drive a business's new product performance

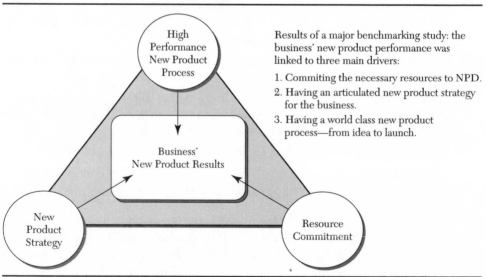

Results of a major benchmarking study: the business' new product performance was linked to three main drivers:

1. Commiting the necessary resources to NPD.
2. Having an articulated new product strategy for the business.
3. Having a world class new product process—from idea to launch.

Other Benchmarking Results

In another study, new product processes were found to be central to a business's NPD success. The PDMA's most recent best practices study[8] begins with a comprehensive review of a number of industrial benchmarking studies that repeat a similar theme: "New product processes are vital." The study concludes that although new product development processes are a relatively recent phenomena, they are seen as being necessary to effective new product development. Over the years, "The focus has moved from defining the process to assuring implementation, to better managing the upfront portion, to measuring the process better, and to continually improving the process." Approximately 60 percent of firms were found to use a Stage-Gate system; this percent was even higher among the best performers (68 percent), consumer goods firms (69 percent), and larger firms (69 percent).[9]

WHY WINNERS WIN

Before we discuss the details of a Stage-Gate process, consider some of the success factors—behaviors, practices, common denominators—that have been found to separate winning project teams from losers and businesses that do well at product development from the poorer performers. Much research has been undertaken to uncover these success factors—research that often compares larger samples of successful projects or businesses to poor performers.[10] The following sections describe some of these best practices and success factors.

1. Differentiated, Superior Products

The top success factor is delivering a *differentiated product* with *unique customer benefits* and *superior value for the user.* Such superior products with *compelling value propositions:*

- Meet customer needs better than competitive products (but often customers do not know what they need).
- Are higher quality products; however, the customer or user defines quality.
- Solve a customer problem with existing products.
- Save the customer or user money—better value-in-use.

Note that the product must be differentiated and offer superior value *in the eyes of the customer or user* (not just in the eyes of the developer or R&D department). Thus, building in a user needs-and-wants study (voice of customer [VoC] research) along with competitive analysis and constant testing with the customer are ways to achieve such winning product designs.

2. Upfront Homework

Too many new product projects move from the idea stage right into development with little or no upfront homework. The results of this "ready, fire, aim" approach are usually disastrous. Solid predevelopment homework drives up new product success rates significantly and is strongly correlated with financial performance. Sadly, firms devote on average only 7 percent of a project's funding and 16 percent of the person-days to these critical upfront homework activities.

Recommended upfront homework activities in a significant new product project include:

- Undertaking an in-depth market analysis—size, growth, trends, segmentation.
- Building in *a voice of customer study* (see next section) to determine customer needs and wants.
- Doing a solid competitor analysis: players, products, performance, and strengths.
- Undertaking a detailed technical assessment—technical risks, probable solutions, and costs to achieve; environmental, health, and safety issues; and intellectual property protection.
- Performing a detailed operations or source of supply assessment—probable production route, costs, and equipment requirements.
- Undertaking a concept test with users or potential customers—to determine interest, liking, preference, and purchase intent.
- Finalizing the product definition (see item 4).
- Building the business case: financial analysis and business rationale for the project.

3. Voice of the Customer

Successful businesses and teams that drive winning new product projects have a slave-like dedication to the voice of the customer. VoC research means face-to-face and in-depth interviews or visits with customers or potential users to determine their needs, wants, and preferences in a new product. Such customer interviews should be undertaken by the project team itself, including the technical members from R&D or engineering. These VoC interviews are designed to probe the customer's *unmet or unarticulated needs*—not just to focus on desired product features and specifications. Questions that comprise the "conversation guide" for the visit include:

- What is your current solution?
- Why are you doing it that way?
- What problems do you have with the current solution—what really annoys you?

- Can you think of a better way?
- Why do you want that feature—what does it allow you to do?

On the basis of such customer or user insights, the project team is in a much better position to begin the design of a truly superior product—item 1 discussed previously.

New product projects that feature such high-quality VoC market research are blessed with more than double the success rates and 70 percent higher market shares than projects with poor marketing information. Sadly, a strong market orientation and customer focus is noticeably lacking in many businesses' new product projects and is consistently rated one of the weakest areas in projects: The project team thinks it already understands the customer's problem or needs, doesn't do the study, and jumps immediately to a solution—often the wrong one.

4. Sharp, Stable, and Early Product Definition

A failure to *define the product and project* before development begins is a major cause of both new product failure and serious delays in time to market. In spite of the fact that *early and stable product definition is consistently cited as a key to success,* firms continue to perform poorly here. Terms such as *unstable product specs* and *project scope creep* describe far too many new-product projects. It is essential that the project team define the product and project before moving into development (prior to Stage 3 in Exhibit 11.1). This product and project definition includes:

- Project scope.
- Target market—at which market segment the product is aimed.
- Product concept—what the product will be and do.
- Benefits the product will deliver to the customer—the *value proposition.*
- Positioning strategy (versus competitive products, including target price).
- Product requirements, features, and high-level specifications.

In addition, this product definition must be fact-based (items 2 and 3) and offer a compelling value proposition (item 1).

5. A Well-Conceived, Properly Resourced Market Launch

Not surprisingly, a strong market launch underlies successful new products. For example, new product winners devote more than twice as many person-days and dollars to the launch as do teams that fail. Similarly, the quality of execution of the market launch is significantly higher for winners. The need for a quality launch—well planned, properly resourced, and well executed—should be obvious. However, in some businesses, it's almost as though the launch is an afterthought—something to worry about after the product is fully developed.

6. Tough Go/Kill Decision Points in the NPD Process—A Funnel, Not a Tunnel

Too many projects move far into development without serious scrutiny: After a project begins, there is very little chance that it will ever be killed. The result is that many marginal projects are approved, with the improper allocation of scarce resources. Many companies have moved toward effective *portfolio management,* where each new product project is viewed as an investment. Here, tough go/kill decision points are built into the new product process in the form of gates that successively cull out mediocre projects. The result is a funnel (by contrast, "tunnels" occur when a set of projects is initially approved and none is subsequently killed, even though the project's prospects have turned negative). Similarly, consistent, rigorous criteria are employed at these gates to rate and rank projects at the gates to promote better decision making.

7. True Cross-Functional Projects Teams

Good organizational design is strongly linked to both success rates and shorter times to market. This means that a project is organized as a cross-functional team that is led by a strong project leader, is accountable for the entire project from beginning to end, and is dedicated and focused (as opposed to spread over many projects). While the ingredients of a "good team" should be familiar ones, surprisingly many projects are found lacking here.

8. Attacking from a Position of Strength

This may be an old adage, but it certainly applies to the launch of new products. The new product fares better when it leverages the business's core competencies. Leveraging core competencies means having a strong fit between the needs of the new product project and the resources, strengths, and experience of the company in terms of marketing, distribution, selling, technology, and operations. For example, projects with technological leverage—where the new product builds from internal R&D, engineering, technical, and manufacturing strengths—have about triple the success rates versus those where the in-house technical strengths are absent; and those projects that build from the business's internal marketing strengths—sold to existing customers, via the same channel or sales force, and so on—have double the success rate as those that do not leverage the firm's marketing resources.

9. An International Orientation

New products aimed at international markets (as opposed to domestic) and with international requirements built in from the outset are more profitable.

By contrast, products that are developed for domestic markets and sold locally yield lower profits. In addition, the strategy of "design for local needs, and adjust for export later" also does not work well; the product is usually compromised.

Some of the action implications of this international approach include:

- Defining the market more broadly than just the domestic market from the beginning—not halfway through the project.
- Ensuring that people from foreign affiliates are on the project team.
- Undertaking some VoC research and competitive analysis in other countries—not assuming that domestic results apply internationally.
- Building foreign requirements (e.g., standards, specs) into the product design.
- Possibly developing a global product—where one size fits all, globally.
- But, more likely, arriving at a "glocal" product—essentially the same product, but locally tailored to suit the unique requirements of different regions of the world or even countries (e.g., a European version, an Asia-Pacific version, and a North American version of the same product).
- Undertaking product tests, beta tests, field trials, and test markets with potential customers in different countries.
- Designing a global roll-out or launch strategy—possibly sequential launches country by country but ideally concurrent launches globally.

10. Speed and Reducing Time to Market

Speed is a vital competitive weapon. Speed yields competitive advantage, the notion that "first to market wins"; it means less likelihood that the market or competitive situation has changed by the time you launch; and it means a quicker realization of profits. So the goal of reducing the development cycle time is admirable.[11] Most firms have reduced product development cycle times over the past five years, with the average reduction being about one-third.[12]

A word of caution: *Speed is only an interim objective.* The ultimate goal is profitability. Too often, the methods used to reduce development time yield precisely the opposite effect and can be very costly: Shortcuts are taken with the best intentions but far too frequently result in disaster. For example, the PDMA's best practices study found that the best firms actually took a little longer to develop new products than the average performer, perhaps a reflection of both the more challenging projects undertaken and the desire to do a better quality job.

There is a dark side to accelerated product development, according to Crawford:[13]

- Shortcutting certain key activities: moving in haste through the early phases of a new product project but missing voice of customer inputs and defining the wrong product, or shortening the customer-test phase, only to incur product reliability problems after launch.

- Focusing only on easy, quick hits, such as line extensions and minor modifications, resulting in a lack of significant new products.
- Setting unrealistic time lines to achieve launch deadlines, only to create frustration and morale problems among project team members when milestones are invariably missed.

Here are six *sensible* ways to reduce cycle time—ways that are totally consistent with good management practice and are also derived from the critical success factors previously outlined:

1. Do the upfront homework, and get early and stable product and project definition based on facts rather than hearsay and speculation. This saves time downstream.
2. Build in quality of execution at every stage of the project. The best way to save time is to avoid having to do it a second time.
3. Effective cross-functional teams are essential for timely development. "Rip apart a badly developed project and you will unfailingly find 75 percent of slippage attributable to: 'siloing,' or sending memos up and down vertical organizational 'silos' or 'stovepipes' for decisions; and sequential problem solving."[14]
4. Use *parallel processing*. The relay race, sequential, or series approach to product development is antiquated and inappropriate for today's fast-paced projects.
5. In combination with parallel processing, use *spiral development*, a series of build-and-test spirals, constantly checking the product with the customer or user. This series of iterations begins with the concept test in Stage 2 (see Exhibit 11.1) and ends with the full field trials (beta tests) in Stage 4.
6. Prioritize and focus—do fewer projects but higher value ones. By concentrating resources on the truly deserving projects, the work will be done not only better, but also faster.

11. The Role of Top Management

Top management support is a necessary ingredient for product innovation. Top management's main role is to *set the stage* for product innovation, to be a "behind-the-scenes" facilitator, and much less an actor, front and center.

Senior management must make the long-term commitment to product development as a source of growth; it must develop a vision, objectives, and strategy for product innovation. It must make available the necessary resources to product development and ensure that they are not diverted to more immediate needs in times of shortage. Management must commit to a disciplined game plan to drive products to market.

Most important, senior management must be engaged in the new product process, reviewing projects, making timely and firm go/kill decisions, and if "go," making resource commitments to project teams. Management must empower project teams and support committed champions by acting as mentors, facilitators, "godfathers," or sponsors of project leaders and teams.

Building These Success Factors In

These and other success factors and best practices have been uncovered in countless studies of successful projects, project teams, and businesses. The analogy is one of observing winning football teams (versus the losers), watching successful touchdown marches, and then trying to uncover what made for success. After these success factors are identified, the coach then sits down with the team and starts to map out plays and a game plan or *playbook*. That's exactly what happens here: Management should take these success factors and build them into the new product process or methodology. The next section discusses how the process works and how these success factors should be built in.

WHAT THE STAGE-GATE™ PROCESS OR PLAYBOOK LOOKS LIKE

The Stages

The Stage-Gate process breaks the new product project into discrete and identifiable stages, typically four, five, or six stages, as in Exhibit 11.1. These stages are the *plays*—where players execute prescribed actions. Each stage is designed to gather information and undertake tasks needed to progress the project to the next gate or decision point. Some key points:

- Each stage is cross-functional. There is no "R&D stage" or "marketing stage"; rather, every stage is marketing, R&D, production, engineering, and so on.
- Each stage consists of a set of parallel activities undertaken by people from different functional areas in the firm—that is, tasks within a stage are done concurrently and in parallel, much like a team of football or rugby players executing a play.
- The activities in a stage are designed to gather critical information and reduce the project's unknowns and uncertainties. Each stage costs more than the preceding one: The process is an incremental commitment one. But with each step increase in project cost, the unknowns and uncertainties are driven down, so that risk is effectively managed.

The flow of the typical Stage-Gate process is shown in Exhibit 11.1. The stages are:

Discovery: Prework designed to uncover opportunities and generate NPD ideas.

Scoping: A quick, preliminary investigation and scoping of the project—largely desk research.

Build the business case: A much more detailed investigation involving primary research—both market and technical—leading to a *business case,* including product and project definition, project justification, and a project plan.

Development: The actual detailed design and development of the new product and the design of the operations or production process.

Testing and validation: Tests or trials in the marketplace, lab, and plant to verify and validate the proposed new product and its marketing and production/operations.

Launch: Commercialization—beginning of full operations or production, marketing, and selling.

There is one additional stage: *strategy formulation,* an essential activity. This strategy formulation stage is omitted from the Exhibit 11.1 flow diagram, not because it is unimportant, but because it is macro and all encompassing in nature—strategically oriented as opposed to process or tactics. Thus, strategy formulation is best superimposed over (or atop) the model in Exhibit 11.1; it is a prerequisite to an effective Stage-Gate process.

The Gates

Preceding each stage is a gate or a go/kill decision point. The gates are the *scrums* or *huddles* on the rugby or football field. They are the points during the game where the team converges and where all new information is brought together. Gates serve as quality-control checkpoints, as go/kill and prioritization decision points, and as points where the path forward for the next play or stage of the project is decided.

The structure of each gate is similar. Gates consist of:

1. A set of required *deliverables*—what the project leader and team must bring to the decision point (e.g., the results of a set of completed activities). These deliverables are visible, are based on a standard menu for each gate, and are decided at the output of the previous gate. Management's expectations for project teams are thus made very clear.

Gates have a common format:

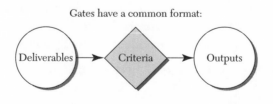

2. *Criteria* against which the project is judged. These can include "must meet" or knock-out questions (a checklist) designed to weed out misfit projects quickly. For example:
   - Does the proposed project fit our business's strategy?
   - Does it meet our environmental, health, and safety (EH&S) policies?

   There are also "should meet" criteria or desirable factors which are scored and added (a point count system) and which are used to prioritize projects. For example:
   - The strength of the value proposition or product's competitive advantage.
   - Ability to leverage core competencies.
   - Relative market attractiveness.
   - Size of the financial return versus the risk.

3. Defined *outputs,* for example, a decision (go/kill/hold/recycle), an approved action plan for the next stage (complete with people required, money and person-days committed, and an agreed time line), a list of deliverables, and date for the next gate.

Gates are usually tended by senior managers from different functions, who own the resources required by the project leader and team for the next stage. They are called the *gatekeepers* and are a predefined group for each of the five gates. For example, for larger projects, Gates 3, 4, and 5 are often staffed by the leadership team of the business—the head of the business and the heads of marketing/sales, technology, operations, and finance.

A WALK THROUGH THE STAGE-GATE™ PROCESS

The following sections describe the Stage-Gate™ process on a high level—an overview of what's involved at each stage and gate. This is shown stage by stage in Exhibit 11.1.

Begin Stage: Discovery

Ideas are the feedstock or trigger to the process, and they make or break the process. Do not expect a superb new product process to overcome a deficiency in good new product ideas. The need for great ideas, coupled with a high attrition rate of ideas, means that the idea generation stage is pivotal: You need great ideas and many of them.

Many companies consider ideation so important that they handle this as a formal stage in the process, often called *discovery.* They build in a *defined, proactive idea generation and capture system.* Activities in the discovery stage include:

- Undertaking directed but fundamental technical research, seeking new technological possibilities.[15]
- Working with lead users (innovative customers) to uncover unarticulated needs.[16]
- Using creativity methods (such as brainstorming).
- Strategic planning exercises to uncover disruptions in the marketplace leading to identification of gaps and significant opportunities.[17]
- Idea suggestion schemes to encourage ordinary employees to submit new product ideas.

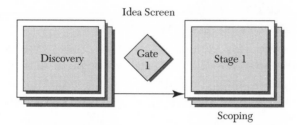

A good summary of many ideation methods is provided in Cooper's *Winning at New Products*.[18]

Gate 1: Idea Screen

Idea screening is the first decision to commit resources to the project: The project is born at this point. If the decision is "go," the project moves into the scoping or preliminary investigation stage. Thus, Gate 1 signals a preliminary but tentative commitment to the project: a flickering green light.

Gate 1 is a "gentle screen" and amounts to subjecting the project to a handful of "must meet" and "should meet" criteria. These criteria often deal with strategic alignment, project feasibility, magnitude of opportunity and market attractiveness, product advantage, ability to leverage the firm's resources, and fit with company policies. Financial criteria are typically not part of this first screen. A checklist for the "must meet" criteria and a scoring model (point count rating scales in the form of a scorecard) for the "should meet" criteria can be used to help focus the discussion and rank projects in this early screen.

Stage 1: Scoping

This first and inexpensive homework stage has the objective of determining the project's technical and marketplace merits. Stage 1 is a quick scoping of the project, involving desk research or detective work—little or no primary research is done here. Stage 1 is often done in less than one calendar month's elapsed time and 10 to 20 person-days' work effort.

A *preliminary market assessment* is one facet of Stage 1 and involves a variety of relatively inexpensive activities: an Internet search, a library search, contacts with key users, focus groups, a quick competitive analysis (e.g., Web pages), and even a fast concept test with a handful of potential users. The purpose is to determine market size, market potential, and likely market acceptance and to begin to better define the winning product concept.

Concurrently, a *preliminary technical assessment* is carried out, involving a preliminary in-house appraisal of the proposed product. The purpose is to assess development and manufacturing (or source of supply) routes; intellectual property (IP) issues; technical and manufacturing operations feasibility; possible times and costs to execute; and technical, legal, and regulatory risks and roadblocks.

Stage 1 thus provides for the gathering of both market and technical information—at low costs and in a short time—to enable a cursory and first-pass financial and business analysis as input to Gate 2. Because of the limited effort, and depending on the size of the project, very often Stage 1 can be handled by a team of only a few people—perhaps from marketing and from a technical group—and in one calendar month.

Gate 2: Second Screen

The project is subjected to a second and somewhat more rigorous screen at Gate 2. This gate is essentially a repeat of Gate 1: The project is reevaluated in the light of the new information obtained in Stage 1. If the decision is "go" at this point, the project moves into a heavier spending stage.

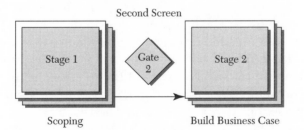

At Gate 2, the project is again subjected to the original set of "must meet" and "should meet" criteria used at Gate 1. Here additional "should meet" criteria may be considered, dealing with sales force and customer reaction to the proposed product, potential legal, technical, and regulatory "killer variables," based on new data gathered during Stage 1. Again, a checklist and scoring model (scorecard) facilitate this gate decision. The financial return is assessed at Gate 2, but only by a quick and simple financial calculation (e.g., the payback period).

Stage 2: Build the Business Case

The business case opens the door to product development. In Stage 2, the business case is constructed. This stage is a detailed investigation stage, which clearly defines the product and verifies the attractiveness of the project before heavy spending. It is also the *critical homework* stage—the one so often found to be weakly handled.

The definition of the *winning new product* is a major facet of Stage 2. The elements of this definition include target market definition; delineation of the product concept; specification of a product positioning strategy, the product benefits to be delivered, and the value proposition; and spelling out essential and desired product features, attributes, requirements, and specifications.

Stage 2 sees *market* and *market research studies* undertaken to determine the customer's needs, wants, and preferences—that is, to help define the "winning" new product. Here the project team undertakes *voice of customer* research to better understand the user or customer's unarticulated needs, wants, and desires and what the user sees as a *benefit*. Such research is usually instrumental in arriving at a *compelling value proposition*.

Competitive analysis is also a part of this stage. Another market activity is concept testing: A representation of the proposed new product is presented to potential customers, their reactions are gauged, and the likely customer acceptance of the new product is determined.

A detailed *technical appraisal* focuses on the "doability" of the project. That is, customer needs and "wish lists" are translated into a technically and economically feasible solution on paper. This translation might even involve some preliminary design, modeling, or laboratory work, but it should not be construed as a full-fledged development project.

A *manufacturing (operations or source of supply) appraisal* is often a part of building the business case, where issues of manufacturability, source of supply, costs to manufacture, and investment required are investigated. If appropriate, detailed legal, intellectual property, and regulatory assessment work is undertaken to remove risks and to map out the required actions.

Finally, a detailed *business and financial analysis* is conducted as part of the justification facet of the business case. The financial analysis typically involves a discounted cash-flow approach (NPV and IRR), complete with sensitivity analysis to look at possible downside risks.

The result of Stage 2 is a *business case* for the project: The *product definition*—a key to success—is agreed to and a thorough *project justification* and *detailed project plan* are developed.

Stage 2 involves considerably more effort than Stage 1, and it requires input from a variety of sources. Stage 2 is best handled by a team consisting of cross-functional members—the core group of the eventual project team.

Gate 3: Go to Development

This is the final gate before the development stage, the last point at which the project can be killed before entering heavy spending. Once past Gate 3, financial commitments are substantial. In effect, Gate 3 means "go to a heavy spend." Gate 3 also yields a sign off of the product and project definition.

The qualitative side of this evaluation involves a review of each of the activities in Stage 2 and a check that the activities were undertaken, the quality of execution was sound, and the results were positive. Next, Gate 3 subjects the project once again to the set of "must meet" and "should meet" criteria used at Gate 2, but this time with much more rigor and with benefit of more solid data. Finally, because a heavy spending commitment is the result of a "go" decision at Gate 3, the results of the financial analysis are an important part of this screen.

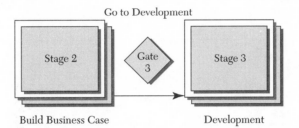

If the decision is "go," Gate 3 sees commitment to the product definition and agreement on the project plan that charts the path forward: The development plan and the preliminary operations and marketing plans are reviewed and approved at this gate. The full project team—an empowered, cross-functional team headed by a leader with authority—is designated.

Stage 3: Development

Stage 3 witnesses the implementation of the development plan and the physical development of the product. Lab tests, in-house tests, or alpha tests ensure that the product meets requirements under controlled conditions. For lengthy projects, numerous milestones and periodic project reviews are built into the development plan. These are not gates per se: Go/kill decisions are not made here; rather, these milestone checkpoints provide for project control and management. Extensive in-house testing, alpha tests, or lab testing usually occurs in this stage as well. The deliverable at the end of Stage 3 is an internally tested prototype of the product.

The emphasis in Stage 3 is on technical work. But marketing and operations activities also proceed in parallel. For example, market analysis and customer feedback work continue concurrently with the technical development, with constant customer opinion sought on the product as it takes shape during development. These activities are back-and-forth or iterative with each development result—for example, rapid prototype, working model, first prototype, and so on—taken to the customer for assessment and feedback. Some experts call this iterative process *spiral development.* Meanwhile, detailed test plans, market launch plans, and production or operations plans, including production facilities requirements, are developed. An updated financial analysis is prepared while regulatory and intellectual property issues are resolved.

Gate 4: Go to Testing

This postdevelopment review is a check on the progress and the continued attractiveness of the product and project. Development work is reviewed and checked, ensuring that the work has been completed in a quality fashion and that the developed product is indeed consistent with the original definition specified at Gate 3.

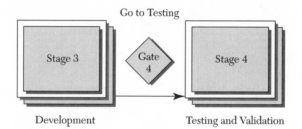

This gate also revisits the project's economics via a revised financial analysis based on new and more accurate data. The test or validation plans for the next stage are approved for immediate implementation, and the detailed marketing and operations plans are reviewed for probable future execution.

Stage 4: Testing and Validation

This stage tests and validates the entire viability of the project: the product itself, the production process, customer acceptance, and the economics of the project. It also begins extensive external validation of the product and project. A number of activities are undertaken at Stage 4:

- *In-house product tests:* extended lab tests or alpha tests to check on product quality and product performance under controlled or lab conditions.
- *User or field trials of the product:* to verify that the product functions under actual use conditions and gauge potential customers' reactions to the product—to establish purchase intent.

- *Trial, limited, or pilot production:* to test, debug, and prove the production or operations process and to determine more precise production/operations costs and throughputs (often, production equipment is acquired and tested here).
- *Pretest market, simulated test market, full test market, or trial sell:* to gauge customer reaction, measure the effectiveness of the launch plan, and determine expected market share and revenues.
- *Revised business and financial analysis:* to check on the continued business and economic viability of the project, based on new and more accurate revenue and cost data.

Sometimes Stage 4 yields negative results, so it's back to Stage 3. Iterations back and forth through the Stage-Gate process are possible.

Gate 5: Go to Launch

This final gate opens the door to full commercialization—market launch and full production or operations start up. It is the final point at which the project can still be killed. This gate focuses on the quality of the activities in the testing and validation stage and their results. Criteria for passing the gate focus largely on expected financial return and appropriateness of the launch and operations start-up plans. The operations and marketing plans are reviewed and approved for implementation in Stage 5.

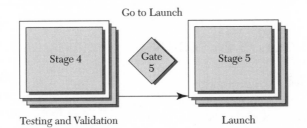

Stage 5: Launch

This final stage involves implementation of both the marketing launch plan and the production or operations plan. Given a well-thought-out plan of action and backed by appropriate resources, and barring any unforeseen events, it should be clear sailing for the new product—another new product success.

Postlaunch Review

At some point following commercialization (often 6 to 18 months), the new product project must be terminated. The team is disbanded, and the product

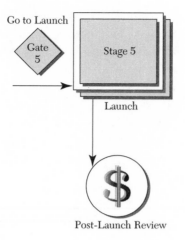

Post-Launch Review

becomes a regular product in the firm's product line. This is also the point where the project and product performance is reviewed. The latest data on revenues, costs, expenditures, profits, and timing are compared to Gates 3 and 5 projections to gauge performance. Finally, a postaudit—a critical assessment of the project's strengths and weaknesses, what can be learned from this project, and how the next one can be done better—is carried out. This review marks the end of the project. Note that the project team and leader remain responsible for the success of the project through this postlaunch period, right up to the point of the postlaunch review.

BUILT-IN SUCCESS FACTORS

The logic of a well-designed new product process, such as Stage-Gate in Exhibit 11.1, is appealing because it incorporates many of the critical success factors—the drivers of success and speed—that were highlighted earlier in this chapter. For example:

1. The process places much more emphasis on the homework or predevelopment activities. Stages 1 and 2—the scoping and build business case stages—are the essential homework steps before the door to development is opened at Gate 3.

2. The process is multidisciplinary and cross functional. It is built around an empowered, cross-functional team. Each stage consists of technical, marketing, operations/production, and even financial activities, necessitating the active involvement of people from all of these areas. The gates are cross functional, too: Gates are tended by gatekeepers from different functions or departments in the firm—the senior managers who own the resources needed for the next stage.

3. Parallel and spiral processing speeds up the process. Activities in each stage are undertaken concurrently, rather than sequentially, with much interaction between players and actions in each stage. In addition, there are constant checks of the product with the customer as it takes shape.

4. A strong market and VoC orientation is a feature of the process. Marketing inputs begin at the discovery stage and remain an important facet of every stage from beginning to end of the project. Projects cannot pass the gates until the marketing actions have been completed in a quality way. This extensive VoC emphasis often leads to the unique, superior product with a compelling value proposition, yet another key to success.

5. A product-definition step is built into the process at Stage 2, *build the business case*, so that the project scope and product specs remain stable from Gate 3 onward. This product definition is a key deliverable to Gate 3; without it, the project cannot proceed to development.

6. There is more focus. The process builds in decision points in the form of gates, with a clear locus of decision making and visible go/kill criteria. These gates weed out poor projects early and help focus scarce resources on the truly deserving projects. The gatekeepers are the decision makers at each gate. At earlier gates (1 and 2), often the gatekeepers are mid-level management; but for Gate 3 and on, gatekeepers are typically the leadership team of the business.

7. There is a strong emphasis on quality of execution throughout. The stages and recommended activities in each stage lay out an "activity plan" for the project leader and team: There is less chance of critical errors of omission. The gates provide the critical quality control checks in the process. Unless the project meets certain quality standards, it fails to pass the gate.

TO WHAT TYPES OF PROJECTS DOES STAGE-GATE™ APPLY?

The specific model described previously and in Exhibit 11.1 has been designed for new product projects. Here, a *new product project* is defined as one where technical development work is applied to a market need to deliver a new or improved product or service that is visibly different from previous products. The result can be a radical innovation, a significant product improvement, or merely a line extension—all these types of new product projects are handled by the Stage-Gate approach.

Stage-Gate is used by producers of physical products—both consumer goods (such as Procter & Gamble and Pillsbury-General Mills) and industrial goods (such as DuPont, ITT, and Nortel Networks)—and service providers (such as banks or telephone companies).

Some companies have extended the use of the Stage-Gate approach—the concept of stages with defined tasks and resulting deliverables, together with gates, defined gatekeepers, and visible go/kill criteria—to a wide variety of investment decisions. Besides new product projects, these other applications of Stage-Gate include:

- New business developments outside the current market and technological boundaries of the firm.
- Alliance and partnership projects.
- New *process* developments where the deliverable is a new or improved manufacturing process.
- Fundamental research or science projects.
- Platform developments.

Stage-Gate Express for Smaller Projects

Some companies have developed abbreviated versions of the five-stage model in Exhibit 11.1 to cope with smaller, lower-risk projects. The Stage-Gate process is not a hard-and-fast set of rules. Rather, each project can be routed through the process according to its specific risk level and needs. Stages can be omitted and gates combined, provided the decision is made consciously, at gates, and with a full understanding of the risks involved. The new product process is essentially a *risk-management process,* and, thus, the risk level, the uncertainty, and the need for information dictate what steps and stages need to be done and which can be left out.

The result is a shortened version of Stage-Gate, such as the three-stage, three-gate process in Exhibit 11.3. But this short-cut process should be reserved for low-risk projects only—extensions, fixes, improvements, and product renewals; the routing decision is made at the previous gate, often as early as Gate 1.

For example, at one of North America's largest banks, a five-stage, five-gate new product process is used, very similar to the process in Exhibit 11.1. But senior management uses a *triage approach* and has defined three categories of projects based on project scope, investment, and risk level:

1. *System change requests,* which are relatively minor product changes and improvements, often in response to a request from a major corporate client. These go through a two-stage, two-gate version of the model.
2. *Fast-track projects,* which are medium-cost projects and feature some risk (less than $500,000 development cost, but impact multiple customers). These moderate-risk projects are tracked through a four-stage version of the model which collapses the two homework stages into a single stage.
3. *Major projects,* over $500,000, are considered higher risk, and pass through the full five-stage model.

EXHIBIT 11.3   Stage-Gate Express—a 3-stage version for lower risk, simpler projects

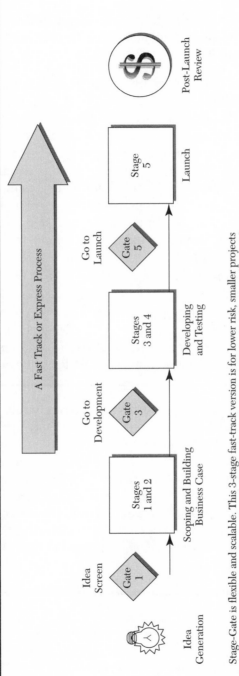

Idea
Generation

Idea
Screen

Gate
1

Stages
1 and 2

Scoping and Building
Business Case

Go to
Development

Gate
3

Stages
3 and 4

Developing
and Testing

Go to
Launch

Gate
5

Stage
5

Launch

Post-Launch
Review

A Fast Track or Express Process

Stage-Gate is flexible and scalable. This 3-stage fast-track version is for lower risk, smaller projects where there are fewer unknowns: line extensions, product improvements, modifications, fixes, and where costs and times are less.

What about Fundamental Research Projects or Platform Developments?

Stage-Gate systems, in modified format, also apply to less well-defined development projects, such as fundamental research and platform developments. First, here are two definitions:

Platform projects build a capability. The analogy is that of building an oil well drilling platform in the ocean at great cost.[19] Once in place, many holes can be drilled from the one platform, each at much less cost. In new products, the platform establishes the capability; and this capability spawns many new product projects—much more quickly and cost effectively than starting from the beginning each time. Examples include a deposit software platform in a bank from which many different end-user deposit products can be developed; a new engine-transmission-frame assembly for an auto company from which many new car models can be developed; and a new catalyst in the chemical industry which might spawn an entire new family of polymers.

Fundamental research projects are those where the deliverable is new knowledge. When the project begins, there may be no specific new product (or new manufacturing process) defined or even in mind. Rather, the scientist initiates some experiments with the hope of finding some technical possibilities and discoveries that might yield ideas for commercial products or processes. These are also called *science projects* and *technology developments*.

The main difference between these and a new product project—for which Stage-Gate in Exhibit 11.1 was designed—is that science projects and platform developments are often more loosely defined at the outset than is the typical new product project. For example, in a fundamental research project, it may take months of technical research before it is even clear what might be technically possible. Therefore, undertaking market analysis in Stage 1 (see Exhibit 11.1) and detailed market studies in Stage 2 is difficult when you cannot even define the resulting products. In addition, the criteria for project selection are different from a very tangible, well-defined new product project.

Similarly, platform projects are often visionary in scope, with little concrete defined in the way of tangible products. Rather, management is building a capability that it hopes will lead to multiple new product projects. Again, it is difficult to undertake detailed market analyses and full financial projections when only the first or second product from the platform is even envisioned—the rest are "yet to be defined." Therefore, the decision to move ahead must be largely a strategic one that looks at what this platform *might yield* in terms of multiple new products, most of which are unknown.

Some companies have *adapted and adjusted Stage-Gate* to handle these types of projects. The stage-and-gate approach seems to work, but the spirit of the stages and the specific criteria used at gates are different from those described previously and in Exhibit 11.1. Some examples follow:

- Rohm and Haas, the chemical company, has expanded its Stage-Gate process to accommodate science or exploratory research projects.
- Exxon Chemical has published a synopsis of its Stage-Gate process to handle fundamental research projects.[20]
- DuPont has modified its new product process to handle business developments—that is, projects that are beyond the typical new product project in the sense that they involve both new markets and new technologies to the company.[21]
- The Japanese company, Dai Nippon Industries, has adapted its regular five-stage process for new products to handle fundamental research projects.

The nature of a Stage-Gate process for technology developments or science projects is different from a standard product-oriented process outlined earlier in this chapter, with much more experimentation allowed.[22] We call the process *StageGate-TD*, for *technology developments:* projects where the immediate deliverable is *not* a new product or new manufacturing process but is new knowledge or a capability that may spawn new products or processes. The model in Exhibit 11.4 is a composite example of a technology development process for science projects (taken from a number of leading firms). Note that there are only two stages and three gates. Gate 3—the Application Path gate—may be combined with Gates 1 or 2 in the standard new product process of Exhibit 11.1. In effect, the two processes are merged or overlapped.

The gate criteria in *StageGate-TD* are much less financial and more strategic in nature than for the standard new product model. For example, Toray Chemical in Japan (developers of breakthroughs such as microfiber and Ultrasuede fabrics) uses the following rating criteria for judging its *technology development* projects:

- Degree of strategic fit and strategic importance to the corporation.
- Ability to achieve strategic leverage (e.g., platform for growth, impact on multiple business units).
- Potential for reward (value to the company, if successful).
- Likelihood of technical feasibility.
- Likelihood of commercial success (e.g., competitive advantage, existence of in-house competencies).

IMPACT OF INSTALLING A STAGE-GATE™ PROCESS

Most best practice firms appear to have a Stage-Gate™ new product process, or one like it, in place, according to the PDMA best practices study noted

EXHIBIT 11.4   Technology Development projects use a 2-stage, 3-gate process, that then links into the usual 5-stage Stage-Gate NPD process

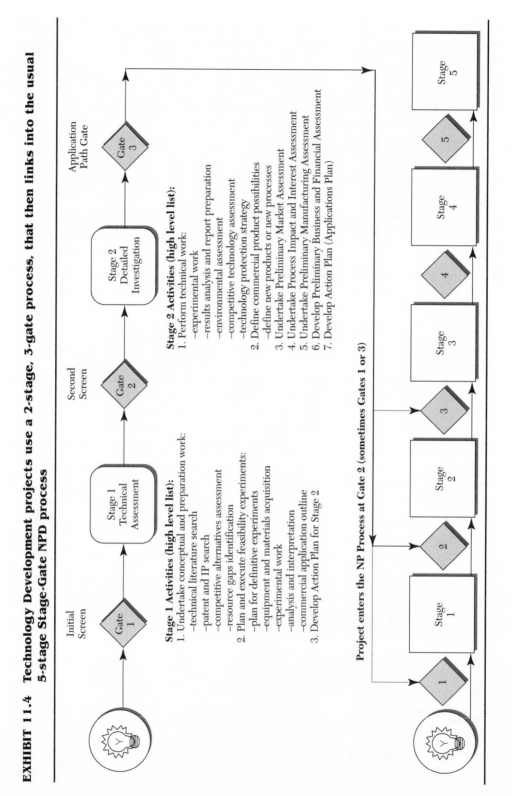

previously. Indeed, more than half the companies in this study had adopted a Stage-Gate process.

Properly implemented, Stage-Gate processes really work, according to the managers who took part in an in-depth study of their firms' new product processes.[23] "Top of mind" comments yielded the following three areas of major impact:

1. Improved product success rates, higher customer satisfaction, and meeting time, quality, and cost objectives are the most frequently cited areas of positive impact (see Exhibit 11.5). More than one-third of managers indicated that the process's strongest impact was on the *success rate* of new products and on the *customer satisfaction* achieved. Managers revealed that a much stronger market orientation had been built into their new product process and that key activities, such as market studies and concept tests, were now an integral facet of their product development efforts.

2. Being *on time and on budget*—that is, meeting project and product objectives—is seen as another payoff from formal processes, also cited by 34 percent of managers. New product processes brought discipline into product development, where previously there had been chaos; and more attention was focused on time schedules, deadlines, and project costs and objectives.

3. Being *faster to market* and obtaining *better profit performance* from new products are other comments volunteered by the study's participants (see Exhibit 11.5). There were almost no negative comments in this open-ended discussion of the impact of the formal new product process.

These top-of-mind comments provide some assurance that Stage-Gate approaches do work. The *degree of improvement* in six key areas was rated to provide quantitative measures of performance impact. The results, shown in Exhibit 11.6, reveal that on all six dimensions of performance there was significant improvement:

1. *Improved teamwork:* Managers saw significant improvement in interfunctional teamwork. The fact that new product processes stress cross-functional activities and use multifunctional criteria and gatekeepers at each gate promotes and demands this teamwork.

2. *Less recycling and rework:* The amount of recycle and rework was greatly reduced. New product processes generally have a number of quality checks built into the process to ensure that critical activities are carried out, and in a quality fashion, thereby reducing the incidence of recycle.

3. *Improved success rates:* Managers noted that the proportion of new products that succeeded was higher, and the profitability from new products was also better. The fact that Stage-Gate processes build in better project evaluations at the gates (hence cull out potential failures earlier) and

EXHIBIT 11.5 Top-of-mind comments from senior managers about impact of Stage-Gate™ new product process on performance

How to read chart: 34% of managers interviewed, with no prompting, cited "improved success rates"; 34% also said "on time, cost, and quality targets" as the major impacts of a Stage-Gate new product process.

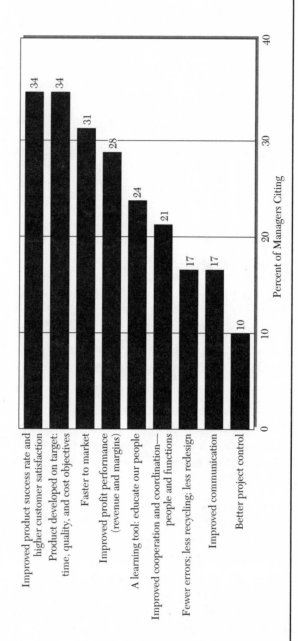

Category	Percent
Improved product success rate and higher customer satisfaction	34
Product developed on target: time, quality, and cost objectives	34
Faster to market	31
Improved profit performance (revenue and margins)	28
A learning tool: educate our people	24
Improved cooperation and coordination—people and functions	21
Fewer errors; less recycling; less redesign	17
Improved communication	17
Better project control	10

Percent of Managers Citing

EXHIBIT 11.6 Rated impacts of implementing a Stage-Gate™ NPD process

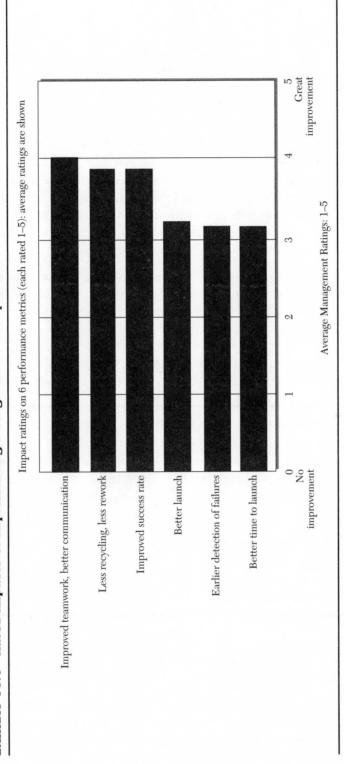

Impact ratings on 6 performance metrics (each rated 1–5): average ratings are shown

focus more attention on key success activities, such as market studies, sharper and earlier product definition, and customer tests, accounts for this improvement.

4. *Earlier detection of failures:* Potential failures were spotted earlier and either were killed outright or steps were taken to avert disaster. The use of gates with clear go/kill criteria, typical of most firms' processes, helped to sharpen the project evaluations.

5. *Better launch:* Marketing planning and other market-oriented activities are integral to most firms' new product processes, resulting in more involvement in the project by marketing and a better launch.

6. *Shorter elapsed time:* This result is surprising. The common view is that a more thoroughly executed new product project takes a longer time. Not so, according to the managers interviewed. Better homework, more multifunctional inputs, better market and product definition, and less recycle work all serve to shorten the idea-to-launch time.

This conclusion on cycle time reduction, although somewhat of a surprise, has also been backed up by yet another study—this one an extensive internal study in one firm.[24] Here, the time to market for a large number of new product projects was considered, both before and after the implementation of a formal new product process. Cycle times depend on project complexity; therefore, a measure of complexity was developed, and cycle times are plotted against this measure. The results:

- The stage-and-gate process reduced the cycle time by about one-third for simple projects and by considerably more than one-third for more complex ones.
- The formal new product process also made the complexity-time relationship much more predictable. The unexplained variance, "noise" or unpredictability in time to market, was reduced from 65 percent to 35 percent.

IMPLEMENTING STAGE-GATE™

The design and implementation of a Stage-Gate™ process is not an easy task. Thus, considerable care, planning, and effort must go into the design and roll-out of a Stage-Gate process. This proceeds in three main steps:

Step 1: The Foundation—Defining the Process Requirements

Understanding the problem is the first step to a solution. The purpose of Step 1 is to understand what needs fixing and to map out the specs for the new process. This step is often skipped over by process redesign task forces with negative results. Key tasks in Stage 1 are:

1. *Seek senior management commitment: Installing a Stage-Gate process must be led from the top.* Every effort must be made to secure executive sponsorship of the Stage-Gate design and implementation effort and, most important, to commit the necessary resources. For a larger business, Stage-Gate design and implementation can cost in the hundreds of thousands of dollars.

2. *Assemble a cross-functional task force.* This effort must be a *business* effort (not an R&D initiative) and requires the inputs of key people across functions. This should be a representative team of leaders in your business who are charged with the design and implementation of your new Stage-Gate system.

3. *Seek outside help.* Outside expertise may add to the cost initially, but it will save you in the end. Outside experts can help your task force move through the difficult design phase much more quickly and lend credibility to the process. They also bring resources to the initiative that help on implementation—for example, IT and training resources.

4. *Hold a kick-off seminar/workshop to generate awareness and the beginning of organizational buy-in.* In this way, you begin to engage the eventual users of the process and, at the same time, provide a forum for listening to their concerns.

5. *Conduct an internal audit of NPD current practices: what works, what does not, what needs fixing, and problems that must be addressed as you design your new product process.* The Product Benchmarking and Evaluation (ProBE) diagnostic tool is a questionnaire-based diagnostic that enables your business to benchmark your new product practices against hundreds of other companies.[25]

6. *Benchmark other firms.* This allows your task force to see Stage-Gate in action and to discuss with others the problems and pitfalls along the way. Note that benchmarking can take much time, so look to published benchmarking studies to help you.

7. *Conduct a thorough literature review.* Investigate the countless studies over the past decades into new product practices and performance.

8. *Map the next steps.* These are the task force's mandate and action plan for Steps 2 and 3, discussed later.

9. *Secure senior management sign-off.* Make sure that they are still on board and support the action plan.

Step 2: Design Your Stage-Gate Process

There are three goals in Step 2:

1. Designing a world-class and robust NPD process.
2. Seeking feedback and buy-into the process from the potential user community.
3. Designing an implementation plan for roll-out.

This step usually proceeds in a series of rounds consisting of task force meetings, typically two days per round, each round occurring about three to four weeks apart. The task force meets and, round by round, maps out the details of the process. A typical sequence of rounds might be:

Round 1: The conceptual design or skeleton of the process.

Round 2: The first draft of the detailed design of stages and gates.

Round 3: The next draft of stages and gates, along with roles, responsibilities, and expected behaviors of key players—teams, leaders, gatekeepers, process manager.

Round 4: The finalized process on paper, along with the implementation plan.

Between each round, the task force members share the evolving process with their colleagues, seeking feedback and concurrence.

Via these successive rounds, your detailed Stage-Gate model takes shape and includes:

- *Stage descriptions:* Specifically, what actions or activities are required at each stage? What best practices and success factors should be built into each stage? Often, an overview of each activity or practice is developed to provide the user (the NPD project teams) with a flavor for what is expected and to better incorporate current best practices.

- *Stage deliverables:* What deliverables are the result or endpoint of each stage and what will be delivered to each gate? In what level of detail? Some task forces develop guides and templates for many of the deliverables. (For example, if you decide to move immediately to a paperless or Web-based process, you likely need to develop some forms with *designated fields* for the deliverables, simply so the project documentation can be conveniently and electronically prepared and stored.)

- *Gate descriptions:* What are the gate criteria—the "must meet" and "should meet" items as outlined previously? Many task forces develop scorecards to be used at gate meetings by the gatekeepers. Other issues to address: How will projects be prioritized? When a project is given a "go" decision at a gate, is this a firm and binding decision (or can the project be reprioritized in a month or two if a better project comes along)? And how do gates mesh with quarterly reviews of projects, project milestones, and annual budget setting? Finally, how do you begin to integrate *portfolio management* into your new product process (NPP)?

- *Gate procedures:* Who are the gatekeepers for each gate? How is the meeting run—for example, is there a chairperson, a referee, or a facilitator present? What method should gatekeepers use to score the project against the criteria? How are decisions made? Should the project team be present for the entire meeting?

- *Organizational:* What should the composition of cross-functional teams be? Where in the process should the team be formed? Who does the work on the project before this point? Who should the project team leaders be? Is it the same leader from beginning to end of the project? How much empowerment should the team be given? How should team members be relieved of their normal duties? Who does the annual performance evaluation of each team member? How are team members recognized and rewarded?
- *What's "in" the process?* Which projects does this new process handle? All projects or just some types? What about process developments (where the project may result in an improved manufacturing or operation process)? How are platform projects and science or exploratory projects handled? What about small projects—extensions, fixes, and modifications? Do they go through the full process, or perhaps you should have a three-stage version of the process for low-risk projects. How much flexibility is there?

The desire to move quickly has led some firms to novel approaches to getting Stage-Gate up and running more quickly. Thus, instead of spending three or more months on the design of the process, they merely purchase an off-the-shelf Stage-Gate model from another firm or outside vendor.[26] Invariably, the company must still modify and adjust the process to suit its own culture and organization. But the result is usually a better process (if you start with a world-class process, you're likely to end up with one) in place much faster. In this way, the task force can spend its energies where the real challenges are— implementing the process.

Step 3: Stage-Gate Implementation

Implementation is by far the longest, most difficult, and most expensive phase. Implementation consists of a set of events and activities designed to inform people about the NPP and train them in its use, to seek buy-in and commitment from the organization, and to bring projects—both new and existing— into the new system. Typical action items include:

1. *Bring projects into the NPP.* It is important to get most of your existing projects into the new process as quickly as possible. Waiting around for only the "new" projects means it might be more than a year before anything is launched via Stage-Gate. "Welcome gates" are recommended as an easy way to introduce project teams working on existing projects (welcome gates are more lenient gates which recognize that the project team has not been following any particular process to date).
2. *Get commitment and buy-in.* One of the toughest jobs is securing buy-in from everyone who must use the new process. This includes both senior management and mid-management, who control the resources, and project team members and leaders, who must execute the projects. Here are some suggestions:

- Position the NPP as one facet of your ISO-9000 or Six-Sigma program.
- Sell everyone on the need for more new products.
- Use facts to underpin the potential benefits of the NPP (for example, the performance data outlined previously).
- Deal with the barriers and preconceptions; often "push back" is the result of a lack of understanding of the process.
- Buy-in starts top down; therefore, be sure to work closely with the business's leadership team as the process takes shape in Step 2.
- Get the commitment to the new process written into the business's mission and strategic plan.
- Most important, get the implementations and use of the new process written into individuals' personal performance objectives.

3. *Use pilots.* As the process comes together in Step 2, start testing the process with some pilot projects. Ideally, the project leaders of these pilots are on your task force. The result is that by the time implementation is well underway, at least some teams and some projects will be already in the Stage-Gate process.

4. *Communicate your new Stage-Gate process.* People will not use what they don't understand, so effective communication is critical to a successful Stage-Gate roll-out. Typical tasks include:

- Designing a promotional brochure for your Stage-Gate process—a four-page, color brochure (for use both at training sessions and for the sales force to share with customers).
- Producing a users' quick guide—perhaps an 8- to 12-page overview.
- Designing a user-friendly instructional manual: the details of the process, complete with templates, scorecards, and "how to" guides. Such a manual is necessarily a fairly thick, onerous one when produced in hard copy; move immediately to a Web-based or e-guide where the user sees only what he or she needs.
- Develop a professional live presentation package; chances are, your task force will be called on to make many presentations to various groups in the company.
- Come up with a good name for the process. Good names include Guinness's *Navigate Process*, Kennametal's *ACE Process* (achieve a competitive edge), and Bayer's *STARGate Process* (strategic applications and research gate process).

5. *Provide training.* Stage-Gate may seem intuitively obvious, but there are many details that need explanation to potential users. Moreover, training also creates excitement and buy-into the process. Most firms provide training for both project team members and gatekeepers.

6. *Install a process manager.* No process, no matter how good and how logical, ever implemented itself. It needs someone to make it happen—that's

the role of the process manager. For larger companies, this is a full-time position. The process manager facilitates gate meetings, coaches project teams, provides for training, enforces discipline to the process, is the keeper of the database, continuously improves the Stage-Gate process, ensures that its documentation is up-to-date, and measures the results— in short, everything needed to ensure a successful implementation.

7. *Develop IT support for the process.*[27] Most often, IT includes:

   - An electronic manual or e-guide, Web-based.

   - A paperless process, where all templates are available online; multiple team members can prepare the same document jointly, and deliverables are automatically sent to gatekeepers on completion.

   - IT tracking of projects, which enables the process manager, executives, and gatekeepers to track progress of projects, review work or deliverables in progress, and spot projects or tasks in trouble or behind schedule.

   - Gate facilitation in the form of electronic scorecards, where gatekeepers' ratings of projects are displayed instantly, and pipeline data displays at gate and portfolio review meetings (e.g., displays of the current portfolio of projects and current resource breakdowns).

   - A projects database, which is essential if you plan to measure results and track projects. Here, vital statistics on projects, timing, resources allocated, progress achieved, and performance results are stored.

   - A one-stop shopping toolbox for product development: tools such as project management or time line software (e.g., MS-Project™, the NewProd™, and SG Selector™ diagnostic models);[28] standard financial models with probabilistic capabilities, such as Crystal Ball; resource allocation software; and so on.

   - Automated NPD software systems—comprehensive software that handles all of these IT tasks, plus more (e.g., Accolade™).[29]

8. *Put metrics in place.* It's never too early to start thinking about new product metrics. Remember the adage "You cannot manage what you cannot measure." New product and Stage-Gate metrics are of two major types:

   a. *Postprocess metrics:* These answer the question "How well are you doing at new product development?" They are "postprocess" because they can be measured only after the product is launched. These include both short-term metrics (measurable immediately after launch; e.g., "the proportion of products launched on time") as well as longer term metrics (that might take several years after launch to determine; e.g., "the proportion of launches that became commercial winners" or the popular "percentage of your sales from new products, launched in the last three years").

   b. *In-process metrics:* These answer the question "Is your new product process working well?" These in-process metrics can be measured almost immediately, and they capture how well new product projects are unfolding—for example, whether they are on time at gates and whether deliverables to gates are in good shape. Achieving high scores on these metrics is not the ultimate goal, but they are immediately measurable. Think of these as *intermediate metrics* and early warning signals about eventual NPD results.

9. *Implement portfolio management.* Shortly after implementing Stage-Gate process, many companies face another problem, namely, the management of new product resources. A gating process does an excellent job of scrutinizing individual projects, one at a time. Ultimately, however, the entire set of projects must be considered, and that's the role of portfolio management. Portfolio management answers the broad questions: Where should the business spend its development resources? Which set of projects should the business invest in? Portfolio management should be piggybacked atop the new product process, and it, thus, becomes a key task during implementation.[30]

DOING IT RIGHT

NPD is one of the most important endeavors of the modern corporation. The message from both Wall Street and Main Street is "innovate or die." Customers, as well as shareholders, seek a steady stream of innovative new products—customers want innovative products because they demand value for money, and shareholders seek the organic and profitable growth that innovations provide. Without a systematic new product process, however, often the NPD effort is a shambles—a chaotic, hit-and-miss affair. Stage-Gate processes act as an enabler or guide, building in best practices and ensuring that key activities are completed and decisions are made better and faster. However, a Stage-Gate process is considerably more complex than the simple diagram in Exhibit 11.1 suggests; there are many intricacies in the details—both the "whats" and the "how to's." In addition, implementing the process is a major challenge. Many leading companies, however, have taken the necessary step and designed and implemented a world-class NPD process, such as Stage-Gate, and the results have been positive: better, faster, and more profitable new product developments.

NOTES

1. Stage-Gate™ is a trademark of R. G. Cooper and Associates Consultants, Inc. in many countries.

2. This chapter is taken from many sources: R. G. Cooper, *Winning at New Products: Accelerating the Process from Idea to Launch,* 3rd ed. (Reading, MA: Perseus

Books, 2001); R. G. Cooper, "Doing It Right—Winning with New Products," *Ivey Business Journal* (July/August 2000): 54–60; R. G. Cooper, "Overhauling the New Product Process," *Industrial Marketing Management,* vol. 25, no. 6 (November 1996): 465–482; R. G. Cooper and E. J. Kleinschmidt, "Stage Gate Systems for New Product Success," *Marketing Management,* vol. 1, no. 4 (1993): 20–29; R. G. Cooper, "The New Product Process: A Decision Guide for Managers," *Journal of Marketing Management,* vol. 3, no. 3 (1988): 238–255; R. G. Cooper, "Stage-Gate Systems: A New Tool for Managing New Products," *Business Horizons,* vol. 33, no. 3 (May/June 1990): 44-54; and R. G. Cooper, "A Process Model for Industrial New Product Development," *IEEE Transactions in Engineering Management,* EM 30 (February 1983): 2–11.

3. *Stage-Gate* is a term coined by and trademarked by the author; see note 1, 1988. Second-generation processes are what many companies began to implement toward the end of the 1980s; the third-generation processes of the late 1990s have improved time efficiencies; see note 2, *Winning at New Products;* R. G. Cooper, "Third-Generation New Product Processes," *Journal of Product Innovation Management,* vol. 11 (1994): 3–14.

4. A. Griffin, *Drivers of NPD Success: The 1997 PDMA Report* (Chicago, Product Development & Management Association, 1997).

5. See note 2, *Winning at New Products.*

6. See note 2, *Winning at New Products.*

7. R. G. Cooper, "Benchmarking New Product Performance: Results of the Best Practices Study," *European Management Journal,* vol. 16, no. 1 (1998): 1–7.

8. PDMA: Product Development and Management Association; see note 4; A. Griffin, "PDMA Research on New Product Development: Updating Trends and Benchmarking Best Practices," *Journal of Product Innovation Management,* vol. 14, no. 6 (1998): 429–458.

9. See note 4.

10. A good review of success factors is provided in R. G. Cooper, "New Products: What Separates the Winners from the Losers," *PDMA Handbook for New Product Development,* ed. Milton D. Rosenau Jr. (New York: Wiley, 1996); see also M. M. Montoya-Weiss and R. J. Calantone, "Determinants of New Product Performance: A Review and Meta Analysis," *Journal of Product Innovation Management,* vol. 11, no. 5 (November 1994): 397–417.

11. Section taken from R. G. Cooper, *Product Leadership: Creating and Launching Superior New Products* (Reading, MA: Perseus Books, 1998).

12. See note 4.

13. C. M. Crawford, "The Hidden Costs of Accelerated Product Development," *Journal of Product Innovation Management,* vol. 9, no. 3 (September 1992): 188–199.

14. T. J. Peters, *Thriving on Chaos* (New York: Harper & Row, 1988).

15. R. G. Cooper, S. J. Edgett, and E. J. Kleinschmidt, "Optimizing the Stage-Gate Process: What Best Practice Companies Are Doing: Part I," *Research-Technology Management* (September/October 2002): 21-27.

16. E. A. Von Hippel, S. Thomke, and M. Sonnack, "Creating Breakthroughs at 3M," *Harvard Business Review* (September/October 1999): 47–57.

17. R. G. Cooper, "Product Innovation and Technology Strategy" in the "Succeeding in Technological Innovation" series, *Research-Technology Management,* vol. 43, no. 1 (January/February 2000): 28–44.

18. See note 2, *Winning at New Products.*

19. See definitions in appendix of *PDMA Handbook for New Product Development,* ed. Milton D Rosenau Jr. (New York: Wiley, 1996); see also note 2, *Winning at New Products.*

20. L. Yapps-Cohen, P. W. Kamienski, and R. L. Espino, "Gate System Focuses Industrial Basic Research," *Research-Technology Management* (July/August 1998): 34–37. See also note 15.

21. R. A. Karol, R. C. Loeser, and R. H. Tait, "Better New Business Development at DuPont"—I, *Research-Technology Management* (January/February 2002): 24–30; and R. A. Karol, R. C. Loeser, and R. H. Tait, "Better New Business Development at DuPont"—II, *Research-Technology Management* (March/April 2002): 47–56.

22. See note 15.

23. R. G. Cooper and E. J. Kleinschmidt, *Formal Processes for Managing New Products: The Industry Experience* (Hamilton, Ontario, Canada: McMaster University, 1991). See also R. G. Cooper and E. J. Kleinschmidt, "New Product Processes at Leading Industrial Firms," *Industrial Marketing Management,* vol. 10, no. 2 (May 1991): 137–147.

24. A. Griffin, "Metrics for Measuring Product Development Cycle Time," *Journal of Product Innovation Management,* vol. 10, no. 2 (March 1993): 112–125.

25. ProBE: Product Benchmarking and Evaluation; available from the Product Development Institute Inc., www.prod-dev.com.

26. For access to off-the-shelf Stage-Gate models, see, for example, www.prod-dev.com.

27. Automated software packages exist that handle all of these IT requirements; see, for example, Accolade available from www.sopheon.com.

28. MS-Project is a trademark of Microsoft Corporation; NewProd-3000 and SG Selector are trademarks of Product Development Institute Inc., www.prod-dev.com.

29. Accolade is a trademark of Sopheon Inc., available from www.sopheon.com.

30. R. G. Cooper, S. J. Edgett, and E. J. Kleinschmidt, *Portfolio Management for New Products,* 2nd ed. (Reading, MA: Perseus Book, 2002).

12 ENTERPRISE PROJECT MANAGEMENT: THE PATH TO MATURITY

Denis Couture

Project management maturity can be elusive. In fact, the notion is so new, there is not even a common understanding of the concept. The widespread interest in project management maturity is related to the growing recognition and acceptance that projects, for most industries, have become the primary way of getting work done. These project-driven firms acknowledge that the discipline and techniques associated with project management can, in fact, improve performance on projects. They realize that the net result of this is higher customer satisfaction, increased market share, and a direct impact to the bottom line.

Most major organizations have gone to great lengths and expense to implement project management within their culture. Why then do many of these organizations experience the same symptoms as those that have done nothing? These symptoms include:

- Budget overruns.
- Schedule delays.
- Inefficient resource utilization.
- Misleading and confusing project status.
- Misaligned project portfolio.

Mature project-driven organizations have overcome these problems. What is their secret? Which combination of the right things have they put in place to make them superior performers, leaving the competition wondering "What are we doing wrong?"

This chapter answers those questions by describing what real project management maturity is. In addition, it goes one step further by providing you with a model for achieving project management maturity and the steps for implementing that model in your organization.

MATURITY AND BEST PRACTICES

Background on Maturity

No standardized definition of project management *maturity* exists in the industry to date. Models have been developed over the past several years, some of which are variants of the Capability Maturity Model (CMM) developed by the Software Engineering Institute (SEI).

At the very least, these models have attempted to give practitioners in project management some quantifiable criteria and measurement by which to evaluate their environment and practices. Many of the models adapted from the Software Engineering Institute's CMM use the same scale to measure maturity. The scale is an ascending one, beginning at 1 and progressing to 5. A level 1 maturity represents the lowest level of maturity an organizational entity can have and is descriptive of little or no formalized project management capability, hence the term *ad hoc* used by the CMM model to describe this level.

At the opposite end of the scale is level 5, which is descriptive of organizations that have achieved a superior level of project management capability, with the ability to continuously improve and monitor their performance over time, hence the term *sustained* used by the same model. We believe that these maturity models will evolve and perhaps eventually achieve a level of standardization. For the time being, however, the exercise of defining a numerical scale to measure maturity is better left to the academics in our profession.

Maturity Equals Best Practices That Achieve Results

The major focus of this section is to identify the best practices that contribute to a high level of project management capability, performance, or *maturity* in an organizational entity, whether it be a department, division, or an entire organization. The term *best practices* is often loosely used by practitioners without any basis or documentation to support the claim that a practice really is a best practice. As such, you might argue that trying to define *best practices* is just as elusive as trying to pin down *maturity*. In defining these practices, then, we provide you with the tools to apply them toward higher and higher levels of project success.

What does a high-maturity score on a scale of 1 to 5 really accomplish, or what will superior performance in project management do for the organization? These are difficult questions to answer, yet they are the most frequently asked questions across industries before organizations commit the required funds for implementing project management. The answer to these questions is often found in anecdotal evidence such as the IT director who claimed, "Before we had project management, 8 out of 10 projects were delayed and over budget; now we successfully bring in 8 of 10." However, this doesn't prove that project management was the contributing factor for turning this problem around.

Survey Data to Strengthen the Argument

Because of this lack of objective data, in 2000, the pci group, a project and portfolio management firm based in Troy, Michigan, sponsored a benchmarking and best practices study to determine whether implementing specific project management practices produced actual project performance improvement. The survey involved 26 companies of varying size across multiple industries. The survey used to administer the study was developed in conjunction with the American Productivity and Quality Council (APQC), internationally known for its benchmarking and best practice studies. Results of the survey showed that companies with the best practice attributes described in the next section consistently scored better than their counterparts in the following four dimensions:

1. Actual cost of projects as a percentage of budgeted cost was 6 percent better for best practice companies.
2. Best practice companies had a 25 percent better rate of completing projects on budget.
3. Best practice companies had a 29 percent better rate of completing projects on time.
4. Actual hours as a percentage of budgeted hours was 15 percent lower for best practice companies.

   Heretofore, the value of project management was either speculative or supported with anecdotal evidence at best. The quantitative data removes any doubt that project management best practices have a direct impact on a company's bottom line.

PROFILE OF A BEST PRACTICES COMPANY

The data garnered from the best practices study enables us to develop a profile of a mature project management organization. As we analyze the data, we find that the enablers and practices observed in the best practice companies can be isolated into a few core best practice attributes found in these companies. These include:

1. *Formal project management structure:* Best practices companies have some type of project management structure, whether a program management office, project management office, project support office, or project

knowledge center. Distinctions among these various offices can be found in the pci best practices report available on the pci Web site, www .pcigroup1.com. Of the best practice companies surveyed, four out of eight have a program management office. What differentiates the program management office from other project management office structures is its responsibility for the delivery of programs, as opposed to strictly an administrative support role. In addition, the program management office is generally responsible to a vice president or director level with program managers directly assigned to this office. Data indicated that the program management office has a higher success rate than other project management structures in percentage of projects completed on time and on budget.

2. *Defined repeatable processes:* Companies with defined repeatable project management processes had a higher rate of project success. Processes in these companies included the nine Project Management Body of Knowledge (PMBoK) areas.

3. *Executive involvement in project management:* The best practices study found a high correlation between companies with a high degree of project success and those whose executives were actively involved in project management. The aspects of executive involvement with the greatest influence on project success consisted of:

   • Alignment of projects to corporate strategy.
   • Visible executive management sponsorship.
   • Existence of an organizational structure that promotes and supports project management.
   • Executive management that prioritizes projects.

   The most commonly accepted vehicle that demonstrated executive involvement was *alignment of projects to corporate strategy.* The companies studied had greater success with the percentage of projects completed on time and lower actual primary hours as a percentage of budgeted hours. It also demonstrates that best practices companies are using strategic planning methods to align projects to their day-to-day corporate functions, ensuring that work is being done on the highest priority initiatives. *Visible executive management sponsorship* showed a higher success in percentage of projects completed on time and for actual primary project hours as a percentage of budgeted hours. Executive management strongly indicates to personnel the importance of the project and that on-time and at-budget completion is a priority, which, therefore, contributes to a high degree of project success.

4. *Project management information technology:* As might be expected, best practice companies all used some form of information technology or project management tools to enable them to support their projects. The tools varied considerably among participant companies, and data indicated that

the tools were closely integrated with the project management processes. The greatest area of consistency of tool use was in scheduling; 88 percent of respondents use some kind of scheduling tool, with more than 65 percent using Microsoft Project. Again, the survey data showed that companies using project management tools had a higher degree of success than those who did not.

5. *Experienced project managers:* Finally, hiring qualified people was found to be the single most important success factor in the companies studied. The skills that were identified for project managers included:

- Experience in project management.
- Ability to see the big picture.
- Excellent communication skills (verbal and written).
- Willingness to do what it takes.
- Valuing of team members.
- Positive attitude.
- Ability to work well with the customer.
- Organizational skills.
- Leadership ability.
- Creation of a positive team/project environment.
- Ability to solve problems.
- Ability to collaborate and cooperate.

Some of the best practices companies hired people with these skills, while others provided the mentoring and training necessary to develop the project manager's skills and expertise. Overall, the *ability* of the project manager was the attribute among best practice companies that had the greatest impact on project success.

Cornerstones of Success

The five attributes previously described, found to be common in highly mature organizations, can be grouped into three main areas—organization, process, and information technology.

Each of these cornerstones represents an essential component in the development and implementation of a highly mature project management organization. The old adage of the three-legged stool applies here. If any one leg of the stool is missing, the stool is unstable and can topple over at any time. Likewise, to truly achieve a high level of project management maturity for the enterprise, each of these cornerstones must be present in some fashion. We frequently encounter organizations that are heavily focused on one or two components. The comment we invariably encounter from these organizations is "I've spent thousands of dollars implementing (a new organization structure, new processes, new tools, new training—take your pick; it's never the combination of all combined), and I'm still no further ahead with making project management work in my environment." The reason it's not working, which is not so obvious to novices, is the lack of understanding that no one component can stand on its own. It takes all three working together in an integrated fashion to reach the desired level of maturity that only best practice organizations have achieved. It is not about the right tool, the right training, the right processes, or the right organizational structure. It is about all of these dimensions being present and working together in an integrated fashion.

ENTERPRISE MODEL OF A
HIGH-MATURITY ORGANIZATION

Organizations that achieve superior project results share three common attributes: They have a clearly defined set of project management processes, an organization responsible for project management practices, and effectively use information technology to apply their processes. Together, these three components integrate the strategic, program, and project perspectives as illustrated in Exhibit 12.1.

Process

A formal set of processes (often called a *methodology*), is used to perform the major project management functions of *scheduling, cost, risk, change control, and communication.* This methodology provides a road map for performing these project functions and is key to consistency in the planning and execution of projects. Without some kind of formalized methodology to govern project management operations, employees are left to their own devices, which leads to confusion and a degradation of quality in project work.

Organization

Best practice organizations all possess some kind of formalized structure used to conduct their project management practices. The organizational type and complexity varies depending on a number of factors including company size, industry, and function. These varying structures perform different project management functions and are given different names, for example:

- Project management office.
- Program management office.
- Project support office.
- Project center of excellence.

The names, however, are not as important as the fact that there is some "ownership" for the corporate project management function. That alone carries

EXHIBIT 12.1 Enterprise project management

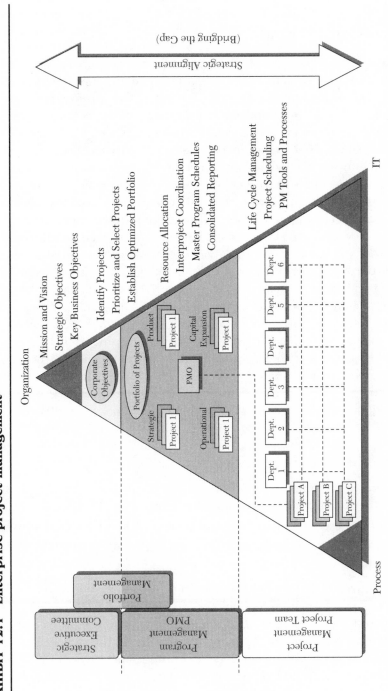

much weight and sends a strong signal to employees that executive management is committed to making project management work in the organization.

Information Technology

Information technology is the enabler to the processes previously described. It has provided a significant boost to project management, particularly in the area of communication. An important point is that *project management has been around a lot longer than information technology.* Before the advances of technology, many organizations could be considered high-maturity, best practice firms. The bar for project management maturity has been raised since the advent of information technology. In today's environment, information technology has done so much to increase the speed and efficiency of information processing and communication that this component has become essential to achieving a level of high maturity and superior performance.

A wide variety of project management tools is used by all high-maturity organizations. Though these tools vary from one company to another, these superior-performing organizations understand one thing about tools: "The path to project management maturity is not exclusively dependent on tools." This is a mistake commonly made by organizations in their search for project management superiority. High-maturity organizations recognize the value of information technology as enablers to project management processes. Processes can be executed without tools. Tools simply increase the efficiency of those processes. The proper selection and integration of information technology with the appropriate processes significantly enhance the project management capability of organizations, thereby leading them to higher levels of maturity.

The Enterprise Project Management model establishes an infrastructure that links every project undertaken in an organization with the organization's long-term vision and objectives. Key characteristics of the model include:

- Strategic alignment of the organization's projects from the vision and strategy level through the individual project level.
- Priority-based selection and routine health checks of project investments.
- Multiproject coordination and reporting through a program management office.

This three-tiered model provides the framework by which organization, processes, and information technology capability required for maturity can be implemented in an organization. Each level is critical to the successful integration of project data from the strategic level down to the project level. Most organizations struggle with effectively integrating data between these levels. The greatest benefit accrued from doing this successfully is the assurance that all project work can be tied to one or more strategic objectives, thereby eliminating the probability of non-value-added projects.

Three Levels of Integration

Strategic

Level 1, the top level of the model, represents the strategic level of the organization. The governing body at this level is often a strategic executive committee whose role is to define the organization's vision and mission. In most organizations, the organizational vision and mission are further detailed into key business or strategic objectives. These objectives are the drivers; they determine which projects or initiatives an organization should select to accomplish its higher level vision and mission.

Program

Level 2, the middle level of the model, represents the program management level. This level is the integration point between the portfolio of projects selected by the strategic executive committee and the individual projects represented in level 3. It serves to bridge the gap between the strategic level of the organization, where the portfolio of projects is established and the project management level where project work is executed.

Project

Level 3, the lower level of the model, represents the activities associated with project management. Organizations performing any kind of project management function are generally operating at this level. The functions performed at this level are operational in nature and are focused on the mechanics of planning and executing projects as described in Parts Two and Three of this book.

In the context of this discussion, the *enterprise* refers to a larger organizational entity. It should be noted, however, that many of the attributes previously discussed can be applied to lower-level organizational units, even departmental levels, with ensuing benefits. The model described previously has the greatest impact on project success at the corporate or divisional level because corporate strategy, project prioritization, and executive support generally take place at these levels. In our earlier discussion, we noted that *executive involvement* was one of the attributes of best practice companies that contributed to project success. Therefore, when applied at higher levels of organizations, project success is driven throughout the organization and resultant benefits are greatly magnified.

BRIDGING THE GAP

In most organizations, there is a wide communication and information gap between the strategic level and the project management level as depicted in the enterprise model. Bridging the gap between these two levels is a primary challenge in achieving enterprise project management maturity. Companies must establish effective organizational entities, processes, and software tools to enable the seamless interface between the strategic level and project management level.

This is easier said than done. The best way to determine if an information gap exists is to perform a simple data audit trail. For example, as project status data is reported in the project management tools, there should be evidence of this information flowing up through the program and portfolio management tools in a real-time environment. In many organizations, this transparent, seamless flow of information is nonexistent. The order of the day is normally one of using project management data, reentering or re-creating the same data in a different tool to meet some executive's expectations. It's a fire drill routine that is highly exhaustive, inefficient, and prone to data inaccuracy. If this is typical of your environment, the information gap has yet to be bridged. This gap creates inefficiencies and delays. Executives tasked with making decisions as to how to allocate limited company resources need timely and accurate project status information so that they can decide whether to kill underperforming, low-return, high-risk, or lower priority projects and reallocate resources to other initiatives that maximize the portfolio benefits. High-maturity organizations have bridged this information and organizational gap and can be much more responsive than their counterparts in decision making. This is because of efficiency gains realized through an effective enterprise model such as the one previously described.

Likewise, project managers and teams operating at the program and project management levels need appropriate information and strategic direction from the executive team. They need to understand the big picture and how their projects support the company strategy and objectives. This communication promotes a more cooperative, team-based environment, which results in more successful projects.

The Program Office: The Link That Bridges the Gap

Best practice organizations all have some kind of project management organizational structure in place. These structures vary by name including *project office, program office, project support office,* and *project center of expertise.* Functions performed by these various structures vary as well; however, their primary focus is generally the same: increase the success of projects. This structure serves as the focal point of project management activity in the enterprise. We previously noted that many of the attributes of high-maturity organizations can also be applied at lower levels of the organization such as a division, business unit, or even department. In either situation, the program office still plays a critical role in bridging the gap between the strategic or executive level and the project management level.

PROCESSES AND ORGANIZATION WITHIN EACH TIER

There are several perspectives from which to understand the Enterprise Project Model. Our first perspective, above, was at a high level, which helped us understand the relationships between the three tiers. Here, we switch our perspective to a detailed examination of the processes and organizational structures required within each tier. We'll start at the lowest level, the project tier, and work our way up.

Project Tier: Processes

Project management processes focus on the planning, execution, and control of the individual projects in the portfolio. They are designed to integrally connect to higher level program and portfolio management processes, linking all projects to the corporate strategy. This ensures that only approved projects supporting corporate objectives are undertaken. Further, these consistent processes increase the predictability of project performance. Establishing and maintaining project management processes is generally the responsibility of departmental or business unit level functions or project offices. These processes are consistent with the Project Management Institute's (PMI) processes as described in the PMBoK and the chapters in Parts Two and Three of this book.

Project Tier: Organization

The governance of these functions is often performed by a *project management office* or a *project support office,* which is subservient to the *program management office* described later. In larger organizations, several project management offices may exist at divisional or departmental levels. Project management information collected by these individual offices is consolidated by the corporate program management office depicted in level 2. The corporate program management office often sets the standards and operating procedures governing the project management offices.

High-maturity organizations have consistently implemented program and project management offices. Project management offices generally administer and govern the execution of processes in a single organization such as a department or business unit. Program management offices are focused on the administration and governance of processes and projects at a higher organizational level or at the enterprise level.

Program Tier: Processes

These processes are largely focused on the coordination, consolidation, and management of multiple projects across the enterprise. The processes synchronize resource allocation across projects, coordinate activities between projects, and consolidate reporting for the multiple projects in the portfolio. They are generally applied at higher organizational levels as opposed to departmental or business unit levels and are performed by a corporate program management function or office.

Common program management processes found in high-maturity organizations include:

- *Multiproject coordination:* In most organizations, projects are often interrelated, with some projects or project activities being dependent on others. This process addresses the relationships between projects and ensures that the proper coordination of resources and dependencies between these projects takes place.

- *Project consolidation and reporting:* One of the major functions performed by program management is the consolidation of project information across multiple organizational units. This process addresses the collection, summarization, and reporting of project data to ensure that project information is communicated efficiently and in the proper format to all relevant parties throughout the organization.

- *Resource optimization:* The resource optimization process is one of the major functions performed by the program management office. At the enterprise level, the program management office is well positioned to oversee all projects, evaluating resource requirements and making resource allocation recommendations based on the priorities and objectives of the organization.

- *Project health status review:* At regular intervals, the program management office reviews the health of projects in the portfolio. This includes schedule, cost, return on investment, and other project metrics deemed useful to the organization. After careful analysis of the projects, status updates are provided to management with recommended actions to take on projects.

- *Project initiation:* This process addresses steps required for initiating a project and adding it to the project portfolio. Project objectives, goals, and key milestones are also communicated to the organization as part of the project initiation process.

- *Project closeout:* Each project should officially be declared complete. The project closeout process defines these steps. An important step in this process is defining the release of resources from the completed project and the reallocation of these resources to new projects. Depending on the structure of the program management office (PMO) and its relationship to the rest of the organization, resources may be released to their respective functional groups and reassigned to other projects.

- *Project cancellation:* Occasionally, projects are cancelled for a number of reasons, including declining return on investment, resource prioritization, failed objectives, or misalignment with strategic objectives. The decision to cancel projects is generally the responsibility of senior or executive management. The PMO, in its role of project oversight, defines the required steps for officially canceling and communicating this to the organization.

- *Supporting processes:* In its project oversight role, the PMO owns and maintains some project management supporting processes. Although these processes are secondary to those previously mentioned, they are important to the ongoing integrity and continuance of project management in the organization.

  —*Project management standards:* This process defines the steps needed for the continued enhancement of project management standards, procedures, templates forms, and reports.

  —*Project management software and tools:* Project management software and tools change on a regular basis. Over time, significant improvements are made to these tools, which contribute significantly to the efficiency of managing projects. High-maturity organizations have a process in place for researching and evaluating the latest technology and trends and making recommendations to the organization on which direction to take. Existing software and tools also need to be maintained and configured to achieve maximum results for the organization. This process also addresses the steps needed to do this.

  —*Lessons learned:* Over time, valuable lessons are learned on projects. These can be captured and applied to future projects, resulting in tremendous savings and efficiency gains to the organization. High-maturity organizations have a process for capturing these lessons in a database and using them for the benefit of future projects.

  —*Project management training:* High-maturity organizations provide project team members with the training needed to sustain high performance on projects. The PMO as the focal point for all projects should play a key role in the development and instruction of this training. Some organizations have an established training group to administer training. The PMO should provide the subject matter expertise and provide advice to this group on the kind and level of training needed for project team members. This process should be developed in advance of delivery to ensure that all project management training needs are met.

In many organizations, the functions performed in this level are nonexistent. As a result, there is an information gap between the project management activity and the strategic level activity. Executives who are involved in the strategic selection of projects are often in the dark as to whether project objectives are being met and proceeding according to plan. With accurate, reliable information about the status of projects, better executive decisions can be made concerning the continuance and funding of existing projects.

Program Tier: Organization

The program tier serves to bridge the gap between the project and portfolio tiers, and the PMO is responsible for the governance and execution of processes on projects used across multiple organizational units.

The organizational component also defines the charter, position descriptions, and roles and responsibilities for all project, program, and portfolio management activities throughout the enterprise.

In high-performing organizations, the PMO is frequently viewed as a center of expertise (COE) or center of excellence for project management. In this capacity, the PMO is often tasked with the role of providing or administering project management training for the rest of the organization. Some high-maturity organizations also use the PMO as a mentoring and coaching center, providing skilled project management personnel as consultants, who offer project guidance and direction to internal groups.

Portfolio/Strategic Tier: Processes

These processes are focused largely on the development of the project portfolio. Processes at this level are generally the responsibility of the strategic executive committee. It is important that these processes be fully integrated at the interface points to ensure proper application. Specific portfolio management processes include:

- Define and validate portfolio.
- Prioritize portfolio.
- Select portfolio.
- Update portfolio.
- Evaluate portfolio.
- Revise portfolio.

The term *portfolio management* is often misleading and conjures up a variety of thoughts. You could argue that the processes described under *program management* such as project initiation, resource optimization, and project health status review all address functions of managing the project portfolio. We agree. They do not, however, address the functions of prioritization and selection of projects. The processes described in this section address these specifically. These functions, until very recently, were not addressed in the context of project management but were mostly performed at strategic levels of the organization. Over the past several years, more and more organizations, including high-maturity companies, have recognized the importance of this function and have included them in the scope of project management. Using a formal prioritization process ensures that projects are aligned with corporate goals and objectives, which ensures that the optimal project portfolio has been selected by the organization. Studies have shown that this can significantly increase the return on investment for companies. As a result, enterprise project management will become viewed increasingly as a strategic function in companies.

Key factors affecting portfolio decisions include:

- Alignment of projects to enterprise objectives.
- Economic value of project.
- Mandatory requirements.
- Project and portfolio risk and return.
- Balance of resources across the enterprise.
- Health of existing projects.

High-maturity organizations perform these steps as part of implementing an enterprise project management infrastructure. Recent studies have shown that the value and return on investment gained by optimizing the project portfolio can offset a significant portion of the total project management costs.

Examples of some common key business objectives include:

- Reduce cost by 20 percent.
- Increase market share by 10 percent.
- Limit maintenance projects to 25 percent of overall project budget.

In best practice organizations, projects are linked to corporate objectives and prioritized before selection. Higher priority projects are selected over lower priority ones. With priority scores used as a basis for project selection, the strategic executive committee can now make much more informed decisions about which projects to select. The final set of projects selected constitutes the portfolio of projects for the given organizational unit. This portfolio represents the optimal mix of projects that ultimately provides the organization with the greatest value from several perspectives, including the accomplishment of its strategic objectives and financial goals.

In many best practice organizations, the PMO is the focal point for collecting and disseminating information. It also provides the function of integrating data between the strategic and project management levels.

Portfolio/Strategic Tier: Organization

As depicted in Exhibit 12.1, the strategic level of the organizational structure includes a strategic executive committee responsible for portfolio selection and ongoing monitoring of the project portfolio. Many high-maturity organizations have a committee operating at this level providing the strategic guidance and direction on project strategy to the lower levels of the organization. Depending on the size of the organization, some organizations have also appointed portfolio director(s) responsible for managing the portfolio management activity at this level.

The establishment of a *portfolio governance board* is an important first step in portfolio management. This board generally consists of executives whose function is to meet regularly to evaluate the portfolio of existing projects and consider requests for new projects. These decisions are generally based on project priorities, resource availability, funding requirements, and projected rates of return.

Board members must have the authority to approve, reject, and fund projects. They generally are division or department heads (depending on the organization) or their representatives who can act on their behalf. Typical portfolio board members include the CEO, CFO, CIO, and directors of functional groups.

INFORMATION TECHNOLOGY INTEGRATES THE TIERS

Information technology tools found in higher maturity organizations cover the full spectrum of the enterprise model from the strategic level to the project management level.

Exhibit 12.2 depicts an array of tools, starting with lower level project management functions and increasing to higher level functions. This array

EXHIBIT 12.2   Information technology tools

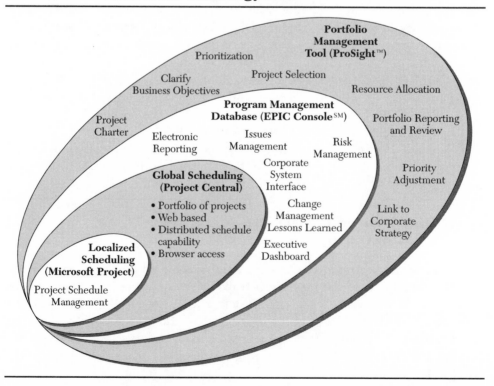

closely parallels the three levels of the enterprise model. Tools represented in the smaller ellipses are generally found at the project management level while those represented in the middle and upper ellipses are found at the program and strategic levels of organizations.

The requirement for information technology at the project level is generally fulfilled by reliable, readily available project management software tools. These applications perform many of the required functions needed at all three levels of the enterprise model. For this reason, discussion of information technology for all three levels is limited to this section only.

Required functions for all three levels should be considered when purchasing the software, as a way of limiting the number of software systems and keeping expenses to a minimum. When selecting enterprise project management software, the requirements of each of the three levels of the model need to be considered. Select a software solution that meets as many of these requirements as possible. Major software functions required for each of the three levels include:

1. Project
   - Project scheduling.
   - Resource scheduling.
   - Cost scheduling.
   - Project reporting.
2. Program
   - Multiproject coordination and summarization.
   - Resource scheduling, aggregation, and optimization.
   - Multiproject reporting.
3. Portfolio
   - Project prioritization.
   - Multiple portfolio creation.
   - Project and portfolio analysis metrics.

Many currently available products support both the project and program functionality. You may have difficulty finding a software application that performs all three of these functions to your satisfaction. Identify the key functions needed in your environment and select one that meets most of these. You can always fill the voids with alternative software.

THE PATH TO MATURITY/GUIDELINES FOR IMPLEMENTING THE MODEL

Identifying the key success factors that lead organizations to high levels of project management maturity is the first step in getting there. Building these into a well-established, mature, and often politically driven organization is the next challenge. This section addresses the required steps for implementing project management best practices that lead to superior performance and a higher level of maturity. In the following sections, we demonstrate that increasing project management maturity in your organization can be done in a timely manner. The days of having to wait five years, or even three years, for results are gone. If tangible results are not observed within three to six months, management will contend: "We need to be looking for something else."

No Universal Path to Maturity

As described earlier, enterprise project management consists of three levels: strategic management, program management, and project management. Often, companies are faced with these questions: What is the best way to achieve project management maturity? Do we take a top-down approach and start from the strategic level, or take a bottom-up approach and start from the project management level? In a purely academic world, the top-down approach might make more sense logically because projects first need to be prioritized and selected before they can be managed. In the real world, however, starting with a clean sheet of paper is seldom the case. In most instances, organizations find themselves managing a multitude of simultaneous projects often in a very ad hoc manner. Their desire is to improve their capability in planning and delivering those projects in addition to becoming more effective in the way they prioritize and select their projects. The answer to the question "Do we take a top-down approach and start from the strategic level or take a bottom-up approach and start from the project management level?" is a matter of priority. It comes down to what is more important to your organization right now:

- More effective management and control of projects.
- More effective prioritization and selection of projects.

If your answer is the first choice, start with a bottom-up approach. If your answer is the second choice, start with a top-down approach. Regardless of the approach, the three cornerstones of success previously described need to be addressed in each level of the enterprise model. Either way, if your goal is to ultimately get to a higher level of maturity and superior performance, you eventually end up with the entire solution. It just comes down to where your highest priority is.

Bottom-Up Implementation

This approach suggests that your organization may be struggling with the management and execution of projects. In this case, your initial focus in becoming a high-maturity organization is to enhance or build your project management best practices as described in level 3 of the enterprise project management model.

Existing projects are committed investments. Therefore, attention must first be given to improving the project management functions to eliminate project inefficiencies and increase the likelihood of successful project execution.

The required steps for implementing or enhancing the project management functions in your organization are described in the section titled Phase 3.

Top-Down Implementation

In some instances, organizations may have adequate project and program management capability already in place. In terms of priority, their greatest need initially may be at the strategic level where better decisions about the prioritization and selection of projects need to be made. Organizations in this situation should consider a top-down implementation approach as the first step in the quest to achieve project management maturity. For example, organizations that are involved in funding major high-risk projects may have a more pressing need to establish an optimized project portfolio with the assurance that they are providing the greatest value to the organization. An actual example of this involved an advance technology organization in a major automotive company that was interested in improving its project and portfolio management operation. This organization was primarily responsible for making funding decisions on advance technology projects. Funded projects were managed by other groups, who provided regular project status updates to the advanced technology group. Although the organization identified a need for improved and consistent project management practices across all projects, the more immediate challenge was ensuring that accurate portfolio decisions were being made. This consisted of prioritizing and selecting the right projects while considering various factors such as economic, market, technical feasibility, risk, return, regulatory requirements, competition, and alignment to the organization's strategy. In this case, the organization decided to focus on the strategic level and move along the maturity path by first improving its portfolio management processes and tools.

Experience Makes a Difference

Identifying opportunities and best practices and implementing them requires a dedicated and objective effort. Organizations may need to make a significant transformation in their practices if they truly want to experience superior project performance and achieve a high level of maturity. Frequently, the lack of internal resources and/or knowledge and expertise hinder these efforts. Organizations committed to achieving enterprise project management maturity should consider using experienced professionals with a record of successful enterprise project management implementations. The proper selection of externally qualified personnel provides significant benefits, including neutrality, objectivity, and the knowledge of many best practices as a result of having performed numerous implementations across multiple industries.

FIVE PHASES TO MATURITY

Our focus has been to define a high-maturity project management organization. This section describes how to get there. Often, it's the little things—the guidelines, techniques, and nuances—that are left unsaid in project management texts that make the difference between success and failure. We point out some of these critical factors that will make your efforts successful.

We have previously noted the differences between a top-down versus bottom-up approach to implementing enterprise project management. We indicated that the main criteria depend on the organization's priority—more effective management and control of projects or more effective prioritization and selection of projects. The discussion in the following section assumes that the management and control of projects is of higher priority; therefore, implementation of project management precedes that of portfolio management in terms of sequence of phases. The major phases on the path to maturity in enterprise project management are:

1. Conducting an organizational project management assessment (OPMA).
2. Developing and implementing a program management infrastructure.
3. Developing and implementing project management processes.
4. Developing and implementing portfolio management processes.
5. Selecting and implementing information technology.

In the sections that follow, we describe the required steps for achieving high project management maturity at the *enterprise* level. Some variation in these steps may exist when implementing the model at lower organizational levels. We note the differences as they occur. In addition, we assume that the organization in question has virtually no project management capability in place. Organizations that have some components of the enterprise model in place may have to modify their approach when applying this model.

Phase 1 Organization Project Management Assessment (OPMA)

Taking stock of your organizational inventory provides you with a baseline to determine how far you have to go to get to your desired state. The process of understanding the difference between your current state and your desired state is known as a *gap analysis*. An effective OPMA consists of three steps:

1. Current situation analysis.
2. Visioneering.
3. Road map.

Current Situation Analysis

The focus of this step is to get a solid understanding of the kind of project management activity currently being conducted at the enterprise level, from the perspective of the three cornerstones of success already described:

- *Organization:* During this exercise, information about the current organizational structure is gathered. The following questions are asked:

    —Describe the current organizational structure.

    —How are projects currently managed?

    —Which organizational group currently has responsibility for projects?

    —How are project teams organized?

    —Describe the level of project management knowledge in the company.

    Information of this kind is helpful in conducting the gap analysis to determine the level of organizational restructuring needed to reach the desired state of maturity. In high-maturity organizations, organizational structure addresses the needs of each of the three levels of the enterprise model.

- *Processes:* This aspect of the current situation analysis focuses on the existing project management processes. This step is conducted to establish the existence, use, and effectiveness of any processes that can be used to increase project management maturity in the enterprise. Information identified in this step includes:

    —Existing project management processes.

    —Redundant processes.

    —Undocumented processes.

    —Templates, forms, and reports.

    As with the organizational component, processes need to be assessed from the perspective of the three levels of the enterprise model: portfolio, program, and project management. If processes at any of these levels are missing or incomplete, project management maturity is compromised.

- *Information technology:* This aspect of the current situation analysis focuses on the use of information technology. As with the processes, an audit is performed to document existing information technology used in project management. In many organizations, this step is fairly simple because information technology is often limited to the use of a scheduling application. In larger organizations, a greater focus is needed on the many legacy systems that provide components of project management information. The source and flow of this data needs to be documented. This becomes important during visioneering and Phase 5 (IT Implementation) when recommendations on software selections are made, particularly when the software needs to interface to existing component systems.

Visioneering

- *Organization:* The purpose of this step is to create the vision for project management in the organization. Again, the vision is based on the three cornerstones of success: organization, processes, and information technology. Organizationally, the vision establishes the framework for defining the new organization structure needed to achieve a high level of project management maturity.

  Several organizational models that best support project management exist. The more notable types are the *functional, matrix,* and *project oriented.* Many factors determine the type that best suits a given organization, including project size, project complexity, and project span of function. Two of the primary issues that surface when creating the organizational vision of project management are location and ownership of resources. In cases where there is no formal project management structure in place, the decision of where to place it organizationally can be controversial. Functional groups often lobby to have project management as an extension of their organization. The basis for this position is that administration costs can be kept to a minimum as a result of not creating a new organizational entity. The downside is that a project management group too closely tied to a functional group may not be in a position to report information as objectively as it could on its own. Best practice organizations recognize this and create project management groups or offices that are independent from the functional groups and report to a nonfunctional executive level of the organization.

  For more information on organizational models, see *The Fast Forward MBA in Project Management,* by Eric Verzuh.

  In addition, a variety of project office forms exist, including: *project management office, project support office, program management office,* and *center of excellence.* Each of these office types has varying degrees of project responsibility. (Exhibit 1.5 in Chapter 1 describes the various forms and possible functions of a project management office.) Research on the best form of project office for your organization should be done before implementation. Ownership of resources is another issue that is often a point of contention. In a project-oriented structure as described in the previously mentioned reference, resources are owned by the project with functional departments that exist within the project structure. In a more traditional matrix or functional organizations, resources are on loan to projects by the various functional groups. When the project is complete, project resources return to their functional homes or are reassigned to other projects. Organizations implementing a project management environment for the first time are reluctant to create a project-oriented structure and reallocate functional resources to an entirely new group. This is a major leap of faith. New project management environments should consider a less drastic approach initially, such as a matrix structure. As experience and acceptance of project management is gained over time, the organization may then shift to a project-oriented structure. This decision should be based on factors described in the reference noted previously. The type of structure is not a determinant of high-maturity organizations. Project management maturity is evident in multiple organizational types. Select the structure that best meets the needs of your organization.

Recommendations for organizational changes can be controversial and often political. It is important that this step be carefully analyzed before making any recommendations for changes. Consult senior executives in the organization for input and buy-in. Develop a solid business case for the changes being recommended. Justify and support the recommended changes with data from best practice organizations that have demonstrated success on projects. This is one area where you need to spend time doing the research and due diligence.

- *Processes:* The vision for project management processes is also defined in this step. Depending on the current level of project management maturity in the organization, some or all processes need to be developed, implemented, or revised. At this point, the processes recommended for the high-maturity organization simply need to be identified. The detail can come later. Building a strong business case advances your cause. Justify the reasons for the development and implementation of any new processes. This takes time and money, and senior management will be reluctant to commit the funds unless there is sufficient value to be gained from this.

- *Information technology:* The vision for project management information technology is cast in this step. The recommendations for information technology are based heavily on the information gathered during the current situation analysis. Your recommendations for information technology will be heavily scrutinized, especially by internal IT groups. You must build a solid business case to either justify new software expenditures or eliminate existing systems. This step needs to address the various systems and software being recommended. A high-level process flow showing the various systems and their interfaces helps to communicate the IT vision. Justify your reasons for selecting software and how they interface with one another. A clearly documented vision and business case goes a long way toward communicating to the organization that you have done your homework and have an effective IT plan for the organization.

Road Map

The last step in the OPMA is the development of the road map. The road map is a high-level plan describing the major components of implementation for an organization to reach its desired state of maturity. Components of the road map include:

- Scope statement.
- Work breakdown structure.
- Summary project plan.
- Detail project plan.
- Risk plan.
- Cost estimate.
- Organizational change plan.
- Benefits.

After obtaining buy-in of the vision from executive management, the road map is the most important step in the OPMA. This document is the communication vehicle to the organization, describing the activities that will take place to develop a best practices, high-maturity organization. It should describe the impact of change on the organization, both positive and negative. Change can be unsettling to employees, particularly when they are uncertain about the future of their jobs and responsibilities. Make every attempt to communicate the changes that will take place, individuals and groups that will be affected, and the duration of such change. Emphasize benefits that will be realized from these changes, for both employees and the organization, if possible. When properly developed, the road map helps to ensure a smooth transition from the current state to the desired state.

Key Guidelines for Conducting This Phase

- *Use an existing model for conducting current situations analysis.* Many good models are available for conducting the *current situation analysis.* Some consulting firms or many of your project management colleagues may share some of their diagnostic tools and templates, which greatly simplifies this step. For a copy of an organization project management assessment form, contact the pci group at (248) 813-1300 or by e-mail at solutions@pcigroup1.com.
- *Involve a horizontal and vertical cross-section of the organization.* For some employees, the OPMA may be their first exposure to project management and what the organization is trying to accomplish. Use this phase as an opportunity to educate and inform employees about the objectives of the project and the benefits to be gained. Interview teams from different organizational and group levels such as project team members, project managers, functional managers, senior managers, and executives. This provides a balanced perspective of the current thinking and potential resistance to change. This is a simple step, but it goes a long way to garner support for project management from employees. Keep them working with you, not against you.
- *Validate the use of existing project management processes.* While conducting the assessment, many versions will emerge about the way things are

currently being done. These are often in conflict with one another. Be sure to ask for evidence of documented processes and validate their use by asking different people. You often find that verbal information is colored by people's bias, background, and perception. You may even consider observing the project management process as it is executed. This is a telltale sign of what's really happening.

- *Don't get caught up in the politics.* After employees catch on to what you're trying to do, you'll catch every opinion on the subject of project management. This ranges from organizational structures that should be in place to recommendations on which software to use. Some of these opinions may be legitimate input, while others are purely political and self-serving. As the consultant and expert on the project, take everything with a grain of salt. Conduct a careful objective assessment and analysis of the data before making your recommendations. Solicit the input of project management practitioners and experts who are not involved in the process and stand nothing to gain by giving you their professional advice.

Phase 2 Program Management Organization Infrastructure

We previously noted the importance of the program management level denoted by level 2 of the enterprise model as the integration point in an enterprise project management organization. It serves to bridge the gap between the strategic level of the organization, where the portfolio of projects is established and the project management level where project work is executed.

The steps specified in this phase relate to organizations looking to implement project management across several departments or groups in an organization. Therefore, the establishment of the PMO is in order, as described in level 2 of the enterprise model. The scope of the PMO is broader than the project management office, in terms of both organizational responsibility and the processes it manages. The following steps also apply to the project management office, with the major difference that the project management office generally resides at a lower organizational level and focuses on projects in a single organizational entity. The PMO is responsible for multiproject coordination and multiproject resource allocation across several organizational groups.

The program management organization infrastructure is the glue that holds the practice and discipline of project management together in high-maturity organizations. Without a formal organizational entity in place to take ownership for project management, there is no governance of the project management practice or point of accountability. Without it, project management as a formal method of managing projects languishes and eventually becomes ineffective and fails. High-maturity organizations recognize this and have made the upfront commitment to establishing a formal program management infrastructure. The infrastructure is generally developed and implemented within the framework of a PMO.

Depending on the needs of the organization, PMOs exist in different forms and may perform a variety of functions. The findings of the OPMA determine this.

The major steps required to establish a program management infrastructure are:

- Create PMO structure.
- Define PMO charter.
- Define roles and responsibilities—PMO staff.
- Determine staffing requirements.
- Identify and appoint PMO manager.

The establishment of a formal PMO lays the groundwork for the implementation of the next phases of project management maturity. In addition, a formally established PMO sends a powerful message to the organization that management is committed to achieving superior performance in the execution of projects.

Key Guidelines for Conducting This Phase

- *Use existing project management organizational models.* Many proven project management organizational models already exist. Do not make the mistake of thinking your organization is so unique that you must invent another. For examples of some of the more common models, see *The Fast Forward MBA in Project Management,* by Eric Verzuh.
- *Don't overstaff.* The initial tendency is to overstaff the PMO. Start small and work your way up. After the PMO is fully functional and has been tested, proving all the processes in the project management cycle, you will be in a better position to assess more accurately the resources required to operate the PMO.
- *Select qualified resources.* One of the most common mistakes made by organizations is the appointment of unskilled staff to the PMO. When properly defined, the roles and responsibilities of the PMO staff can serve as a guideline to the proper selection of staff. Project management is a discipline requiring people with the right skills. No one would debate the need to have a properly trained and skilled surgeon in an operating room. Yet, organizations are all too quick to find a readily available body to staff the PMO. Arguably, one of the major reasons for the failure of project management in organizations is the inadequacy of its staff.

Phase 3   Enterprise Project Management Processes

Processes are the road map to the successful execution of projects. A formal methodology that prescribes the steps by which to perform the required project management functions is essential to becoming a high-maturity organization. Without this governance, inconsistency and chaos reign.

Project and program management processes described in this phase are generally implemented in parallel. High-maturity organizations implementing project management at the enterprise level have both sets of processes.

In this discussion, we are assuming a bottom-up implementation, with project and program management processes implemented first, followed by portfolio management in Phase 4.

Project and Program Management Processes

The major steps required to implement project and program management processes are:

- Identify and document applicable processes (see project and program processes in previous section and PMBoK).
- Develop process maps.
- Identify process owners.
- Communicate processes to stakeholders.
- Develop and conduct process training.

Do not underestimate these critical steps. Processes serve as the basis for defining the project management operations. When properly developed, they also serve as inputs to a training manual by which to inform and train employees about project management and responsibilities expected of them.

Phase 4   Portfolio Management

The three major steps required to implement portfolio management in an organization are:

1. Establish a portfolio governance process.
2. Define metrics and measures.
3. Conduct portfolio review.

The governance process addresses the business case for developing the project portfolio. Every organization undoubtedly has its own process and criteria by which to justify the selection of its projects. For organizations adopting a formal portfolio management process for the first time, this may be a painful and very controversial step. During the establishment of this process, the strategic executive committee determines the basis by which the organization prioritizes and ultimately selects projects. This takes many hours of deliberation, but once established, it guides the organization into selecting projects on a much more objective basis, ensuring that projects are more aligned with corporate strategic objectives and eliminating much of the subjectivity in the process. This is a continuous process for organizations looking to achieve high levels of maturity. The first pass in developing this process will undoubtedly change, and organizations striving to be best in class will look for improved methods of achieving the optimal project portfolio.

Defining the metrics and measures is the next major step in portfolio management. Much of the work in this step can be conducted in parallel with the governance process. Metrics and measures are used to prioritize projects and determine which projects are selected as part of the portfolio. Financial metrics include return on investment, payback, internal rate of return, and net present value. Nonfinancial metrics include risk, alignment to corporate objectives, and market penetration. In addition, some of these same measures are used during project execution to measure project results and identify trends. Caution should be exercised in this step. Identify and define as many metrics and measures as necessary to enable projects to be adequately prioritized and selected. There may be a tendency to create far more metrics than are needed. This overly complicates the process and adds confusion. Start with a limited number of metrics and work through the process. You can always add more later, if needed.

Portfolio review is the ongoing process of reviewing the project metrics and analyzing the results of the project portfolio against objectives and expectations. Best practice organizations convene the strategic executive committee on at least a monthly basis to perform this function. During this meeting, key decisions are made about funding projects, canceling underperforming projects, and reallocating corporate resources.

This process defines and documents the steps required to formally develop the organization's portfolio of projects.

Key Guidelines for Conducting Phases 3 and 4

- *Document processes.* Processes are the road map to the proper execution of project management best practices. To ensure their continuous improvement, they need to be documented. Documented processes with proper version control serves as the baseline by which to revise and improve the processes over time.

- *Leverage existing processes.* In most organizations, project management functions are already being performed to some degree. Make the best use of these. Do not create new processes if existing ones are working or can be slightly modified.

- *Use cross-functional teams.* Processes tend to be cross-functional in nature. The more involvement you get by various cross-functional groups, the greater the likelihood of acceptance and success for project management.

- *Use established project management processes.* Countless hours have been spent by project management professionals in developing and refining the core project management processes. These are published in many books and in the PMI's *A Guide to the Project Management Body of Knowledge* and are readily available for use. These processes have been tried and tested over time and serve as excellent models to begin building processes in your organization.

Phase 5 IT Tools

Information technology tools were described in the Cornerstones of Success section. In this phase, information from the OPMA is used to determine the kind of information technology needed to meet the specific needs of the organization. More in-depth analyses of the various tools may be undertaken before their implementation in this phase. Depending on the technology selected, the software may need to interface with existing corporate systems. When implementing information technology, care should be taken to ensure compatibility with the processes implemented in earlier phases. Let the process drive the tools, not the other way around.

Discussion of information technology in most organizations can be highly controversial and political. As is often the case with information technology, users of project management software are seldom the ones making decisions about which software to buy. Consequently, inadequate software that does not meet the needs of the organization may be purchased. Project management groups and practitioners need to be involved in setting the vision for project management information technology. This is one of the cornerstones of success for high-maturity organizations. Project management groups in best practice organizations play a key role in influencing buying decisions about project management software. The project management background and expertise of these groups should drive the selection of the software to ensure that superior performance can ultimately be realized. Project management practitioners should develop a strong business case for their recommended software. This is too important an area to leave solely to the information technology professionals. The processes described previously are key drivers for the selection of the right software. The business case should state the processes, functions, and requirements that need to be satisfied by the software. Use information obtained from other best practice organizations to reinforce your case.

Key Guidelines for Conducting This Phase

- *Reference PMI's annual project management software report.* Commercially available software is identified and ranked based on requirements and functionality. This is an invaluable source for narrowing down the list of software before conducting a detailed analysis.
- *Use cross-functional teams (see previous discussion).*
- *Select integratable software.* Be especially mindful of the three-tiered enterprise model when selecting software. Data needs to be communicated through all levels of the model. If different software is used at different

levels to accommodate specific needs, ensure that data can be easily transferred and integrated between software.

SUMMARY

Superior-performing organizations have uncovered the mystery as to what it takes to consistently excel at delivering projects on time, under budget, and at desired quality levels. These few steps can make a significant and positive impact on organizations' customer satisfaction, market share, and bottom line when properly executed.

To effect successful change, an organization must:

- *Conduct an organization project management assessment.* There's no point in trying to figure out where you're going if you don't know where you currently are. Taking stock of your current organizational inventory is the essential first step to maturity. With that understanding, you now know the adjustments necessary to lead you up the maturity curve.

- *Establish a program management organization infrastructure.* This is the glue that holds the practice and discipline of project management together in high-maturity organizations. Without it, there is no governance or point of accountability for project management. This infrastructure is generally developed and implemented within the framework of a program management office (PMO). This includes creating the structure, defining the PMO charter, defining the PMO roles and responsibilities, determining PMO staffing requirements, and appointing the PMO manager.

- *Develop and implement enterprise project management processes.* Processes are the road map to the successful execution of projects. This formal methodology prescribes the steps by which to perform the required project management functions that are essential and evident in all high-maturity organizations. Without this governance, inconsistency and chaos reign. These processes include program management processes, which are largely focused on the coordination, consolidation, and management of multiple projects across the enterprise. Also included are project management processes, which focus on the management and execution of individual projects and are consistent with the processes described in the Project Management Institute's (PMI) Project Management Body of Knowledge (PMBoK). High-maturity organizations implementing project management at the enterprise level have both sets of processes.

- *Implement a portfolio management methodology.* High-maturity organizations understand the importance of having projects linked to corporate goals and objectives. Using a formal prioritization process ensures that projects are aligned with corporate goals and objectives. The establishment of a portfolio governance board to oversee the portfolio management activities is an essential first step to a successful portfolio management methodology. Once in place, portfolio management processes that define and document the steps for managing the organization's portfolio can be developed and implemented.

- *Select and implement appropriate information technology.* These tools, enablers to the processes, need to function in concert with them. Adequate time should be dedicated to understand the organization's project management system requirements and ensure that these requirements can be delivered with the software selected. Make sure to select the right tools from the beginning.

As organizations strive to be best in class, they need to consider the basic elements required for sustained superior performance on the path to project management maturity.

CREATING AN ENVIRONMENT FOR SUCCESSFUL PROJECTS IN *YOUR* ORGANIZATION

13

Robert J. Graham and
Randall L. Englund

Bold moves are needed to develop project management in most organizations. The person leading the change is likely to be going against tradition, fighting inertia, and attempting to overcome fierce resistance to change. Many organizations halfheartedly attempt to add project management to existing organizations. But to do it right requires that someone in senior management wants the change to happen. Without the backing of at least one person in senior management, any number of excuses can be found to justify not making the change; but it is also true that if only one senior manager wants to implement proper project management, and wants it badly enough, then it can happen. At Hewlett-Packard (HP) the chief operating officer made excellence in project management a priority, and it came to pass. One senior manager definitely committed to the process of implementing project management and bold enough to begin it, may bring forth all the power and magic necessary to pull it off.

This chapter outlines a process of implementation and provides examples, many of which are from large organizations. However, the process can also be used in smaller organizations, though the project management office may not be as extensive and the project manager's development curriculum may need to be purchased rather than developed.

IMPLEMENTATION PROCESS OVERVIEW

The overall implementation process is shown in Exhibit 13.1, where the ovals are steps in the process and the arrows indicate the consequences of not

378

**EXHIBIT 13.1 A process for success and defaults
for nonaction**

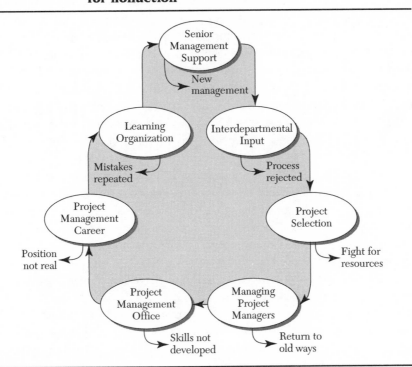

successfully implementing a step. The process begins with developing senior management support. If this is not accomplished, most of the succeeding steps will fail and the organization will require new senior management. The next step involves developing a project management process using interdepartmental input. Without this input, the process will fail because the departmental cooperation needed for good project management will probably not be forthcoming. The next step involves developing a process for project selection. If this is not done correctly, there will be massive fights for resources among competing projects. The following step involves developing upper managers' abilities in managing project managers. Without this, there will be a return to the old ways of managing and not an advancement to project management. Subsequent steps involve developing a project management office to help in developing project skills, determining a project management career ladder so that the position is considered real, and finally creating a learning organization to help ensure that past mistakes are not repeated.

Step 1: Developing Senior Management Support

The first step is to develop senior management support for a project management program. If the managers at the top echelon of an organization are forward-looking, this should not be too difficult. If upper managers, the people at the middle levels of an organization, are not forward-looking, they usually become enlightened after several project failures. For example, at Chevron a project management program was developed after a benchmarking study found that, on average, Chevron projects were taking longer and costing more than those of competitors.[1] At NCR, a project management program was started after several projects lost money.[2] The organization may follow the path of the revitalization process and enter the period of cultural distortion before realizing that significant effort is needed to break people out of their old departmental management habits and instill practices that support project management. However, it is not absolutely necessary to wait for a large failure in order to develop senior management support and senior management resolve. There are other ways.

One possibility is to hold a project inventory meeting. To do this, have all senior managers list the projects going on in their organization. When all the projects are put together, the managers may be amazed at how much total project work is going on in the organization. Determine how many projects there are in total, and then list those that were recently finished or canceled. Understand why the canceled projects were canceled. Are there any runaway projects? Have any languished for years, never canceled but never finished, always with an excuse? Experience indicates that the senior management group may be struck by how many total projects exist and how much money is being wasted on poorly run ones. In addition, there may also be several potential runaway projects— projects that have the potential of wasting still more money. A runaway project is described as one that has one or more of the following characteristics:

- It is way behind schedule.
- It is grossly over budget.
- When and if finally implemented, it subjects the enterprise to risk of a substantial financial loss.

Research by Martin suggests that at any time there is a runaway in every Fortune 200 company and that one-third of all companies have a runaway in progress.[3] Usually technology is conveniently blamed as the cause of the runaway. Blaming one factor is an example of the man on the dock approach to explaining organizational catastrophes. However, technology is usually not the only cause; more than 80 percent of the time, organizational, planning, or management problems are responsible. Thus, project runaways are much more of an upper-management issue than they are a project management issue. Projects that have run away, languished, or been recently canceled will probably lack a project sponsor, indicating that no one in senior upper management really wanted them to happen. Do any current projects lack an upper-management sponsor? If so, you might as well cancel them now; they will probably be canceled later anyway.

However, remember that the function of a project inventory meeting is to examine the state of projects and the management of the project portfolio. The next step is to look at how many person-years per year each of those projects requires and find the total person-years being consumed by the entire inventory. Are that many person-years available to be devoted to projects in your organization? Are there that many person-years in total in your organization? The normal result of a project inventory is that senior management sees for the first time that too many projects are being attempted, that they are not coordinated in any way to effectively reach organizational goals, and that they cannot possibly be accomplished with the resources of the organization.

Now examine how important project management is in your industry. In a commodity industry that produces standard off-the-shelf products that rarely change, project management may not be very important. However, if many projects are already under way in your organization it is a sign that project management is becoming very important in your industry. If you are experiencing increasing changes in products with a corresponding decrease in product life-cycles and increasing need for product quality and customer acceptance, then project management is certainly becoming essential to your organization's survival.

The normal result of a project inventory is that senior management realizes that management of the project portfolio is essential for the survival of the company, that the current portfolio probably does not represent the optimum use of resources to reach organizational goals, and that a coordinated effort to properly manage the portfolio of projects as well as the individual projects themselves is necessary for future survival. With this realization the senior managers should be ready to support a project management response.

An alternative to having a project inventory is to hire someone into senior management who has worked in another company and understands what needs to be done to have more effective projects. For example, an insurance company that was having trouble with information technology projects hired a senior manager from a leading computer firm as its information technology (IT) director. This person convened a senior management meeting to discuss IT project problems and how they had been solved in the computer firm. A consultant was brought in to discuss the role of upper management in creating the environment for successful projects and to indicate how these problems had been solved in other organizations. This approach got senior management attention, and a project management program was begun.

Another approach is to have upper managers attend training courses with the project managers and then create a senior management review based on the comments from those courses. This can work well. In designing a project management course for an engineering firm, for example, the members of the technical committee (who were upper managers) were challenged to attend the course, one at a time, with the project managers. Thus, they heard the pain caused by upper and senior management firsthand from the lower-level participants. A survey instrument was also used to generate data about how bad things were in this company. Summarized and presented to the senior managers, these experiences and data allowed them to finally see the problems through the eyes of their own project and upper managers, and the project management program was expanded throughout the organization.

If your organization does not have a tradition of challenging upper management, you may not get good results from having upper managers in courses. In organizations where open communication is not the norm, the presence of upper managers in courses tends to restrict conversations and the true expression of perceived problems. If so, having a project inventory or getting the view from a respected outsider may work better. It is much less threatening to have an outsider talk about senior management problems in general than to have data from insiders reveal senior management problems in particular. Remember that the important result of this step is to get attention to a problem, not to threaten the senior management team. Choose a method that will work in your organization.

If you are not able to get senior management support at this time, simply wait. Project failures will continue to grow; competitors who have adopted a project management approach will begin to develop superior products, better customer response, or better product service in much less time. Your organization will founder as its sales decrease and it enters the period of cultural distortion. Then a new CEO will be appointed who will no doubt trumpet the virtues of project management, and you will then have senior management support for change.

Step 2:   Develop a Structure for Interdepartmental Input

It is important to develop a project management program, often called a project management office or initiative. It guides the development of project management practices throughout the organization. As the program affects all parts of the organization, all parts of the organization should be represented. Therefore, the first step is to develop cross-organizational teams that can help guide and implement the project management effort.

Two important levels of questions will probably require two different levels of teams. The first level has to do with what projects to attempt; these questions should be addressed by a senior- or upper-level management team. The second level is more operational, concerned with which project practices to adopt and how they will be implemented; such questions should be answered by a team of upper managers and project managers.

Hewlett-Packard uses the council concept as one mechanism to establish a strategic direction for projects spanning organizational boundaries. A council may be permanent or temporary, assembled to solve strategic issues and thus typically involving upper managers. Standard council roles are setting directions, managing multiple projects or the project portfolio, and aiding in cross-organizational issue resolution.

3M also developed an interdisciplinary team to help improve project management. The company held a focus group with some top project leaders from different parts of the organization to find out precisely what problems they were experiencing on projects. From this came a list of more than eighty areas of difficulty grouped into 10 major categories of critical success factors. These factors became the basis for developing a project management process.[4]

A financial services firm realized it had a problem after several software project failures—a classic way to get management attention. Case studies were developed for these projects and a senior management team, including the CEO, was convened to study the causes and cures. As a result, an ad hoc team of senior managers from the information technology, operations, and management development departments was developed to research solutions. This team developed and supported a cross-organizational project management program. See Graham for additional details.[5]

The important point here is that any sort of cross-departmental effort requires input from the different departments involved in order to help ensure its eventual acceptance. For people in various departments to embrace any set of standard procedures, they must first have some say in the design of those procedures. Some project management practices may not make sense from the point of view of an individual department, but if department representatives were part of a team that developed those practices, they could explain the rationale to members of their department. Understanding the reason for recommended practices is critical to cross-departmental acceptance, so it should be facilitated from the beginning by forming cross-departmental teams to help define the total project management program.

Examine your organization to see how cross-departmental efforts are coordinated. Many organizations have a council structure that can be used; others use ad hoc teams. Whatever structure is available, it can help gain input from those who will be affected by the output. Without performing this important step, the people affected do not own the resulting process and the probability of failure of the final effort is greatly increased.

Step 3: Develop a Process for Project Selection

Project selection will normally be done by an upper-management team. This team must ensure that the projects selected are those that best fit the organizational strategy. First they determine which types of projects will be supported; not all projects will be R&D types that break new ground or develop new product platforms, and not all projects will be add-ons that modify current products or procedures. The team of senior and upper managers decides on the mix of types of products for both the long term and short term.

The Pillsbury Project Portfolio Management process attempts to develop a mix of projects that represent balance, business benefit, and alignment.[6] Balance is defined as the trade-off between urgency and importance, short term and long term, and developing competences and core competences. The business benefit assesses the profit potential for all activities, calculating the return on the joint R&D-marketing investment. Alignment questions consider the degree of shared objectives, cross-functionality, common understanding of requirements, and ability to integrate into the total business plan. This is one example of a management team determining the most important criteria for selecting projects to meet the goals of the organization.

Once the criteria for projects are determined, the potential projects are prioritized according to their ability to meet the desired objectives. The upper-management team assesses the ability of each project to meet the stated goals. Pillsbury does this with a priority assessment form. For each project to be considered, the team lists the project goal, the strategic basis for interest, the business benefit, the R&D investment needed, the implementation timing, toughest hurdles, and odds of success. Based on these, priorities are assigned to each of the potential projects.

NCR looks at a risk-to-payback analysis in evaluating potential professional services projects. An upper-management team from project management, sales, professional services, and risk assessment, plus technical subject matter experts, prepares a risk analysis. This package describes the project opportunity, risks, a high-level technical design, and a business case. Sales and professional services management then decides whether to pursue the project by weighing the rewards against the risks.

Many organizations use a business case approach for each potential project. The business case includes a project narrative and a financial analysis. The narrative explains the business process the project is designed to address, the linkage to corporate strategy, the time frame of the project, resource requirements and risks, and issues associated with the project. The financial analysis provides a project cost summary by year reflecting the costs required to complete a proposed project. In addition, it reflects on the financial benefits that successful accomplishment of the project will achieve. Finally, the analysis calculates the net present value, return on investment, and the discount period based upon the cost and benefit streams. The purpose of the business case is to provide the senior management team with an overview of the project that enables it to make go/no-go decisions on projects submitted for approval.

Other organizations use the priority assessment method. Chevron uses the Chevron Project Development and Execution process, where multifunctional teams meet during the initial phase of the process to test project ideas for strategic fit. Many other methods are probably in use as well. The point is that upper managers determine the most important criteria for project selection and then rank potential projects accordingly. The rank of a particular project then becomes that project's priority. Once the projects are in priority order within categories of project types, they are selected according to the available resources. HP uses the in-plan/out-plan document for recording this selection. When a project is selected, a project sponsor should be assigned.

If an organization's project selection process is not properly executed, its strategy suffers because too many projects will be launched in a scattershot manner. This causes a massive fight for resources among the competing projects, a Darwinian scenario where those who fight the hardest get resources for their projects and the other projects die. *Survival of the fittest* would not appear to be the appropriate upper-management tactic for implementing organizational strategy. Projects should be chosen for their contribution to strategy, and it is upper management's responsibility to make that happen.

Step 4: Develop Upper Managers' Abilities in Managing Project Managers

The most critical step in implementing the chosen projects is developing upper managers' abilities in managing project managers. Without success here, all other efforts are wasted. Throughout the land, project managers complain that upper managers will not let them do what they are trained to do. As a result, all the time, effort, and training that goes into developing project managers is wrecked on the rocky shores of some upper manager's mismanagement. Yet despite its importance, this is the step most often forgotten or ignored. Ignore it at your peril.

Developing abilities can be done only over time. Even if upper managers realize the importance of project management and follow the project selection step just described, they must not think their influence is over. The behavior of upper managers has a profound effect on project success, and they must be educated in the best practices. For example, the NCR executive team responsible for implementing the GlobalPM methodology attended executive project management education and attained certification as project management professionals (PMPs). The team understood that leading by example was the best measure of success, and they expected nothing of their associates that they did not expect of themselves.[7] In this way the NCR team members increased their skills in managing project managers and showed that they can *walk the walk* as well as *talk the talk.*

Like project managers, upper managers need time to practice any new skill they learn. The most likely vehicle for learning best practices is some combination of courses, conferences, refreshers, and discussions. To begin, a course or executive overview should be developed as a part of the project management office. This course could cover all of the ways upper managers help the project management function. Normally this includes what upper managers should ask for in terms of a project plan, goal statement, staffing plan, and so on. The HP Project Management Initiative developed such a course. Such a course might cover why upper managers are so important in the change to project management and explain best practices so that the upper managers can support the project management process.

One interesting way to teach best practices is to let the upper managers discover the effects of their actions themselves. One approach taken at HP was to let the upper managers go through the Complete Project Manager simulation as if they were project managers.[8] This simulation helps project managers learn to deal with team building, stakeholder management, and other project issues by solving a sequence of problems that affect project success. As the upper managers went through the problems in the simulation, they became just as angry and upset as real project managers normally get at the problems caused by the upper managers in the simulation. In the feedback discussion, they were asked who causes these problems in their organization and, of course, it is themselves. As they were angry and upset at the simulated problems they encountered, they could easily understand how their actual project managers could also be angry and upset. It was important for upper managers to go through the simulation themselves and experience the frustrations. Otherwise, discussion of the problems they cause is just an intellectual exercise that is not internalized. Having experienced the problems themselves in the simulation, they were ready to listen to solutions and best practices.

Another way to develop upper managers' abilities is to hold an upper-management conference. Conferences like these gather together many upper managers to network among themselves and listen to some of the best experts discuss problems and suggest solutions. When properly designed, these conferences are well attended and even sought out by upper managers.

If management conferences are not normal procedure in your organization, it may be best to hire a consultant to help upper managers understand how they affect project success. Experience indicates that upper managers tend to listen to outside experts more than they listen to insiders with the same information. This is especially true if the consultant has experience in other organizations that are similar to yours. The consultant should interview upper managers and project managers to see which practices are prevalent in your organization and then show the consequences of those practices in other organizations. The consultant should be able to show the results from applying best practices in the best organizations.

The important point is to note that upper managers need to change along with project managers in order to make the move to project management successful. This cannot be done by executive fiat, so a development plan is needed; it should be developed to fit the customs of your organization. If none of the above methods seems to fit, consider developing an internal upper manager–project manager team charged with developing a list of best practices.

If this step is not successfully implemented, the benefits of the first three steps will not be realized. This is because a change in practices must be reinforced by upper management on a daily basis. If upper managers say they want new practices but continue to use old practices themselves, the project managers sense this lack of integrity and revert to old practices too.

Step 5: Establish a Project Manager's Development Program

Motorola undertook a very large system development project involving satellite communications. It represented a significant shift away from familiar military projects into work-for-hire on a massive commercial project. A senior manager initially established self-managed teams as the modus operandi, believing them empowered to make all decisions unhindered by management meddling and delays. Chief Planner Darrell Blackburn describes the resulting scenario as similar to team members inside a large number of tubs lashed together by long ropes.[9] The mission was for all tubs to reach the other side of a wide river. Everybody rowed like crazy to complete the mission, but without project and program managers each tub went off in its own direction, fighting the current as best it could. Members were fiercely loyal to their mission but impervious to the needs and wishes of other teams. The long tethers occasionally snapped, and people were jolted by the miscues of poor communication.

They corrected this situation by positioning project managers in each project and establishing a program management office. This shortened the ropes between the project "tubs" so that project managers took ownership not only for their own projects but for the whole program as well. They served as communication liaisons between projects and to the program office. All became closely synchronized, the efforts of each were supported by the efforts of others, and rapid progress for all became evident.

Upper managers must determine what they think are the most important attributes for potential project managers, then inculcate them through training. This would usually be the job of the project management development office, a group like the Project Management Initiative at HP that is most often staffed by experienced project managers. However, it could also be a part of normal training and development; if so, it could be done more cheaply as there is no need to establish an entire new group, and project manager development becomes part of regular management development. But done this way, certain possibilities may be missed, such as project management conferences, the ability to incorporate the latest developments, and having people who have been there transfer knowledge based on experience. If these are not important to your organization, do project manager development as part of the organizational development program.

A good example is 3M's development of its competence model and curriculum. Honeywell is also developing a total curriculum, as is Chevron. Lucent Technologies has a project management department to oversee project management development and project management practice. All these companies put together a development program and course curriculum. All have a basic course in project management fundamentals and further courses that develop other skills, including business skills. Project management curricula tend to feature courses in the following areas:

Project techniques: Project management fundamentals courses teach basic project planning, estimating, and risk analysis techniques. When participants finish such a course, they know how to put together a project plan.

Behavioral aspects: These courses cover such areas as team building, motivating team members, developing effective project teams, and dealing with upper managers, contributing department managers, and other stakeholders. Many of these courses use simulations to help teach the effects of project manager behavior on team development and other matters.

Organizational issues: These courses cover techniques for managing across organizations when the project manager has all the responsibility but none of the authority. They teach participants how to get projects done in spite of the rest of the organization.

Business fundamentals: Many project managers have a technical background but lack basic business knowledge. These courses teach the business of the organization, how decisions affect the bottom line, and how to run a project as if it were a business.

Marketing and customer issues: In the end there must be a market—a set of customers—for the final product of the project. This is true even of internal projects. Courses on these issues focus on the techniques of defining and developing a market as well as understanding the needs and desires of the customers and end users.

Not all courses need be developed from scratch. Some project management skills are similar to regular management skills, so it may be possible to use courses that already exist in the organization to teach project managers about such subjects.

Project managers must know the company's business if they are to act as if they are managing their own business. Project managers understand business better if they have had a variety of assignments before becoming project managers; in designing any curriculum it is important to understand what skills current project managers have and what they lack.

Project forums are an opportunity for practicing project managers to get together to discuss a particular topic, such as work breakdown structures. These can be half-day sessions to review basics, cover advanced applications, and discuss problems with application in the organization.

The ability to do this depends on the culture of your organization. The idea is to design meeting places where project managers can learn from the experiences of one another. Increasingly, there will be Internet forums on the World Wide Web where people can share experiences. Be careful, however, not to expect impersonal technologies to take over for the personal touch that people need.

Smaller organizations may not have the resources to develop the competence models and complete curriculums described here. The curriculum can then be developed by choosing from the array of public courses that are readily available. Encourage people to attend universities that now offer master's degrees in project management. Many organizations offer complete curricula and will tailor them to fit the needs of smaller organizations. The easiest way to determine available courses is to attend a national project management conference such as the annual seminar and symposium of the Project Management Institute and visit the vendor displays. By doing so, smaller organizations can develop the same caliber of project management as larger organizations.

Step 6: Make Project Management a Career Position

Any organization that is serious about projects will make project management a career position, not just an add-on to peoples' regular responsibilities.

At NCR Professional Services, for example, project management is now defined as a career position. Project managers run all aspects of their projects using NCR's GlobalPM methodology. They are assigned to their position at the end of the concept phase of proposal development, and they remain on the project until the end. The best performers have superior skills in specifying project requirements, meeting customer needs, and managing change. To handle larger efforts, NCR has defined the program manager role. A program is a set of individual projects that are integrated to accomplish a customer's objectives. The program manager oversees the multiple projects that are included in the program, supports the project managers, and resolves conflict as needed. The program manager also provides a planning and control function to ensure that individual projects come together as needed at completion.[10]

A project management career track based on the roles just mentioned was established to emphasize the value NCR places on project management skill. Project managers are expected to advance their capabilities through ongoing company-supported formal training and certification. Certification as a project management professional is mandatory for individuals aspiring to rise on the project management career track.

Where many organizations draw project managers from the ranks of technical or engineering professions, AT&T has assembled a large section of professional project managers drawn from various areas of the company.[11] Upper manager Dan Ono developed a distinct career position for people aspiring to advance within the organization. They make significant contributions by focusing strictly on project management issues to coordinate cross-organizational projects. Many of them did not have advanced professional training before joining this organization; they followed a course of study leading to the project management professional certification given by the Project Management Institute. They continue advancing in the profession by completing a series of increasingly complex projects and by attending conferences and networking with other project managers.

In the field of electronic commerce, many businesses are scrambling to develop Internet-specific business practices. There is an explosive growth in the need for system integrators who can provide services ranging from reselling hardware and software to architecture design and business-process consulting. Businesses sometimes look to integrators to assume total responsibility for their business applications and the business processes they support. There is a question about how ready businesses are to turn over mission-critical functions to outside firms, and the answer often lies in talking to people who have been through a similar experience. In an extensive survey of information systems managers, *ComputerWorld* gathered the criteria into three categories: business practices, project management, and technical performance.[12] Project management expertise, according to the survey, becomes significant when clients are looking for a global integrator that can attack a worldwide challenge with a common set of methodologies and practices while being sensitive to cultural differences.

These projects pair hundreds of professionals together from client and consulting firms, handling project management, applications development, business function analysis, and technical support. The projects require more than passing interest from upper managers; without a sense of urgency and enough full-time people on the integration job, "projects tend to fail," according to one participant. Said another about a positive experience: "Management backed the project with dollars and freed up senior people in the organization to make it happen."

Project management criteria in the survey broke out into areas such as integrators' knowledge of clients' business, integrators' project management skills, integrators' systems integration experience, and integrators' level of flexibility. Even the business practices criteria included project management areas such as integrator communication processes and problem resolution processes. Technical performance criteria included actual versus scheduled completion time and compatibility with other systems.

If project management is not made a career position, it will not be perceived as a job of importance to the organization; the best people will not be drawn to it and the organization will most likely revert to the *accidental project manager* approach, which is known to be a recipe for failure. Upper management must ensure that project management is a desirable position and that it is indeed a school for leaders.

Step 7:   Develop a Project Learning Organization

Developing a project learning organization is something that everyone agrees is important but that few attempt. Learning through projects could be the responsibility of a project office, but that requires project reviews, most of which are sporadic at best. Some organizations require reviews of all projects, but the information is shared only within the team. Few organizations have a mechanism to share the learning of one team with another. Information is basically free at the end of a project, and everyone seems to agree that sharing it is an important way to increase project management skills in the organization. But few organizations actually avail themselves of this free yet priceless information. Why not?

One reason is organizational perversity. Some upper managers say they want people to learn from other projects but do not reward or support the necessary reviews of those projects. Ideally, they would ask for reviews of all projects and support the idea and process of sharing learning with other project managers.

However, a more important reason may be that though people learn from their mistakes, sharing project learning also reveals project mistakes. Only the rare organization rewards people for mistakes; thus most people hide them and try only to show the "right stuff." Most people have a public self that they show to others and a real self that they hide from public view. As organizations comprise people, they too exhibit a public persona and a private persona. The public persona usually requires that everything be done right—that there be no mistakes. Thus, any mistakes tend to be hidden from customers and others, who are fed a steady stream of the right stuff. Employees learn this from senior managers, and if the senior managers are seen hiding the truth, they tend to do the same. This reinforces the notion that hiding behavior is natural, which is another example of organizational perversity: what is desired is a learning organization, but what is rewarded is covering up mistakes.

Too few organizations reward learning, because true learning requires leadership of the kind that goes against well-established norms and that rewards what is really best for the organization. O'Toole describes this as value-based leadership, which is based on what is morally right even if it goes against the norm.[13] For example, Jesus Christ is often considered a value-based leader because his message of forgiveness went against the norms of his times. Likewise Mahatma Gandhi's message of nonviolence went against the behavioral norms of his time and place. Yet both were able to effect massive social change, mainly because their message was morally right and they stuck to it despite assaults from all sides. Says O'Toole (p. 11): "In complex, democratic settings, effective leadership will entail the factors and dimensions of vision, trust, listening, authenticity, integrity, hope and, especially, addressing the true needs of followers. . . . Such a philosophy must be rooted in the most fundamental of moral principles: respect for people."

For the value-based project management leader, the vision should be one of an open organization where mistakes are openly discussed and the learning value of the error is appreciated. This is particularly necessary in a project organization where people are constantly doing something new, which is where mistakes are most likely. Mistakes, it must be understood, are merely after-the-fact judgments of decisions made with incomplete knowledge. The line between hero and goat is often very thin; a decision may be a big success or a huge failure depending on how subsequent events unfold. So the first step in developing true learning from experience is to avoid labeling erroneous decisions as mistakes, but rather to consider them as decisions that did not work out as planned. Beyond that, discussion should center on why things went other than as planned: from this, learning occurs.

Developing trust in this vision is difficult. If the company has a long history of berating people for mistakes, it may be almost impossible. Trust builds only after a long period during which upper managers repeatedly and consistently discuss mistakes with an open mind and with the goal of maximizing learning from them and not maximizing the guilt of some scapegoat. Honestly perusing the reasons why a decision did not work out is the best way to ensure better decisions in the future. Hanging a scapegoat merely ensures that the reasons for failure will never be discovered; thus the same mistake might be made again and again. Upper management will not be trusted until it sees that people who discuss mistakes are no longer made the scapegoats.

The change to open discussion must be made with authenticity and integrity or it will never take hold. Organization members are very well tuned to the flavor of the week approach to management: If upper managers do not really mean what they say about understanding the reasons for mistakes, people will assume that the new management style is just a fad and that things will soon return to normal. In other words, no change will happen.

Integrity in this context means that upper managers actually do something with the project learning information they receive to help make things better in the future, rather than fire or otherwise berate the messenger. They adopt new learnings into their values and belief systems, adapt them to the current situation, and apply them consistently—not just until a new idea or crisis comes along. Simply put, authenticity and integrity mean that upper managers really want what they ask for and will do what they said they would do. It seems so simple, but most organization members seem to think that their upper managers lack authenticity and integrity. When that feeling is prevalent, trust cannot possibly develop and the learning organization remains a fiction.

The final part of value-based leadership is meeting the true needs of organizational members. Most project managers and most people in general truly need little more than the authenticity and integrity just described.

THE COMPLETE UPPER MANAGER

Hewlett-Packard Executive Vice President Rick Belluzzo expressed his commitment to project management at HP by his presence, his words, and his willingness to answer the tough questions presented to him at the company's Project Management Conference.[14] This event provided him the opportunity to share his values, beliefs, hopes, and concerns with those closest to managing the action throughout the company. He emphasized the "concept, belief, strong principle I have about *focus*. It can be applied to everything we do. There is so much more value that if there are ten things you can do, pick one or two to do extremely well, and then go on to the third one. This is so much more valuable and so much more rewarding than trying to cover everything and doing a mediocre job." In his statements, he demonstrated values-based leadership, shared his thought processes, provided one answer to the issue of doing too many projects, and empathized with the desire of all to accomplish great results through projects. It is heartwarming when we can point to managers who act with authenticity and integrity.

The Successful Complete Upper Manager

- Conducts an inventory of all projects under way and optimizes the project portfolio.
- Examines how important project management is to the organization.

- Develops a project management program or office.
- Uses an assessment and prioritization process to select projects.
- Gets training or outside assistance to improve the ability to manage project managers.
- Recognizes the profession of project management and invests in training project managers.
- Learns from mistakes, avoids organizational perversities, and builds a trusting, open organization.

NOTES

1. D. Cohen and J. Kuehn, "Navigating between a Rock and a Hard Place: Reconciling the Initiating and Planning Phases to Promote Project Success." Paper presented at the Project Management Institute 27th annual seminar/symposium (Boston, 1996).

2. J. Kennel, "Creating a Project Management Culture in a Global Corporation," *Proceedings of the Project World Conference* (Santa Clara, CA: December 1996).

3. J. Martin, "Revolution, Risk, Runaways: The Three R's of IS Projects," *Proceedings of the Project Management Institute 25th Annual Seminar/Symposium* (Upper Darby, PA: Project Management Institute, 1994).

4. R. Storeygard, "Growing Professional Project Leaders," *Proceedings of the Project Management Institute 26th Annual Seminar/Symposium* (Upper Darby, PA: Project Management Institute, 1995).

5. R. J. Graham, "A Process of Organizational Change: From Bureaucracy to Project Management Culture," *The AMA Handbook of Project Management*, ed. P. Dinsmore (New York: AMACOM, 1993).

6. T. Abraham, "Leveraging the R&D Marketing Interface: Finding and Exploiting the 'C' in R&D," *Proceedings of the Product Development and Management Association International Conference 1995* (Bloomington, MN: October 14, 1995).

7. See note 2.

8. R. J. Graham, "The Complete Project Manager," Software (Philadelphia: Strategic Management Group, 1991).

9. D. R. Blackburn, "And Then a Miracle Happened: Cost/Schedule Performance Management on the Iridium Program," *Proceedings of the Project World Conference*, Session D-4 (Santa Clara, CA: December 14, 1996).

10. See note 2.

11. D. Ono, "Implementing Project Management in AT&T Business Communications System," *PM Network* (October 1990): 9–19.

12. *ComputerWorld* (February 26, 1996): SI 14–19.

13. J. O'Toole, *Leading Change: Overcoming the Ideology of Comfort and the Tyranny of Custom* (San Francisco: Jossey-Bass, 1995).

14. R. Belluzzo. Paper presented at the Hewlett-Packard Project Management Conference 1996 (San Diego, CA: April 1996).

INTEGRATING PROJECT MANAGEMENT INTO THE ENTERPRISE

14

Eric Verzuh

In the successful project-based organization, project management disappears.

Disappearing is not the same as ceasing to exist. Many of the systems we rely on in our lives, from the skeletons in our bodies to the transmissions in our cars, are invisible to us. We do not even think of them until they fail us. Project management systems should be just as invisible to our project-driven organizations.

In this chapter, we discuss the systems or *capabilities* required in the project-based organization. We also take a snapshot of the discipline to understand the current frontiers faced by project-based organizations that are closing in on making project management invisible. Together, these perspectives provide a global view of where project management fits into the organization and what remains to make it fit.

INVISIBLE PROJECT MANAGEMENT SYSTEMS

The transmission in my car is a mystery to me, but not to my mechanic. I want the transmission to be invisible—I don't want to think about it. The purpose of my car is not to use a transmission; it is to transport me to work, school, the grocery store, and so on. In the same way, the purpose of the project-driven enterprise is not to hone project management capabilities, it is to deliver products and services. If your firm is trying to improve its ability to deliver projects, it focuses on the three tiers of an enterprise project management system described in detail in Chapter 12 and briefly recapped here:

394

- *Project tier:* This tier includes the tools, processes, and organizational support necessary to consistently manage projects well. The focus at this level is the individual project and the ability to apply the classic project management discipline described in Parts Two and Three of this book. All project managers and teams have solid project plans; they control the project schedule, budget, and scope; they actively manage risk; and project managers consciously build a positive team environment.
- *Program tier:* This tier includes the tools, processes, and organizational structure required to coordinate multiple projects. The focus at this level is found in three primary categories: deploying limited resources—particularly personnel—among many projects, tracking the relationships (dependencies) between projects, and creating a consistent view of project status so that management can usefully monitor all projects even though they come in a range of sizes and complexity. (The term *program* is not universally used with this meaning. The other common meaning for program refers to managing all the projects that support a related goal—such as capturing a contract to design and build a satellite. In this chapter, we consistently refer to program as it is used in the enterprise project management system.)
- *Strategic or portfolio tier:* This tier includes the tools, processes, and organizational structure necessary to connect the firm's strategy to its projects. This tier focuses on the capability to select and prioritize projects so that the limited resources of the firm are applied to its strategy.

As indicated in Exhibit 14.1, there is a relationship between each of these tiers. The data required at the program and portfolio levels rely on the levels below them; that is, project data must be accurate for program management activities, and program management data must be accurate to support portfolio management activities. Likewise, the priorities and clarity of oversight that the upper tiers provide benefit the lower tiers. Project managers get better sponsorship and more realistically staffed teams because of the portfolio and program management activities.

Implementing each of these levels is not effortless. Chapter 12, by Denis Couture, contains the guidelines for implementation at each level. It is also clear that the information systems, process methodologies, and organization structures can be established in a reasonable time (Couture suggests three to six months), but it takes practice to achieve competence. As Couture also points out, however, these three levels of enterprise project management can be implemented concurrently; a firm does not need to develop competence at one level before it attempts to implement the next.

Will all of these activities, tools, and people be invisible? Not completely, and certainly not to the people carrying out the projects or the people whose entire responsibilities are to keep the tools and processes working. But to the executives of the firm, the infrastructure of enterprise project management

EXHIBIT 14.1   Information travels between levels of the enterprise project management system

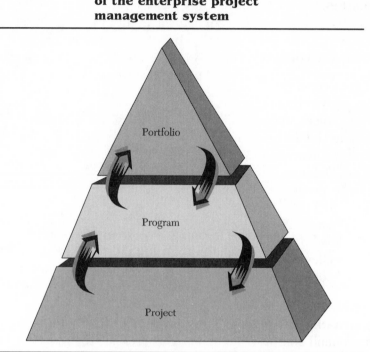

will become like my transmission—a dependable linkage between my intentions and the operation of the vehicle. To the degree that the infrastructure is dependable, it disappears, enabling them to focus on steering the enterprise.

CAPABILITIES OF THE PROJECT-BASED ORGANIZATION

Given that this entire book is about capabilities of a project-based organization, what is left to say? Plenty. While the preceding chapters all addressed important capabilities in the project management discipline, a project-based firm has other necessary capabilities outside the discipline. The auto designer must understand the entire automobile to optimize the performance of the transmission. In the same way, leaders of the project-driven firm must have a vision of the whole enterprise to optimize—and make invisible—project management functions. Understanding these other capabilities and their relationship to project management provides a vision of the complete infrastructure necessary in the project-driven firm.

In this chapter, we use the term *capability* to describe a consistently followed process that produces specific useful results. For instance, nearly every business needs an accounts receivable capability—a known method of issuing invoices and ensuring those invoices are both accurate and paid in a timely manner. Together, the capabilities of a firm dictate its competitive strengths and weaknesses.

The First Capability Model

Terms such as *capability* and *maturity* are becoming more commonly used as companies analyze themselves in their attempts to improve the way they operate. In the project management profession, the use of these terms can be traced back to the Software Engineering Institute (SEI), a research organization located at Carnegie Mellon University, which is sponsored by the U.S. Department of Defense. In 1987, SEI released what has become a landmark report on the proposal of a Capability Maturity Model for Software (SW-CMM). In it, SEI described *capabilities* that a software development organization should possess. The model listed five levels of *maturity* (level 1 was least mature and level 5 most mature; see Exhibit 14.2 for a brief description of these maturity levels). The model made two huge contributions to organizations that developed software or purchased custom software:

1. It delineated a set of capabilities required to deliver software products. By separating these processes—such as project management, quality assurance, and configuration management—the model provided a detailed breakdown of all the capabilities required by a software development organization. By viewing software projects as a set of related processes, firms could focus on improving specific capabilities and be able to link that improvement to specific results. Without this ability to focus, improvement initiatives are too diffused, trying to do everything better. This focus on breaking the software process down into many processes is a direct application of the quality management principle of process improvement.

2. The model's five levels of maturity provided a road map for incremental progress. Few, if any, software development shops could start with no defined processes (level 1) and transition to having all the necessary capabilities in one great leap. The model's maturity progression shows where to put the focus first and describes the related benefits of formalizing each process. According to SEI, a firm should stabilize at each level before taking on the effort to move to the next level of maturity. For instance, the model emphasizes that project management process—the ability to plan and manage a plan—is a necessary competence before a firm can begin to establish the standard practices for design and development.

The SEI SW-CMM has been responsible for much of the focus on project management in IT and software organization, but its application is universal. The fundamental principles of being able to delineate all necessary processes and create a sequence for their formalization have been applied in every field,

EXHIBIT 14.2 Software engineering institute capability maturity model overview

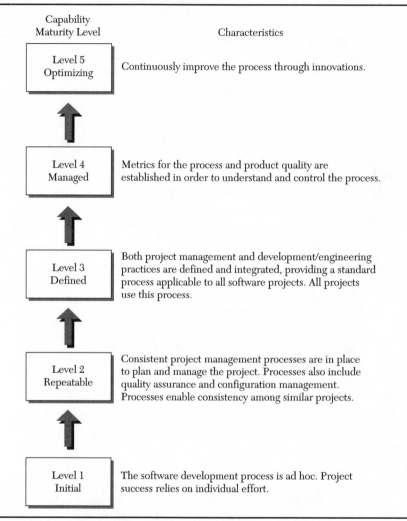

Capability
Maturity Level

Characteristics

Level 5
Optimizing

Continuously improve the process through innovations.

Level 4
Managed

Metrics for the process and product quality are established in order to understand and control the process.

Level 3
Defined

Both project management and development/engineering practices are defined and integrated, providing a standard process applicable to all software projects. All projects use this process.

Level 2
Repeatable

Consistent project management processes are in place to plan and manage the project. Processes also include quality assurance and configuration management. Processes enable consistency among similar projects.

Level 1
Initial

The software development process is ad hoc. Project success relies on individual effort.

Source: Technical Report CMU/SEI-93-TR-24, Software Engineering Institute.

from construction to health care. In every case, project management processes are recognized as a foundation, a concept we explore further in the remainder of this chapter.

With this brief grounding in the concept of capabilities and maturity, we analyze the project-based organization.

Capabilities and Infrastructure

A business infrastructure is commonly understood by professional managers but rarely considered a core competitive capability. Like the skeletons in our bodies, accounting, finance, human resource, and inventory management systems are necessary for basic survival. Infrastructure is typically taken for granted until—as in the spectacular accounting scandals of 2002—we find it is broken and the failure draws our attention.

This phenomenon is responsible for the intense focus on project management that began in the 1980s and 1990s. Many firms experienced a dramatic increase in the number of projects they undertook, and far too many projects were failures. As seen throughout this book, the discipline of project management definitely provides part of the answer to this problem. However, it is now time to view the organization from the proper perspective. Project management represents just *one* capability, and it is not the primary purpose of the project-driven firm. The purpose of a project-based organization is to *deliver* products and services.

What capabilities, then, are necessary to deliver products and services in such a way that the project-based firm is judged successful? Exhibits 14.3 and 14.4 demonstrate these capabilities and the role played by project management practices. Exhibit 14.3 shows three primary capabilities: strategic, business case, and technical; each is described in detail in the following discussion. Exhibit 14.4 demonstrates how the enabling disciplines of project management and quality management add strength and rigor to the primary capabilities. Placing project management in this context balances its importance in the organization. We see that project management is important, but it is not the only thing that is important.

Before describing this model in detail, there are three important points:

1. Project-based organizations exist across the economic spectrum—from the U.S. Army Corps of Engineers, to information systems departments in any business, to small consulting firms—so that any model must be general in its nature.

EXHIBIT 14.3 Primary capabilities of the project-based organization

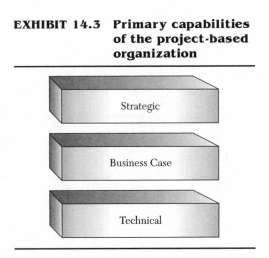

EXHIBIT 14.4   Primary and enabling capabilities

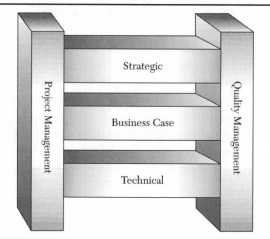

2. The distinction between *primary* and *enabling* is not intended to place one as more important than the other. The point is that primary capabilities need enabling capabilities.

3. The model does not address the infrastructure functions previously noted, such as accounting, because these are not typically the biggest challenges to the project-based organization.

Primary Capabilities

Primary capabilities are the functions that enable the organization to meet its primary purpose. Simply, these are the abilities to determine the strategic goals of the organization, to establish tactical goals, and to deliver on those goals. Primary capabilities are not defined by functional boundaries. If a project-based organization comprises multiple disciplines, the capabilities will rely on cross-functional participation.

Strategic Capabilities

This is related to the capability described earlier in this chapter as the top tier of a project management system. It includes strategic planning and prioritization of the firm's resources. It is easy to see how this capability applies to internal projects, such as information technology improvements. For a firm that derives its revenue from delivering projects, such as a construction company, the strategic capability includes choosing the markets where the firm pursues new business.

Another facet of the strategic capability is selecting long-term directions of *how* strategic goals are achieved. One example is selecting standard database architecture for information systems. Another example is forming alliances with other firms to develop new markets. These decisions ultimately affect many projects. The project-based organization must be able to link these strategic decisions to project decisions.

The skills and techniques used for strategic decisions are not necessarily within the project management discipline. Market analysis, financial planning, setting long-term technical architecture directions—these activities require more than project management has to offer. The connection between the strategic capability and the portfolio management tier is that portfolio management ensures that strategic decisions are based on accurate data and that the strategic decisions are firmly linked to project action.

Given the nature of these activities, it is no surprise that most of the processes and skills required for the strategic capability are fulfilled by top-level management.

Business Case

Creating a bridge between the strategic goals and the technical implementation of any project is the business case. Through a comparison of features, benefits, cost to produce, and schedule sensitivity, the firm decides whether to pursue the project. Every project-based organization must attend to this balance, though it is manifested differently depending on the firm. Here are some major categories:

- In a consumer product company, these decisions are shepherded by product managers. The Stage-Gate™ process described in Chapter 11 presents this perspective. The essential challenge in these firms is to determine what product to produce, based on an understanding of the demand for the product. Cooper's process emphasizes that striking the balance of features, benefits, and costs is actually a series of decisions spread throughout the product development process.

- Firms that earn their revenue through project delivery have a slightly different perspective. They often have a person or department responsible for business development whose focus is to capture new project work. A small general contractor in residential construction may spend part of his or her evenings preparing bids. A giant defense contractor such as Boeing, Grumman, or Lockheed Martin has teams of people developing proposals and may spend years winning a new contract. This team needs to do more than win the contract, however. First, it submits a bid that balances the effort to deliver with the need for profitability. After the contract is awarded, the team must also monitor and control changes to ensure that profits are retained. The relationship between business development and the ability to deliver is pretty clear in these cases—the most talented project team ever assembled will have nothing to do if it cannot capture any profitable projects.

- Service organizations also manage this function, with Information Technology (IT) providing some good examples. Whether IT is supplied via an internal department or an external IT services firm with a long-term contract, each request for a service addition or enhancement must be managed. A common name for this role is *account manager.* He or she must understand the requirements and the benefits to the users and be able to respond with cost and schedule estimates to determine whether the service really is cost effective. The account manager ensures that the customer will understand and be willing to pay the cost of delivery.

- Nonprofit agencies need this capability to weigh the benefits of any undertaking against the potential costs. Rather than assess the potential profit of a project, they estimate the benefits to their constituents and make sure it outweighs the costs of delivery.

In each of these cases, the project-driven organization must manage the value equation—the balance of cost, schedule, and benefits—throughout the life of the project. This may seem like the triple constraint of project management (on time, on budget, conformance to specifications) and it is. The job of the product manager, the business development team, and the account manager is to manage the business risk—to set the cost, schedule, and quality goals so that every project and every product is cost effective. (The project manager then validates the triple constraint and delivers on it.) Without this capability, an organization could find itself delivering terrific customer satisfaction but without any profit, with each successful project driving it closer to extinction.

All of this may seem obvious, but consider the following scenarios and see how the lack of this capability affects these project teams:

- A company that designs and installs computer networks relied on its sales staff to size up projects and prepare fixed bid proposals. Because the projects required network design and implementation services, it was far too common for the actual scope of the work to be far different from the way the salesperson had envisioned—making the majority of projects over budget or far behind schedule. To rectify this, the business development process was revamped. Rather than provide a fixed bid for design and development, the firm provided a bid for only the design work and, after the design was complete, prepared a separate bid for the network implementation. Customers appreciated the additional flexibility of this approach, and the firm benefited because it meant every project would have a profit.

- Winning a huge aerospace contract meant many millions of dollars in revenue and a thousand or more jobs retained. Pressure was intense on the business development team to develop a winning proposal, and the team was constantly asked to find a way to reduce the bid amount. It should come as no surprise that the pressure to win the contract resulted in a bid that was sure to be unprofitable. After too many of these experiences (and it doesn't take many for it to hurt), an aerospace business instituted nonadvocate bid reviews as part of the proposal process. Other experts from the business, but outside the team, reviewed the bid to make sure it was in the best interests of the company.

- A computer hardware manufacturer pushed a project team to speed up delivery of a new printer. Through Herculean efforts and excellent project management, the printer was delivered on time and with high quality. Customers, however, did not see the printer as being much different from previous, less expensive models, so sales were slow and the product was pulled after six months.

The breakdown in each of these examples underscores the importance of a known, effective approach to managing the business case.

Technical Capability

Every project-based organization has a technical competency that makes it valuable to its customers. These are the areas of technical specialization necessary to design, build, test, or operate a product or service. For an aerospace firm, it includes engineers who can successfully translate a requirement to a design for a new aircraft or satellite. For an advertising firm, it is the skills to design and produce a television commercial. Technical skills are the reason we hire accountants, technical writers, software developers, photographers, and so on.

During project management's decade of growth, it has been noted repeatedly that technical competence was insufficient for a project's success. Clear goals, communication, scope management, detailed planning, and management support are often cited as project success factors, and these are increased by employing the project management discipline.[1] None of these comparisons of project management and technical ability should imply that technical capability is not important. When Lockheed Martin Corporation won the contract to build the Joint Strike Fighter (JSF)—a program that could be worth up to $200 billion over 25 years—one of the major factors cited by the Pentagon was the aircraft's ability to meet the short takeoff vertical landing (STOVL) requirement: The airplane will be able to land vertically, like a helicopter.[2] Lockheed Martin accomplished this through a unique and revolutionary design approach. In short, a major factor in Lockheed Martin's success was its technical capability. Another example comes from the SEI Capability Maturity Model where level 3 focuses on having consistent software development practices—in other words, a focus on the technical practices for design, development, and testing of software products.

Finally, technical capability is often composed of a wide range of technical specialties. The more complex the product or service that is being delivered, the more disciplines are likely to be required.

Enabling Capabilities

Enabling capabilities improve the performance of the organization and directly strengthen primary capabilities. Exhibit 14.4 graphically shows project management and quality management reinforcing and building bridges between each primary capability.

All the chapters of this book have spoken to the benefits project management provides to the primary capabilities:

- Good project management improves the performance of the project team (the people with the technical capabilities). It provides the coordination and unity of purpose that magnify individual technical skills to solve huge problems.
- Planning techniques provide the methods of analysis to produce realistic estimates that product managers and account managers use to oversee the business case. Project control information serves to keep the business case up-to-date, maintaining the value equation.
- Finally, the strategic/portfolio capability is supported by the project management discipline in two ways:
  1. Accurate project reporting systems enable top management to see how the firm's resources are being deployed against the strategy and the actual progress against specific strategic goals.
  2. Project performance is more predictable, which in turn makes strategic planning more accurate.

Quality management is also a discipline composed of principles and methods. The overview of this important discipline in Chapter 7 was brief, but it points out that its principles also directly improve the primary capabilities we discuss in this chapter. Its focus on the customer affects the attitudes and actions at every level and in every role in the enterprise. Process management methods provide specific techniques to measure and improve every aspect of the organization. Finally, the emphasis on how to manage and motivate the people of the organization overlaps the project management concepts of building successful team environments.

MANAGING THE CAPABILITIES OF A PROJECT-BASED ORGANIZATION

What is most important? Our technical expertise? Strategy? Quality? Project management? The question doesn't make sense. All serve the same cause, and all are essential. Improving our ability to successfully deliver the right project demands we focus on the entire firm—all the capabilities and their relationships to each other.

After the leader of a project-based organization accepts this notion of *necessary capabilities,* the analysis can be extended toward improving all the factors that affect project success. While the five capabilities listed so far apply to every firm, other essential capabilities are driven by the purpose of the firm. For example, real estate developers, whose portfolio of projects may be worth billions of dollars, rely on well-established financing systems that enable them to concurrently pursue multiple projects and ride out the long periods of expense that precede any revenue generation. Major defense contractors such as Boeing and Lockheed Martin view themselves as systems integrators; their success as prime contractors relies on their ability to manage and integrate a wide range of subcontractors.

The list of related capabilities can go on and on. During the final selection process for the Joint Strike Fighter program, the Pentagon team used literally hundreds of criteria to assess the final two bidders. In addition to the technical merits of its airplane, Boeing presented its advanced manufacturing capabilities as a significant advantage.[3]

Project management is essential to project-based organizations. But it is not the only essential capability. Recognizing and delineating between all the necessary capabilities begins the cycle of improvement. Like the SEI Capability Maturity Model described earlier, it provides a framework for analyzing a firm's strengths and weaknesses, and it provides focus. Within the scope of this book, understanding this framework is necessary to complete the integration of project management into the enterprise. We now explore the frontiers that remain to making project management fit seamlessly in the firm.

PROJECT MANAGEMENT FRONTIERS

Frontiers can be boundaries or opportunities for further exploration. Project management frontiers are both; they represent the challenges of integrating the discipline into the organization. The remainder of this chapter discusses challenges and strategies for four major frontiers:

1. Melding the separate but complementary capabilities of business case management, project management, and technical knowledge.
2. Developing a project management career path in the firm.
3. Reconciling the structures of the permanent organization to temporary projects.
4. Matching the cultural change to the systems and process changes.

The nature of frontiers is that they are not the same for every firm. For some, creating the integrated information systems described in Chapter 12 is a staggering obstacle; for others, the implementations have been smooth. You may not recognize all of the four major frontiers as challenges for your firm. If none of these frontiers exist for your firm, your organization has successfully integrated project management into the enterprise.

Frontier: Melding the Separate but Complementary Capabilities of Business Case Management, Project Management, and Technical Knowledge

If my project produces the requested product on time and on budget, is it successful? That depends on whom you ask. The project manager and team met the goals. But what if the goals were wrong? This frontier emphasizes the distinctions created earlier in this chapter between the capabilities of business case, project management, and technical knowledge.

We have already established the distinction between these capabilities; Exhibit 14.5 shows their relationships, representing the three capabilities as separate *gears*. The business case gear represents the skills and principles for balancing the cost, schedule, features, benefits, and profit. The project management gear contains the skills and methods for controlling scope, planning, tracking cost and schedule progress, communicating with customers, and assigning and controlling work on the project team. The technical gear contains the knowledge, abilities, and methodologies necessary to create the product or service. Notice how the project management gear provides the linkage between the business case and the technical capability. Even though it is not

EXHIBIT 14.5   Separate but complimentary disciplines

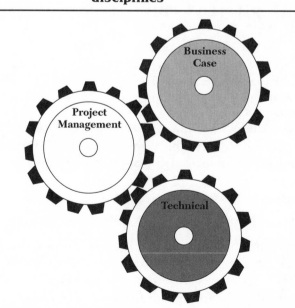

represented in the diagram, it is easy to grasp how the strategy gear would mesh with the business case.

This concept is important because so many firms do not recognize these as separate but complementary disciplines, each with its own processes and knowledge requirements. The mistake they make is creating a single, linear methodology that ties all of these disciplines together. The resulting process is appropriate for some projects but is completely unrealistic for others. Rather than multiple gears, they have one large gear. The advantage of multiple gears is obvious to anyone who has ridden a 10-speed bike: Use the appropriate combination of gears for the project.

Two examples show how this works in reality:

1. An IT group in a bank serves the mortgage business unit. The IT manager responsible for customer contact (an account manager) is responsible for developing proposals for any service enhancement requested by the customer. During the same day, the account manager analyzes a business case for developing a Web site for internal communication and a business case for changing the electronic funds transfer process with the Federal Reserve Bank. In each case, the account manager uses a similar analysis process and produces proposals with similar formats. Once the project manager gets involved, the differences between the nature of the two projects start to emerge. The heavily regulated project with the Federal Reserve Bank demands much more formal communication planning and reporting, for example. At the technical level, the project teams are completely different: They use different programming languages, different development environments (intranet server versus mainframe database), and one uses a sequential waterfall development process while the other employs an iterative prototyping approach. The business case gear was the same, the project management gears were similar, but the technical gears were completely different.

2. To revisit the original question in this section: If the project team produces the requested product on time and within budget, are they successful? If you apply this question to an earlier example, the new laser printer whose features didn't sufficiently distinguish it from its predecessor, the attention gets focused on the right place: the business case gear. The other two gears did a great job of producing what they were asked for. The benefit of the multiple gear analogy here is that by separating these disciplines, we improve the correct process.

A variation on this issue is making your methodology for project delivery distinguish between development and deployment.[4] In this context, *development* refers to the full scope of activities to take a product or service from idea to use. *Deployment,* on the other hand, refers to the actions required to implement a design. A real estate developer who starts with a strip of land in the desert and ends up with a retirement community is managing *development,* and the contractor who constructs the roads and buildings is managing *deployment*. Exhibit 14.6 is a conceptual representation of the three disciplines required during the development of a single product. For the sake of understanding the model, imagine that it is a product or service that your firm delivers. It could be an IT solution, a television commercial, or a component of an aircraft:

- The business case life cycle represents multiple decision points necessary to balance the cost, schedule, features, benefits, and profit associated with the product/service.

EXHIBIT 14.6   Conceptual view of multiple complementary disciplines

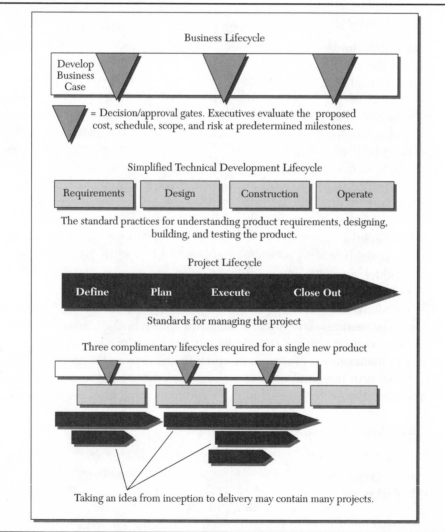

- The technical life cycle represents the activities, techniques, and skills required to document the requirements, develop a design, construct the product, and turn it over to whoever will operate it. (Many would argue that this is an inaccurate representation of the technical activities because it is completely linear. That is a fair objection. For the purpose of this example, we keep this model simple. If you add the iterative reality that many technical problems experience, it strengthens the case for the multiple complementary disciplines perspective.)

- The project life cycle is labeled with the phases of the work from the perspective of the project management discipline. The *define* activity means documenting the goals, stakeholders, communication plan, and so on; *planning* is building the action plan and includes developing a risk management plan; *execute* means the work is actually performed; *close-out* is the postproject reporting to management, customer, and team.

Notice that the business case life cycle spans the entire development process. This is the same concept that Robert Cooper presents in describing the process for managing new product development in Chapter 11. Why multiple decision points? Because the technical work represents discovery. That is also the reason multiple projects are shown. Another reason for showing multiple projects is that as the product passes through design and begins construction, the effort can be distributed to multiple independent teams. Each smaller project, whether it is market research, product design, production engineering, or systems integration, will be more effective if managed with the project management tool set.

Product development companies such as Procter & Gamble and Microsoft have understood this concept for years, which is why they distinguish between product managers (responsible for the business case) and project managers (responsible for delivering components of the solution).

In project management literature, commonly used terms that relate to this concept are *phased estimating*[5] and the *rolling-wave*.[6] Both describe the same problem and present essentially the same answer. So why is it considered a frontier? Because so many project-based organizations that are trying to formalize their project management processes are making the one-methodology mistake.

The goal is to integrate project management into the enterprise. The key is to recognize the separate but complementary nature of these three disciplines. Each requires formal processes (methodologies). Together, they define an idea-to-delivery capability.

Frontier: Developing a Project Management Career Path in the Firm

Project management is an important skill in the workplace and certainly in a project-driven firm. We want all employees and, particularly, management to value this skill set, and we recognize that people have varying levels of project management ability. Project leadership is often the specific responsibility of a single person in a project. For all these reasons, project-based organizations are attempting to develop project management career paths.

First, we explore this frontier by looking at the reason that a project management career path is important. A career path implies two things: There is a progression of positions of responsibility, and each of those positions has articulated requirements. Such a career path benefits recruitment, retention, and staffing decisions. Two of these benefits are enjoyed in the near term; the other, in the long term.

The near-term benefits are staffing decisions and recruitment. Because our project-based organization is filled with unique projects, each of which is temporary, there is an ongoing need to match people to project leadership positions. That means that for an internal project management career path to be useful, the position descriptions make it easier to assign people to projects. The related test of usefulness is whether the position descriptions lend themselves to assessing potential candidates from outside the organization. Considering that project staffing is one of the major challenges of the project-driven firm, finding both temporary and permanent personnel to manage projects is an ongoing activity.

The long-term benefit of a project management career path is retention of good personnel. For purposes of this chapter, we assume your firm wants to retain project managers who consistently deliver good results. The inherent problem with being this kind of project manager is that you are constantly working yourself out of a job. If nobody in the organization is showing an interest in what happens to you after the project, your survival instincts will force your own commitment to the firm to diminish. Or you may try to get a more stable position, such as a functional management role. Either way, the firm loses a good project manager. So this is the other test a career path must face—does it encourage the best project managers to stick with the company by addressing their long-term career concerns?

Organizations have made substantial headway on this frontier in some areas and are bogging down in others. What seems to be working is that project managers are being given long term "homes" in the project management office (PMO). From a career and administrative standpoint, they report to the PMO. For their day-to-day responsibilities, they manage one or more projects and are responsible to the project owner or sponsor. This structure allows them to rub shoulders with other project managers and to have a long-term relationship with the manager of the PMO. That is also a benefit to the project owners because they have a source of qualified project managers. On the other hand, if the project starts to fall apart, the project owner can go directly to the PMO manager to ask for additional support for the project manager.

What is proving to be a stickier problem is articulating the requirements for project management positions and developing the training plans for these positions.

During the first big wave of enthusiasm for project management in the 1980s and 1990s, the tendency was to look to external entities for guidance. Project management was new to many firms, and the certifications offered by universities and professional organizations provided an immediate answer to the question, "What makes a good project manager?" Let's briefly review what external entities are offering:

Universities offer graduate degrees and certificates in project management. The degreed programs are what you would expect: challenging, broadscoped, and represent a significant time investment for the student. Like any university program, the actual quality of the experience varies with the university, but they all meet certain minimum requirements of academic rigor. The certificate programs have a far wider variation in their format, scope, and value. These certificates are merely records that a participant attended training for a specified number of hours. The training is rarely presented by college faculty, and the requirements to earn a project management certificate range from a few days of training to eight-month programs that require more than 200 class hours plus homework. It is not at all uncommon for a university offering such a program to completely outsource it—including curriculum development and delivery—to a professional training company. That is not to say these programs have no value, but it must be understood that any certificate is only as good as the individual program offering it.

Professional associations are also trying to fill the gap. At the risk of offending those institutions we do not mention, we look at the approaches from three widely recognized project management professional associations:

- The Project Management Institute (PMI), headquartered in the United States, has successfully promoted the acceptance of its Project Management Professional (PMP) designation, with more than 40,000 PMPs certified around the world. The requirements for achieving this certification include experience leading a project and passing a rigorous test on general project management knowledge. In 2002, PMI also instituted a new designation, the Certified Associate in Project Management (CAPM). The CAPM requires experience as a project leader (though less than the PMP designation) and a minimal amount of project management training.[7]

- The International Project Management Association (IPMA) has its headquarters in The Netherlands and serves many countries in Europe, Asia, and Africa. IPMA has established four levels of certification. The lowest level requires knowledge of project management, while the highest level designates the ability to direct all projects of an enterprise or all projects of a program. Achieving each level of certification requires a combination of experience, often documented by actual project results and successful completion of an exam.[8]

- The Australian Institute for Project Management (AIPM) has established three levels of project management competence. Gaining certification at any level requires applicants to demonstrate their competence primarily by providing evidence of their performance in the workplace. Although AIPM does not use an exam in its certification program, it does base the requirements for each level on the *Guide to the Project Management Body of Knowledge* (PMBoK), which is produced and maintained by PMI.[9]

A significant benefit of the certification programs offered by these institutions is their broad recognition and acceptance. Their professional designations mean the same thing in every country and every organization. Another advantage is that they were developed by the very people who need them: practicing professionals. These professionals bring their real-world needs to designing these certifications.

Finally, private, for-profit training companies offer their own certifications. Like the certifications provided by universities, these certificates usually represent attendance at one or more classes. As with the university certificate programs, the value of the certificate varies with the provider.

With all of these training and certification resources available, why does establishing meaningful project management job descriptions and training plans continue to present a challenge? The answer is in the challenge of managing projects. The Australian Institute of Project Management reveals the issue in the guidelines that describe its certification process:[10]

> The standards are Common Standards and are thus generic in nature and are not necessarily appropriate for direct usage in all industries or enterprises. In most cases, users of the standards will need to adjust them to suit the particular context in which they are to be applied.
>
> Where an industry or occupational sector wishes to establish project management competency standards, these generic standards may be used as a foundation upon which the industry/sector can develop its own specific standards, which would reflect the industry/sector context.
>
> Similarly, individual enterprises may wish to develop standards for internal use. In such cases, either the generic standards or the industry standards, where available, can be used as a basis for development in the specific enterprise context.

AIPM is saying that not all projects are the same; therefore, relevant standards for your firm should be based on the factors that make your projects successful. As we have already discussed, managing a project requires a combination of disciplines. That reality quickly shows why those firms trying to use PMP certification as a guarantee for project success are so often disappointed.

A more complex, more realistic response is to match the job requirements to the nature of projects that exist in the organization. For nearly every project, the project manager requires at least three dimensions of skill competency, as illustrated in Exhibit 14.7 and described here:

- The pure discipline of project management exemplified by the specific techniques described in Part Two of this book.

EXHIBIT 14.7   The project environment dictates skill requirements for project managers

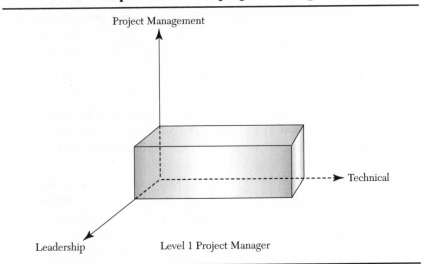

Project Management

Technical

Leadership

Level 1 Project Manager

- The leadership skills required to create positive team environments, to draw out the best from a variety of people, and to navigate the political realities in your environment.
- The technical knowledge specific to the project.

As you define the progression of project leadership responsibilities, the number of dimensions will grow—gaining the ability to manage the business case is a common example. With this in mind, design a career path that matches skills to the complexity of projects. Here are some guidelines to follow:

1. Categorize your projects by the complexity of managing them. Start with a list of active projects, add the biggest challenges of the past year or two, then add any other unusual ones you can envision for the future. Now lump the projects by difficulty to manage—a subjective judgment, but you know which ones were the biggest challenges.

2. Recognize the various disciplines a project manager should master for each of these project types. Within each discipline, establish some level of expertise that corresponds to the project category. Either plot it as in the Exhibit 14.7 model, or just describe it. But make sure you can differentiate between the skills required for one category of project and another.

3. Do not be surprised if the progression has more to do with adding new disciplines than refining the pure project management skills.

4. Allow for the intangible but essential leadership characteristics such as tenacity, the ability to perform under pressure, and contagious enthusiasm.

5. Finally, do not rely on a university or professional association to certify a project manager. Require him or her to demonstrate the skills. There is a big difference between taking a class and demonstrating the ability.

Designing a career based on a progression of responsibilities and associated skills is not revolutionary. In fact, it is just plain logical. It's the same approach used to define a purely technical career path or a functional management career path.

With this approach to defining position requirements, the training path becomes more apparent. Yes, your project managers probably need a project management class so they understand the techniques to plan and control a project. After practicing the basics, attend a course on risk management. Add negotiating, communication, and team leadership skills, too. Problem solving and basic business case analysis are equally important. Of course, all along we assume their technical skills are adequate. Ongoing technical education makes sense, too.

If there is a place for external certifications, it is in this training path because those certifications describe specific education accomplishments. The key is that training and certifications are dictated by the position requirements.

When project management skills were new to the firm, we struggled with this position of project manager. Now that we see project management for what it is—another complementary discipline—we can consciously choose who needs the skills and the level of expertise they need.

Integrating a project management career path into the enterprise has one more benefit. Specific, useful position requirements connect job performance to the defined processes of the firm, reinforcing the processes and the firm's commitment to their use.

Frontier: Reconciling the Ongoing Requirements of the Permanent Organization to the Temporary Nature of Projects

A significant frontier for many firms is the boundary between their projects and their ongoing operations. The struggle here is to create organizational structures that are optimal for both the temporary project work and the ongoing operation.

Some project-based organizations literally do nothing but work on projects. In these firms, only the administrative staff required for infrastructure activities, such as accounting, is uninvolved in project delivery. But that is a rare situation. More commonly, projects make up somewhere between 20 percent and 80 percent of the budget or revenue of the organization. The rest represents ongoing operations that are every bit as important as the project work. The classic example is an information technology department that builds, updates, and operates its systems. When restructuring the department to improve project performance, it is not acceptable to compromise the production systems that must be running 24 hours a day, seven days a week.

The challenge of reconciling the permanent organization to temporary projects is epitomized by three specific problems that occur in project-based organizations. We start by understanding these problems and then discuss the strategies being used to mitigate them.

Problem One: Maintaining and optimizing resources that benefit many projects

These aren't just personnel, but long-term company assets; for example:

- Every firm needs reliable, cost-effective suppliers. For firms that run projects as a prime contractor who brings many subcontractors to the team, the ability to find and retain the best suppliers is a significant competitive advantage. This capability cannot be left up to individual projects or programs. Even firms that perform much of their own work use external specialists. In either case, having to seek out the best supplier on every project is not efficient.
- Another example is specialized equipment or facilities. An advanced technology test environment could be essential to project performance but far too expensive for one project or program to afford.

Problem Two: Maintaining and increasing institutional knowledge

The product of many project-driven firms is specialized knowledge. The value to their customers is that they have successfully delivered many similar projects. This is true for internal projects—such as product development teams—and is always true for project teams that are external to the customer's firm. That makes institutional knowledge a core strategic asset. The problem is that temporary, project-oriented teams are terrific at generating new knowledge but are lousy at passing it on. It is an issue of institutional knowledge when you hear someone ask: "I think the Excalibur Project had to handle this—what did they do?" Traditionally, it was the functional groups—accounting, marketing, engineering—that maintained this knowledge. So how do we transfer the wisdom from one project team to the others?

Problem Three: Project management capability is required throughout the enterprise

Processes die without process owners. If everybody is responsible for using project management, but nobody owns the systems and methodologies, we end up where we started: with ad hoc approaches and incompatible tools. On the other hand, when projects exist across the enterprise, the methodologies and tools hit the "no one size fits all" problem. Who, then, should *own* the project management capability?

For a small, specialized, project-driven service firm such as a landscaping company, maintaining project management standards and growing project leadership skills can be the responsibility of a single person or team. But many project-driven organizations have a broad range of products, services, and locations. At Microsoft, Bank of America, Lockheed Martin, or even smaller firms with 50 or more employees, the problem is more complex. Who is responsible for the project management capability?

These are not the only problems arising from the temporary-permanent frontier, but they suffice to show why it is a challenge. Because the problem is one of structure (How does a permanent structure accommodate temporary structures?), the solutions are found in the way we structure our organization. Achieving the permanent structures that best fit your project-based organization has two dimensions: how we define the boundaries of the project-based organization and establishing a permanent unit responsible for project management methods, systems, and skills.

The first issue of boundaries is a classic one for projects. Because so many projects are cross-functional, how do we organize the enterprise? The first part of the answer is to allow for a large, multifaceted organization to have multiple project-based organizations within it. For example, a major health maintenance organization (HMO) with dozens of hospitals and clinics contains at least two project-intensive groups: the facilities group responsible for expansion and maintenance of the HMO's many buildings and the IT group. Aside from the fact that these groups are both project-intensive, they do not have much else in common, so let them operate as independent, project-based organizations within the enterprise. In this case, their separate technical/functional capabilities were the basis for drawing the project-based organization boundary.

The enterprise project management model presented in Chapter 12 may evoke an image of top-down centralized control, but that does not have to be the case. Centralized versus decentralized organization factors also influence the proper structure. Many firms, for instance, find it better to decentralize around their customer and products rather than centralize along functional lines of expertise. Exhibit 14.8 shows how a software product company organizes around its products and allows redundancy of functions among product groups. Exhibit 14.9 demonstrates how a company with just a few major programs balances a program focus with the need for shared resources and maintaining institutional knowledge.

Therefore, the first part of the answer is to establish organization boundaries on factors other than the fact that they all use project management. The second part of the answer is to allow shared, coordinated ownership of the project management capability by having more than one style of PMO to fulfill different needs. This is not an attempt to make it more complicated—if you can get by with one organization that takes responsibility for project management, go ahead. Larger, complex organizations have found that multiple PMOs balance the need for process ownership and decentralization.

EXHIBIT 14.8 Software product company organization

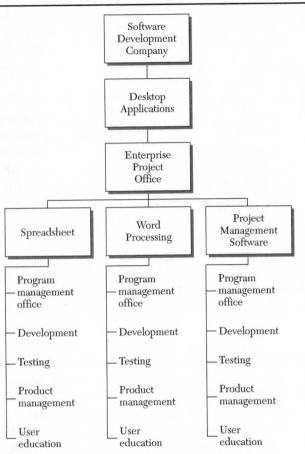

Product-oriented units are project based organizations. Since the units are focused on developing new releases, most of their work is project oriented.

Making decisions about how many and what kind of PMO you want begins with stating that the typical PMO can provide a range of services:

- Maintaining the project management methodology.
- Maintaining the standard information technology tools.
- Providing project management expertise.
- Coordinating personnel and other resource deployment among multiple projects.
- Consolidating status from individual projects to present portfolio status information.

EXHIBIT 14.9   Organization structure balances temporary and permanent structures

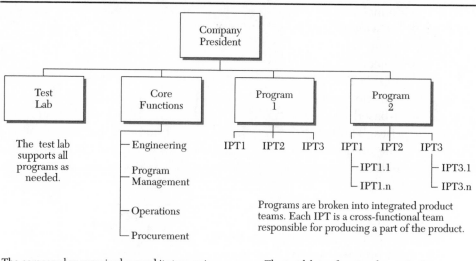

The test lab supports all programs as needed.

Programs are broken into integrated product teams. Each IPT is a cross-functional team responsible for producing a part of the product.

The company has organized around its two major programs. The test lab is a functional organization because it is too expensive to create a test lab for each program. The core functions group is responsible for maintaining and communicating institutional knowledge.

Now ask, "How many of these services must be consistent across the entire enterprise?" If you have multiple business units or product groups (as in the software company example in Exhibit 14.8), total consistency can be counterproductive. In that case, you want multiple PMOs, some with unique functions and others with overlapping responsibilities.

In Chapter 12, Couture describes two types of PMOs, the program management office and project management office. The project PMO serves the individual projects, primarily with project management expertise. The project PMO could be directly accountable for project success, or it may just provide a permanent "home" for some of the organization's project managers who are then loaned out to projects. The program PMO at the middle tier of the organization has different responsibilities: collecting and consolidating status from all projects, overseeing and coordinating personnel and resource deployment among projects, maintaining the methodology, and maintaining the information technology tools. This two-tier structure might be appropriate for a single product group or business unit that has many projects.

Another combination of PMOs was found in the IT group at a Fortune 500 corporation. This corporation had many business units, each of which had its own internal IT group. The firm chose to maintain a central PMO that was responsible for methodologies, training, and offering consulting to projects. Each IT group within a business unit had its own PMO that was accountable for all projects. The business unit PMO was a home for project managers, managed the projects, maintained its own information technology tools, and coordinated personnel among projects. The central PMO's duties also included facilitating knowledge sharing across the business units and formalizing the training program.

Some project-driven firms add a third type of PMO, the *enterprise project office* (EPO).[11] This EPO is necessary for very large, decentralized organizations. We use the term *enterprise* to describe the organization that contains many project-based organizations within it. Exhibits 14.8 and 14.9 represent such enterprises. The focus of the EPO is those functions that should be the same across the enterprise such as methodology and, particularly, information technology tools and processes that enable portfolio management activities. The IT EPO in a major bank also coordinated cross-business unit projects, particularly when a change in one system rippled through other information systems.

Keep it simple, but not too simple. If your firm is big and multifaceted, spreading the PMO functions across multiple PMOs strike a sustainable balance between process ownership and decentralization. As the PMOs mature, their presence and their function blends seamlessly into the enterprise.

Frontier: **Matching the Cultural Change to the Systems and Process Change**

The simplest to understand yet most difficult frontier to cross is related to every frontier we have examined. In any organization, it is easier to implement new tools and processes than to change the habits and values of the people they are designed to serve.

Integrating the project management discipline into the enterprise requires a dual understanding of the term *discipline*. A discipline is a body of knowledge with accepted principles, methods, and tools. This is the common understanding of the term when we speak of "implementing project management." In the beginning of Chapter 9, Neil Whitten provides another definition: *Discipline is the act of encouraging a desired pattern of behavior.* For those who are leading the project-based organization, both definitions are essential. We implement the discipline *with discipline.* Whitten's remarks about the importance of establishing and maintaining discipline on the project team extrapolate directly to the entire firm. The people in the organization must be held accountable to the new processes for the new ways to take root and mature.

In Chapter 13, authors Graham and Englund present another facet of leading this cultural change: the need for visible commitment from top management. They stress the importance of championing the new direction with specific, observable actions that demonstrate they are leading by example.

I add another facet to the efforts of leading cultural change that brings us full circle in this chapter. This is a message to the leaders of the shift to project management processes—senior project managers, leaders of the PMO, and even the executive sponsors who are so important in leading the change. The message is this: *Serve the people who are serving the projects.*

Your customers, to use the language of quality management, are those people who work on project teams, who select and cancel projects, as well as the people who benefit from project outcomes. Listen to them. If they do not understand the methods or the value (the how or the why), you need to stick with them. Change your methodology if that's what it takes. Again applying quality management principles, stay close to the people who are doing the work. The methods and tools that are most useful are the ones that have been customized through use.

Is this flexibility in conflict with Whitten's emphasis on discipline and accountability? Absolutely not! Leading cultural change is not accomplished with our heads down and our eyes shut. Our commitment to implementing the project management discipline is not blunted when we listen to our stakeholders. Instead, the value of our new processes is heightened, and our customers' commitment leaps when they see we will use both our determination and our intelligence to make this change work.

SUMMARY—INTEGRATION INTO THE ENTERPRISE

This book is about leading the project-based organization, whose ultimate goal is better delivery of the right projects. Integrating our project management systems and processes into the enterprise takes the focus away from project management and puts it on the enterprise.

Viewing project management as an enabling capability acknowledges that, for the firm to thrive, it must have many capabilities. That is true for a government agency, a nonprofit service firm, an IT department, a consulting business, and every other type of project-based firm. Project management benefits our strategic decisions and leverages our technical skills. Like the transmission in my car, my project management capability either magnifies or constrains the performance of my other systems, and it achieves its peak performance when it meshes so perfectly with the other systems that it recedes from view.

Your job is to implement the project management discipline in the firm, and your success will lead to powerful results. As you lead this change, remember that project management is an enabling capability. The purpose of your organization is to deliver results. The people in your firm want to maximize their own effectiveness using whatever tools and standards make them more productive. To the extent that project management serves these purposes, it will be embraced and accepted. As long as you are serving the people—from the executives to the project team to the vendors and customers—your systems and processes will lead to change.

NOTES

1. Eric Verzuh, *The Fast Forward MBA in Project Management* (New York: Wiley, 1998), pp. 7–8.

2. James Fallows, "Uncle Sam Buys an Airplane," *The Atlantic Monthly* (June 2002).

3. See note 2.

4. Gregory D. Githens, "Manage Innovation Programs with a Rolling Wave," *PM Network* (May 2001).

5. See note 1.

6. See note 4.

7. Project Management Institute Web site www.pmi.org.

8. International Project Management Association Web site www.ipma.ch.

9. Australian Institute for Project Management Web site www.aipm.com.au.

10. AIPM Web site www.aipm.com.au/resource/guidelines.pdf.

11. Jean Miller, personal conversation (Seattle, WA: October 10, 2002).

Index